Canada's Pacific Gateways
REALIZING THE VISION

Canada's Pacific Gateways
REALIZING THE VISION

By Dr. W.B.M. Hick

PRINCE RUPERT PORT AUTHORITY
Prince Rupert, B.C.

Prince Rupert Port Authority
200–215 Cow Bay Road, Prince Rupert, British Columbia V8J 1A2

Library and Archives Canada Cataloguing in Publication

Hick, W. B. M.
    Canada's Pacific gateways/W.B.M. Hick.

Includes bibliographical references and index.
ISBN 978-0-9733894-1-8

    1. Port districts--British Columbia--Pacific Coast.
2. Harbors--British Columbia--Pacific Coast. 3. Port
districts--British Columbia--Pacific Coast--History.
4. Harbors--British Columbia--Pacific Coast--History.
I. Title.

HE554.A6H53 2011   387.1'2097111   C2011-903148-5

Editing: Lynne Graham, *Northwest Business Writing Solutions*
Design and Print Production: Toni Serofin, *Sanserofin Print Production Studio*

This book is a non commercial enterprise and has been prepared as a public service. Neither the Prince Rupert Port Authority, as publisher, nor the author desire or intend to profit from its sale.

Printed and bound in Canada by Friesens Corporation

FOREWORD

When I first joined the Port of Prince Rupert organization in 1987, Dr. Hick was a member of the Board of Directors. I well recall his words of advice when I was struggling to understand the economic rationale and commercial justification for certain decisions being made in the transportation of Canadian grain. "The Grain Business," Dr. Hick aptly stated, "is 14 percent protein and the rest politics." What I learned over the years was that this adage also explained so many of the anomalies in other areas of the port and transportation industry. But as Dr. Hick clearly illustrates in this meticulously researched study, political influences and human intervention, while important, have often had to take a back seat to the more dominant forces of major world events and economic factors; factors that have helped mold and shape the complexion of the maritime transportation industry on Canada's West Coast for 150 years.

I was very appreciative when Dr. Hick finished his first book, *Hays' Orphan* because it provided a detailed account of the historical development of the Port of Prince Rupert. But of course, the story of port development in Prince Rupert is incomplete without an understanding of its historical context. Thus the need for what will truly become a companion volume to *Hays' Orphan, Canada's Pacific Gateways — Realizing the Vision*.

I must, once again, thank Dr. Hick for providing additional understanding of the port industry, as it was not until I read *Canada's Pacific Gateways — Realizing the Vision*, that I gained a more complete picture of the unfolding history of Canada's West Coast Gateway Ports. It is the cascading effect of world events, political influence, and human intervention that have chosen winners and losers and has ultimately molded the shape of the Port of Prince Rupert and the rest of Canada's Pacific Gateway ports.

Few readers would think of Victoria harbour as being the first of Canada's Pacific Gateways, but that is where Dr. Hick begins his story. And although New Westminster at first competed as the gateway to mainland British Columbia, it was Vancouver that ultimately won the railroad lottery and benefited from the political winds that provided economic support and investment to the newest maritime gateway. However, despite its vision as the prime gateway for Orient trade, the Port of Vancouver's first great impetus to growth came from the opening of the Panama Canal and the concurrent growth of grain trade to Europe through terminals provided by the federal government. The Port of Prince Rupert with its alternate rail corridor seemed to be born into a state of suspended animation, where it stayed for the first seven decades of its history. It arrived on the scene late and its influence was immediately marginalized by world wars, economic depressions, and world trade patterns that did not favour the northern port.

But the story of the Pacific Gateways, as foretold by Dr. Hick, is really just now getting underway. Today, there is a great deal of interest shown in Canada's Pacific Gateway Ports by both the public and by politicians of all stripes. British Columbia and Canada have a lot to gain from their relative proximity to the rapidly expanding economies of the nations of east and south Asia. For Canada — a nation whose economic prosperity depends upon selling its resources and manufactured goods to the world and, more specifically, to China and India in the coming decades — the advantage of having strong and healthy Pacific Gateway port structures served by two world class rail corridors will be critical to its success in capitalizing on this opportunity.

Dr. Hick provides us with a very insightful documentation of the way that the Pacific Gateways have emerged to their current position, but their story is ever changing. Dr. Hick, I know, struggled to close the manuscript of this book because there was always something new to be said. As we move through the current decade, geo-political influence and economic power will continue their dramatic growth in East and South Asia. This will be accompanied by growing political and industry recognition of the advantageous location of the Gateways for moving trade goods between these areas and the heartland of North America. With the commercialization of the transportation industry — whether it be the railroads or the port authorities themselves — and the consequential evolution toward more business-based decisions, it is easy to predict that the next 150 years belong to Canada's Pacific Gateways.

It is no wonder that the last word about the Pacific Gateways has not yet been written. The last and, I believe, the most exciting chapter is yet to be played.

Don Krusel, President and CEO
Prince Rupert Port Authority

ACKNOWLEDGEMENTS

This book originated in a decision taken in 2008 to update *Hays' Orphan* — a book describing the history of the Port of Prince Rupert — in light of the recent, substantial changes in the development and activity at that Northern Gateway Port. With the unfailing support of Don Krusel, President and CEO of the Prince Rupert Port Authority and his staff the project expanded to include a study of the development of the Southern Gateways at Victoria, New Westminster, and Vancouver with some emphasis on the political decisions that directly impacted the growth, or lack thereof, of each of the four ports.

The material for this book has been drawn from many published sources and I record my appreciation for the assistance provided by staff at the Vancouver Public Library, the Vancouver Maritime Museum, and both the Vancouver Fraser and Prince Rupert Port Authorities during the three years it has taken to complete this project.

As noted in the individual credits, the photographs assembled in the two pictorial sections have come from multiple sources, including the Vancouver and New Westminster Public Libraries, the Royal B.C. Museum, the Vancouver, North Vancouver, West Vancouver, New Westminster, Prince Rupert and Victoria Archives, the Vancouver Maritime Museum, ILWU Canada, Westshore Terminals and the Vancouver Fraser and Prince Rupert Port Authorities.

My thanks to Lynne Graham for her meticulous editing of the manuscript and captions, and to Toni Serofin for the excellence of her work preparing the book for publication.

Finally, my sincere gratitude to my wife Lillie for putting up with my three-year dedication to the research and writing of this book.

TABLE OF CONTENTS

CHAPTER ONE

Rail Corridors Through the Cordillera
to Canada's Two Pacific Gateways

CHAPTER TWO

CHAPTER THREE

PHOTO PLATES — SECTION 1

CHAPTER SEVEN

The Gateways 1970 to 1985 —
A Tentative Response to the "Container Revolution". 197

CHAPTER EIGHT

PHOTO PLATES — SECTION 2

CHAPTER NINE

CHAPTER TEN

CHAPTER ELEVEN

ABBREVIATIONS

AMP	Alternate Marine Power	IMO	International Maritime Organization
APGCI	Asia Pacific Gateway & Corridor Initiative	JRI	James Richardson International
B.C.	British Columbia	LNG	Liquefied Natural Gas
BCDC	British Columbia Development Corp.	LPC	Local Port Corporation
		MTBE	Methyl Tertiary Butyl Ether
BCR	British Columbia Railway (1972–1984)	NAFTA	North American Free Trade Agreement
BCRIC	B.C. Resources Investment Corp.	NHB	National Harbours Board
		NWHC	New Westminster Harbour Commission
BNSF	Burlington Northern Santa Fe Railway	NWMP	North West Mounted Police
CGMM	Canadian Government Merchant Marine	PCT	Pacific Coast Terminals
		PGE	Pacific Great Eastern Railway
CWB	Canadian Wheat Board	PMV	Port Metro Vancouver
CM&S	Consolidated Mining & Smelting Co.	PRPC	Prince Rupert Port Corporation
		RTI	Ridley Terminals Inc.
CNR (CN)	Canadian National Railways	RCN	Royal Canadian Navy
CNP	Canadian Northern Pacific Railway	SWP	Saskatchewan Wheat Pool
		TEU	Twenty Foot Equivalent Units
CPC	Canada Ports Corporation	UGG	United Grain Growers
CPR (CP)	Canadian Pacific Railway	U.K.	United Kingdom
ECA	Emission Control Area	U.S. (U.S.A.)	United States of America
FRHC	Fraser River Harbour Commission	U.S.S.R.	Union of Soviet Socialist Republics
FRPA	Fraser River Port Authority	VDWWA	Vancouver & District Waterfront Workers Association
FWS	Foley, Welch & Stewart		
GNR	Great Northern Railway		
GTR (GT)	Grand Trunk Railway	VHC	Vancouver Harbour Commission
GTP (GTPR)	Grand Trunk Pacific Railway		
HMCS	His/Her Majesty's Canadian Ship	VHCTR	Vancouver Harbour Commission Terminal Railway
HBC	Hudson's Bay Company	VPC	Vancouver Port Corporation
ILA	International Longshoremen's Association	VPA	Vancouver Port Authority
		VW&Y	Vancouver Westminster and Yukon Railway
ILWU	International Longshore and Warehouse Union		

PREFACE

Canada is exceptionally fortunate in having a superb natural harbour at each end of its Pacific Coastline. Over the past century these two harbours have been developed into national ports and with their vital rail corridors they have become key components in facilitating Canada's overseas trade, albeit at dramatically disparate growth rates.

The questions of why, where, and when developments serving overseas trade took place at each Gateway Port and its main corridor, the pervasive political influences that supplied historic and current senior government funding for port infrastructure and development, the effects of changing global markets, and the impact of economic cycles are considered in the context of explaining the present status of these two national ports.

China's spectacular entry into the world marketplace in recent years has stimulated intense focus at the highest levels of both the federal and provincial governments on the potential for Canada to play an expanded role as a North American entry point for transpacific trade. Achievement of that goal must involve careful consideration of where public funds can be applied most economically to assist in providing the most effective new capacity. It must also recognize and resolve the risks inherent in continuing to channel most of that trade through one corridor to one port. To this end the strengths and weaknesses of each corridor and gateway, together with its potential for further development, are explored.

Coastal domestic trade is not considered; neither are the ports on Vancouver Island or the valuable, rail served, private Port of Kitimat.

Where feasible, weights and measures are recorded in metric with imperial conversions but, where appropriate, terms that were in vogue prior to 1978 are used. Abbreviations are spelled out in full the first time they are used in each chapter. Place names and their spelling reflect those current at the time.

CHAPTER ONE

Rail Corridors Through the Cordillera to Canada's Two Pacific Gateways

INTRODUCTION

The first rail line to cross North America was completed at Promontory, Utah on May 10, 1869. For the next four decades there was enormous popular enthusiasm in the United States (U.S.) for new railways to "open the west" and connect to the Pacific Coast. To subsidize their construction 60 million hectares (150 million acres) of western lands were granted to railway entrepreneurs who eventually completed nine major routes to the West Coast from the Midwest and southern parts of the country.

Seven months after the last spike ceremony at Promontory, Utah, the infant Dominion of Canada purchased Rupert's Land (the vast central plain drained by rivers emptying into Hudson's Bay) for $1.5 million and then on July 20, 1871, British Columbia (B.C.) became part of the Canadian Federation with the promise to commence a rail connection to Central Canada within three years. As a consequence, the urgent need to construct at least one transcontinental line became the major issue for Canada's first government led by Sir John A. Macdonald.

Macdonald was determined that the route of the new rail link to the West Coast must be all Canadian, despite the exceedingly difficult terrain north of Lake Superior. He further insisted that the railway must be solely financed by Canadian and British private capital, supported by government grants of lands and money. Thus began the inextricable link between railways and politics in Canada, and later in B.C.

The political imperatives were clear. There was the commitment to B.C., the very real threat of annexation of the West by the U.S., the need to populate the central plains with immigrants and, in the face of high U.S. tariffs, the need to have ports on both coasts united by rail to foster overseas trade, especially with the Orient. The concept of a land bridge to Europe from Asia had its origins during this time, creating another reason to get on with the railway. Canadians caught the U.S. mania for railway building and it, too, lasted for over 40 years.

Railways became highly politicized and many leading politicians doubled as railway promoters. It would soon become evident that building railways in Canada was much more profitable than operating them in this sparsely populated land. Massive government support was needed to induce private capital to invest in railway ownership.

Though aware of the monumental task ahead, the infant Dominion had committed to build the longest railway in the world, over some of the most difficult terrain ever encountered by railway builders anywhere. Surveys commenced to find a practical route for the "Pacific Railway," while Macdonald sought out reputable capitalists or financial institutions willing to back the project.

He first approached the owners of Eastern Canada's existing main line, the Grand Trunk Railway (GTR). At the time of Confederation, this company's lines formed the world's largest railway network with 2,055 km (1,277 miles) of track and, by the late 1880s, its main line extended from Sarnia to Halifax with additional lines into the U.S., including Chicago and the port of Portland, Maine.

Though at first strongly supportive of the GTR, the Canadian public had become disillusioned and viewed it with contempt and hostility because of its perceived bad labour relations and endless importuning of government for cash grants, guaranteed interest on railway bonds, land grants, rebates, and rights of way. Construction costs, absentee management, and failure to generate anticipated traffic levels left the GTR debt-ridden and unable to adequately upgrade its line or equipment.

The GTR head offices were in London, England, where most of its financing had been raised. The British owners and operators were only interested in building a line west across the continent if it were to be routed via Chicago. They would not consider an all-Canadian route until the population in the West had grown sufficiently to support such a line.

An initial offer to arrange financing for the railway from Montreal ship owner and financier, Sir Hugh Allan, was unacceptable as it involved assistance from the American financier Jay Cooke, who was building the Northern Pacific Railway across the U.S. There was strong resistance in Canada to any U.S. sourced capital. This related directly to concern that such involvement could mean long delays and, perhaps, even a contrived postponement of construction, while U.S. railways sent multiple tracks north to siphon off traffic, economically controlling Canada west of the Lakes, and thereby eventually absorbing the country.

Further negotiation with Allan and his partners finally resulted in a deal to build the railway. It would be called the Canadian Pacific Railway. There would be no U.S. capital involved, there would be directors from the provinces, and the company would receive cash grants and millions of acres of land from the government. Rejected U.S. capitalists were furious and retaliated by circulating rumours of excessive government favour to Allan. Macdonald won re-election in 1872, but it soon became public that some of his re-election campaign funds had come from Allan and he was forced to resign. In late 1873, the Liberal (ex-Reform) government took power with Alexander Mackenzie the new prime minister.

Mackenzie did not share Macdonald's vision of the strategic importance of a railway to Canadian nationhood. He dismissed B.C. as a land of "superlative difficulties," and viewed the railway project as "a bargain to be broken." He professed surprise that B.C. viewed the rail line as a sacred trust and tried to renegotiate the federal commitment to complete the rail line by 1881. This produced a strong protest in Victoria with threats of joining the U.S. and public demonstrations demanding that the B.C. Government stand firm. Mackenzie faced not only losing B.C., but also a resurgence of the Metis problem in Manitoba. He vacillated, feeling that the Tory commitment was preposterous, and proposed that the government build only rail links between navigable waterways, thus abandoning the sector north of Lake Superior.

In opposition, Macdonald articulated his "National Policy" of high tariffs, a sea-to-sea railway, and settlement of the West. He insisted that only with the pursuit of these goals could Canada be assured prosperity.

There was at least some progress in the sea-to-sea railway, albeit in the East. In 1876 the Intercolonial Railway was completed, fulfilling a 40-year-old Maritime desire to secure a railway link to Central Canada. It was wholly government owned and soon became a sinkhole for public funds and patronage.

BUILDING THE CANADIAN PACIFIC RAILWAY (CPR)

In the West, two issues remained to be settled, the route through the mountains and the Pacific terminus. Though no track had yet been laid, much route surveying had been completed. Sir Sanford Fleming, Canada's most eminent railway surveyor and civil engineer, recommended the route through the Yellowhead Pass, then south to Kamloops, and on through the Fraser Canyon to a terminus at Port Moody on Burrard Inlet. Other options included taking the line west from Yellowhead to Port Simpson, or taking a southern route through Kicking Horse Pass. The latter was strongly supported by those who feared incursions into the southern sectors of the province by U.S. Railroads.

The question of the ocean terminal was politically difficult. The capital city Victoria, still dominant in provincial overseas trade, had been promised that it would be the terminus of the "Pacific Railroad." It wanted the line to reach tidewater at Bute Inlet and thence by ferry to Vancouver Island with a terminus at Esquimalt. Rival New Westminster, which had lost its bid to be the provincial capital, very much wanted to be the terminal city, or at least have the line pass through en route to Burrard Inlet. Richard Moody, by this time a major general, was brought out of retirement in England to adjudicate the issue. He chose Burrard Inlet over Bute Inlet and a Victoria terminus, to keep the Fraser Valley and southern B.C. from domination by the U.S. rail lines to Puget Sound.

With B.C. threatening to pull out of the Confederation and Sir John A. Macdonald back in power in 1878, priority was given to his "National Policy" goals. To compete with the U.S. for immigrants, land grant policies for homesteaders were developed that were at least as attractive as those south of the border. Protective tariffs were raised and a new attempt made to get the "Pacific Railway" underway. Port Moody was designated the Pacific terminus, replacing the earlier promise of Esquimalt. The government contracted Andrew

Onderdonk, an American, to start work in the Fraser Canyon section and construction began at Yale in May 1880. This contract preceded both the conclusion of negotiations with Allan's Canadian Pacific (CP) Syndicate and a decision on the route through the mountains. Undoubtedly, it was awarded to placate the separatists who were becoming increasingly vocal in B.C.

The deal to build the railway was negotiated by Tupper, the federal Minister of Railways, with a syndicate of Canadian financiers including George Stephen, President of the Bank of Montreal, his cousin Donald Smith, J.J. Hill, R.B. Angus, and John S. Kennedy. Hill, a Canadian, had built an impressive record in the U.S., particularly in the rescue of the St. Paul and Pacific Railroad. Its subsidiary, the St. Paul, Minneapolis and Manitoba Line, extended to the Canadian border south of Winnipeg.

Negotiations between the federal government and Allan's CP Syndicate resulted in a contract to complete and operate the "Pacific Railway" that was signed on October 1, 1880. Salient points of the agreement included:

- An all Canadian route
- A grant of $25 million cash and 10 million hectares (25 million acres) of lands "fairly fit for settlements," in the "fertile belt." (The latter being unlike the U.S. land grants to railways, which were made without regard to quality.)
- No new lines connecting east to west to be chartered for 20 years
- No taxes for 20 years
- Freedom from any rate regulation until a minimum 10% profit achieved
- Sections already contracted to be turned over

Legislation confirming the contract was passed February 15, 1881 after weeks of debate with the Liberals who opposed every clause.

In assessing the magnitude of this project, it is noteworthy that the Union Pacific, which opened up the American West, had only to build 1,760 km (1,100 miles) of track through a known and relatively easy route, while backed by the resources of a great power. Canadian Pacific had to build 4,000 km (2,500 miles) of line and cross multiple mountain ranges, while backed by a nation of only 4 million people — almost all located in the East — and with a depleted national treasury.

Hill's main contribution to the future Canadian Pacific Railway (CPR) was his recommendation of the American, William C. Van Horne, as general manager of the project with Thomas G. Shaughnessy as his assistant. Later, Hill pulled out of the syndicate when he found he could not convince his partners or the government to confine the construction to a line from Port Moody east to Winnipeg, there to connect south with his St. Paul line. Failing to complete the line north of Lake Superior would of course have meant abandoning the basic principle of an All Canadian Line. Hill soon became the fledgling CPR's chief rival by extending his U.S. line to the Pacific as the Great Northern Railway (GNR) with multiple branch lines into Canada. So began the irony of the personal duel between Hill, the Canadian known in the U.S. as the "Empire Builder" for transforming the U.S. Northwest, and Van Horne and Shaughnessy, the only two Americans knighted for their work in the interest of the Dominion of Canada.

Van Horne at once abandoned the Yellowhead route chosen by Sanford Fleming, in favour of a more southerly line, and pressed for speedy completion — in contrast to those that favoured progress at the rate of settlement. He also believed strongly that trade with the Orient would be crucial to the Railway's solvency. The route through the Kicking Horse Pass was finally chosen and Onderdonk's initial government contracts (by now assumed by the CPR) were extended to connect the line from Yale to Port Moody and build east from Savona.

The choice of the shorter (by 120 km [75 miles]) southern route was primarily motivated by awareness that settlement density, and therefore traffic in both B.C. and the prairies, was greatest near the U.S. border and certainly well south of the much easier Yellowhead route. Only by choosing a route near the border could the CPR forestall its aggressive rival, Hill's Great Northern Railway, from siphoning off much of the potential traffic with numerous branch lines crossing the boundary. The price paid, of course, was in having to cope with the problems relating to the excessive grades on this southern route. These were overcome in stages over the next century, but only after the expenditure of many hundreds of millions of dollars.

By the fall of 1883 the line was nearing Kicking Horse Pass. West of the Pass, grades of 4.5 percent at the "Big Hill" forced westbound trains to slow to 10 km per hour. After many disastrous run-a-ways, this grade was substantially reduced with construction of the Spiral Tunnel in 1906 and the Connaught Tunnel in 1916.

Early in 1885 the railway was out of funds, though only a few gaps remained to be built north of Lake Superior and in B.C. Oddly enough, Louis Riel saved the day!

Some Metis had accepted Canadian law in Manitoba, while others had moved west to the banks of the South Saskatchewan River at Batoche near the new river town of Prince Albert. There, 2000 of them under their leader Gabriel Doumont, formed a government of sorts. When Canadian government and railroad surveyors arrived to carve up the land, all the fears and frictions that had produced the Red River Rebellion resurfaced.

Since being paid to stay out of Canada, Riel had busied himself teaching Indian children to read and write at a Catholic Mission in Montana. He was now an American citizen and possessed of a vision that he was David, of Biblical fame. To Dumont and his Metis at Batoche, Riel was the Messiah. They called for him and in 1884 he returned to Canada.

The Northwest Mounted Police (NWMP) increased forces on the Saskatchewan River to the fury of the Metis. Riel's mind was clouded with messianic visions, megalomania, and anger. Strains finally exploded in March 1885 at Duck Lake when the Metis ambushed 95 members of the NWMP, killing 12 and wounding 11 more.

Macdonald now had a second Metis War to deal with and turned to the CPR. Van Horne promised to get troops to the scene in 11 days via the rail line despite the gaps — a vast improvement on the 96-day trek west of troops sent to the first rebellion 15 years earlier. After several more skirmishes and massacres, Batoche was finally taken, Riel surrendered, and Dumont was escorted to Montana. Riel was tried for his role in the revolt. His defence was insanity. Despite strong intervention on his behalf by Laurier (who was responding to an incensed Quebec public) and appeals to the Privy Council and Queen, he was hanged in November 1885. Before execution, Riel wrote to President Cleveland urging the U.S. to annex the Canadian West. His fate was deeply resented by French Canada and, eventually, the issue would destroy the Tory grip on government.

However, the Batoche incident saved the CPR. Its role in the speedy transfer of troops to the Northwest Rebellion was proof enough of its vital importance to national integrity and enabled Macdonald to get acceptance of further government appropriations to complete the line.

On November 1, 1885 the last spike was driven. The "Northwest Passage" was now open and the Canadian Nation became a viable entity. On July 4, 1886 the first transcontinental train arrived in Port Moody from Montreal. Though the line was complete, the financial strains on the CPR at this point were great. The company owed the federal government $9.9 million on loans of $29.9 million and was forgiven that amount on the surrender of one-quarter of its land grants.

On Vancouver Island another railway was underway. It had its origins in Macdonald's promise to make Esquimalt the terminus of the "Pacific Railway." B.C. coal magnate and politician, Robert Dunsmuir, was granted three-quarters of a million dollars by Ottawa and 800,000 hectares (2 million acres) of the best land on Vancouver Island (one-fifth the total) by the province to build a rail line from Esquimalt to Courtney with branches to Port Alberni and Lake Cowichan. Macdonald came to B.C. for the first and only time to drive the last spike in the line on August 13, 1886. The CPR later purchased the line in 1905, complete with its land grants, though only after the province declined an offer to acquire the line.

With news that the CPR was to be extended west another 20 km (12 miles) from Port Moody, the tiny settlement of Granville was incorporated in 1886 with the new name Vancouver. The first train arrived there on February 23, 1887, though officially not until May 23, 1887. Soon large quantities of lumber, salmon, and refined sugar were moving east by rail and the new land bridge service to Europe began based on cargoes of tea and silk from the Orient that were initially brought to the Port Moody terminus in chartered vessels. In 1891 the first of three new *Empress* passenger/cargo liners arrived from Britain for the CPR's transpacific service and U.S. rail lines were shocked by this lively, new, and potent competition. By this time Vancouver's population had reached 13,685 and the metamorphosis from tent town to metropolis was well underway.

THE CANADIAN NORTHERN RAILWAY

While the transcontinental CPR was being built, two Ontario contractors, Mackenzie and Mann, who had built large sections of that line, saw opportunities for "colonization" rail lines in the "Fertile Belt" of Manitoba. Between 1884 and 1890 three companies that they formed for this purpose received land grants of 4 million acres. Although these lines were built only as traffic warranted and to a very modest standard (with promise to upgrade), they became known as the "Farmers' Friend" and were combined to form the Canadian Northern Railway in 1899. A line was built to connect Winnipeg to Port Arthur on Lake Superior. Grain elevators were built there and freight rates were generally lower than those demanded by the CPR. The lines were financed with federal, provincial, and municipal loans and bond guarantees, and their construction was strongly motivated by the desire to create competition to the perceived CP monopoly.

Government largesse in awarding huge land grants to stimulate railroad building was coming to an end. In the U.S., where 60 million hectares (150 million acres) of land had been granted to various railways, exploitative tendencies soon appeared which irritated and alarmed western settlers. As a result, there were no further U.S. land grants after 1871.

In Canada, too, opposition to land monopoly eventually brought a halt to further grants and forced some to be cancelled for non-performance of the obligations agreed to by their recipients. Support for railway development via government loan guarantees instead of grants became the vogue. The CPR had been a national building project of supreme importance. The precedent of huge land grants did not need to be repeated. To do so could encourage rivals to the CPR and negate the spirit of the Syndicate contract.

LAURIER AND THE LIBERALS

Final rejection of incentive land grants coincided with the election of the Liberals under Laurier in 1896, giving them the opportunity to denounce the Tories and concurrently be seen as the friend of homesteaders who fancied themselves perennial victims of the CPR. Indeed, Laurier's incoming government began that great Canadian political tradition of having to be seen to be upset with all the previous government's decisions and, wherever possible, to overturn them, or at the very least change direction.

In 1891 Macdonald won re-election with his "National Policy," especially because of his stand on tariffs. He knew that reciprocity was the best policy, but protectionism was very strong in the U.S. Congress so, to survive, Canada had to erect a barrier of high tariffs. Macdonald feared, first economic and then political union with the U.S. if the Liberal ideas of "unrestricted reciprocity" were allowed. Laurier and his Liberals were to learn that the Canadian public would oppose at the polls any policy that threatened independence, regardless of how economically beneficial it might appear. Thus reciprocity lay dormant for

20 years, only to awaken and destroy Laurier in 1911. Macdonald died on June 6, 1891 and was followed by four Tory prime ministers in five years: Abbott, Thompson, Bowell and Tupper.

In 1893 stock markets crashed, an event followed by a major economic slump in North America. In Canada, the provinces became restive and Nova Scotians talked of secession. The period 1895–1909 began and ended in economic recession with euphoric heights in between.

Macdonald's "National Policy" was confirmed in spades by the Liberals who found that despite high tariffs, Canada was still selling nearly half its exports to the Americans who were becoming increasingly dependent on Canadian raw materials. To the Liberals, the CPR was a creation of the hated Tories, so when they came to power, the close contact of the government with the CPR and the sense of obligation to the spirit of the Syndicate contract weakened considerably.

Canada entered the twentieth century fully recovered from depression. The economy was booming and Laurier proclaimed that the new century "belonged to Canada." Historians in the U.S. have called the first decade "The Good Years." In Canada, enthusiasm and euphoria were epidemic and public pressures led to more and more plans for new railways to open the relatively unpopulated West.

In 1901 the population of B.C. stood at 179,000 — a tremendous increase from the 50,000 recorded in 1883. It would double over the next decade, reaching 400,000 by 1911.

Laurier's Liberals, who had attacked the building of the CPR as madness, began to reverse course in response to public demand. They decided to replace land grants to railway builders with incentives through loan guarantee.

By the turn of the century 30,400 km (19,000 miles) of track had been laid in Canada. Railways owned land areas greater than many European countries and railway building had made many millionaires, especially in Montreal. The CPR was at least profitable, despite the challenge from the Great Northern across the border. Hill had committed his railroad to a Pacific extension to Puget Sound with branch lines to the south bank of the Fraser River and into the Kootenays to benefit from the mining boom there. To protect its interests in southern B.C. the CPR asked for and received $3.3 million in aid from the federal government to build a line through the Crowsnest Pass just 40 km (25 miles) north of the border. The resulting famous (or, eventually infamous) 1897 agreement included the Crow rate for grain transportation, a monstrosity that distorted western agriculture development and haunted the railways for the next 86 years. In response to the Great Northern line entering coastal British Columbia, CP built a line south from Mission to connect with the Northern Pacific Railway, thus robbing Hill of cross border traffic. Further friction developed between the CPR and GNR as Hill attempted to tap into the Orient trade, which up to then had been an almost exclusive preserve of the CPR.

In the populating of the West one name stands out, that of Sir Clifford Sifton, Laurier's

Minister of the Interior. This Prairie lawyer was determined to create conditions attractive to massive immigration and he succeeded. Essential to this success was the development of the "Marquis" wheat variety, capable of maturing in the shorter growing season of the northern plains. Free land in the U.S. was no longer available and many Americans, as well as returning expatriates, entered Canada to create the next immigrant invasion from south of the border after the United Empire Loyalists.

Between 1898 and 1904 over 60,000 European farmers and 120,000 from Britain arrived, adding to the influx of 180,000 from the U.S. They all needed the products of the industrial complexes developing in the St. Lawrence Valley, as well as transportation by rail to move these goods to their homesteads and to export their agricultural products.

Railways became a Canadian obsession. They were essential to the cultural and economic development of the Great Plains and basic to their history. Their success and that of the communities they served were inextricably linked. Communication by telegraph followed the rail lines. Settlers resented the CPR monopoly and it was apparent to them that relief was available if governments and moneylenders provided funds to encourage new and competing lines. In 1900, the covenant between the CPR backers and Ottawa that precluded, for 20 years, a federal charter for a second transcontinental railway expired, opening the way for new lines to be built.

From all this exuberance, Canada was to get its second and third transcontinental rail lines. The race to complete the second line began when the Grand Trunk directors, chagrined by what they had missed, began to reconsider their former position. They had timidly rejected Macdonald's offer to build the "Pacific Railroad" in 1880 and so had lost the bonanza of land grants and cash later given to the CP Syndicate. They were jealous of the phenomenal and unexpected success of the CPR and acutely aware that it was draining traffic from their mature lines, which extended west only as far as North Bay, Ontario. Well aware of the shift in political winds in Ottawa and of the revised thinking of his Board of Directors in London, Charles M. Hays, recently reengaged as general manager of the Grand Trunk Railway, formed a subsidiary in 1902, the Grand Trunk Pacific Railway (GTP). He announced that a new line would be built from North Bay across northwest Ontario and the Prairies, through the Rockies, and thence across B.C. to a new Pacific port on the coast that would be closer to the Orient than CPR's Vancouver terminus. Such a port would, in Hay's view, capture substantial Orient trade. In addition, Hays indicated the intention to build a deep-sea fleet to further challenge the CPR. This land bridge vision was, he proclaimed, the "All Red Route" of the British Empire.

CHARLES MELVILLE HAYS

In 1895 the Grand Trunk directors named Charles Melville Hays general manager of the railway. Hays was a native of Rock Island, Illinois and started his railroading career at age

17, as a clerk in the passenger department of the Atlantic and Pacific Railway. Gaining experience with increasingly responsible positions with the Missouri Pacific Railway and the Wabash & St. Louis Pacific Railway Company, his advancement was rapid.

During his initial engagement from 1895 to 1900 as general manager of the Grand Trunk Railway, Hays initiated a massive upgrading program for the company's lines, including double tracking from Montreal to Sarnia, curve and grade reductions to improve efficiency, and reconstruction of bridges, yards, and buildings. He at once took on the Canadian Pacific in the East and soon restored the GTR to viability and profitability.

Hays left the GTR in 1900 to take a position as president of the Southern Pacific Railway Co., but unhappy differences with its new owners, coupled with a call from Sir Charles Rivers Wilson, GTR president, brought him back to Montreal in late 1901, as second vice president and general manager of the GTR. His connection thereafter with the GTR and its subsidiary Grand Trunk Pacific Railway was continuous, until his demise in April 1912. In October 1909 he was appointed president of the parent company.

Hays was very clearly a driven man, possessed of great energy, ambition, and ability. He was, however, a micromanager, addicted to the power of undivided control. This led too often to mediocre and inept lower level management. His dubious practices in dealing with the acquisition of rights of way and town sites located on Indian reserves along the planned route of the Grand Trunk Pacific Railway, has left a sad legacy of strained relations with a number of First Nations to this day, especially in the Prince Rupert Harbour area. His reactionary policies towards labour led to intense strife in the operation of the GTR and later in the construction and operation of the GTP. Miserable pay and working conditions during construction of the latter resulted in strikes and inability to secure an adequate labour force, with the consequence of at least a year delay in completion of the railway. Hays' response to labour troubles was to demand that Ottawa change its exclusion policy so that he could bring in Asian labour to work on the line. Laurier refused. He was combative and aggressive and antagonized both federal bureaucrats and the provincial government in Victoria. He browbeat the first City Council in Prince Rupert over property assessments with the result that the Bank of Montreal cut off the nascent city's credit, until they settled with the railroad.

Sir Wilfrid Laurier called him "a valuable acquisition to Canada," but one of his Ministers described Hays as "heartless, cruel, and tyrannical," and an Edmonton magistrate declared that the GTP's treatment of its workers was disgraceful. Perhaps Laurier was influenced by the Grand Trunk's new hotel in Ottawa being named the Chateau Laurier!

PLANS FOR TWO NEW TRANSCONTINENTAL RAILWAYS

Laurier was now enthused with the prospect of a new railroad across Canada. He and his Liberals, who had so vehemently opposed the Tory-backed CPR, now wanted to make their mark as builders of a second "Liberal" line across Canada. Even Van Horne agreed it was a good idea, there being "enough for all" in his view. His former assistant Shaughnessy, by 1899 president of the CPR, opposed the line, as did the City of Vancouver and the Canadian Northern Railway of Mackenzie and Mann. Opposition from established interests on the South Coast would continue to plague the development of the new rail line and new port for many years to come.

By 1902, the Canadian Northern Railway, the "Farmers' Friend," was operating 2,100 km (1,300 miles) of track in Manitoba and in what would soon become the Province of Saskatchewan. These lines connected to Port Arthur on Lake Superior. They were Manitoba's counterweight to the CPR and exclusively served 130 communities. Plans were in hand to extend the lines further west into what would become Alberta. Faced with the GTP's announcement of intent to build a new transcontinental line, Mackenzie and Mann abandoned their concept of being a regional railroad in favour of creating a third railway to the Pacific.

They had the unique advantage of planning their transcontinental line *after* they had developed a strong prairie system of branch lines. Furthermore, they enjoyed strong local support. The CPR had also finally built up an extensive branch network to feed its main line. The GTP, however, forged ahead with its main line west without any supporting network of branch lines and this would become one of the reasons for its eventual downfall.

Consumed with their new vision, Mackenzie and Mann moved their base to Toronto and rejected offers from both the GTP and CPR to be bought out, even though the GTP was prepared to make Mackenzie its president. In 1903, Laurier tried to persuade the Canadian Northern and the GTP to amalgamate, but failed to apply the pressure needed and available to achieve this result. At one point Mackenzie and Mann offered to build a jointly owned section from the end of the Grand Trunk at North Bay to Port Arthur, whereupon their railway would develop to the west, while the Grand Trunk developed in the east. This offer was rejected. They, along with Hays, were swept up in the euphoria of the times and failed to realize that two more Trans-Canada lines were "too much railway for too few people."

By early 1903, the GTP was considering building a line to extend from Quebec City to a terminus on the West Coast somewhere between Bute Inlet and Port Simpson. It would cross the Rockies through the Pine, Peace, or Yellowhead Passes.

Laurier became involved with the planned Liberal-supported second Atlantic to Pacific line. He conceived of a "National Transcontinental Railway" from Moncton to Winnipeg via Quebec City and thence west to the Pacific at Port Simpson. This was, at least partly, in response to Maritime pressure for a second line via Quebec to Central Canada. From Moncton, there would be links to Halifax and St. John. With two-thirds of Canadian grain exports then shipped via U.S. ports, it was deemed most desirable to re-route this trade over Canadian lines to Canadian ports.

Laurier proposed that the federal government would build the line east to the Atlantic from Winnipeg, while the GTP could build west to the Pacific with Ottawa guaranteeing bonds for most of the construction costs. The GTP planned to construct the main line west to the Pacific first and then add a network of lines on the Great Plains to collect grain for export to East Asia, thereby balancing prospective imports of tea and silk. Laurier further proposed that the Grand Trunk Pacific provide rolling stock for the entire coast to coast hybrid system and, after seven years, lease and operate the government built eastern portion.

The National Transcontinental Railway bill passed the House, September 2, 1903 over strong Tory opposition. Their leader, Robert Borden, had proposed a government buyout of the CPR line from Sudbury to the Lakehead with running rights open to all. That would have linked the Canadian Northern in the west with the Grand Trunk network in the east and been a much more rational approach.

The politics of the situation are fascinating. The federal Tories were basking in the success of "their" railroad, the CPR. Laurier was determined to have a Liberal-sponsored line and chose the hybrid National Transcontinental as the vehicle to achieve his goal. The Canadian Northern was strongly supported in the West, where Saskatchewan and Alberta were about to become provinces (1905), and it was also favoured by the Tory government in B.C.

Mackenzie and Mann received funding, bond guarantees, and land from local governments to extend their lines across the prairies and, by 1905, the Canadian Northern had reached Edmonton, capital of the new Province of Alberta.

McBride, B.C.'s Tory Premier gave strong support to the builders of the Canadian Northern based primarily on their choice of Burrard Inlet for its western terminus. He called the Canadian Northern a "thoroughly Canadian system controlled by Canadians," as opposed to the London based directors of the GTP and the dominantly British owned CPR. As the GTP was so closely aligned with the federal Liberals, it was to receive only token help from B.C. Mackenzie and Mann, recognizing the nuances in politics west of the Rockies, were astute enough to call their proposed line in B.C. the Canadian Northern Pacific Railway (CNP).

During the 1904 federal election campaign, Tory leader Borden came out strongly in favour of a "People's Railway." The new Trans-Canada lines should be wholly owned and controlled by the people of Canada. Borden vehemently opposed Laurier's hybrid National Transcontinental as far too favourable to the GTP. In his view, if Canadian taxpayers had to underwrite 90 percent of the project, they might as well pay the rest and own it outright. The major issue of the 1904 election became public versus private (with massive government support) ownership of the second sea-to-sea railroad. Borden lost and berated voters for a verdict against themselves in favour of corporate interest.

Meanwhile, Hays was having problems convincing the London directors of the GTR to accept Laurier's plan. They were still smarting from the folly of rejecting the massive support offered 25 years earlier to build the "Pacific Railway." To their chagrin, land grants were a thing of the past and no longer available. Attempts to sweeten the deal further were dismissed by Laurier who could always turn to the eager and willing Mackenzie and Mann if the GTP backed out.

A primary motive behind the GTR board's eventual decision to build a western extension to their eastern rail network was the desire to capture a share of the rapidly expanding wheat exports from the central plains. Moreover, the producers there needed manufactured goods from the east, produced on lines served by the existing railway. By stressing this potential, Hays was able to convince the GTR president and directors of the viability of a western extension to the mountains.

The London directors were more skeptical, however, toward the concurrent building of a line from the Pacific Coast, east across B.C. to the prairies. The GTR president, Sir Charles Rivers Wilson, believed that there was little prospect of revenue from the B.C. section of the line and wished to leave its construction until later.

Hays, however, was convinced that the proposed line across the mid-section of B.C. could lead to rapid exploitation of large coal deposits and timber resources. He was further persuaded that the completion of his line to the North Coast, 804 km (500 miles) closer to Asia, would result in the capture of much of the rapidly expanding Orient trade. He was not the first with this vision. An eastern promotion, the Trans-Canada Railway Company, had sought government support for a north line from Quebec City to Port Simpson since 1895 and one proposed option for the CPR had been through the Yellowhead Pass to the same port.

Hays further pressed his case for an early start on construction from the Pacific Coast eastward by predicting large exports of prairie grain to Asian markets, as well as the prospect of substantial utilization of the completed line as a land bridge from Alaska to the lower states.

Eventually Hays managed to override the concerns of the GTR president and the more cautious members of his London board, committing the parent company to the entire project and its construction schedule. The entire line was to be built to a very highest standard, very much higher than the more frugally built Canadian Northern "colonization" lines. This requirement was spelled out in the contract drawn up between the railroad and the federal government which, among other things, insisted that the entire transcontinental main line be built to the high standard of the existing GTR line from Montreal to Toronto. This meant ruling gradients of 0.4 percent, curvatures of no more than 6 percent, use of 80-pound rail, and the use of concrete and steel in the construction of bridges over major rivers. Hays agreed to this without complaint, based on his firm belief that the extra costs would be recouped many times over in much reduced operating costs, especially when competing with the CPR main line in the south. Later though, when the railway was in deep financial trouble, he complained about the high and costly standard that had been imposed on the GTP by the federal government. Clearly, the design standard for most of the National Transcontinental was much too good for the traffic it could attract.

Added to his very optimistic and imaginative predictions for traffic, Hays was convinced that immediate and handsome returns would be obtained from the sale of subdivided property in town sites developed along the railway's route. Denied land grants by both federal and provincial governments, Hays established a subsidiary, the GTP Town and Development Company in 1906 (later called the GTP Development Company) to acquire land for this purpose. A major problem for all railway builders eager to reap early returns from the sale of land was deflecting speculators and opportunistic rivals in town development. Secrecy in planning town locations and speed and stealth in land acquisition were all-important.

Hays expected that the most important town site on the entire line would be at the Pacific terminus. He further expected that the sale of lots there and at other town sites would recoup the costs of land acquisition many times, and thereby provide immediate capital for additional development.

PROPERTY ACQUISITION
FOR THE NEW TERMINAL PORT CITY

In 1904, Kaien Island, which formed the south shore of the magnificent harbour then shown on Admiralty charts as Tuck's Inlet, was finally chosen over Port Simpson or Kitimat as the Pacific terminus for the new transcontinental rail line. B.C. Premier McBride, under considerable public pressure, repudiated his predecessor's promise to grant lands to any railway building a line to the coast, but did facilitate — by secret order in council — the GTP's May 1904 purchase of 4,000 hectares (10,000 acres) on Kaien Island. The purchase price was $10,000 and included a reversion right to the province of one-quarter of the land and waterfront. In return for this bargain, McBride demanded an early start to construction eastward from the Kaien Island terminal, rather than wait for the more sensible westward progression from the prairies as traffic expanded with settlement. A year later, using intermediaries, the railway acquired Ridley Island, as well as several small land parcels that controlled the limited practical approaches to Kaien Island.

In addition to the provincial crown grant of land on Kaien Island, the GTP considered it essential to acquire the portion of the Tsimpsean Indian Reserve No. 2 that constituted the entire west coast of the island. Early in 1906, company agents began negotiations with the Metlakatla Band for the acquisition of the west coastal strip of Kaien Island, as well as for parcels on Digby Island and the north shore of the harbour. These lands had been part of the Band reserve since 1888. After a week of bargaining, agreement was reached between the Band and the GTP for the sale of 13,567 acres in three parcels at a price of $7.50 per acre, for a total figure of $103,202. The local Indian agent considered this a very good deal for the Band and Anglican Bishop DuVernet presided over the signing of the provisional agreement on February 7, 1906. The deal was then subject to approval by the Department of Indian Affairs (DIA) in Ottawa.

The federal government asked the Province of B.C. to waive its reversionary interest in the land to be removed from the Indian Reserve, a request the B.C. Cabinet rejected outright. In Ottawa, the Tory opposition protested that if the land would soon be worth $100–1,000 per acre, as the Liberals had boasted, the DIA had robbed the native people by not reserving a quarter of the land parcels for the original owners, as the province had done on the Kaien Island land sale to the GTP. In Victoria, the government insisted that the three parcels alienated from the native reserve by Ottawa on behalf of the GTP belonged to the province, even though by then the GTP had paid the full-agreed amount to the DIA on behalf of the band. None of the funds, however, had yet reached the band and, by April 1907, they were becoming increasingly upset and blamed the local Indian agent for the delay.

The province used the club of its reversionary right to extract further concessions from the GTP and a final agreement on further terminal land acquisitions between the railway and the province was not signed until February 29, 1908. In return for waiving its right to the 13,567 acres removed from reserve lands, the GTP would pay the province $2.50 per acre, allow B.C. to select for provincial ownership one quarter of the these additional lands and waterfront (as in the original 1904 purchase by the GTP on Kaien Island), promise to commence continuous construction eastward from its terminal by March 1, 1908 and, finally, purchase all possible construction materials and supplies in B.C.

With this agreement, the GTP now owned more land at its Pacific terminus than the CPR did at theirs. In the fall of 1907, the GTP corporate secretary estimated that the railway would receive over $25 million from the sale of these lands. Later events were to prove this a wildly optimistic figure.

TWO NEW RAIL LINES HEADING WEST

In 1905 the GTP began building west from Winnipeg, locating their line south of the newly built Canadian Northern Line. In that same year Laurier turned the first sod for the Moncton to Winnipeg portion of his National Transcontinental. Progress was slow on the GTP line westward. It finally reached Edmonton in 1909, four years after the Canadian Northern. Both lines selected the Yellowhead Pass for their route through the Rockies. The GTP reached their final decision in September 1906 after extensive surveys of three possibilities: the Pine, Peace, and Yellowhead Passes. The choice of both railways confirmed the recommendation of Sir Sanford Fleming to the CPR in 1870. Hays was satisfied that the Yellowhead offered the most direct and economical line for the operation of a transcontinental railway.

From the Yellowhead Pass the two railroads were to take very different paths to an ocean terminal. The GTP had decided on their terminus in 1904 and had negotiated the initial purchase of crown land on Kaien Island. Mackenzie and Mann, too, had originally considered building their line to reach the coast at a point 800 km (500 miles) north of Vancouver. The

GTP's terminal choice caused them to look further south. Moreover, their strong supporters in the provincial government did not want their line to terminate that far north, thus creating a rival port to Vancouver and Victoria. Indeed, the Conservative government of Premier Prior in 1903 had attempted to persuade Mackenzie and Mann to bring their Canadian Northern Pacific line out to the coast at Bute Inlet, and thence by bridge crossings to Vancouver Island for a terminus in Victoria. That old idea was still not dead!

The main issue of the B.C. election in 1909 was public endorsement of the contract between the province and the CNP guaranteeing principle and interest on construction bonds for the B.C. portion of the line. A stipulation required that one-sixth of the new tracks had to be built on Vancouver Island. McBride's whole platform for that election was based on railroad development and his re-election, by a landslide, confirmed the popular enthusiasm of the day for such projects.

The Canadian Northern did receive some support from Ottawa. Though their lines served half the prairie grain elevators, the railway had no link to Central Canada or the Atlantic coast. It had failed in an attempt to buy the Intercolonial Railway but did manage to purchase 2,600 km (1,600 miles) of track in Ontario, Quebec and Nova Scotia as part of its goal to complete a third sea-to-sea line. Laurier, though favouring his pet National Transcontinental, was persuaded to provide funds to build a link connecting Port Arthur to those purchased eastern lines.

BUILDING THE GRAND TRUNK PACIFIC EASTWARD

Two years after driving the pilings for the first tiny wharf at its nascent ocean terminus, the railway commenced construction of the main line eastward. In the following year, 1909, work began on the westward line from a point 193 km (120 miles) west of Edmonton. The 1,339 km (832 mile) line between that point and Prince Rupert had been designated the "Mountain Section," and the railway had received a federal government guarantee covering 75 percent of its construction cost. Though delayed for a year by labour shortages and strikes, construction crews from east and west finally met at Fort Fraser for a "last spike" ceremony on April 7, 1914 and the first train through-train from Winnipeg arrived to a tumultuous welcome in Prince Rupert on April 8.

The principle contractor for the GTP rail line was the firm Foley, Welch and Stewart, the largest railway builder in North America at that time. They were also major contractors for the CPR, Canadian Northern, and the Pacific Great Eastern. The final cost of the line from Winnipeg to Prince Rupert was $109,828,588 of which $78,269,721 was attributed to the "Mountain Section." This turned out to be 1.76 times the initial estimated cost. This escalation looks modest, however, when compared to the 3.26 times increase over estimate for the government-built eastern half of the National Transcontinental, or the 3.36 times increase over estimate for the Pacific Great Eastern in B.C.

Labour problems plagued the line's construction and a strike lasting from July 18, 1912 to January 9, 1913 cost most of the 1912 season and set back completion for a year. Labour shortages were acute and Hays' desire to import Asian labour ran afoul of the strong exclusion policy of the B.C. and federal governments. The GTP had to give Premier McBride a written undertaking that only white labour would be used, unless otherwise permitted by Cabinet.

Hays insisted that all the GTP labour problems were the fault of labour. In this regard, he may well be considered a successor to the likes of Robert Dunsmuir or Andrew Carnegie! With wages of $2.50–3.00 for a 9-hour day and minimal to poor camp conditions, it is not surprising that the GTP had great difficulty keeping a labour force to construct their line that was anywhere near adequate or productive. Evidently, Hays gave little or no consideration to the long-term benefits that might have accrued from a more flexible and conciliatory labour policy.

THE THIRD TRANSCONTINENTAL

With strong support from the Province of B.C. the Canadian Northern's B.C. subsidiary, the Canadian Northern Pacific, chose a route south from Red Pass Junction (west of the Yellowhead Pass) to Kamloops. From there, the line ran parallel to the CPR main line to a yard at Port Mann near the mouth of the Fraser River. Through sections of the route in the Fraser Canyon, the CNP line had to build on the most difficult topography because the CPR had selected the least formidable passage years before. The last spike on the CNP line was driven near Ashcroft on January 23, 1915 and the first passenger train arrived at the railway's new Vancouver terminal on August 28, 1915.

Mackenzie and Mann, like Hays, planned to build a fleet of deep-sea ships to bring Orient trade to their line. The Great War and the deteriorating finances of both companies intervened to terminate these plans with the result that the CPR would keep its monopoly of the land bridge from the Pacific to the Atlantic for many more years. However, the "Farmers' Friend" had, indeed, come a long way. In 20 years Mackenzie and Mann had built a transcontinental railway with over 16,000 km (10,000 miles) of track, albeit built to a very great extent with government land grants and guaranteed bonds.

TROUBLE AHEAD

By late 1911, both government and public enthusiasm for building railways was waning and disillusionment began to appear. The CPR was viable, even though it was never in favour with the Laurier Liberals in Ottawa. GTP construction was two years behind schedule and its costs had escalated substantially. Hopes were beginning to fade that their line's substantial grade advantage over the CPR could compensate for the extra distance to their new northern port. As far back as 1905, Hays had become convinced that the GTP had to have a connection to the booming port of Vancouver and he continued to actively pursue that goal. The Canadian Northern Pacific was a full year behind the GTP and was having major difficulty building the line from Kamloops to Vancouver on the least favourable side of the all-river route.

The public began to comprehend that Canada, with a population of only 6 million neither needed, nor could afford three coast-to-coast railways. For hundreds of miles, these lines ran parallel through virtually empty country. Though neither of the two new lines had yet reached financial collapse, both were running into increasing resistance to their recurring demands for government guarantees on financing.

Laurier lost the election of October 1911. His 15-year run was over and with his defeat the Grand Trunk Pacific/National Transcontinental lost its champion. The public was disillusioned with his railway policy and his concessions to the Canadian Northern that allowed building of the third line. He had vigorously pursued his vision of Canada as a "land-bridge" (or interrupted Northwest Passage) from the Orient to Europe and saw Pacific Rim trade as a way to reduce dependence on the U.S. Unquestionably, Laurier's biggest failure was his reluctance to force the amalgamation of the GTP and the Canadian Northern, even if only where their lines paralleled each other. Such an arrangement might have saved the GTP and Prince Rupert. Insofar as both lines opened up new areas for grain production, they succeeded, but both failed miserably in their other objective, Orient trade.

Prime Minister Borden and his Tories, patrons of the CPR and friendly to the Canadian Northern, were now in power. He was to stay at the helm for nine years, leading Canada through the 1912 depression and then World War I.

THE PACIFIC GREAT EASTERN RAILWAY (PGE) AND ITS RELATIONSHIP TO THE GRAND TRUNK PACIFIC

Beginning in 1905, the Grand Trunk Pacific Railway under Hays' leadership played a major role in promoting and sponsoring the construction of a fourth major railway line within B.C.

Railway mania in Canada had never been confined to transcontinental routes. The government and people of B.C. very much wanted a rail line north through the Cariboo to Prince George or Hazelton and from there on into northwest B.C. and the Yukon.

The idea of a route north was not new. After the discovery of gold in the lower Fraser, a trail from Harrison to Lillooet provided access to the interior of the province, until the Royal Engineers could finish the Cariboo Road in 1864. New impetus for a rail line into the interior was provided by the Atlin and Klondike gold stampedes. Many charters were granted between 1897 and 1910 to build rail lines on a variety of routes to satisfy the perceived need. Most planned to utilize Vancouver, or its environs, as their southern terminus.

In addition to these newly chartered companies, most of which were promotions without substance, there were three large players that showed clear interest in being involved in such a line. Each of these had a transcontinental line already built, or in progress. James J. Hill, whose Great Northern Railway just south of the border had long been complete, was anxious to extend lines north into B.C. to tap its resources for transfer to his main line. Mackenzie and Mann, favoured by the B.C. Government, finally selected their route from the Yellowhead south through Kamloops, though this could not satisfy the public's desire for a line northwest through the centre of the province. In 1906 the Grand Trunk Pacific had obtained a charter for a branch line to Vancouver from Prince George.

Among the charters granted for a rail line north from Burrard Inlet was one granted in 1901 to the Vancouver, Westminster, and Yukon (VW&Y) Railway Company. It was another element in Hill's rivalry with the CPR and was promoted by Vancouver industrialist John Hendry, acting as a front for the Great Northern. Though it never materialized, its planned route via Hazelton to Teslin and Dawson City attracted Hays' attention and, in 1905 he proposed to link his planned line to the VW&Y at Hazelton. However, by 1907 Hays had become disillusioned with this Great Northern proxy, as it appeared to be making no progress with its line. At that time, too, Hays was concerned that the Canadian Northern Pacific might continue its new line to Prince George before turning south to Vancouver.

As the VW&Y faded into memory, Hendry, in 1907, acquired a new Dominion charter for the Burrard, Westminster and Boundary Railway and Navigation Company. Its board included a high official of the GTP and its aim was to keep the Canadian Northern Pacific from building into B.C. Its charter granted a route north via Yale, Lillooet, and the Cariboo to Tête Juane Cache, but also allowed for a route north from Squamish.

Another company, the Howe Sound, Pemberton Valley and Northern (later changed to Howe Sound and Northern, and later still the B.C. Central) began surveys on their route and planned to have rail laid to Lillooet by 1911 and thence on to Prince George.

By the fall of 1908, the GTP had completed surveys for its planned branch line to Vancouver, mostly over the route chosen by the VW&Y Railroad and, early in 1909, the Province newspaper printed a map produced by the GTP that showed the planned branch line from Prince George to Vancouver via Pemberton and Coquitlam Lake. With McBride's campaign for re-election in 1909 emphasizing his pledge to subsidize the CNP line from the Yellowhead Pass to Vancouver, Hays lobbied hard for matching help for his planned line connecting the GTP to Vancouver from either Prince George or Tete Juane Cache. He pointed out that the route south from Prince George would traverse much better country than that chosen by the CNP. Hays' entreaties were rejected by McBride, but at least his desire to connect his main GTP line to Prince Rupert with the lower mainland, via the Cariboo, put him on the same path as McBride's newly re-elected government.

Hays became increasingly concerned with the growing importance of Vancouver and the urgent need to connect his GTP main line in the north to that rapidly developing port by a better route than that chosen by the CNP. Indeed, the general manager of the GTP now acknowledged that there were limited prospects of immediate returns from traffic on the main line within B.C., but that big tonnage would be available if a branch line were built south to Vancouver from Prince George.

Another attempt in September 1911 to get McBride's support for the GTP's proposed line from Prince George south failed because Hays refused to relinquish control of rates to the province. However, some of McBride's ministers agreed that the GTP choice of routes for the north to south line was the best possible. They suggested that the premier might be amenable to support a corporate entity formed to build the line that was independent (at least in appearance) from both the GTP and the CNP.

Following up on this suggestion, D'Arcy Tate, the GTP solicitor, proposed a deal whereby the railway contractors, Foley, Welch and Stewart (FWS) would form a company to build the line and give the province full control of rates. However, unbeknown to McBride, Tate and Hays had pre-arranged a private deal between FWS and the GTP that gave Hays effective control by insisting on a traffic agreement whereby "all passengers, freight, express and mail traffic originating on the new line, the routing of which is under the control of that company, shall be routed over the GTP… and all passengers, freight, express and mail originating on the GTP destined for Vancouver shall be routed over the PGE." That private arrangement also gave the GTP a monopoly over the supply of materials and labour for construction of the new line. Stewart, on behalf of FWS, paid Tate $500,000 and one-quarter of the stock in the new company to secure its relationship with the GTP. Tate also was appointed vice president of the new company.

Unaware of the "side deal" with the GTP, McBride awarded the newly incorporated Pacific Great Eastern Railway Company (incorporated February 27, 1912) a provincial government bond guarantee of $35,000 per mile. He easily won the election in March 1912 on the main plank of linking southern B.C. to the Peace River country.

Thus, not many months before his death, Hays finally secured the provincial subsidy he had sought for a decade, albeit by stealth and only for the "branch line" to Vancouver. It would be built largely at provincial expense.

When it was announced that the province would provide very substantial subsidies to construct the line south from Prince George, newspapers in Prince Rupert protested. The Daily News fumed that the new line "would reduce by half the traffic this port had every reason to expect." Certainly, events after the PGE finally reached Prince George in 1952 demonstrated that their concerns were valid.

The name Pacific Great Eastern (PGE) was chosen because of the substantial financial backing the company received initially from the Great Eastern Railway in England. One of its first moves was to acquire the Howe Sound and Northern Railway, which had built 14 km (9 miles) of track north from Squamish. Construction commenced in October of 1912, using equipment borrowed from the GTP, and completion was scheduled for July 1915. By

January 1, 1914 the first 19 km (12 miles) were open for service between Lonsdale Avenue in North Vancouver and Whytecliff.

All these actions directed toward constructing a south to north railway unquestionably jeopardized the future of the infant port at Prince Rupert. The Conservative McBride government clearly supported the CPR and Canadian Northern Pacific over the GTP/National Transcontinental favoured by the federal Liberals and showed little interest in the development of a new port on the North Coast. Hays was becoming increasingly desperate to connect his line to Vancouver. After the VW&Y, sponsored by the Great Northern, failed to construct their planned line north, he had, by 1912, arranged a private deal to achieve his goal with the government subsidized Pacific Great Eastern group. Four decades later, the PGE finally reached Prince George and so began the predicted drain of traffic from central and northern B.C. to southern ports. This fact, unquestionably, stunted the growth of the long-delayed Fairview General Cargo Terminal, which was finally completed in 1977 at Prince Rupert.

FROM BOOM TO GLOOM:
THE GENESIS OF THE CANADIAN NATIONAL RAILWAY

At the beginning of 1912, railroad construction in B.C. was booming. Premier McBride's spring election campaign focussed on an even more comprehensive rail development plan than the one that gave him a landslide win in 1909. That program included more aid to the CNP, plus support for the CPR lines in the south of the province and for the construction of a new rail line to extend from south to north through the centre of the province.

A snapshot of the status of railways built and building in B.C. in early 1912 reveals:
- CPR: The CPR was still having very serious grade problems, only partially relieved by the Spiral Tunnel built in 1906. Their Pacific terminus at Vancouver was booming.
- GTP: The GTP was building from both east and west, but was still two years from completion and plagued with labour problems. They had two coastwise ships in service and were planning for a grand hotel in Prince Rupert, a shipyard and dry dock, and a fleet of deep-sea ships to operate on the Pacific.
- CNP: The CNP was a year behind the GTP and having great difficulty building their line through the Fraser Canyon.
- PGE: The PGE, in effect, a proxy for the GTP, was incorporated February 27, 1912 with plans to start constructing a line from North Vancouver to Prince George.

Historians have referred to the first decade of the twentieth century in North America as "The Good Years." The booming economy of those years ended with a world recession by 1912. Soon, boundless optimism changed to pessimism, disillusionment, and depression. Tensions were rising in the Balkans and European investors lost interest in railroad stocks and bonds. The long period of railway mania had ended. Federal and provincial governments found they might have to honour their bond guarantees on both interest and principle, and very soon they had to finance a World War.

Both the CNP and the GTP had seriously underestimated both the costs of construction and the time required to complete their projects. Inflation during the 1910–1913 period added even more to their cost overruns. Both lines needed more help from governments.

Laurier lost the October 1911 federal election, and on April 15, 1912, Hays was among those lost in the sinking of the *Titanic*. He was returning from England to attend the opening of the Grand Trunk Railway's new Chateau Laurier in Ottawa, scheduled for April 26, after spending weeks working in London on further financing — and probable reorganization — of the GTR and GTP railways. His plans went down with him.

Thus, in early 1912, both Laurier, the proud sponsor of the GTP/National Transcontinental "Liberal" railroad, and Hays, the president of the Grand Trunk and driving force behind the GTP, were both out of the picture. Popular perception insists on the romantic myth that the loss of Hays led to the downfall of the GTP and with it Prince Rupert's glowing future as equal and rival to Vancouver. This is clearly untrue. Unquestionably, Hays realized that the GTP was heading into deep trouble and his moves to connect the main line at Prince George to Vancouver are certain evidence of this. The loss of Laurier's support only made the situation worse.

Though both lines were well into a downward spiral of financial woes, the GTP did manage to complete their main line on April 7, 1914 and the CNP finished theirs nine months later. The section of the National Transcontinental built by the federal government from Moncton, N.B. to Winnipeg was completed in 1913, albeit at over triple its estimated cost. Indeed, those costs were so high that the GTR declined the offer to lease the line, leaving the federal government to operate it. Two-thirds of its track ran through unpopulated wilderness and, like the GTP, it had built to extravagantly high standards.

After Hays demise, company principals persisted in their optimistic predictions for traffic on the GTP. The chairman of the GTR insisted that the line would pay its operating expenses by 1916. The railway expressed confidence that resources of coal and lumber, plus transpacific trade, assured viability and profitability on the "Mountain Section" (mostly in B.C.). They predicted that agricultural developments within reasonable distance of the B.C. section of the line could support a population of 350,000. Hays had made the remarkable statement that when the Panama Canal opened in 1914, the GTP would be hauling 2.7 million tons of wheat annually from the prairies to Prince Rupert, for shipment to Europe. He had said, "We can deliver wheat to Europe at the same cost and in almost the same time as via the Lakes and Atlantic ports." Company promotional material insisted that Prince Rupert was destined to be a duplicate of Vancouver within a very few years. Doubtless, the top executives of the GTR and GTP continued to make these and other optimistic predictions to mollify their questioning shareholders and to keep funds and loan guarantees flowing from the — by now far less supportive — Tory government of Robert Borden.

Much less sanguine was the GTP's chief engineer, Kelleher, who admitted, "The only justification for building the line through the mountains and across B.C. was to reach the coast." In 1915 the line within B.C. was producing a miniscule amount of revenue, as freight traffic between Prince George and Prince Rupert warranted only two trains a week in each direction.

After only one year of operations, A.W. Smithers, chairman of the Grand Trunk in London, asked the Canadian Government to take over the GTP and relieve his company of all its obligations to the subsidiary, which it could no longer support financially. This plea resulted in a further series of government loans that enabled the parent company to continue operations for a further three years.

Both the Canadian Northern and the GTP traded securities for cash from Ottawa, so that by 1917, the federal government was effectively the owner of both lines. These two western lines were not alone in their financial woes. In the eastern half of the country the Intercolonial Railway, the National Transcontinental, and the Prince Edward Island Railway were also in deep trouble. Clearly, the railroad building mania had produced far more track than the country needed and the extensive and costly duplication of lines cried out for consolidation.

Since Confederation, governments and railways had become so entangled, with so many tax dollars spent, that nationalization was both logical and inevitable for the failed lines. In just over a decade, the picture had changed from manageable costs and moderate expansions to almost absurd over-extension with trackage doubling to 61,142 km (38,000 miles). Governments had provided about half the construction costs of all these lines by way of subsidies, loans, and guarantees. That well was now dry.

Borden inherited this railway mess from Laurier. In 1915 he appointed a Royal Commission to advise him of the best solution to the problems of the Canadian Northern and the GTP. The same year the government formed a new entity, Canadian Government Railways, to operate the Intercolonial and the National Transcontinental.

The Royal Commission majority report in 1917 recommended nationalization of the GTR, GTP, and Canadian Northern and the amalgamation of these lines with the recently created Canadian Government Railways. Borden welcomed the report and moved quickly to implement it. He had long been a strong proponent of a mix of private (CPR) and public ownership. First to go was the Canadian Northern in November 1918. Then on December 20, 1918 the new title Canadian National Railway (CNR) was authorized and the company was incorporated June 6, 1919. The GTP went into receivership in March 1919 and its management, thereafter, was entrusted to the CNR Board of Directors. Then, despite its reasonably successful eastern Canadian operations, the Grand Trunk Railway itself was finally dragged into default because of its guarantees on GTP securities. It, too, was nationalized and amalgamated into the CNR on January 19, 1923. Thus the CNR was cobbled together from six railway companies, all of which had failed, despite government encouragement and support for their construction.

FACTORS RESPONSIBLE FOR THE COLLAPSE OF THE GRAND TRUNK PACIFIC AND THE PORT OF PRINCE RUPERT'S DELAYED DEVELOPMENT

Many factors contributed to the financial failure and nationalization of the Grand Trunk Pacific Railway and the consequent long delay in the development of Prince Rupert as Canada's second West Coast gateway. Contrary to popular myth, probably the least important of these was the demise of Hays on the *Titanic*.

- The CPR and its Pacific port terminal at Vancouver had a 27-year head start on the GTP and had developed a very firm monopoly position on the transpacific passenger, silk, and tea trade, which not even West Coast U.S. ports had been able to break.
- During the "Good Years" of the first decade of the twentieth century, public enthusiasm for more and more railways across the country led malleable politicians to guarantee financial support for lines that never should have been built. This was especially evident in Laurier's unwillingness to force the Canadian Northern and GTP to jointly build and operate a single line where their routes paralleled each other over great distances. Much of this failed political leadership stemmed from his determination to have an "All-Liberal" transcontinental railroad to compete with the Tory-built CPR.
- Western Canada's tiny population was huddled along the U.S. border near CPR lines and the GTP had no land grants to offer to new settlers along its northern line. The new (1905) provinces of Alberta and Saskatchewan were in no position to help subsidize the northern rail line. Furthermore, due to economic recession and the Great War, there was a marked reduction in immigration to the Prairies after 1911. Certainly, there were far too few people to support three railways across the Great Plains.
- Unlike the Canadian Northern, the GTP had no pre-existing system of branch lines in place on the prairies to collect traffic for its main line. Anticipated resource traffic on the B.C. section of the GTP was a figment of Hays' imagination and did not materialize.
- Extravagantly high construction standards were imposed on the GTP/National Transcontinental by the federal government, as a term of its support. Hays appears to have done little or nothing to object, presumably thinking of lower operating costs on the better built line.
- Construction and maintenance costs, especially in the "Mountain Section," were much higher than anticipated.

- The sponsor and chief supporter of the GTP/National Transcontinental railroad, Prime Minister Wilfrid Laurier, was defeated in the 1911 election and replaced by Robert Borden's Tory government who had vigourously opposed the hybrid railway.
- There was no enthusiasm or support from McBride, the Tory Premier of B.C. (1903–1915) for either the railway, or its terminal city, Prince Rupert. His government had opposed the GTP from the start and favoured the CPR, the Canadian Northern Pacific railway, the building of the PGE, and the Southern Gateway Port at Vancouver.
- Recession in the North American economy started in 1911. The 40-year mania for more and more railroads in North America collapsed and the fickle public turned against the politicians that they had elected on a platform to build more rail lines.
- The London Directors of the parent Grand Trunk Railway were, at best, lukewarm to the company's subsidiary and especially to its construction west of the Rockies.
- Hays' one-man management style was not conducive to attracting, or keeping the best people at mid- and lower levels of management. His combative and hardnosed approach to labour, city governments, federal bureaucrats, the provincial government, and First Nations was counterproductive and resulted in long term problems for the railway and its terminal port.
- Hays became more and more concerned with the growing influence and importance of Vancouver and, from 1905 on, was increasingly preoccupied with connecting the GTP line at Prince George with the Southern Gateway Port. He played a major role in the development of the PGE.
- The onset of World War I in 1914 made huge demands on government finances. During the war, emphasis was directed at getting materials and supplies railed to Atlantic ports for shipment to Europe. Shipping was mobilized for war priorities and transpacific trade dried up almost completely. The Northern Gateway Port was considered unattractive by shipping companies, unless they were paid a substantial premium over Vancouver.
- In contrast to Hays' wildly optimistic predictions, traffic failed dismally to materialize, especially in the "Mountain Section." In its fifth year of operation, the GTP main line revenues were only 5 percent of the CPR's and less than 15 percent of the Canadian Northern's. Grain from the prairie section constituted most of its freight movement and this could be moved to markets more cheaply via the Lakehead than through Prince Rupert. The potentially lucrative carriage of frozen fish from Prince Rupert and Alaska to eastern markets was severely hampered by inadequate specialty car supply and by competition from Puget Sound ports. Movement of lumber and mineral products from the mountain section never amounted to more than a trickle. The extra distance to Prince Rupert from Edmonton versus that to Vancouver had to be absorbed by the railway, after the Prince Rupert Board of Trade successfully insisted on equalization of rail tariffs to the two ports.

- After World War I, the effective opening of the Panama Canal "made" the port of Vancouver, but was of no help to Prince Rupert inasmuch as virtually all trade from the West Coast was destined to the United Kingdom (U.K.) and Europe. Prince Rupert's advantage related solely to trade with Asia.
- In 1924 the CNR, formed from six bankrupt railroads, designated the line in the Northern Corridor from Red Pass Junction to Prince Rupert a branch line; with the main line going to Vancouver using the Canadian Northern line route south through Kamloops and the Fraser Canyon.
- In 1920 Prince Rupert's Ocean Dock was completed and, in 1926, the new grain elevator opened. However, the dock saw little use until 1942 and the elevator, after its initial year of operation, was virtually unused for the next 25 years.
- During the 1930s, Asian wars and the Great Depression militated against growth in transpacific trade, where Prince Rupert had a clear distance advantage.
- The 1932 report of Sir Alexander Gibb, commissioned by the federal government to examine Canada's port system, recommended, *"that Vancouver should be protected from the establishment of a competitive port further north."* There was no time limit to this recommendation and the report became the basis for the creation and policies of the National Harbours Board in 1936.
- Prince Rupert's tiny population lacked political clout and received no active support from the CNR until 2004.
- There was overt and covert opposition from Vancouver maritime interests, the Vancouver Board of Trade, and the CPR to development of a rival port at Prince Rupert.
- Completion of the PGE railway to Prince George in 1952 and the associated political imperatives resulted in traffic that would logically go to Prince Rupert being siphoned off to southern ports.

THE CANADIAN NATIONAL RAILWAY: 1919 TO 1929

The CNR was incorporated on June 6, 1919. Its creation flowed from the recommendations of a Royal Commission appointed by Prime Minister Borden to advise the federal government of the best solution to the railway mess his government had inherited. By early 1923 the new company had absorbed the assets and problems of six failed Canadian railway companies. These included the Grand Trunk Pacific, its parent Grand Trunk, and Mackenzie and Mann's Canadian Northern.

As the process of integration and rationalization of all these lines progressed, it soon became apparent that large expenditures were needed to consolidate lines, buy new and repair old equipment, and rehabilitate retained lines. By 1924 the former GTP line within B.C. was designated a branch line off the main CNR line to Vancouver. The latter line utilized the Canadian Northern Pacific's track south from Red Pass Junction and, mainly, the GTP line eastward from that point. This action by the national railway reduced Prince Rupert to a minor port at the end of a little used line.

In 1920, a depression year during which all North American railways suffered, the CPR, greatly upset by the government takeover of the GTP, offered to sell its tracks to them. This offer was spurned. However, Canada certainly needed much less trackage and far more people to support the lines remaining after the consolidation that formed the CNR.

Borden focused on Canada's export trade potential to give the depressed economy a boost and, to this end, formed the Canadian Government Merchant Marine to build and operate ships to expedite the movement of Canadian exports worldwide. This new entity was operated by the CNR and grew to a 66-ship fleet totalling 391,212 tons deadweight. These ships were built to vintage designs and were slow, small, and coal fired. All were constructed in Canadian yards, including two in Prince Rupert's shipyard. One of the prime export objectives was the carriage of lumber from B.C. to overseas markets. In 1922 trade across the Pacific was developing rapidly, especially in lumber and grain. Silk imports were virtually a CPR monopoly until 1925, when both the CNR and the Great Northern at Seattle were finally able to break into that lucrative business. Hays' expectation of funnelling some of that trade through Prince Rupert was, however, never realized. CN gave top priority to their modest share of this coveted traffic. Their "silk trains" reached New York in four days via a connection with the New York Central Railway.

The *CNR Act* of 1919 proclaimed that the railway's annual deficit was to be covered by the federal government. Borden also insisted that there be no patronage, or political interference connected to the CNR, but the railway's importance to national and regional growth inevitably resulted in political pressures. Thus, instead of a board of directors of businessmen concerned only with the health of the company, regional representatives were soon appointed whose primary interest was to benefit their constituency. Furthermore, the government owner never clearly enunciated guidelines for relationships between politicians and the "People's Railway." A policy of freedom from interference was hard to define and even harder to carry out.

The 10-year Tory era ended with the election of Mackenzie King and his Liberals in December 1921. King picked Sir Henry Thornton to head the CNR as chairman and president. When in opposition, King had demanded that the CNR divulge its business on demand. Now in power, King gave solemn promises of no political interference in the affairs of the railway. One of the first directors of the CNR was a wholesale grocer from Prince Rupert, Fred Dawson — a prominent local Liberal who was later accused of bootlegging by the Tories!

In 1924 a new and heavy burden was dealt the railway. The federal government imposed the 1897 Crow rate for moving grain on the CNR, despite the fact that, unlike the CPR, neither it nor any of its antecedents had derived any commensurate benefit from Ottawa to balance this long-term penalty. It would be many decades before this dubious subsidy to Prairie farmers would finally be withdrawn.

THE DEPRESSION YEARS: 1930 TO 1939

The boom years of the 1920s reached a peak in 1929. Suddenly optimism and prosperity dissipated, along with the great stock market crash. Gloom and misery followed for the next decade. Responding to worldwide trade wars, R.B. Bennett, who became prime minister in August 1930, raised tariffs sky-high with the intent of effectively closing Canada's borders to imports. Many other nations did likewise in a round of protectionist "beggar thy neighbour" policies with the result that the world economic depression deepened. The British Empire was beginning to metamorphose into the Commonwealth and at the Imperial Economic Conference of 1932, held in Ottawa, a system of preferential agreements increased trade between components of the Empire. By 1934 the U.S. was ready to reduce its high tariffs, and by 1935 a new Canada-US Trade Agreement had been signed.

Orient trade, however, was on a progressive decline as Japan embarked on its program of conquest by invading Manchuria in 1932. After a trade war with Canada early in the decade, Japan restricted imports of no military value, so that only steel and base metals were allowed entry duty free. Even that trade terminated in 1939–1940 as Canada followed others in trade embargoes on commodities destined for military use. Silk was now carried to Europe via Panama, and Australia had captured the Japanese grain market. In 1937 Japan seized Shanghai, and by 1941 Pacific trade ended. This had been one of the major reasons for building both the GTP and Canadian Northern. Thus ended a trade that had been a boon to Vancouver's port, the railways, and the country as a whole. A tumultuous decade would pass before it began again.

Attempts were made to combat the serious economic effects of the depression on the railways. Between the two World Wars, Canada's two remaining transcontinental railways underwent a long period of evolutionary adjustment with many lines abandoned and very few new lines built. R.B. Bennett was a proponent of retrenchment and sought the amalgamation of the CN and CP as a measure to eliminate extensive duplication of trackage. The CPR now resisted this, even though a decade earlier they had offered to sell their rail line to the federal government for integration into the new "People's Railway." Though revenues had dropped by half, the CNR still had a huge debt to service and this could only be met, in the face of heavy losses, by Canadian taxpayers.

A few things materialized to offer hope. With wheat prices down 80 percent, the federal government in 1935 established the Canadian Wheat Board, giving it impressive powers to control Canadian Wheat trade and increase returns to the desperate western farm community.

King, who returned to power in October 1935, was a Harvard trained economist and a friend of F.D. Roosevelt. Together with Britain, they worked out a new tariff deal in 1938, the North Atlantic Triangle. Trade wars were now over — to the mutual benefit of the participants. Some semblance of sanity was returning in world trade, but it was too late to halt either the rise of the Nazi and Fascist powers in Europe, or the triumph of the militarists in Japan who were set on controlling East Asia.

THE CANADIAN NATIONAL RAILWAY: 1939 TO 1978

World War II stimulated full utilization of both passenger and freight facilities for both Canada's major railroads. Between 1940 and 1943 the dire shortage of shipping, resulting from losses to U boats in the Atlantic and Mediterranean, meant that bulk commodities such as grain could no longer be moved to Europe from the West Coast via Panama. Inasmuch as a precious vessel could make three trips across the Atlantic in the time taken for one trip from Vancouver to Europe, it fell to the railways to move virtually all western grain for export to Canadian and U.S. east coast ports. This put a tremendous strain on tracks, locomotives, and rolling stock. Furthermore, manufacturing facilities used in peacetime to produce rails, locomotives, and freight cars were now mostly converted to provide the steel, engines, and parts for the massive shipbuilding program underway in Canada.

Even the "orphan" line from Red Pass Junction to Prince Rupert came alive in mid-1942, after the Japanese occupation of Kiska and Attu in the Aleutians prompted the U.S. Army to use and develop Prince Rupert as a sub-port of embarkation for troops and supplies to the Pacific Theatre. Freight trains, troop trains, ammunition trains, and even an armoured train put quite a strain on the old GTP line, which had been little used or maintained since its completion 28 years earlier. By the summer of 1943 the Japanese had been evicted from the Aleutians and, thereafter, activity on the northern rail line and at the port gradually waned, returning to pre-wartime somnolence by late 1945.

After 1945, change was the order for Canada's railways. They lost interest in carrying passengers, as new highways were increasingly utilized for short trips and air travel became the vogue for long trips. Rolling stock and trackage were in dire need of repair or replacement, after their exceptionally heavy wartime use. The diesel locomotive replaced steam and centralized traffic control allowed much longer trains at closer intervals. Sidings were lengthened and rail yards expanded. The railroad's role evolved to focus on becoming the primary mover of huge tonnages of bulk commodities, at least until the advent of container trains.

In Vancouver during the mid-fifties, the CNR started to improve its position vis-à-vis the CPR by much improved access to the North Shore of Burrard Inlet with its several bulk terminals for grain, coal, sulphur, and potash. This was not helpful to Prince Rupert, as the CNR committed itself to the shorter of its two rail routes to the Pacific Ocean. The CPR had no direct access to the North Shore, but was initially the clear bulk-tonnage winner when it secured contracts for hauling coal from the newly developed Crowsnest Pass mines in the 1970s. Its old rival, the Great Northern, had an easier route to the coast, but had abandoned its old line into the Pass and could not revive its old charter to re-enter Canada.

For the western divisions of both major railways, the decade of the 1970s was dominated by coal. The movement of huge tonnages of this low value material to the new ocean terminals on the lower mainland required further upgrading of tracks to the highest standards, as well as acquisition of unit trains and slave locomotives. The first coal train from the Smoky River and Luscar mines in west central Alberta arrived at the new Neptune Terminal in North Vancouver over CN lines February 23, 1970 and the first coal from the Kaiser mines, tributary to CPR lines in the south, reached the new Roberts Bank terminal April 30, 1970. Trackage to Roberts Bank was built in 1969 by the B.C. Harbours Board to connect the new terminal to the CPR and CNR main lines. This 37 km (23 mile) line was taken over by BC Rail in 1984.

With the development of the northeast B.C. coalfields in the early 1970s and the construction of the new Tumbler Ridge electrified line by BC Rail, the CNR line from Prince George to Prince Rupert was extensively upgraded with centralized traffic control and with 138-pound rail able to handle unit trains. The first unit train of coal arrived at the newly built Ridley Terminal in November 1983 and, by early 1985 long unit trains of grain were rolling over this massively refurbished line to the recently opened grain terminal.

As a federal Crown Corporation from 1919–1995, the CNR was essentially a social and economic tool of government. Ottawa policies dictated CNR decisions. Political imperatives trumped business-like policies. Vast numbers of hopelessly unprofitable, low volume branch lines had to be maintained and operated, and politicians ensured that rail, rolling stock, and locomotives had to be purchased from Canadian manufacturers, regardless of price or suitability.

Troubled enough at its birth by having to attempt to create a "silk purse from the sow's ear" of six inherited bankrupt lines, the CNR became, over succeeding decades, the reluctant repository for such losing government created entities as Trans-Canada Airlines (Air Canada), CN Marine's operations in the Maritimes, as well as real gems like the Newfoundland Railway ("Newfie Bullet"), among many others. Like most government enterprises, it was sheltered from accountability and the need to perform well. Burdened with debt, riddled with inefficiencies, and beset by labour strife it was perceived as the "sad sack of continental railroading." The federal government's commitment to cover all CN's losses resulted in the infusion of $17 billion in subsidies between 1945 and 1995. In fact, at the time of privatization in 1995, a review of the railway's financial history estimated the total federal support for the carrier from 1923 to 1993 at $95 billion in 1995 dollars! Despite this largesse, the CNR still had an accumulated debt of $2.5 billion in 1995.

CANADIAN NATIONAL'S RENAISSANCE

As a perennially troubled railroad, the CNR had plenty of company. The industry in the U.S. was in dire straits, hopelessly burdened by regulatory restraints and competition from trucks. The 1980 passage of the *Staggers Act* resulted in the removal of most restraints and regulations, thereby allowing flexibility to adjust rates and tailor services to meet shipper's needs and revenue requirements. The railways responded with a massive restructuring, and mergers reduced the number of Class One lines in the U.S. from 40 in 1980 to just four serving the whole country. No longer crippled by a surfeit of regulations and restrictions, the U.S. lines soon tripled their productivity, while reducing rates by 60 percent, which more than met their trucking competition.

In Canada the suffocating burden of regulation was lifted in stages, starting with the deregulation of freight rates (except for grain) under the *National Transportation Act* of 1967. The CNR began divesting itself of non-core entities with the aim of becoming a purely rail freight operation. Air Canada and CN Marine were spun off to separate Crown Corporations in 1977 and the next year all passenger services went to Via Rail. Over the next decade trucking subsidiaries, hotels, telecommunication networks, and real estate were sold off with the proceeds applied to reducing debt.

Allowing little used branch lines to be abandoned was a difficult political issue for the government, especially on the prairies. Resistance was often very strong in the area affected. However, gradually, grossly underutilized lines were allowed to be discontinued and finally, in 1987, the last restrictions were removed allowing abandonment, or sale to short line operators of thousands of kilometres of branch lines across the country.

After recapitalization in 1978, the CNR started to operate much more efficiently, assuming its own debt, utilizing better accounting practices to allow depreciation of assets, and having access to financial markets for capital. It was now charged with operating as a "for profit" Crown Corporation and, as such, it did manage a profit in 11 of the 15 years between 1978 and 1992, paying $371 million in cash dividends to the federal government.

The measures taken to improve the lot of the CNR during the seventies and eighties led inexorably to a decision in 1992 to prepare the railway for privatization. A management team led by former senior civil servants Paul Tellier and Michael Sabia emphasized the need for greatly increased productivity, through aggressive cuts in the inefficient management structure, major reductions in the bloated workforce, and further abandonment or sale of branch lines. During 1993 and 1994, Canadian Pacific proposed a merger with the CNR, whereby CP would take over all CN lines from Ontario east and all CN lines in the west would be sold to Burlington Northern. Ottawa rejected this scheme outright. Finally, on July 13, 1995 the *CN Commercialization Act* became law and in November of 1995 an initial public offering resulted in all CNR outstanding shares being sold to the public at $27 per share. There were two major reservations attached to this offering:

- No individual, or corporation could hold over 15 percent of CN's shares
- CN's headquarters must remain forever in Montreal, assuring that it would always be a Canadian corporation.

Those astute enough to recognize the potential of the newly liberated CN and to take advantage of this offer have been richly rewarded!

With privatization and freedom from regulation the CNR undertook an aggressive network rationalization, which included shedding more branch lines by sale, or outright abandonment, leaving a core east-west, freight-only rail line from Halifax to Vancouver and Prince Rupert, plus lines to Chicago from both Winnipeg and Ontario.

The North American Free Trade Agreement (NAFTA) between Canada, the U.S., and Mexico came into effect on January 1, 1994. This created the largest trading block in the world and the CNR set out to become *the* NAFTA railroad, capable and ready to respond to the anticipated large increases in north-south trade and investment within North America. CN had long owned railroads in the northeast U.S., including lines into Michigan, Illinois, Ohio, Indiana, and Minnesota. It had disposed of the old Grand Trunk line to Portland Maine in 1989, but retained the Central Vermont line down the Connecticut Valley to Long Island Sound. In 1997 it opened a large new intermodal terminal in Chicago.

With a renewed focus on north-south expansion in response to NAFTA, CN purchased the Illinois Central Railroad in 1998, thus acquiring access to the Caribbean at New Orleans. A strategic alliance with the Kansas City Southern Railway gave the CN access to Mexico. An attempted merger with the Burlington Northern Santa Fe was blocked by the U.S. government. Nonetheless, the CNR has developed a very smooth and efficient rail route into and through the U.S. heartland, from Winnipeg to Chicago and on to Memphis and New Orleans, through the purchase of the Wisconsin Central Railway in 2001, the Great Lakes Transportation system in 2004, and finally the Elgin, Joliet and Eastern Railway in 2008.

In 2004, CN acquired the operations of BC Rail. This purchase focussed the railway's attention on B.C. and the potential for development of the "Pacific Gateways" and especially the underutilized Northern Corridor and port. This interest resulted in the CNR's enthusiastic support for the development of the Fairview Container Terminal that came on stream in October 2007. With this new access point for trade from Asia connecting to the newly upgraded and highly efficient north-south route to the U.S. Midwest and south, the CNR has come full circle from its predecessor, the GTP, which created and then abandoned the north coast port.

From being the "sad sack" of continental railroading, the CN has become a leader in North American railroading with a geographic reach greater than any other line. It is now very profitable and highly respected with an operating ratio (expenses as a percentage of revenue) well below average for the industry. Its role in the future of Prince Rupert as a major Pacific Gateway is crucial and the port can only benefit from its connection to this newly enlightened and well managed colossus.

THE PACIFIC GREAT EASTERN RAILWAY: 1914 TO 1949

The Pacific Great Eastern Railway could hardly have been incorporated at a less auspicious time than early 1912. The world economy, booming through the first decade of the twentieth century, was sliding into depression. War clouds were appearing, soon to lead to World War I. The mania for railroad building that had gripped the North American public for 50 years was rapidly waning and politicians, who had been elected on a platform promising even more trackage, were now deserted by those who had elected them with large majorities.

In B.C. 3,840 km (2,400 miles) of track had been laid between 1910 and 1916, mostly by four major railroads. Three of these were failing and their impending collapse left governments stuck with their bond guarantees. Some lines were dropped, including most trackage on Vancouver Island. The CPR did, however, complete its line across southern B.C. to fulfill the provincial dream of a "Southern Railway." The Great Northern abandoned its border crossing tracks in the Kootenays, after J.J. Hill died, and the CPR did the same. The long feud between those two companies was finally over.

By 1915 the PGE, scheduled for completion by July 15 of that year, had only reached Chasm, a point 281 km (176 miles) north of Squamish, and was running out of money for further work. It failed to pay interest on its bonds in 1915, forcing the province to honour its guarantee of both interest and principle on all PGE issues. Plans to connect Horseshoe Bay to Squamish were dropped.

The newly elected Liberal government of Premier Brewster (1916–1918) and his Minister of Railways, John Oliver, announced an investigation into the affairs of the PGE, which was fast becoming the "Province's Greatest Expense." The incoming Liberals alleged that some of the funds transferred to the railway to prevent default on their bonds had, instead, found their way into Conservative Party campaign coffers. The inquiry committee reported its findings on May 1, 1917 with many accusations of wrongdoing by the Tory McBride government and the contractors. This report inflamed public opinion against both. The new government took Foley, Welch and Stewart to court to recover $5 million of allegedly unaccounted funds.

In October of 1917 Premier Brewster travelled east to discuss a possible takeover of the PGE by the CPR. Little interest was shown. This was only the first of many efforts by future B.C. premiers to unload their unwanted albatross. To resolve all issues between them Foley, Welch and Stewart agreed to pay the government $1.1 million and turn the railway over to the province. At that point, February 22, 1918, two separate sections of track had been completed. The first connected North Vancouver to Horseshoe Bay and the second took the line north from Squamish to Clinton.

John Oliver was now premier of B.C. and made a second attempt to sell "the waif on my doorstep" to either the CPR or the federal government's soon to be formed CNR. Prime Minister Meighen already had a surfeit of problems with failed inter-provincial and transcontinental rail lines across the country. He hardly needed another failed, wholly provincial line in the far west to add to the collection, so showed no interest. Neither did the CPR indicate any desire to lift the burden from B.C.

Finding no takers, Premier Oliver commissioned work to extend the line further north and, by 1919 rail had reached Williams Lake. After Oliver's re-election, provision of more provincial funds enabled a further extension to a point 15 miles past Quesnel by July 1921. The track north of Quesnel was later removed. Though Oliver supported further extension on to the Peace River country, it would be 31 years before the line even reached Prince George. Resources were simply not available for new construction, especially during the Great Depression of the 1930s or during World War II.

The line that ran "from nowhere to nowhere" was mockingly referred to as the "Premier's Greatest Eadache," or the "Puff, Grunt, and Expire"; pejoratives unlike the happier "Farmers' Friend" (Canadian Northern), or the "People's Railway" (Canadian National).

The province sought advice from the CPR. Their chief engineer insisted that no other railway would absorb the line and he advised against extension north to Prince George. He further suggested that much of the existing line should be abandoned. His prime advice was for the PGE to build a connection from Clinton to either the CP or CN main line at Ashcroft. For years to come this "Ashcroft-Clinton Connection" idea was to rear its head, especially with regard to the perception on the prairies that it might solve the bottlenecks in the movement of grain to Vancouver's ocean terminals.

In 1923 the opposition Peoples' Party of B.C. (a grassroots party) demanded a royal commission to investigate allegations of impropriety between "Honest John" Oliver's government and the PGE. None were found.

In the election of June 1924 all three party leaders were defeated, though Oliver later won a seat in a by-election. He was determined to shed the PGE, now known as the "Please Go Easy" but again neither the CP nor CN wanted any part of B.C.'s white elephant. To assist in getting the line extended to Prince George, Oliver tried and failed to force the CN to honour the line's 1912 agreements with its predecessor, GTP. The public now dubbed the line the "Prince George Eventually."

Oliver died in 1927 and John D. MacLean became Premier. He insisted that any takeover of the PGE must guarantee completion to the Peace, though it was clear that there would be no offers even without that condition. The B.C. portion of the Peace River "Block" was connected by rail at Dawson Creek in 1931, not to B.C., but to Alberta via the Northern Alberta Railway, jointly owned by CP and CN.

In 1932, Premier Simon Tolmie formed a committee of the legislature to investigate and advise on the future of the railway given the parlous state of the province's finances. They recommended abandonment of the PGE. Others called again for the disposal of the line on any terms that would ensure completion to the Peace River area, which was then filling with homesteaders. Still others wished to persuade the federal government to extend the PGE north as a relief measure. T. D. Pattullo, elected Premier in 1933, insisted the PGE must be Canadian owned and tried again, in 1937, to unload the line on Ottawa. The offer was again spurned. During WW II, the line was busy and even made money for the first time. After the war, John Hart, Premier since 1941, had surveys done for an extension to Dawson Creek, where it would link with the Northern Alberta Railway.

THE PGE FROM 1949 TO 1977
AND THE BENNETT-JAMIESON "GRAND PLAN"
FOR A NORTHERN BC RAIL NETWORK

Between 1945 and 1949, U.S. groups made several overtures to the B.C. Government to buy the PGE and extend it into Alaska. All were rejected. On February 11, 1949 Premier Byron Johnson's coalition government announced plans to start a northern extension. The projected cost was $13 million with a paltry $1.25 million contribution from Ottawa. Plans to connect the line to North Vancouver raised the ire of the West Vancouver residents who were appalled to find that the PGE had never abandoned its right of way there, even though service on that sector had been discontinued in 1928.

A major change in the B.C. political scene took place with the election in August 1952 of a Social Credit government led by W.A.C. Bennett. For the next 20 years B.C. was to have a leader who was a man of vision and action. He was also most fortunate to "ascend the throne" during a time of burgeoning economic activity in the province. His policies encouraged and nurtured those activities.

The line finally reached Prince George ("Prince George Egad") in late 1952. Newly elected Premier W.A.C. Bennett paid tribute to the efforts of Premiers Hart and Johnson for their contributions to the achievement of the long sought goal. Bennett then discussed the future of the PGE and its proposed extension into the Peace with Donald Gordon, head of the CNR. Bennett felt it was imperative that the PGE become integrated with a national system and, to achieve this, was quite willing to sell the line. Gordon, however, was not interested, being convinced that the jointly owned CP/CN Northern Alberta Railroad could quite adequately serve the Peace. A further attempt to interest Prime Minister St. Laurent in buying the line was rebuffed.

Despite discouragement and rejection from Ottawa, Bennett remained determined to push the PGE into the Peace and connect Squamish to North Vancouver. He insisted that the line would no longer be a bad joke, but would be turned into a viable north-south trunk route for B.C. Wall Street would provide the needed funds as British Columbia guaranteed bonds.

Between 1918 and 1953 the PGE had been a financial nightmare for the province. Its accumulated debt had reached $152 million — three-quarters of the total provincial debt! Bennett wrote off the uncollectable interest and took shares for the principle, thereby finally putting the railway on a viable financial footing.

Re-elected in June 1953 with a strong majority, Bennett announced his decision to extend the line north to the Peace and south from Squamish to North Vancouver. For this project Ottawa magnanimously granted another $1.25 million. Work at both ends proceeded rapidly with the link to North Vancouver opening in the summer of 1956. In mid-1958 the first trains from the south arrived in Dawson Creek and Fort St. John. Now the PGE became the "Province's Greatest Enterprise," after so many years of "Patience Guts and Endurance." An ebullient Premier expressed his intent to push the line on into the Yukon and Alaska, a revival of an old idea, which began to look like its time had come. No longer would the line be dubbed "Past God's Endurance" or the "Please Go Easy."

In 1956 a wealthy Swedish promoter, Axel Wenner-Gren, proposed a "Pacific Northern" monorail line from the south end of the Rocky Mountain Trench to the Yukon border in return for exclusive resource rights over the area tributary to the line. Within a year, his interest switched to the development of a massive hydroelectric development on the Peace River. As a private enterprise, especially one owned by a foreigner, neither project was acceptable to the B.C. public. However, the interest in the hydro potential of the Peace River received the full attention of Premier Bennett and became the basis of his "Two Rivers Policy" which eventually built both the Peace and Columbia dams.

A start was made on a 400 km (250 mile) extension of the main line north to Fort Nelson and, after five years of construction, this became operational in September 1971, but was plagued thereafter with frequent derailments, due to questionable construction standards. A spur line was built in 1966 to serve the new pulp mill at Mackenzie and a branch line pushed west from mile-31 north of Prince George to reach Fort St. James in 1968.

Bennett viewed the PGE as an instrument of public policy, not as a business venture. He retained the president's chair and appointed directors and managers who would carry out his vision. That vision certainly included further rail development in the north of the province. Late in 1969, the government decided to extend the line from Fort St. James, a further 660 km (412 miles) northwest to Dease Lake and Cassiar, B.C. The next stage after this "Dease Lake Extension" would take the line into the Yukon. Work on the extension commenced in the early seventies, along with rebuilding and renewing the main line with heavier rail and steel bridges.

On February 18, 1971, Ray Williston, a senior B.C. cabinet minister representing Prince George, announced that the province was ready, willing, and able to take over the CN north line and to develop port facilities on the North Coast. This, coupled with the increasing interest from multiple sources in port development at Prince Rupert and Kitimat, prompted Don Jamieson (federal Minister of Transport 1968–1973) to request a meeting with Premier W.A.C. Bennett to discuss rationalization of rail and port development in Northern B.C. Jamieson, it might be added, was a refreshing change from his recent predecessors as Minister of Transport in Ottawa, Pickersgill and Hellyer. Pickersgill was a master peddler of pious platitudes and Hellyer's short tenure was marked by his refusal to even visit Prince Rupert to assess the question of the long delayed northern port development.

From the subsequent meeting between Jamieson and Premier Bennett came plans for the CNR and PGE to work together to provide new rail infrastructure to open up northwest B.C. with eventual extension into the Yukon. A link was planned from the CN main line at Terrace to connect with the planned PGE extension south of Dease Lake. By mid-1972 extensive consultations and negotiations were underway between Ottawa and Victoria regarding responsibility for constructing these tracks and the matter of reciprocal running rights between the two railways. At this point, W.A.C. Bennett dropped from the picture with the election of the Barrett government on August 30, 1972.

In October of that year, a study by the consulting engineers, M.W. Menzies Group Ltd., reported that enhancing Prince Rupert as a port would cause a significant loss to the recently renamed British Columbia Railway (the PGE, until April 1972). It predicted that the line would lose 80 percent of its traffic over a major part of its system because virtually all the waterborne export traffic generated from existing and planned British Columbia Railway (BCR) lines north of Clinton would move via the CNR north line to Prince Rupert. The report concluded that if the BCR were to manage, or possibly own and manage the CN line from Prince George to Prince Rupert, it could equitably divide up traffic between its own system and the CNR.

Negotiations between the federal and provincial governments continued and by mid-1973 Jean Marchand, the new Minister of Transport in Ottawa, and his B.C. counterpart announced a $325 million plan for rail, port, and resource development that was designed to usher in a new period of economic growth in northwest B.C. The plan called for the two governments to share the cost of building five distinct lines in northwest B.C., as well as large-scale port developments. The CNR would be able to run trains over BCR tracks from the point where its new link from Terrace joined the BCR extension to Dease Lake. Thus the CNR could reach the Yukon, once BCR had reached Lower Post on the sixtieth parallel. In return, CN would allow BCR to operate over its main line from Prince George to Prince Rupert and both lines would have equal access to south-bound traffic from Dease Lake to Prince Rupert. In 1969 the CNR completed an initial study and evaluation of two feasible routes from Terrace to Watson Lake with connection to the BCR extension at Dease Lake. Subsequent to this, preliminary surveys were undertaken.

Meanwhile, the Barrett government in Victoria (1972–1975) became aware of mounting problems on the Dease Lake extension project of the British Columbia Railway. Costs had escalated and contractors were suing the railway for underestimating fill and rock cuts in their tender calls. Furthermore, the line began to appear increasingly less likely to be economically viable in the light of a world decline in the demand for asbestos and copper, the commodities most likely to use the service. In addition, the Cassiar Highway (Highway 37) from Highway 16 and the Port of Stewart had been recently upgraded as far as Dease Lake and offered an outlet to products from the far northwest of the province.

In December 1975, the Socreds, led by W.R. Bennett, were returned to office. The new Premier declined the role of chairman of the railway, a post held for so long by his father. Instead he appointed a board of nine directors from private business circles and, in 1978, Mac Norris was appointed President and CEO. A new era of relative freedom from political interference had begun for the railway.

Work on the Dease Lake extension was halted in April 1977. Premier W.R. Bennett appointed a Royal Commission to examine the railway's financial affairs and make recommendations for its future. Track had been laid to a point 423 km (262 miles) northwest of Fort St. James and all but 62 km (39 miles) of the remaining 238 km (148 miles) of roadbed was partially prepared. Expenditures on the extension to that point totalled $360 million, more than twice its original estimated cost. The federal government had agreed to contribute 38 percent of the cost of the extension, but still owed the province $117 million on that commitment. Now, however, Ottawa offered to contribute $81 million, if the province suspended the project.

The Mackenzie Royal Commission spent 18 months delving into the affairs of the railway, past and present, and made its final report August 25, 1978. The Commission recommended that construction cease on the uncompleted roadbed between Dease Lake and the end of track at Jackson. It further recommended that trains be terminated at Driftwood, just 234 km (145 miles) from Fort St. James with the remaining track to be left in place, but not used. The line to Driftwood operated until 1983 and then reopened in 1991 with a further extension of operations to Chipmunk — a point still 281 km (175 miles) short of Dease Lake. Other commission recommendations included eliminating the railway's debt, insofar as it had been incurred by politically motivated decisions, and abandonment of any future political role for the railway.

With termination of further work on the Dease extension and the premier's hands-off policy toward the railway, the "Grand Plan" that included the Yukon extension, the proposed link south to Terrace, and extensive CNR/BCR trackage interlining came to naught. The result of the plan's collapse was the continued somnolence of the entire northwest sector of the province and the stunted growth of traffic, especially in forest products, for the Port of Prince Rupert's Fairview General Cargo Terminal, which was completed in early 1977. Furthermore, as long as the BCR and the forests of central and northeastern B.C. had a common owner, it was certain that the forest industry would not alter its pattern of shipping by the "approved" railway.

An additional casualty of the collapse of the "Grand Plan" was the prospect for an early extension of the line from Dease Lake through the Yukon and into Alaska, where local citizens had long yearned for a rail connection to the "lower forty-eight."

THE BRITISH COLUMBIA RAILWAY AND BC RAIL: 1978 TO 2004

Early in the 1970s, the provincial government became increasingly aware of the potential for large, new, metallurgical coal sales to Japanese steel mills, but potential buyers insisted that they were only interested if the coal were moved to tidewater by an alternate rail corridor to the southern route through the Fraser Canyon. Extensive exploration of known coalfields in northeast B.C. led to the development of two deposits, the larger Quintette and the smaller Bullmoose. Owners of these deposits secured letters of intent from Japanese steel mills for large coal purchases and, in 1978, the government decided to have its British Columbia Railway build a new branch line into the coalfields. This new Tumbler Ridge subdivision, a 123 km (82 mile) electrified line, cost nearly $600 million and opened in 1983. It has the lowest crossing of the Rocky Mountains of any railway and the line passes through two tunnels totalling 15 km (9.3 miles) in length.

There was much debate over the tidewater terminus for coal from this new line. Pressures were strong to move the coal exclusively on British Columbia Railway track to a terminal at either Squamish, or Britannia Beach. Finally, however, both the federal and provincial governments selected Ridley Island, so trains from the Tumbler Ridge line had to be interchanged at Prince George to the CN north line for onward transit to Prince Rupert.

Though initially profitable, traffic on the line never reached its predicted volume because Quintette developed serious production problems and world demand and price for metallurgical coal declined. In August 2000, the Quintette mine ceased operations and the portion of the rail line between it and the Bullmoose operation was abandoned. The electric locomotives were replaced by diesel. Then in 2003 Bullmoose ceased operating and the remaining 112 km (69.6 miles) of the line was abandoned, although the track was left in place. In 2005, the line reopened for shipment to Ridley Terminals, in response to the development of new, smaller, and more efficient mines coupled with a renewed demand for metallurgical coal and higher prices.

The railway incurred a heavy debt load building the Tumbler Ridge Line and losing operations on that line did nothing to help its finances. In 1984 the British Columbia Railway was restructured and its rail operations renamed BC Rail. This same year it acquired the British Columbia Harbours Board Railway, a 37 km (23 mile) line connecting three Class 1 railways to Roberts Bank.

When Mac Norris retired in 1989, Paul McElligot took over as President and CEO. At this point BC Rail had a relatively efficient and mostly profitable railway, a real estate division, a development plan, and a province-wide telecommunications network. A major thrust to own and operate marine terminals in Vancouver began with the purchase of Vancouver Wharves in 1993. This was followed in 1998 by the acquisition of Casco Terminals (Centerm) and Canadian Stevedoring. These three entities were included under a new division, B.C. Marine, which became a major player on the Vancouver waterfront.

Despite these changes, the railway's political masters still required it to operate a number of money losing services, while in receipt of much reduced government subsidies. Its debt load increased by a factor of six over the period between 1991 and 2001. BC Rail remained a relatively short-line, intra-provincial railway subject to intense competition from trucks operating on parallel highways, as well as from the CNR, CPR, and Burlington Northern, each using affiliated truckers and reload yards. The southern part of the line was plagued with excessive maintenance and operating costs, a result of many miles where gradients were 2.2 percent and numerous curvatures were between 8 and 12 degrees.

Losses in 2001 amounted to $107 million and an additional $617 million, relating to the Tumbler Ridge line, had been written off. Traffic volumes were substantially reduced with little prospect of future profitable operations. The railway's operating ratio (expense as a percent of revenue) was over 90 percent, in contrast to the privatized CNR at 73 percent.

For the nine decades of its troubled history, successive provincial governments had reluctantly borne this railway millstone around their necks. Despite the political sensitivities, the lesson taken from the very successful CNR privatization could not be ignored and it focussed most minds in Victoria on the idea of, once again, trying to dispose of this questionable asset.

Between 1991 and 2001 political ideology constrained the NDP governments from thoughts of disposal, but in May 2001, the Liberal party, under the leadership of Gordon Campbell, took over the reins in Victoria with a mandate for change in many directions. Campbell had promised during the election campaign that he would not sell the railway, but subsequent actions clearly indicated that some form of disposal of this seemingly eternal burden on the province was planned.

The BCR Group, parent of B.C. Marine and BC Rail, announced plans to sell all the components of B.C. Marine in March 2002, with proceeds to be applied to debt reduction. Casco Terminals (Centerm) and Canadian Stevedoring were sold to P&O Ports Canada for $110 million in February 2003. This sale resulted in the transfer of the Canadian Stevedoring lease on Fairview Terminal to the new owner for the remainder of its term, which was due to expire December 31, 2004. Vancouver Wharves proved more difficult to sell. The site was finally leased to Kinder Morgan Energy Partners of Texas, after their purchase of the terminals and above-ground assets in 2007.

On May 13, 2003 Premier Campbell announced that the province would sell the operations of the railway, including all its assets, except the track and the right of way. The latter would be leased. The "fig leaf" of this lease component of the deal allowed the government to insist that it was not really selling the railway.

Sale of the railway's operations to the CNR for one billion dollars was announced on November 25, 2003. The first lease on the right of way would last 60 years and would be followed by 30-year option renewals. Excluded from the deal with CN was the former British Columbia Harbours Board Railway, owned by BC Rail since 1984, the short line that connected Roberts Bank to CN, the CP, and the Burlington Northern Santa Fe (BNSF) lines in the lower mainland. Other B.C. Group assets including some real estate and Vancouver Wharves were also excluded from the sale to CN.

The transfer of operations on the 2,215 km (1,330 miles) of track to the CNR took effect on July 15, 2004 after the Federal Competition Bureau had approved the transaction. Sale of the railway's operations brought the line under federal, rather than provincial regulatory jurisdiction, and responsibility for enforcement shifted to Ottawa.

As one (of a number) of conditions of the sale, CN agreed to spend $4 million to upgrade and reopen their rail line between Dawson Creek, B.C. and Hythe, Alberta. To date, sufficient traffic has not materialized and the line remains closed. It is expected that continuing efforts to develop a transload facility in Grand Prairie, Alberta will eventually consolidate sufficient traffic to provide a daily train service over the reopened line, moving both bulk commodities and loaded containers from the Peace River Block to port facilities in Prince Rupert, rather than via the much longer route to Jasper and Vancouver.

The province assigned $30 million from the sale proceeds toward the conversion of Prince Rupert's Fairview break-bulk and general cargo terminal to a state-of-the-art, intermodal container handling operation — an operation aimed at traffic from Asia to Central Canada, the U.S. Midwest and Southeast. This was one of a number of provincial initiatives aimed at lifting the economic depression that had settled over many of the communities along the Northern Rail Corridor. Prince Rupert, especially, saw reason to hope for an end to the 9-decade drain to the south, over the provincial railway, of resource commodities produced in central and northeastern B.C. — a movement that had severely retarded throughput growth at the port.

OTHER PLANNED RAILROADS IN NORTHWESTERN CANADA

The enthusiasm for planning, promoting, and building railroads in Canada in the late nineteenth and early twentieth centuries was by no means confined to the three giant transcontinental projects. The 1898 gold rushes to the Klondike and to Atlin, plus the subsequent discovery of other very substantial mineral deposits in the northwest, spawned dozens of companies that applied for and received charters from Victoria, Edmonton, Ottawa, and even London, England to provide rail access to and through this area. Most were promotions with little or no substance, but one did succeed and several others are worth noting. Most of the routes entailed a tidewater terminus after traversing the Bear Pass to Stewart, the Stikine River Valley to the head of river navigation at Glenora, the Taku River valley, or the White Pass to Skagway.

While it is well beyond the purview of this book to describe, in any detail, the story of these many projected railways, a superficial look at a few may well interest readers because of their potential relationship to the Northern Rail Corridor and Gateway Port.

In 1887, the great G.M. Dawson envisioned a 1,120 km (700 mile) rail line extending from the mouth of the Stikine River to Fort Simpson on the Mackenzie River. Ten years later, Warburton Pike received a provincial charter with land and mineral concessions to build the "Cassiar Central Railway" from Glenora to Dease Lake. Track was laid a short distance inland from the riverbank, before this project was abandoned. The same year (1897) those inveterate railway builders, Mackenzie and Mann, builders of the Canadian Northern Railway (the "Farmers' Friend"), received a federal charter with liberal concessions to build a line from Glenora to Teslin Lake with a branch line to Dease Lake.

In 1907, the Portland Canal Short Line Railway built and operated a rail line up the Bear Valley from Stewart to serve a copper mine. This line was taken over by Mackenzie and Mann in 1910 and renamed the Canadian Northeastern Railway. Aware of Hays' efforts to connect the Grand Trunk Pacific line with Vancouver via the planned provincial railway south from Prince George (the PGE), the two railway entrepreneurs determined that their Canadian Northern transcontinental line (called the Canadian Northern Pacific in B.C.) must have an outlet to a north coast port. Their plan for the Canadian Northeastern Railway was to build east from Stewart, across northern B.C. with numerous branch lines. The line would then go through either the Peace, or Pine Pass, and then through the Peace River agricultural area and northern Prairies to a final link with their main line at Edmonton. They laid out a railway town site at Stewart and upgraded and extended the former Portland Canal line as far as the Bear Pass, 26 km (16 miles) from the village. The project ground to a halt as financing problems mounted. These were mainly due to heavy cost overruns constructing their main line in the Fraser Canyon section of the corridor to Vancouver and the general collapse of financial and political support for all railway projects with the 1912 economic depression. The Consolidated Mining and Smelting Company, owned by the CPR, acquired the completed 16 miles of the line in 1929 with plans to extend the line east to Fort Grahame on the Finlay River. This plan collapsed in the 1929 stock market crash and the subsequent depression of the 1930s. The tracks were finally removed during World War II.

First references to the extensive anthracite coalfields of the Klappan plateau near the headwaters of the Skeena and the Nass Rivers date back to 1900. By 1911 the entire area, which starts 152 km (95 miles) northeast of Stewart, had been staked and 21 charters granted to railway companies to build lines through, or close to this resource. In recent years, there has been considerable interest in this coalfield and studies have been undertaken to determine the best way to move the very high quality product to tidewater.

The White Pass and Yukon Railway was the one line completed. Backed by British capital, this line reached Whitehorse from Skagway in 1900 and has been operated, albeit in a variety of modes, for most of the years since.

Though many of the projected rail lines entailed plans for a west to east routing, others focussed on a generally south to north direction, starting at points as disparate as Alberta, southern B.C., or one of a number of a number of tidewater points on the north B.C. coast, or the Alaska Panhandle. Furthermore, a number of the proposed south to north routes were planned to include, eventually, extensions through the Yukon and into Alaska. Some proposals — and they reappear from time to time — even entailed extensions across Alaska to the Bering Straits with a crossing to Siberia, for onward links to Europe. Interestingly, this last idea was first proposed in 1845, well before the 1867 purchase of Alaska by the U.S. In 1942, Stalin pressured Roosevelt to build a railway across Canada and Alaska to expedite the movement of supplies, under the Lend-Lease Program, to the hard pressed Soviet military. Instead of a railroad, the Alcan Highway was roughed out in a remarkably short time and a series of air bases built to facilitate both aid to Russia and the defense of Alaskan territory.

We have noted the 1959 Wenner-Gren proposal to the B.C. Government to build a "Pacific Northern" line via Dease Lake and also the 1969 CNR "Yukon Feasibility Study" in connection with the Bennett/Jamieson "Grand Plan" for a rail network to open up northern B.C. The proponents of the Dease Lake extension project certainly had the longer range objective to extend that line further into the Yukon and finally, into Alaska. The 1978 report of the Mackenzie Royal Commission, however, called the "North to Alaska" project "the stuff of grand political dreams."

The sale of BC Rail to the CNR in 2004 revived hope in Alaska for their long sought rail link to the "lower forty-eight," despite Transport Canada's view that "the business case is frail with benefits to Canada questionable." Certainly, the enthusiasm in Alaska for the "Alaska Rail Corridor" is not matched in Ottawa or even in Washington. If ever undertaken, the shortest, fastest to complete, and cheapest route for such a line would be via Dease Lake and would extend 2,168 km (1,355 miles) from Prince George to Fairbanks at a cost estimated in 2004 at $3.7 billion dollars. The alternate route via Fort Nelson would be 128 km (80 miles) longer, would take an extra year to build, and would cost an estimated $4.22 billion. The latter route, however, could be more viable if associated in a common corridor with a fibre-optic link and the much sought after natural gas pipeline from Prudhoe Bay to the "lower forty-eight."

SUMMARY

The classic literary work *Extraordinary Popular Delusions and the Madness of Crowds* by Charles McKay appeared in 1841. It explored in depth examples of mass human folly such as the seventeenth century "Tulipomania" in Holland and the eighteenth century "South Seas Bubble." Invariably, the "Madness of Crowds" was closely abetted by greedy and unscrupulous promoters and financiers closely associated with malleable or negligent politicians who, too often, seemed more motivated to embarrass their opponents than to show the leadership needed to arrive at commonsense decisions. The history of early rail development in Western Canada is replete with examples of this sort, especially in the later years.

Sir John A. Macdonald built a railway from sea to sea to create a nation. His very real fear of U.S. expansion north, either by occupation, or through financial hegemony forced him to deal with wealthy, but less than scrupulous Montreal financiers and led to the first major political scandal in Canada. His Liberal successor, Alexander Mackenzie, could see only "superlative difficulties" in building the line and his lack of interest almost cost the West. Only Macdonald's return to power saved the day and the CPR was finally completed.

Mackenzie and Mann were the quintessential railway promoters and entrepreneurs. They developed close relations with the governments and people of the prairies, taking full advantage with their "Farmers' Friend" of the visceral hatred of the CPR on the part of the local people and their governments. With that strong local support they then developed a grandiose plan to extend their prairie lines east and west to form a transcontinental line able to compete from sea to sea with both the CPR and the concurrently planned National Transcontinental for land bridge traffic from Asia to Europe.

Laurier's conversion to railway building stemmed from a burning desire to create a second Liberal-sponsored transcontinental line. From this ambition came the hybrid public-private National Transcontinental, the public component being a result of the Grand Trunk directors' refusal to be responsible for the whole route. His great mistake was to allow parallel development of the Grand Trunk Pacific and the Canadian Northern across the vast, near-empty distances west of southern Ontario.

Hays' ambitious and aggressive approach to his London directors partially overcame their better judgement and his alliance with Laurier on the National Transcontinental project was crucial to the extension of the Grant Trunk Railway to the Pacific. His labour policies, nepotism, unwillingness to delegate authority, and unsavoury land acquisitions — especially at the new terminal port — are all black marks on his record. His later eagerness to connect the GTP in B.C. to Vancouver suggests, most strongly, that his interest and support for Prince Rupert had waned.

In B.C. we first see the public insisting that the CPR transcontinental line must end in Victoria (regardless of geography). To calm the public clamour, Dunsmuir was given one-fifth of the land on Vancouver Island in return for building the rail line from Esquimalt to Courtney and Port Alberni. McBride's Tory government in Victoria certainly demonstrated strong support for Mackenzie and Mann's Canadian Northern Railway (called the Canadian Northern Pacific within B.C.) and Vancouver, while showing much less enthusiasm for the foreign owned and Liberal-sponsored GTP, or its terminal port, Prince Rupert. Responding to public demand for a new rail line north through the centre of the province, McBride reluctantly dealt, albeit indirectly, with the GTP to create the Pacific Great Eastern at a most inopportune time — just as the great rail building bubble was about to burst. The fickle public, who had given him a landslide mandate, then deserted him and subjected the new railroad to ridicule and sarcasm.

The W.A.C. Bennett years saw final development of the provincial railroad as a tool for overall development of the province. The Dease Lake extension, however, turned out to be "too far too soon" and the "Grand Plan" for a rail network in northwest Canada, though visionary, proved impossible to justify economically. It is perhaps best remembered as one of the very rare occasions when Premier W.A.C. Bennett and a federal Cabinet Minister worked together amicably on a project!

The great railway building bubble finally burst in 1912. As so often happens, the financiers, promoters, and builders for the most part kept their fortunes intact, or even increased them, while the public was left "holding the bag" over the next nine decades, not only for government guarantees, but also for the ongoing billions in operating losses for both the CNR and the PGE/BCR. The same public who had so enthusiastically encouraged politicians to back the building of more and more railways now turned on their leaders and ridiculed the failing lines.

For the newly created model city of Prince Rupert, the fallout from the collapse of the railway bubble, followed so soon by the Great War and then the Great Depression of the 1930s, was disastrous. Apart from the flurry of port and rail activity for a couple of years during World War II, the rail line from Red Pass Junction west and its Pacific Port languished. Later, when the economy of most of B.C. was booming under Bennett's dynamic leadership, the PGE extension to Prince George and on to the Peace River area was completed and siphoned virtually all the traffic tributary to that line south, to Squamish and Vancouver. In the late seventies and early eighties very substantial investments resulted in state-of-the-art grain and coal terminals, as well as the Fairview General Cargo Terminal in Prince Rupert. The latter's growth, however, would continue to be stunted by the movement of forest products from central and northeastern B.C. to lower mainland ports via the PGE/BCR lines.

As long as the CNR and BCR remained crown corporations, they were subject to overriding political considerations and the resulting monumental inefficiencies. The "liberation" of both railways from these constraints has unquestionably created, at long last, the opportunity for the Northern Rail Corridor and port to show their potential.

The privatization of the CNR has produced a thoroughly rejuvenated entity that is now a model for all North American railroads, a huge success story. Its takeover of BC Rail and its imaginative and aggressive leadership in encouraging the use of the Northern Rail Corridor west from Red Pass Junction to Prince Rupert bodes well for the future of the north coast port. At long last, the orphaned port is recognized at the highest executive levels of the CNR for its potential to serve the ever-expanding trade with Asia. The superb deep natural harbour, so well located on the Pacific Rim, is now linked to the most profitable railway in North America, operating 33,750 km (21,094 miles) of tracks and spanning Canada from Atlantic to Pacific and mid America south to the Gulf of Mexico. It serves the ports of Halifax, Montreal, Vancouver, and Prince Rupert in Canada and New Orleans, Mobile, and Baton Rouge in the U.S. Through its U.S. rail hubs and affiliates, it serves all points in North America. The sorry, overbuilt conglomeration of bankrupt railroads that was cobbled together by Ottawa to create the CNR has become a very successful enterprise, singularly blessed with a grossly underutilized, first-class line to a second Pacific Gateway Port that enables it to take full advantage of the recent, dramatic increase in transpacific trade.

Sir George Foster, Minister of Trade and Commerce in the Robert Borden government is said to have remarked, "Prince Rupert appears to be struggling under a curse." If that were true, it would surely appear that the curse has finally been lifted and the port's future can now be considered secure.

CHAPTER TWO

The First Pacific Gateways to Overseas Trade

INTRODUCTION

Two harbours on Canada's West Coast have the required attributes for a great world port, but neither participated in the early development of maritime trade from the Pacific shores of British North America.

Captain Cook's 1778 visit to Nootka Sound on Vancouver Island triggered the beginning of overseas trade in the Pacific Northwest. Between 1785 and 1825, one hundred and seventy vessels, mostly from New England, exploited the demand for sea otter fur in China until over-harvesting led to total collapse of this resource. One of Cook's officers, George Vancouver, returned 14 years later with two vessels, HM Ships *Discovery* and *Chatham*, and over a three-year period charted 8,045 km (5,000 miles) of the exceedingly complex northwest coastline, commencing in Puget Sound. On June 13, 1792 he entered and charted "Burrard's Channel," named to honour his friend Captain Harry Burrard. For the next 70 years, this fine natural harbour with its substantial native population lay virtually undisturbed.

Early in the nineteenth century, the North West Company established fur trading posts in northern New Caledonia at Fort Nelson (1805), Fort St. James (1806), and Fort Fraser (1806), but their orientation was land-based and directed east. The company purchased the one-year-old Fort Astoria at the mouth of the Columbia River from J.J. Astor's Pacific Fur Company in 1813 and changed its name to Fort George. Then, in 1821, the company was taken over by its old rival, the Hudson's Bay Company (HBC) and, four years later, the headquarters of the combined operation was moved 70 miles upriver to Fort Vancouver.

Recognizing that Britain's hold on the "Oregon Territory" was becoming increasingly tenuous, the HBC governors decided to move the company's principle base further north. Accordingly, in 1825, the HBC trading and supply vessel *William & Ann* was directed to sail up the "inside passage" of coastal New Caledonia as far as Portland Canal to identify good harbours and to explore prospects for profitable trade with the natives. Particular attention was to be paid to finding a suitable site near the mouth of the Fraser River for the proposed new company base north of the forty-ninth parallel. Two years later, another HBC vessel, the schooner *Cadboro*, entered the Fraser carrying the party sent to establish Fort Langley, located 45 km (28 miles) from the river mouth. This same vessel, captained by Aemilius Simpson, established Fort Nass in 1831, though it was later moved to Port Simpson. Fort McLoughlin followed in 1833, Fort Victoria in 1843, and Fort Rupert in 1849. Three years after the signing of the Oregon Treaty in 1846, Fort Victoria became the western headquarters of the HBC.

Operations on the tortuous and confined coastline north of the forty-ninth parallel necessitated the addition of steam powered vessels to supplement the company's fleet of coastal deep-sea sailing ships. The arrival of the paddle wheeler *Beaver* in 1836, followed in 1853 by the propeller driven *Otter*, enabled the company to distribute trade goods arriving via Cape Horn on the annual sailing vessel to their coastal "Forts," as well as collect furs acquired from the native population to ship back to England. In addition to furs, there were shipments of spars to Britain and Australia, as well as salmon — salted and packed in barrels — to Britain and the Sandwich Islands. In 1849, Vancouver Island was established as a Crown Colony with the Royal Navy reinforcing Victoria's position as the main base for British interests on the western Pacific. The colony's second governor, James Douglas, together with the local citizens, jealously guarded Victoria's dominance against erosion from any potential new power base on the mainland.

The discovery of coal on Vancouver Island, as well as gold on the banks of the Fraser River and the Cariboo transformed these outposts on the far fringe of the British Empire. The new mainland colony of British Columbia (B.C.) was proclaimed at Fort Langley on November 19, 1858 with Douglas appointed its first governor, a position he held in addition to that of governor of the Vancouver Island Colony. Douglas chose a site for the new colony's capital on the south bank of the Fraser adjacent to Fort Langley and had his surveyors lay out a town site to be known as Derby. Lots were sold, mostly to Douglas' friends and speculators from Victoria.

A detachment of 225 Royal Engineers under the command of Colonel Moody was sent to the mainland colony from England in 1858/9. They were charged with three objectives: to keep the peace, maintain sovereignty in the presence of so many unruly, mostly American, gold seekers, and to initiate a major program of public works. Moody at once rejected Derby as a practical or defensible site for the colony's capital, choosing instead a better site on the north bank of the river further west. Reluctantly, Douglas agreed and Queensborough was declared the capital of British Columbia on February 14, 1859. The Engineers surveyed the newly planned town site and lots were auctioned in June 1859. Derby was abandoned and relations between Moody and the mainland colonists, and Douglas with his land speculator friends from Victoria, became strained. Victoria citizens were determined to control and suppress the development of any mainland rival, and their protests against the name Queensborough resulted in the capital city being re-named New Westminster. On July 16, 1860 New Westminster was incorporated as a city with its own council; the first incorporated city in Canada west of Ontario. The following year Government House was completed, but Governor Douglas elected to stay in the capital of the older colony, Victoria, which was incorporated as a city in 1862.

Observing the activities of Colonel Moody and his Royal Engineers, Douglas and his Victoria-based clique began to feel a challenge from developments on the mainland. Since the founding of Fort Victoria, all European trade goods had arrived there in sailing ships for trans-shipment on small coastal vessels, including the paddle wheeler *Beaver*, to Fort Langley and up-coast points. Probably the oddest cargo was a shipment of 23 camels that arrived from San Francisco in 1862 to be used for hauling freight on the road to the Cariboo. Attempts by the citizens of New Westminster to promote their city as a port for the mainland colony were thwarted when Douglas imposed a special duty on all goods transported through the river port. As a result, all goods legally brought into B.C. were routed through the free port of Victoria, thereby strangling the nascent mainland port. Vessels en route from Victoria to Hope simply bypassed New Westminster.

During their five-year stay in B.C., the Royal Engineers established the city of New Westminster, surveyed the border with the U.S., upgraded the Douglas Trail from Harrison Lake to Lillooet to a wagon road, built the first road from the Fraser River to Burrard Inlet and, along with private contractors, built the Cariboo Road from Yale to Barkerville. This famous wagon road opened the route through the Fraser Canyon that would later become the first rail corridor to the coast.

In 1859 HMS *Plumper*, a steam-powered vessel commanded by Captain Richards, surveyed and charted Burrard Inlet. The same year the Royal Engineers built a pack trail through 9 miles of dense forest to connect the inlet to New Westminster. Two years later, the trail was upgraded to a wagon road, ostensibly to create an emergency escape route for New Westminster residents in the event of invasion from the south! Before they left the colony, the Royal Engineers undertook preliminary surveys for the town site of Granville on the south shore of Burrard inlet. This remarkable unit of the British Army was recalled to England in 1863, though most of its complement elected to remain in the new colony.

The citizens of New Westminster resented their non-resident governor and his Victoria cronies. This, coupled with Colonial Office's suspicion of Douglas' too close relationship with the Hudson's Bay Company, led to his resignation and replacement by Frederick Seymour, on April 20, 1864. Then, primarily as a cost saving measure, the Colonial Office in London decided to unite the two rival colonies effective November 19, 1866 with New Westminster as capital city. A new 23-member legislative council was formed with majority representation from the more populous, former island colony. The council soon resolved that the capital should be moved to Victoria and, as Governor Seymour refused to override that decision, Victoria was proclaimed capital of B.C. on May 24, 1868, to the bitter disappointment and fury of New Westminster residents.

Despite the handicaps imposed by jealous administrators in Victoria, the citizens of New Westminster continued to aspire to make their city the mainland's premier port, by attempting to attract deep-sea vessels terminating their voyages in Victoria. The first ocean going vessel, Hudson's Bay's side-wheeler *Labouchere*, reached the city in July 1859, but the dangers of navigating the unmarked river convinced deep-sea captains to avoid the port, at least until proper navigational aids were provided. By 1866, a lightship was in place at

Sandheads, supplemented by buoys to mark the main river channel. The $37,150 cost of these navigational aids was paid out of New Westminster harbour revenues. In 1867, the Pilot Ordinance established rules governing marine traffic on the river with requirements that all foreign vessels drawing over 6 feet must carry a pilot provided by the city.

Though mostly unsuccessful in competing with Victoria for deep-sea traffic, New Westminster became the base for a fleet of steam-powered paddle wheelers that operated on the river, as far as Yale, for 50 years, serving not only interior points, but also the thriving agriculture based communities, sawmills, and salmon canneries, which were developing along the lower Fraser River. The black tinsmith John Deas began canning salmon at Sapperton in 1871 and, in 1873, set up his own cannery on Deas Island. By 1878 there were eight canneries on the Fraser River. Canned salmon replaced shipments of salted salmon in barrels and quickly became B.C.'s second most important export commodity. For a time, New Westminster became the prime commercial centre on the mainland. Cannery numbers multiplied, so that by 1905 a total of 48 were operating on the lower river.

New Westminster supported confederation, especially in light of Canada's promise of an early rail connection to the eastern provinces. However, neither the rail corridor, nor the ocean terminus for the planned line had yet been selected. The final choice of the southern Kicking Horse Pass route through the Rockies eliminated Port Simpson as one of the three terminal options being considered. The remaining possibilities were Burrard Inlet, or Victoria via Bute Inlet and a bridge across Seymour Narrows. Victoria, capital since 1868 and the chief entry port for international trade, lobbied hard and expected to achieve its goal. Faced with the strictures of geography, however, it had to accept the consolation prizes of a railway up the island to be built by Dunsmuir (on receipt of an enormous land grant) and the promise of a dry dock, which was finally fulfilled by Ottawa in 1887.

New Westminster citizens were especially delighted that Port Moody was chosen in 1878 to be the terminus of the promised transcontinental railway, rather than its rival Victoria. They were sure that their "outer harbour" on Burrard Inlet was a far better choice. With the arrival of the first two-car transcontinental train in Port Moody on July 4, 1886 (139 hours after leaving Montreal), the city matched funds with the province to build a branch line, the New Westminster and Port Moody Railway, to its waterfront. The first passenger train on this line arrived at the river port on November 1, 1886.

Even before the first train arrived at the CPR's Burrard Inlet terminus at Port Moody, many realized that the line should be extended further west to the tiny logging and sawmill community of Granville. The railway concurred after the province gave it title to much of the waterfront on the south side of the inlet, as well as 25 square km (9.7 square miles) of upland that eventually became the city's business district. Renamed Vancouver by CPR manager Van Horne, the newly dubbed Terminal City was incorporated on April 6, 1886, and officially welcomed its first through train from Montreal on May 23, 1887, just one year after the original settlement had been destroyed by fire.

NEW WESTMINSTER AND VANCOUVER, THE FIRST MAINLAND PORTS

For two decades before the first train arrived at Port Moody, sawmills on both shores of Burrard Inlet had been active exporters of forest products manufactured from local clearings. Graham and Hicks built the first water powered sawmill on the north shore of Burrard Inlet in 1863 and, finally in November 1864, the barque *Ellen Lewis* left the mill wharf after spending two months loading lumber, fence pickets, and railway ties for the Australian market. Later, under the aggressive ownership of Sewell Moody, the mill focused on the export market, loading 33 vessels between January 1867 and June 1868.

Burrard Inlet's second mill was built by Stamp on the south shore at Centerm's present site. "Stamp's Mill" began full production in 1867 and loaded its first lumber cargo on the Aquila, bound for Cork, Ireland. This mill was expanded under the new name Hastings Mill and became the focus of the tiny surrounding company community of Granville, just as Moodyville developed around the mill on the north shore.

The first navigation aids to the harbour approaches were placed in 1865 and that same year Charles Houston was certified to pilot vessels into Burrard Inlet. To assist vessels within the harbour, Stamp ordered the tug *Isobel* from a Victoria yard.

Despite all this activity on the mainland, when the combined colonies entered confederation in 1871, Victoria still dominated deep-sea trade by a ratio of 4:1.

New Westminster did enjoy a boom in river transportation during the years of railway construction, but ocean-going vessels still tended to avoid the river, preferring to terminate their voyage in Victoria. Steamboats still carried lumber (produced on the river since 1869), as well as fish and agricultural products to Victoria where they were loaded on overseas-bound sailing vessels. After B.C. joined confederation in 1871, the federal government became involved in projects designed to create and maintain a navigable channel on the Fraser River, at least as far as New Westminster. Substantial works commenced in 1882 with removal of snags and construction of control works at the river mouth.

To remove logs, tree trunks, and other debris fouling the river, the first of a series of five purpose-built snag scows, the *Samson*, was constructed in 1884. Built of wood at a cost of $14,993 and operated by 9–15 men, this vessel was tasked with keeping the lower Fraser River free of snags and floating debris and maintaining navigation markers from the river mouth to Mission. In 1898 the *Samson* journeyed north to the Stikine River to clear that water route for the steamboats carrying gold seekers to the Yukon. It was replaced by the *Samson II* in 1904. For 86 years the acquisition and operating costs of the five *Samson* snag-clearing vessels were paid by the federal Department of Public Works. Clearing debris was especially important to the operations of the increasing number of salmon canneries situated on the river since the early 1870s.

With limited dredging, the marked channel was prone to shifting and silting up.

However, by 1889 the river was navigable for vessels with a 14-foot draft, allowing cargoes of lumber and canned salmon from twelve canneries and three large sawmills to be loaded at the river wharves in increasing numbers. Continent-wide economic depression, starting in 1892 and lasting five years, upset plans for a deep-water port on the Fraser and, during those years, it became very difficult to secure federal funding to upgrade the main channel, or create major port facilities. With a return to more prosperous times the Department of Public Works acquired a dredge, the *King Edward*, in 1901, to begin the monumental task of creating and maintaining a navigable channel for deep-sea vessels, at least as far as New Westminster. After World War I, *King Edward* was joined by the *Fruhling*, an ex-German dredge built in 1907 (to dredge the Kiel Canal and turned over to Canada after the war as reparations). These two dredges worked on the river, and at times in Burrard Inlet, until well after World War II.

New Westminster did receive one substantial boost with the 1891 arrival of the New Westminster and Southern Railway, on the south bank of the river (in Surrey). This 22-mile branch line off the Great Northern at Blaine had the distinction of being the only Canadian railway built to that date without government subsidy. Its delayed construction was only permitted after negotiation with the CPR that still had the right to block any competing rail operation within 32 km (20 miles) of their tracks.

Sail powered vessels still dominated overseas trade, but required the aid of steam powered tugs to safely navigate the lower Fraser, as well as the passage to newly constructed wharves in Burrard Inlet.

Vancouver, with its new rail connection to the rest of Canada and its fine natural harbour was at once destined to become a port for national trade, rather than a limited regional port. It would, inevitably, eventually eclipse both Victoria and New Westminster as the principal port for both coastal and overseas shipping. Captain John Irving merged his Pioneer Line of Fraser River steamboats with the Hudson's Bay fleet of coastal steamers to form the Canadian Pacific Navigation Company, in 1883, and assume service to many coastal points.

Aware that freight and passenger revenues from the tiny population along its long rail route would, at least at first, be minimal, the CPR aggressively entered transpacific trade. The intent was to capture the movement of tea, silk, mail, as well as passengers from the Orient to U.S. and European markets. Initially, the railway chartered eight sailing vessels to move this high value cargo to the newly built government wharf at the railway's terminus in Port Moody. The first of these vessels to arrive, the *W. B. Flint* off-loaded 17,430 half-chests of tea on July 27, 1886, seven weeks after the great fire on June 13 that destroyed most of the newly incorporated City of Vancouver. It is on record that the tea cargo from that vessel arrived in New York 49 days after leaving Yokahama.

While awaiting the delivery of their own liners, the railway chartered three former Cunard liners, the *Abyssinia*, *Parthia*, and *Batavia* to augment the transpacific service. After a 13-day Pacific crossing from Yokohama, *Abyssinia* arrived on June 14, 1887 at the newly completed wooden dock west of Hastings Mill, just three weeks after the arrival of the first train. Her cargo of tea was transferred to waiting trains which departed at once for Montreal and New York. Part of that tea shipment arrived in London 29 days after leaving Yokahama — an impressive record for surface transport 120 years ago!

In 1889, the ships chartered from Cunard brought 3,231 passengers and 53,217 tons of cargo to the new port from the Orient, while the fast, former tea clipper *Titania*, operated by the HBC, became the first ship to arrive with cargo direct from London, after a record voyage of only 105 days. She returned with the first load of canned salmon shipped to the United Kingdom (U.K.).

The new cargo passenger liners *Empress of India*, *Empress of China*, and *Empress of Japan*, built to order for the transpacific trade, arrived in 1891. The Canadian Pacific's integrated transportation system now allowed it to move mail and passengers from Yokahama to London in 22 days. With these vessels, coupled with aggressive marketing and efficient service, the railway began to establish a near monopoly on transpacific passenger, mail, and cargo movement that would last for half a century.

By 1891 the city's population had risen to 13,685 and it had moved from a tent town to an embryo metropolis with matching political influence.

Two years after the arrival of the Empress liners, the Canadian Australasian Shipping Company's *Miowera* inaugurated a liner-service linking Australia and New Zealand with Vancouver. This passenger, mail, and freight service would outlast the CPR's Pacific services by 14 years, ending with the final sailing of the *Aorangi* in 1953.

The Klondike gold rush of 1897–1899 ushered in a period of frenetic activity in Vancouver and New Westminster (as well as Victoria and Seattle) for outfitting and transporting gold seekers to Skagway. This lifted the spirits of the entire area, after the slumping economy of the previous five years. The CPR participated with two vessels, the *Tartar* and *Athenian*, hurriedly purchased in the U.K. and brought via Cape Horn to Vancouver early in 1898. Though the boom in coastal shipping quickly peaked, it led to the establishment of the Union Steamship Company in 1889 that challenged Irving's Canadian Pacific Navigation Company for coastal trade. It led also to the CPR's takeover of the Pacific Navigation Company, two years later, to form its British Columbia Coast Service. This company's *Princess* ships dominated passenger and freight traffic between major points on the coast of B.C. and the Alaska panhandle for the next 60 years.

One of the first industries in Vancouver that was not founded on forestry or the fishery was the sugar refinery, built just east of Hastings Mill in 1890 by the 24-year-old American, B.T. Rogers. Rogers was supported by CPR directors including Van Horne, by now president of the company, and was subsidized by the infant city. Raw sugar for the refinery was imported from southwest Pacific islands and Australia. False Creek became an early centre of industrial activity and included Alfred Wallace's first shipyard. However, port activity was based, by a very large margin, on the export of lumber from sawmill company wharves on both sides of Burrard Inlet. As a result of this relative dependency on forest products, Vancouver and its port business reflected world economic cycles in resource markets from the outset. The pattern of alternating boom and recession that was established early was directly mirrored in port activity and development over the next 75 years.

In 1908, the Grand Trunk Pacific Railway took over Mackenzie Brothers Steamships and established their *Prince* ships as the third coastal service, albeit with special emphasis on north coast points.

With the completion by the province of the Fraser Bridge in 1904, the Great Northern Railway (CPR's rival for West Coast business), extended its New Westminster and Southern Railway line into Vancouver under the new name Vancouver, Westminster and Yukon Railway. Five years later, it relocated most of that line, now renamed the Great Northern, to a new route from the border through White Rock. In 1914 this railway completed the Great Northern Pier on the south shore of Burrard Inlet.

The North American depression during the mid-1890s slowed Vancouver's growth, but was followed by a decade-long boom at the start of the new century. By 1911 the city had grown from a huddle of shacks and shops adjoining a sawmill to a metropolis with considerable political influence. While the population of the rest of the province merely doubled, Vancouver's population quadrupled between 1901 and 1911, reaching 100,401 for the city and 164,020 for the metropolitan area.

The city was served from the east and south by rail lines and could anticipate, in the near future, a rail link from the north and the completion of a second transcontinental line. The aspiring world port hosted 72 deep-sea vessels in 1909 and, of these, 51 were coal burning steamships, which were now dominating maritime trade. Port revenue that year amounted to $650. The focus of the port's trade had to remain on the Pacific Rim until the Panama Canal opened and facilitated access to the far larger markets for forest products that were available in the U.K. and Europe. Indeed, the ability to use the Panama shortcut to Europe, which removed the handicap of the long and difficult Cape Horne route, was the crucial third factor in the success of the port — almost as important as the coming of the CPR and the fine, natural harbour.

The decade-long economic boom was over by the fall of 1911 and, in the October federal election, Sir Robert Borden's new Conservative government replaced Sir Wilfrid Laurier's Liberals. The Conservatives would lead the country through the coming period of recession, followed by World War. The port city at the western end of the "Tory" railroad now had a very sympathetic ear in both Ottawa and McBride's long-lived Conservative government in Victoria. Vancouver's citizens were astute in electing H. H. Stevens as their member of parliament five times. Of the 24 years he represented Vancouver in Ottawa, 15 were as an influential member, or cabinet minister in the Tory governments of three prime ministers. The health and development of the port were paramount among his interests. In 1913, he introduced the legislation that created the Port of Vancouver as an official entity under the control of a new Vancouver Harbour Commission (VHC). The VHC was charged with administering and developing the port, which included Burrard Inlet, English Bay, and False Creek. Prior to this, there was no central administration and harbour development had depended on private sector interests. There was little accommodation for shipping and the few facilities available were mostly provided by the CPR and the local sawmills, for their own use. The new Harbour Commission would act as trustee for all the foreshore Crown lands that were not in dispute with the CPR.

Stevens' representations in Ottawa resulted in federal funding for port projects. These included more dredging to deepen and widen the harbour's entrance channel at first narrows, additional navigational aids, and the completion of the Government Wharf in 1915 — the first major pier complex east of Hastings Mill. Years later it was named Lapointe Pier, after the Minister of Marine in the first Mackenzie King administration between1922 to 1926. Presumably, this was political retaliation for the splendid new pier completed in 1923 by the VHC being named after Honourable C. C. Ballantyne who had been the Tory Minister of Marine and Fisheries from 1917 to 1921!

Stevens is probably best remembered for "Stevens Folly," Vancouver's first grain elevator, completed adjacent to the new pier in 1916. His enthusiastic support for this project was based on his clear vision that Vancouver could become a major outlet for the movement of Alberta grain to Europe via the Panama Canal. The new Dominion No. 1 terminal with a capacity of 1,125,000 bushels (approximately 30,500 tonnes of wheat) sat idle for most of the next five years because World War I intervened to disrupt world trade and the availability of ships. His foresight became evident later in the post war rush to build more grain terminals, which very rapidly made grain the port's export tonnage leader.

The CPR's transpacific *White Empress* service added two large new vessels in 1913. The *Empress of Russia* and the *Empress of Asia* established speed records for carrying passengers and freight from the Orient to North America. This assured the CPR's continuing dominance on this route, which was being challenged by Japanese services to San Francisco. Added to the regular visits by these prestige vessels were the increasing number of tramp steamers, most of which called at the port to load forest products. In 1915, a total of 237 deep-sea vessels, 225 of them steamers, visited the port, a very substantial increase over the 72 port calls six years earlier. Port revenues that year reached $24,000. In 1916, traffic increased again with 343 vessel calls, but thereafter growth ground to a halt for four years.

Although Vancouver had clearly become the dominant mainland port for deep-sea vessels engaged in overseas trade, New Westminster was certainly not ready to abandon its own port aspirations. At first, potential rivalry was subdued in the common cause of challenging Victoria, both politically and economically. In 1903, forty-four canneries and several large sawmills were operating on the lower river and they needed clear channels to their facilities. The local citizens were rewarded for their wisdom in voting on the side of the Laurier Liberals in power in Ottawa. New Westminster received funding for a new dredger, the *King Edward*, in 1901, a new snag boat, the *Samson II*, in 1904, and the first channel controlling jetties at the river mouth. In the decade after the devastating fire of 1898, the city — with federal assistance — reconstructed and extended its wharves to service deep-sea vessels with cargoes of lumber and salmon. Unlike Vancouver, New Westminster owned and leased most of its waterfront. It also provided and paid river pilots.

Richard McBride became premier of B.C. in 1903 at the age of 32. Born and raised in New Westminster, he was attentive to the needs of his home town during his three terms as government leader. At a cost of 1 million dollars the province completed a combination road and rail bridge across the Fraser River at New Westminster in 1904. At first the bridge linked the Great Northern Railroad to New Westminster and on into Vancouver (as the Vancouver, Westminster, and Yukon Railway). Later, it accommodated the Canadian Northern Pacific, as well as road and interurban rail traffic. When the Pattullo Bridge was completed in 1937, the bridge's road level was removed and ownership was transferred to the federal Department of Public Works. This old rail bridge is still very much in use.

In 1913, the federal government established the New Westminster Harbour Commission to administer port activity on the river in 1913 and the new Commissioner's focus was immediately directed to the further widening and deepening of the river's navigable channel for deep-sea vessels. However, the speculative boom of the first decade of the new century had by then collapsed and markets for lumber, fish, and agricultural products languished. Economic stagnation continued during the war years. In 1918 New Westminster handled only 1.4 percent of West Coast deep-sea traffic. Port activity and growth would not recover until the mid-twenties. New Westminster had cultivated and enjoyed the favour of the Laurier Liberals early in the century, but the succeeding decade-long administration of Borden's Tories coupled with the long Tory administration in Victoria favoured the development of Vancouver, over both New Westminster and Prince Rupert.

THE FAILING RAILWAY PROJECTS

The North American economic depression, which followed the "Good Years," combined with war clouds on the near horizon to substantially increase the problem of fundraising for the two companies that were still building transcontinental railways. Despite these difficulties, however, both managed to complete their main lines, the Grand Trunk Pacific (GTP) in April 1914 and the Canadian Northern Pacific (CNP) 16 months later. Hays' determination to build a branch line to Vancouver from his GTP main line at Prince George had developed into the Pacific Great Eastern Railway, incorporated in 1912. By 1916, work on that line had stopped, although only the Vancouver to Horseshoe Bay section and a line from Squamish to Clinton were complete. Sources of financing were either unable or unwilling to provide further money so, in February 1918, the company surrendered the project to the Province, which became the reluctant owner for many years to come. Premier McBride, disillusioned over this issue, retired in 1915 rather than face the public, even though they were the same electors who had so overwhelmingly supported subsidies for that line three years earlier.

PRINCE RUPERT, THE NASCENT PORT CITY

Though both the Canadian Pacific and the Canadian Northern Pacific used different passes through the Rockies, their lines converged at Kamloops and then followed the same, very difficult, corridor to the Southern Gateway Port of Vancouver. The Great Northern line reached Vancouver from the south. The Grand Trunk Pacific line, like the Canadian Northern Pacific, entered British Columbia via the Yellowhead Pass, but then continued west across the middle of the province by a much easier water-grade corridor to the new Northern Gateway Port of Prince Rupert.

Having selected the site for their terminus and obtained a Crown Grant in 1904 from the province for much of the land and waterfront they required, the GTP now needed a name for their planned port city. They held a contest and, from the 12,000 entries they received from across Canada, they selected the name Prince Rupert in 1905.

By mid-1906, the first small wharf had been built and by 1908 a much more substantial wharf and shed structure had been constructed on the waterfront. Late in 1909, the third and largest wharf and freight shed was complete. Concurrently, an extensive waterfront rail yard was being carved out of the rocky foreshore.

The GTP engaged the Boston landscape firm of Brett, Hall and Co. (Hall was Hays' son in law) to plan the new town site on Kaien Island. Later, the same firm laid out the plan for the new city of Prince George. Their plan for Prince Rupert recommended 50-foot lots, but the GTP reduced the width to 25 feet in the anticipation of greater revenue from double the number of lots. The final town site plan was registered in the fall of 1908 and site clearing and surveying followed, in preparation for initial lot sales.

During this period of waterfront, rail yard and town site development, there were tedious and time-wasting disputes between the province and the GTP. These focused on the selection of the province's agreed quota of a quarter-share of the town lots and water-front. More serious were the railway's difficulties in getting clear title to water lots adjacent to their subdivided waterfront property. As Provincial Crown Grants extended only to the high water mark, the company had to deal with officials of the federal Marine and Public Works department and, because the railway and the Ottawa bureaucracy failed to agree on the terms of water lot transfer, it was 10 years before clear titles were obtained. This did considerable damage to both the port and the railway, as the GTP was unable to generate the anticipated traffic or revenue from the leasing foreshore property, despite high demand.

At least the railway and the province could sell lots in the town site. By March 1909, they had settled the apportionment of the subdivided land and had spent $200,000 on plank roads and sewer pipes, in preparation for their first auction of lots in May of that year.

In the rampant euphoria of that time, there was a tremendous response from Canadians, Americans, and Europeans. Speculation was rife and it drove the market. A 50-foot corner in the designated business district sold for $16,500, far above its upset price at the auction. In addition to the auction in Prince Rupert, the GTP and province each sold another 1,200 lots at an auction held in Vancouver. By late 1909, the GTP had disposed of 4,600 lots for a total of $1.9 million.

The City of Prince Rupert was incorporated in March 1910 and municipal responsibilities were assumed by the first city council, which was elected in May. Very soon the new council was feuding with the GTP over the taxing of railway property and improvements. Council desperately needed tax revenue, as it had embarked on a program of expensive but necessary works that included waterworks, sewers, street grading, and a telephone system. The GTP used the threat of halting all further work on local projects in order to wring huge tax concessions from the City. For the railway however, this was to be a Pyrrhic victory, as it greatly hindered economic development at the new Pacific port.

MORE LOT SALES

Anticipating substantially higher prices than those received in the 1909 auction, the GTP deferred selling further city lots for two years. A second auction was held in 1911 by David Hays (Charles' brother), the local representative of the Grand Trunk Pacific Development Company. The sum of $597,660 was realized from that sale of 583 lots. Prices for City lots peaked at another auction in 1912 when 242 government-owned lots sold for $1.2 million. In total, the company received $2.3 million from lot sales, but by mid-1914 the market had collapsed. Speculators had pushed prices far too high, thereby inhibiting development.

MARINE LINKS TO THE NEW PORT

Hays' plans for the GTP extended beyond the railway and port city. Between 1908 and 1910, the company chartered ships to move freight and passengers up the coast, while two express passenger ships to be named *Prince Rupert* and *Prince George* were being built in Scotland. They arrived on the coast in June and July of 1910. On August 22, 1910, Prime Minister Laurier traveled to the infant city on the *Prince George* and received an ecstatic welcome from the city residents. In his address to an open air meeting of citizens, Laurier admitted that the dream of his career was to see the National Transcontinental Railway complete from coast to coast.

GRAND PLANS FOR THE NEW PORT CITY

After the first auction of town site lots in 1909, the focus of the GTP was primarily directed toward extracting immediate returns from waterfront property. As described earlier, this goal was frustrated by the delays in getting clear title to adjacent water lots from Ottawa. Though most company expenditures were directed toward developing the wharf and rail yard (for which grandiose plans had been drawn by a San Francisco engineer), two new major projects were undertaken. Hays believed that if Prince Rupert was to challenge Vancouver for port supremacy it must have a symbolic grand hotel and a facility to build and repair ships. To achieve the first goal he awarded a commission to Francis Rattenbury to design a 12 story, 450 room grand hotel, which would be the centrepiece of the business district. The designer of Victoria's Parliament Buildings produced a truly elegant and grand design, estimated to cost a million dollars. However, feuding with the new City Council over taxes delayed the hotel's construction and, although excavation of the chosen site commenced in the fall of 1913, the project was never completed. A new plan for a more modest hotel was announced by the CNR in 1930, but this project fell victim to the collapsing world economy.

The second major project, building a shipyard and dry dock, did come to fruition, primarily due to federal government largesse. Because of high tidal fluctuations, the dry dock was designed as a pontoon or floating dock, rather than the more conventional basin type. It would measure 184 m (604 ft.) long and be able to lift ships weighing up to 20,000 tons. Hays prevailed on Ottawa to provide a $2 million subsidy for this project, which had been estimated to cost $2.26 million. The final tally for completing the dock and shipyard, however, came to $2.8 million. The new dry dock lifted its first ship in September of 1915 and, with the shipyard, repaired some vessels during World War I.

With his two fine new *Prince* vessels, Hays planned to compete head on with the CPR's coast services. Furthermore, he fully intended to build and operate trans-Pacific liners (to be named *Dukes*). These would compete with the CPR's *White Empresses* to profitably carry tea, silk, and other commodities to his new port. From Prince Rupert they would be carried by the second land-bridge rail line across Canada. Hays accused the CPR of retarding Canada's trade with the Orient by colluding with other shipping companies to keep rates high. Laurier supported Hays' plan to enter the transpacific shipping business to break the CPR's monopoly on the valuable tea and silk trade.

Fascination with Orient trade has a long history, to which the travels of Marco Polo and Columbus attest.

THE LONG SLEEP AHEAD FOR PRINCE RUPERT AND ITS PORT

The Grand Trunk completed its main line in April 1914 and the Canadian Northern Pacific 16 months later, but by then both companies were caught in a downward spiral of financial woes that finally forced their surrender to the federal government in 1918. Prime Minister Robert Borden's solution to the mess he had inherited was to absorb both railways into the newly created Canadian National Railway (CNR). Faced with far too much rail capacity, especially in the west, the government and the CNR management elected to focus on the Southern Corridor to the Port of Vancouver, which had been established longer and was better equipped.

The development of a port, regardless of how well it may be blessed by nature, is utterly dependent on the enthusiastic support of the transportation organizations operating in its access corridor. Almost as important is the support and favour of the government in power. The Conservative government of Sir Robert Borden had first a depression and then a world war to cope with; it could hardly be faulted for showing little interest in the waif at the western terminus of the Liberal's GTP/National Transcontinental Railway that it had so vigorously opposed in the past. The CNR — created to hold and operate six failed railways — chose to relegate the GTP's Northern Corridor to a little used branch line. It is difficult to criticize the CNR for taking this position.

Within a year of completing the GTP line to Prince Rupert, four rail lines converged on Vancouver from the east, south, and north. The successful transpacific passenger cargo service had been in operation for over two decades. The port was administered under a new and enthusiastic Harbour Commission with extensive plans to build new facilities with federal government money. The railways' private wharves were now complemented by the large new Government Wharf, complete with its extensive warehouse space. The first facility for handling bulk grain was under construction and the 1914 opening of the Panama Canal offered the port post-war access to markets in Europe, as well as the Atlantic seaboard of the United States.

Vancouver's 27-year head start over Prince Rupert was preordained in 1880 when the CP Syndicate was given a 20-year monopoly on transcontinental railway building. By 1914 Vancouver's population had passed 150,000. It repeatedly elected a representative who was both respected and given considerable powers by Ottawa's governing party. Tiny, nascent Prince Rupert had no such political influence. Furthermore, the port-related business elite in Vancouver — strongly supported by both the CPR and Mackenzie and Mann's nearly completed Canadian Northern Pacific — were fully conscious of their potential competitor on the North Coast and both overtly and covertly opposed its development.

Prince Rupert offered a substantially shorter route to Asian markets, but the CPR had dominated this trade since 1887 with their integrated ship-rail service through Vancouver. Not even northwest U.S. ports had been able to break the CPR's hold on this business. The opening of the Panama Canal in 1914 had the potential to greatly benefit Vancouver, but it offered little benefit to Prince Rupert, due to the extra distance involved.

Finally, the Province of British Columbia, under the Conservative administration of New Westminster native Richard McBride (1903–1915) had never shown either enthusiasm or support for the Grand Trunk Pacific or its terminal city. Rather, it favoured the Canadian Northern Pacific, the Pacific Great Eastern, and the Port of Vancouver.

Thus, with little or no support from the senior levels of either federal or provincial government and near abandonment by the successor to the railway that built it, it is little wonder that the orphaned port saw little development and only one short wartime flurry of activity during the seven decades after its first wharf was completed.

DISPOSITION OF THE GTP RAILWAY'S SECONDARY PROJECTS

Chapter One describes, in some detail, the grandiose plans for the new Northern Gateway and outlines the reasons why the Grand Trunk Pacific Railway ended in financial ruin, despite being built across a significantly easier corridor to a harbour with all the natural attributes needed for a great world port.

With its deteriorating financial position, the GTP had to cancel or delay a number of projects that were secondary to its primary goal — completion of the main rail line. The final disposition of several projects was to have a major impact on the future of Prince Rupert.The grand hotel designed by Rattenbury was never built, though excavation for its waterfront location commenced in 1913. The grandiose plans for wharf and rail yard development that were drawn by a San Francisco engineering firm were never implemented. The planned fleet of deep-sea passenger cargo liners for transpacific trade never materialized.

The dry dock and shipyard project did proceed, though very slowly and fraught with problems. Hays had persuaded the federal government to grant a $2 million subsidy for this work, payable on completion. This sum was supposed to cover 90 percent of the project's cost. Work started in 1910, but was slowed by conflicts with the city, shortages of skilled labour, lack of prospective business, and interference by federal bureaucrats regarding subsidy requirements. When finally completed in 1916 the cost had escalated to $2.8 million with the railway responsible for all the cost overruns. In addition, because of bureaucratic nit picking, the federal subsidy was not paid until 1918.

Business was very slow for the new dry dock and the Grand Trunk Railway employed its head office staff in London to persuade the Admiralty to make use of the facility. As a result, HMS *Orbita*, an armed merchant cruiser, arrived at the port on October 21, 1916 for repair and maintenance work. The work performed was considered so unacceptable by the ship's officers that the GTP waived charges for the docking. A sister vessel, HMS *Otranto* entered the dock for a refit on December 9, 1916. The Admiralty brought workmen from Esquimalt for this work at considerable expense and over the protests of local residents and thereafter, shifted work on their Pacific-based vessels to Bremerton Navy Yard in Washington State. It is difficult to be critical of the Admiralty for that decision, given that the GTP chose to refit its own coastwise vessel *Prince Rupert* in Esquimalt in December 1916. The yard in Prince Rupert had been well equipped to build wooden vessels, but lacked machinery for heavy steel work.

In mid-1918 a New York entrepreneur, Newman Eby, began operating the facility and incorporated the Prince Rupert Dry Dock and Engineering Company with the intent to build steel freighters. While negotiating the lease with Eby, it is recorded that the federal Minister of Marine suggested that the dry dock should be towed to Vancouver. Perhaps he was so persuaded by the influential Member of Parliament for Vancouver! Subsequent battles with Ottawa over the terms of the lease and the control of assets, combined with management problems and shortage of capital plagued the new company. It finally went into liquidation in 1921.

Succeeding chapters will relate the very uneven development paths of the Northern and Southern Gateway Ports plus their corridors with special focus on the long struggle ahead for Prince Rupert to arrive at its "place in the sun."

AUGUST 1914, A FRIGHT ON THE B.C. COAST

Britain, her Empire, and the Dominions declared war on Germany at midnight August 4, 1914. Though seemingly insulated by distance from the impending ravages of war, the citizens of coastal B.C. were aware of a real and immediate threat from Admiral Von Spee's formidable squadron of modern, heavy and light cruisers based at Tsingtao across the Pacific. In fact, the only threat that war in Europe posed to the West Coast had long been perceived to be from enemy raider attacks on coastal ports and shipping and, of course, the naval base at Esquimalt.

To defend the West Coast, Canada's four-year-old Navy had one obsolete training cruiser, HMCS *Rainbow*, and two rather ancient sloops, HMCS *Algerine* and HMCS *Shearwater*, which were used primarily for sealing patrol. On August 4, the sloops were off the coast of Mexico, while *Rainbow* prepared to head to sea to engage potential foes lacking high explosive ammunition and manned by only half her wartime crew complement. In short, when war broke out, the B.C. coast was virtually without defence and there was evidence of panic, especially in Victoria. Premier McBride, in an uncharacteristically rapid move for government, succeeded in buying two new submarines from a Seattle shipyard for US$1.15 million and getting them delivered hours before Canada's declaration of war. It would be some time, however, before they were supplied with torpedoes and substantially longer before crews could be trained to operate them. They did, however, boost morale!

Plans were drawn up to protect both the north and south entrances to the Gulf of Georgia with its vital ports. These plans included positioning mines in Johnstone Strait at Malcolm Island and the installation of two 4-inch guns at Seymour Narrows.

In urgent response to Britain's call, her ally, Japan, sent the heavy cruiser *Idzumo* across the Pacific to arrive at Esquimalt on August 25. This formidable vessel was followed five days later by the modern cruiser HMS *Newcastle* from Yokahama.

Prince Rupert, the most exposed port on the coast, had no protection at all. When a three-funnel cruiser was reported offshore the frightened community demanded protection and the old *Rainbow* was sent north on August 19 for a 10 day "visit" to the port. At least by then the obsolete cruiser had a supply of high explosive shells for her guns — and even the fuses to go with them! Her consort on the visit to Prince Rupert was the GTP coastal passenger vessel *Prince George* which had been very hastily converted to a "hospital ship," presumably to deal with casualties from any action the *Rainbow* might be involved in.

For a short time, the threat appeared very real, though post war records indicate that the closest any of Von Spee's warships came to B.C. was when the *Leipzig* reached Cape Mendocino off the north California coast, before turning south to rejoin her squadron. *Nurnberg* was never closer than Hawaii. At the time, however, the threat seemed even more menacing when, on November 1, 1914, Von Spee destroyed Admiral Cradock's two, old, heavy cruisers at the Battle of Coronel off the Chilean coast. One of the ships that escaped this engagement was the armed merchant cruiser *Otranto* which, two years later, visited Prince Rupert for refit work at the dry dock. Coronel was avenged 5 weeks later when Von Spee's squadron was all but annihilated off the Falkland Islands and the sole survivor caught and sunk, in March 1915. The elimination of this powerful naval force removed any threat to the West Coast ports for the remainder of World War I.

CHAPTER THREE

The Gateways 1917 to 1929 — Panama Extends Vancouver's Reach to Atlantic Markets

The boom-depression-war cycle that characterized the first two decades of the twentieth century would be repeated over the subsequent 26 years, albeit with a much greater boom, a far longer and deeper depression, and a longer, wider, and even more terrible world war.

The 1920s were years of great optimism and exuberant growth, especially in North America, which had escaped the ravages of the 1914–1918 war. Public and private capital was lavished on port projects deemed necessary to accommodate the tremendous upsurge in world trade.

On Canada's Pacific Coast, nearly all the spectacular port growth during this decade was confined, however, to developments at the Southern Gateway with particular focus on new Burrard Inlet facilities. In 1924 the Northern Corridor was relegated by its new owner, the CNR, to a little used branch line off the established main northern rail route to Vancouver. That decision condemned the orphaned Northern Gateway Port to a long wait to fulfill its destiny as a major outlet for Canadian overseas trade.

The decade-long boom of the twenties came to an abrupt end with the stock market meltdown in late 1929 and was followed by the decade of gloom and despair that characterized the Great Depression, which ended with the onset of the even greater tragedy of World War II.

VANCOUVER, THE NEW OUTLET FOR PRAIRIE GRAIN

Vancouver finally passed Victoria in port throughput tonnage in 1919. A total of 496 vessels called at the port in 1921 with the result that revenues that year increased to $341,000. Vessel traffic, which had remained static during the war years, increased fourfold, and the waterfront along the south shore of Burrard Inlet became lined with new facilities, many built with federal government funds. Orient trade boomed with scheduled liner sailings increasing from three to seventeen each month by 1925. By 1929 Vancouver hosted 30 steamship lines and had 28 berths available for their use. It was widely recognized as the fastest growing port on the Pacific Coast of North America. The shoreline available for development doubled following the completion in 1925 of a road and rail bridge across the harbour's second narrows to the north shore of the inlet.

The availability of the Panama Canal after the war was second only in importance to the arrival of the CPR on Burrard Inlet as a seminal event in the spectacular growth of the Southern Gateway Port. With its new ability to access transatlantic trade, Vancouver could now tap into the movement of overseas wheat exports to Europe from Alberta and western Saskatchewan, so long the exclusive preserve of East Coast, Canadian and United States (U.S.) ports. By mid-decade this new commodity movement through the all-year port dominated export tonnage and would hold that position until the early seventies. No longer was Vancouver seen as a transit importer of tea and silk, and an exporter of regionally produced forest products, even though those exports increased fivefold between 1920 and 1929.

The single grain terminal — built by the federal government between 1913 and 1916 in anticipation of the opening of the Panama Canal — had been joined by six others by 1929, including those newly completed in New Westminster, Victoria, and Prince Rupert. Vancouver's exports of forest products were matched by the combined loadings from Vancouver Island and New Westminster docks, whereas grain exports became almost exclusive to Burrard Inlet facilities.

Whereas previously, Vancouver, New Westminster, and the Vancouver Island ports had primarily handled exports produced in their vicinity, the new massive movement of grain by rail from another province substantially confirmed Vancouver's destiny as a national, rather than a regional port.

THE PANAMA CANAL

For the Southern Gateway, the positive impact of the opening of the Canal on August 15, 1914 was significantly delayed. The long awaited shortcut to the Atlantic was intermittently inoperable during its initial two years, as a result of slides and other problems. Even more important, overseas trade, with its dependence on available shipping, was extensively disrupted by the war. With adequate shipping again available by 1920, the new shortcut, with its saving of 8,850 km (5,500 miles) on a voyage from Vancouver to London, first benefited lumber shipments to the Atlantic Seaboard ports of the U.S. and to Britain, which at that time was the world's largest wood importer. Stevens' foresight in persuading the federal government to build a grain terminal in Vancouver began to bear fruit when five vessels loaded the port's first bulk cargoes of wheat destined to the United Kingdom (U.K.) during late 1917 and 1918. These trial shipments marked the beginning of a major shift in the route taken by prairie grain destined for overseas markets. Vessel sailings from Vancouver via the Panama Canal to Europe or the eastern seaboard of the U.S. increased from 51 in 1921 to 240 three years later.

SHIPBUILDING

After completion of the Government Pier in 1915 and the Dominion No.1 grain terminal a year later, planned projects had to be deferred until the conclusion of the war. World trade routes had been severely disrupted and priorities drastically changed by the conflagration in Europe. As the war progressed, mounting losses of ships to submarine warfare made the acquisition of new vessels an urgent priority, especially for the U.K. Shipbuilding became the West Coast's primary contribution to Canada's war effort.

Since the earliest days of European settlement, wooden ships had been built in the two colonies that united to form British Columbia (B.C.). These included a considerable number of sternwheelers that were used during and after the gold rush.

No ocean going vessels had been built in B.C. prior to 1917, but the urgent need for new ships to replace wartime losses resulted in government subsidies, loan guarantees, and other financial inducements directed at expanding shipbuilding capacity. As a result 17 new yards were established in the province between 1914 and 1920. During and shortly after the war these yards produced:

- 21 wooden auxiliary schooners
- 69 wooden steamers for the U.K. and France
- 34 steel freighters

Completion of their war orders for wooden cargo vessels meant closure for most of the new yards. Those that remained survived on building wooden fishing vessels, tugs, barges, and small passenger vessels.

Wallace moved his shipyard from False Creek to North Vancouver in 1906 and this yard completed the 3,046 ton *War Dog* for the Imperial Munitions Board in May 1917; the first steel deep-sea cargo vessel built in B.C. A sister vessel, the *War Viceroy*, sailed from Vancouver loaded with wheat for the U.K. on November 13, 1917, the first of several "test" cargoes designed to determine the feasibility of shipping grain to Europe via the Panama Canal shortcut without experiencing spoilage.

By 1918 the Vancouver shipyards employed over 5,000 men out of a total of nearly 10,000 for all B.C. yards. In that year the Canadian Government Merchant Marine (CGMM) was incorporated by the federal government with a view to maintaining shipyard employment, fostering a Canadian flag merchant marine, and enhancing Canada's position in world trade. A total of 63 steel freighters ranging in size from 2,800–10,800 tons were ordered from Canadian yards. Sixteen of these vessels were completed in B.C. yards between 1919 and 1921; thirteen in Vancouver, one in Victoria, and two in Prince Rupert. The CGMM leased the Government Pier in Vancouver from the Harbour Commission and planned to operate the B.C. built vessels on new routes in the Pacific and Indian oceans.

Unfortunately for the new government enterprise, it very soon became evident that world shipyards, especially in the U.S., had built an excessive number of new ships, so that by 1921 ship-owners everywhere were facing very tough times. With the CGMM orders filled and no major orders forthcoming, the West Coast yards either folded or restructured to survive on domestic orders for ferries, barges, tugs, and fishing vessels. The large Coughlin steel shipyard on False Creek was destroyed by fire in 1923 and not rebuilt. Shipbuilding in

B.C. would continue to be minimally active until war intervened again in 1940. The federal government's foray into operating a fleet of freighters on world trade routes ended in failure. The CGMM gradually sold the vessels to relieve the country of the heavy liability of annual operating deficits. By 1933, the only remaining ships operated a West Indies service under the banner of Canadian National Steamships. Accumulated losses reached $82 million by the time the company was disbanded in 1936.

CHANNEL IMPROVEMENTS, NEW PIERS, A WATERFRONT RAILWAY, A DRY DOCK, AND A BRIDGE

The Vancouver Harbour Commission (VHC) had been created by the federal government in 1913 to administer Crown property in the port and oversee port development. The war deferred most of their ambitious plans, though the Government Pier and the grain elevator were completed in 1915 and 1916 respectively.

Dealing with the increasingly unacceptable navigational hazards at the harbour entrance was an early priority for the new Commissioners. Burrard Inlet's fine harbour had gained an unsavoury reputation because of its "indifferent entrance," as described by early mariners. In 1888 the former Cunard liner *Parthia*, chartered by the CPR, struck bottom at what became known as "Parthia Shoal" between Brockton Point and Calamity Point. Many vessels were experiencing difficulty entering and leaving the inlet due to strong currents at the narrows.

In 1910 the bucket dredge *Mastodon*, built in Scotland for the Department of Public Works, arrived in Vancouver after transiting the Straits of Magellan and began a multiyear dredging program at first narrows to widen, straighten, and deepen the channel. However, by 1920 there remained a number of dangerous shoals along with continuing deposition of sand, gravel, and boulders from the adjacent Capilano River. Under pressure from the maritime community and the VHC, the Department of Public Works mounted a second substantial program of dredging and boulder removal between 1921 and 1923, and a further program in 1928. These programs removed more shoals with a view to widening the navigable channel to 540 m (1800 ft.) at the 9 m (30 ft.) low water contour, a marked improvement over the 120 m (400 ft.) wide channel at that depth 15 years earlier. By 1930 these programs had succeeded in substantially reducing the velocity of the current at first narrows. A most unusual and, fortunately, rare hazard resulted from the breakup of ice on the Fraser River in late December 1924 when ice pans drifted into Burrard Inlet and temporarily choked first narrows.

Under legislation passed in 1919, the federal government agreed to provide the VHC with a loan of up to $5 million to build port facilities approved by the Minister of Marine. More funds were promised as requested and were supplied on the issue by the VHC of debentures bearing 5 percent interest. By June 1929, loan authorizations for the port on this basis had increased to $29 million (although events later that year meant that a number of loan applications for planned projects were not given final approval).

Assured of financing, the VHC embarked on its first major project, a fine new public pier built on steel-reinforced concrete pilings at a 225 m (750 ft.) waterfront site just west of the Great Northern Pier. Its dimensions were 350 m (1200 ft.) long by 102 m (340 ft.) wide, with the two outer berths dredged to a depth of 13.5 m (45 ft.). Cranes, tracks, and four double-decked sheds were provided and the $6 million facility opened in 1923. It was named Ballantyne Pier after the long serving Minister of Marine in the Borden Government.

While Ballantyne Pier was under construction, the VHC embarked on a major program of grain elevator construction, jetties to serve them, and a waterfront railway along the south shore of the harbour. The Commission planned to operate the railway, but lease its docks and grain terminals to private interests.

The Vancouver Harbour Commission Terminal Railway (VHCTR), costing $1.4 million, was completed by the Harbour Commission in 1923, in an effort to resolve the complications arising from the need for multiple railways to access the south shore waterfront terminals on Burrard Inlet. Since extending its line from Port Moody in 1887, the CPR had controlled most of the south shore and its access, until the Great Northern line reached the Inlet in 1904 and built its pier in 1914. The Canadian Northern Pacific line — completed in 1915 and then absorbed into the Canadian National in 1919 — had its terminal at Port Mann on the south shore of the Fraser River. To reach Burrard Inlet terminals, 24 km (15 miles) away, CN cars had to travel on Great Northern tracks and cross the tolled provincial bridge at New Westminster to reach their yard at False Creek, then switch again to tracks belonging to the Great Northern, CPR, B.C. Electric, or the Vancouver Harbour Commission Terminal Railway. This limited the ability of the nation's second transcontinental railroad to play its full part in serving Canada's principal Pacific port. The VHCTR was built primarily to ease this situation and it derived three-quarters of its revenue from the CNR.

With the only dry dock on the coast able to handle a vessel of over 4,000 tons located at Prince Rupert, the frustrated Vancouver maritime community vigorously lobbied Ottawa to either move the fine, but little used North Coast facility, south, or assist with financing a new facility for Vancouver. Several years of negotiation, at first with John Coughlin & Sons who were later joined by Wallace Shipyards, resulted in the provision of a $2,618,018 federal subsidy toward the construction of a floating dock on the north shore of Burrard Inlet. The $3.75 million dock, capable of lifting vessels up to 15, 000 tons, was located at the site of Wallace Shipyards, which was renamed Burrard Dry Dock in 1921. It lifted its first vessel in March 1925, two years prior to the completion of the second and much larger graving dock at Esquimalt on Vancouver Island.

Private enterprise soon joined the VHC in providing new wharves and loading facilities for the busy port. The CPR elected to build a new concrete and steel passenger and cargo terminal between their aging wooden piers, A and D. The fine new pier B-C, opened July 4, 1927 and replaced the older piers as the terminal for the transpacific service of the

Empress liners. With the arrival of the new *Empress of Canada* and the *Empress of Australia* (ex *Tirpitz*) in 1922 the old *Empress of Japan* was retired from service. Her name was given to a fine new vessel which commenced transpacific service in 1930.

A number of smaller docks were built specifically to serve the fishing industry, cross-harbour ferries, and coastal vessels. These, along with fuelling facilities and other marine related services, began to fill available waterfront space on the south shore of the inlet. Development of the extensive water frontage between first and second narrows on the north shore awaited provision of road and rail access.

The Burrard Inlet Bridge and Tunnel Company took up the challenge of building a bridge to the north shore at second narrows. The road and rail bridge, completed in November 1925, had a counterweighted lift span near the south shore and very soon gained an unenviable reputation as a menace to navigation. It was described by the maritime community as an "ill conceived, inefficient, wrongly placed and dangerous structure," a classic example of how not to build a bridge over navigable waters. There were even proposals to replace it with a dam across second narrows. The bridge was hit repeatedly by vessels attempting to pass through the second narrows, sustaining varying amounts of damage until, finally, in 1930 collision with a wayward barge collapsed one of the spans. The owners declared bankruptcy and the VHC eventually rebuilt the bridge in 1934 with a centrally placed lift span at a cost of $1 million. The new location of the lift span and greater precautions in vessel transit reduced the frequency of collisions and the bridge survived until 1969 when it was replaced by a new CNR rail bridge.

GRAIN, THE NEW COMMODITY FOR THE PORT

Since the arrival of the railway, sacked wheat and oats had been intermittently exported from Vancouver, mostly to Pacific Rim destinations and South Africa in "parcel shipments" carried in the holds of liner vessels. Before completion of the Panama Canal, no bulk cargoes of grain had moved from the West Coast to the U.K. or other European countries, which at that time constituted the market for three-quarters of Canadian grain exports.

Anticipating the opportunity the canal presented and eager to expand the range of the port's facilities to include a terminal able to efficiently receive, process, and load vessels with bulk wheat from Alberta, the Vancouver Board of Trade, strongly supported by Vancouver's Member of Parliament H. H. Stevens, lobbied Ottawa to fund such a project. The federal government responded by constructing the Dominion No. 1 grain terminal next to the Government Pier (later Lapointe) on the south shore of Burrard Inlet. Though completed in 1916, the terminal saw very little use for another five years and was ridiculed locally as "Stevens' Folly". At first, wartime vessel shortages coupled with intermittent interruptions to passage through the Panama Canal were accepted as reasons for its disuse. However, with the war over it soon became evident that eastern Canadian interests, and especially the Port of Montreal (which had been "made" as a result of its 60 percent share of the overseas export of Canadian grain), would not easily surrender any portion of that traditional movement. Most of the balance was railed to New York, Philadelphia, Baltimore, or other U.S. Atlantic ports for loading onto vessels bound for the U.K. and Europe. This massive movement of Canadian overseas export grain through U.S. ports seemed both illogical and unacceptable to Vancouver port promoters, as it could only be partially explained by the long winter freeze-up of the St. Lawrence River at Montreal. At the very least, they argued, Alberta wheat destined for export could and should be moved through their all-year port. This would substantially reduce dependence on the long railway haul to U.S. ports for Canadian grain exports in the winter months.

The Vancouver maritime community's desire to participate in the grain export trade encountered obstacles on several fronts. First, there was the expected opposition from the eastern terminal operators, loathe to lose any part of the movement of Canadian export grain that they shared with U.S. ports. This opposition was reinforced by the traditionalists who invariably rejected any change. Second, for the first two or three post-war years, there was an acute shortage of shipping with resultant high ocean freight rates. Third, there was a widely held belief that a wheat cargo loaded in Vancouver would spoil in the humidity and heat encountered on the Panama route. To test this concern the Department of Trade and Commerce and the Grain Research Laboratory arranged for bulk shipments of wheat to be loaded in Vancouver on five steel vessels built for the Imperial Munitions Board. The first vessel, *War Viceroy*, loaded approximately 99,209 bushels[1] and sailed for the U.K. via Panama on November 13, 1917. She arrived in London on January 10, 1918 and examination of her cargo indicated damage to a mere 274 bushels. The other four vessels followed in 1918 and all their cargoes arrived at their destination with negligible damage. These five trial shipments totalling approximately 800,000 bushels conclusively proved that grain could be shipped via Panama without loss of quality.

Finally, there was the problem of the railways' "Mountain Differential." Traditional high rail rates to the Pacific Coast were ostensibly related, at least in the case of the CPR, to the difficult grades and winter maintenance problems in the mountain passes on their southern route. Furthermore, the longer the rail haul, the greater the revenue — certainly no inducement to support the relatively short haul to the Pacific Coast.

Vancouver needed lower west-bound rail rates and available shipping at low long-haul ocean rates. Increased rates east-bound and higher transatlantic ocean vessel rates would also help. By 1921 the post-war shortage of ships had changed to a surplus, resulting in a steep drop in ocean rates and ready availability of vessels. The railways found that they now had to haul empties to the West Coast to cope with the heavy eastern movement of forest products. They therefore became more amenable to filling these cars with grain at a lower west-bound haul rate, while compensating by raising charges for eastern rail movement.

---

[1] In the 1920s and 1930s almost all grain exports were wheat with a bushel equivalent of 36.744 to the tonne.

Vancouver promoters had not been idle, disseminating information and correcting misinformation about the advantages of "Wheat via Vancouver."

The combination of lower ocean freight rates, reduced west-bound rail rates, active promotion, and high demand in the U.K. started the movement of Alberta grown wheat to Vancouver's single terminal in the winter of 1920–1921. SS *Effingham* left the port on January 7, 1921 loaded with 88,185 bushels of wheat, the first commercial overseas bulk shipment. A trickle at first, it quickly became a year round flood with shipments increasing from 561,221 bushels in the 1920/21 crop year[2] to 54,619,188 bushels three years later. This rapidly increasing volume had to be received, processed, and loaded to vessels and, until late 1924, the port had available only the Dominion No. 1 terminal elevator to move this commodity. As a result, the harbour became seriously congested with ships sitting idle while waiting for full or partial cargoes of grain. In March 1924 there were 44 ships waiting for a loading berth at "Stevens' Folly," despite the little terminal having turned over its storage capacity five times that month — considered a phenomenal achievement for an ocean terminal at that time.

Such a dramatic increase in so short a time required the rapid construction of new facilities. Solidly backed with federal financing, the VHC led the way. Between 1924 and 1926 they completed two more grain elevators, VHC No. 2 and VHC No. 3 plus an annex to VHC No. 1 (formerly Dominion No. 1). Private capital provided by Spillers, a large British miller and major buyer of Canadian wheat, financed the largest of the new terminals, which was completed in 1924. These railcar unloading, processing, and storage terminals were built at a cost of approximately $1 per bushel capacity. Initially the Spillers terminal and VHC No.1 loaded vessels by using galleries on Lapointe Pier (formerly called Government Pier) pending VHC's completion of Jetty No. 1 that had connections to both Spillers, VHC No. 1, and its annex. Combined, these adjacent terminals offered a total storage capacity of 4.5 million bushels and would eventually be operated as a unit named Pacific Elevators. With a number of upgrades, additions to capacity, and changes in ownership over the years, these old terminals are still in use under the same name.

VHC No.2 terminal, with 1.5 million bushels capacity, initially used galleries on Ballantyne Pier for ship loading, pending completion of a dedicated loading jetty, built by the VHC at a cost of $0.5 million, in 1925. It would be the first terminal on the West Coast operated by the Alberta Wheat Pool under lease from the VHC. In 1966 the Saskatchewan Wheat Pool took over the lease pending completion of their new terminal on the north shore in 1968. It then sat idle for 10 years and was finally demolished in 1979.

Thus, by the 1928/29 crop year, the port's terminal capacity had increased tenfold enabling it to move 95.4 million bushels with ease and exceed Montreal's annual throughput for the first time. Total Canadian overseas wheat exports doubled between the 1921/22 and

---

[2]The Crop year begins August 31 and ends July 31 the following year.

1928/29 crop years. Over that period the Pacific Coast's share of that movement increased from 6 to 29 percent, while the amount directed to U.S. Atlantic ports fell from 67 to 45 percent. Vancouver's gain was clearly at the expense of the U.S. ports.

In addition to these major public terminals, two private facilities were completed by the end of 1925. Columbia Elevator had an initial storage capacity of only 125,000 bushels connected to a small vessel loading jetty. Terminal Dock and Warehouse, a subsidiary of Robin Hood Mills, completed the first flour dock in Vancouver, a substantial facility with a two story warehouse and a three-berth pier equipped with rail tracks. It loaded its first vessel with 3,500 tons of flour in April 1925. Flour, sacked or contained in barrels weighing 196 pounds, became a major new commodity export for the port, increasing from 9,832 tons in 1921 to 170,328 tons in 1928. The Orient supplied 80 percent of the market for Canadian flour, but buyers there eventually began to build their own milling facilities, limiting further export growth.

By mid-1925 the port's major terminals had 13 loading berths, a storage capacity of 6.9 million bushels, and the ability to unload 600 railcars daily. Though this was less than one-tenth the capacity at Fort William and about half that of Montreal, the all-year port estimated that it could now handle 100,000 000 bushels (approximately 2.7 million tonnes) of export wheat annually. Four of the five major terminals and all the shipping galleries with their jetties had, to this point, been built with federal funds provided to the VHC. This was the reverse of the situation in the east, where private capital had built almost all the facilities. This federal largesse toward Vancouver exacerbated the existing strong resistance from many in Winnipeg, the centre of the grain trade, directed against the concept of moving prairie grain destined for overseas export through the West Coast. This resistance often took the form of disseminating misinformation to farmers about the supposed physical and economic perils associated with moving their wheat over the endless mountains to the Pacific Coast, so far removed from the major European markets.

Almost all the wheat moved through Vancouver in the first few years came from Alberta. The Alberta Wheat Pool, formed in 1923, soon realized that it needed to enter the terminal scene in Vancouver. At first the Pool leased and operated the VHC No.2 terminal while planning and constructing a new 2.4-million-bushel-capacity terminal just west of second narrows. Completed with its own galleries and loading jetty in 1928 at a cost of $2.9 million it soon became inadequate and, over the next two years, extra storage was added to increase its capacity to 5.15 million bushels. Further storage additions over the years have doubled that capacity. The terminal, largest on the West Coast, is now owned and operated by Viterra, a company representing the consolidated assets of the former wheat pools and United Grain Growers.

The completion of the road and rail bridge at second narrows in 1925 presented the opportunity for new terminal development on the north shore of Burrard Inlet. Midland Pacific completed a small terminal in 1928 and shortly thereafter expanded its storage capacity to 1.5 million bushels. In 1975, this terminal, then known as Burrard Terminal and owned by the Richardson interests of Winnipeg, was partially destroyed by explosion. It was subsequently rebuilt and modernized, and is currently owned and operated by James Richardson International.

With further additions to three of these terminals the total storage capacity of the port increased from 14 million bushels in 1930 to 19.5 million bushels in 1967, but no new terminals were added until the Saskatchewan Wheat Pool completed its new 5.5 million bushel facility on the north shore in 1968.

By 1929, wheat exports, coupled with the fivefold increase in lumber exports during the 1920s, had made Vancouver the export tonnage leader among Canadian ports. The major market for these exports was, by a considerable margin, the U.K. In 1932 Vancouver's terminals handled 44 percent of Canadian wheat exports, and this movement constituted 73 percent of the total export tonnage of all commodities through the port. Of the remaining 56 percent of overseas wheat exports from Canada that year, two-thirds was loaded onto ocean carriers at eastern Canadian ports and the remaining third went via east coast U.S. ports.

FUTURE PLANS FOR THE PORT

By 1929 the VHC could look back on a decade of spectacular growth in the port's traffic and in the development of the port's facilities. It seemed clear that this trend would continue and that more and better facilities must be provided. In 1929 Parliament approved further loans to the Commission of up to $10 million for projects approved by the Minister. With this new funding the VHC repaid notes issued to purchase Hastings Mill. Plans were developed for a new "Ocean Pier" for that site, even larger than Ballantyne Pier. Each of the Commission's three grain terminals was to be provided with additional storage capacity and new docks for coastwise vessels, fish storage facilities, and adjacent docks for fishing vessels were planned. A lumber assembly facility to be leased to H. R. MacMillan and a terminal railway on the north shore, to be operated by the Commission and connecting to the PGE line, were already underway.

VICTORIA AND NEW WESTMINSTER

Victoria and New Westminster had long been flourishing commercial centres as well as rivals when the first CPR train arrived at the waterfront on Burrard Inlet. Both had been keen to be recognized as the terminus for the Southern Rail Corridor and accordingly, the port of access and egress for West Coast Canadian trade. Due to tradition, politics, and the problems associated with creating and maintaining a navigable channel on the lower Fraser River, Victoria had long been able to hold on to its position as the main port for overseas commerce. Waterborne activity on the Fraser had been mostly confined to river and coastwise traffic, though a few sailing vessels had ventured up the river to pick up cargo at local canneries and sawmills.

VICTORIA

After the 1887 arrival in Vancouver of the first transcontinental train, port development on the south shore of Burrard Inlet gradually began to eclipse activity at both Victoria and New Westminster. In 1918 Victoria handled 4 million tonnes of cargo, Vancouver 3.8 million, Prince Rupert 825,000 and New Westminster a paltry 14,000 tonnes. From 1919 on, Vancouver gained and held the dominant position for West Coast marine traffic.

Victoria had been awarded the prize of being named the capital of the Province of B.C. It benefited greatly as the Pacific base for the Royal Navy and later the Royal Canadian Navy, established in 1910. The first graving dock at Esquimalt, adjacent to the Navy base, was completed in 1887, fulfilling Ottawa's promise to B.C. in the negotiations that led to the colony joining confederation. Upgraded several times since, it is still used by the Navy.

To protect planned docks in the outer harbour the federal government supplied funds to complete a 750 m (2,500 ft.) granite block breakwater in 1916. Two years later, the Ogden Point wharf complex was completed at a cost of $5 million, provided by Ottawa. Immediately after the first Great War the Foundation Company built a series of 3,300 ton wooden freighters for the French Government, but no further large contracts followed for the local shipyards until World War II. The federal government built a second and much larger graving dock on 6.9 ha (17 acres) of land expropriated from the Hudson's Bay Company at Skinner's Cove in Esquimalt harbour. Completed in 1927, this $6 million facility was the largest dry dock on the entire Pacific Rim for many years and continues to prove the most worthwhile federal expenditure on the Victoria port scene.

Eager to participate in the flourishing West Coast grain export business and thereby expand its hinterland reach, the City of Victoria strongly supported the Panama Pacific Grain Company's plan to build a grain elevator in Victoria's harbour. It assisted by providing a favourable lease on a site near Ogden Point and a guarantee for $500,000 of Pan Pacific's bonds. The contrived justification for building a grain terminal at this singularly inappropriate island location was that it could load "parcel shipments" of grain to liner vessels, saving them the extra 128 km (80 miles) transit to Vancouver. A 1-million-bushel-capacity elevator with dock was completed in 1928 at a cost of $0.8 million, but its operation depended on the railways having to barge loaded grain cars to the island under the infamous Crow rate, without compensation for their additional costs. Over the next 48 years the terminal was operated intermittently by Panama Pacific Grain Terminal Ltd., Alberta Wheat Pool, United Grain Growers and finally, the Victoria Elevator Company. Due to its limited storage capacity, vessels loading there usually had to move to Vancouver or Prince Rupert to complete their cargo. It finally ceased operation in 1976 and was demolished. The site is now occupied by a major Canadian Coast Guard base.

NEW WESTMINSTER

Since confederation, New Westminster had been successful in persuading Ottawa to fund programs to upgrade and maintain a navigable channel for deep-sea vessels on the lower river and thus gradually overcame shipmasters' reluctance to use the river port's facilities. However, it became more difficult to obtain grants for these programs in the latter half of the 1890s, a time of continent-wide recession. A pattern then developed of sawmills along the river barging export lumber to Vancouver for loading onto deep-sea vessels.

The completion of the Canadian Northern Pacific Railway (soon to be part of the CNR) in 1915 brought renewed interest in the port. Then, with the opening of Panama, the end of the war, and renewed efforts to improve the navigable river channel, substantial activity began returning to the port. The New Westminster Harbour Commission (NWHC), established in 1913, was now served by three major railways and could offer cheap land that was easy to develop. The fact that the river's teredo free fresh water allowed the use of untreated wooden pilings for wharves was a bonus.

Vessels began to load lumber again at the river wharves in 1921, initially at the private facilities of the major sawmills. During that year 13 vessels called at the port to lift 3½ million board feet (approximately 4800 tonnes) of export lumber[3]. Three years later that figure had ballooned to 119 million board feet with 10–12 vessels loading at river facilities each month. In 1929, a total of 248 vessels made use of port facilities with lumber loadings on the river reaching approximately 204 million board feet, more than a quarter of all overseas shipments from B.C. ports that year.

In 1925 the year-old Fraser River Dock and Stevedoring Company completed a second wharf on the New Westminster waterfront, giving their facility a total of three berths and 2.8 ha (7 acres) of backup land for lumber assembly. In addition to lumber, the port handled significant quantities of lead and zinc metals, canned salmon, and fruit. By 1924, the high water depth of the navigable channel was being maintained at 7.8 m (26 ft.) with plans to increase that eventually to 10.5 m (35 ft.).

No longer seen to be a very minor player, the port's promoters aspired to participate in the booming grain export business. To this end the Harbour Commission selected a site on the south bank of the river at Port Mann for a grain terminal estimated to cost $600,000, which they expected would be operated by Gillespie Grain. When this project failed to materialize a new site was chosen opposite the City of New Westminster. In November 1927, Parliament authorized the NWHC to issue up to $700,000 worth of bonds for the construction of a small grain elevator at this new site. Built on wooden pilings, this 700,000-bushel-capacity terminal was completed in 1928 and leased to the Fraser River Elevator Company. To remedy initial design problems the NWHC issued an additional $100,000 of bonds, and the elevator did not receive its first vessel until June 1929. Interestingly, that vessel unloaded

---

[3]Rough green coastal fir lumber weighs approximately 1.37 tonnes per thousand board feet.

1,818 tonnes (2,000 tons) of Argentine corn. The terminal's operation was fraught with problems and in 1933 the Searle interests of Winnipeg took over the lease. Later, in 1956 Searle assigned the lease to their related company, Pacific Elevators of Vancouver. For almost all its existence, the terminal was primarily used as an "overflow" facility to their Vancouver elevator. After developing a lean in 1968, it ceased operations and was demolished in 1970. Fraser Surrey Docks now occupies the site.

In early 1928, Pacific Coast Terminals was formed and acquired the 7.2 ha (18 acre) central riverfront site of the former Royal City Mills, which had been destroyed by fire in 1913. This company had ambitious plans to build a number of first class facilities, including a large cold storage warehouse, deep-water berths and a second grain terminal on the New Westminster waterfront. The new company was assured very strong support from the CNR, as its chairman, Sir Henry Thornton, was also head of the national railway. Developing New Westminster port facilities offered the railway an opportunity to better compete with the CPR that continued to dominate the Vancouver waterfront. Undoubtedly, federal politics also played a role with the Liberal King government favouring the CNR over the Tory founded CPR!

The City of New Westminster enthusiastically backed Pacific Coast Terminals, providing long term tax relief and a 20-year guarantee for the dividends on $300,000 of the company's preferred shares. In addition, the company received $700,000 in federal subsidies for the cold storage facility. In 1929 the company took over the Fraser River Dock and Stevedoring Company assets, consolidating and extending its wharves and warehouses. Total expenditure on new construction, including the cold storage facility, was $2.38 million. The plan to build a second grain terminal was abandoned.

Pacific Coast Terminals' facilities on the New Westminster waterfront dominated vessel handling on the river for the next 50 years. Then, in the early 1970s, Fraser Surrey Docks built a modern wharf complex on the south shore site of the recently demolished grain terminal. Soon after, Pacific Coast Terminals sold their New Westminster properties to the British Columbia Development Corporation for development as New Westminster Quay. A subsidiary, Pacific Coast Bulk Terminals, continued operations at Port Moody.

PRINCE RUPERT

Canada's new Northern Corridor and Pacific Gateway Port could hardly have become operational at a less auspicious time. Less than four months after the arrival of the first passenger train in Prince Rupert the First World War broke out. For the next four years the war dominated all the activities of the participants. The three-year economic depression that preceded the war and the parlous state of the Grand Trunk Pacific Railway's finances had already resulted in cancellation or deferral of most of the plans for the new port. Furthermore, it certainly appears clear that before his death, Hays had already redirected much of his attention to connecting his Northern Rail Corridor at Prince George to the Port of Vancouver. By the war's end in November 1918, the financial position of the railway had deteriorated to the point that it was forced into receivership in March 1919 with its management taken over by the newly organized CNR. The new owner completed the railway installations and built a passenger station in 1922.

During the first war there had been a few shipments of "airplane spruce" to the UK, organized by H. R. MacMillan, Chief Forester for British Columbia. Thereafter, overseas exports through the port were negligible until the grain terminal opened in 1926. The port's main asset was the new floating dry dock built by the railway with a very substantial government subsidy. Though the second largest dry dock on the west coast of North America, it had been used only six times during the period from its completion in 1916 to the war's end, none of them commercially.

The American entrepreneur who had obtained a 10-year lease on the dry dock and associated shipyard secured an order from the CGMM for two steel freighters. The keel for the first 5,300 ton freighter was laid in November 1919 and by spring 1920, 374 men were working at the shipyard. Poor management and an inexperienced work force resulted in slow progress and within a year the lessee was in financial difficulties. Work stopped on the two ships (the *Canadian Scottish* and *Canadian Britisher*) and the work force was idled. In December 1920, the lessee went into receivership and the CGMM negotiated an arrangement with the bonding company to have Wallace Shipyards of Vancouver finish the two ships at cost plus 8 percent. On completion the shipyard and dry dock reverted to CNR management and, with a minimal workforce, the operation survived by constructing small vessels for local use and repair and maintenance work, mostly on government and CNR owned vessels. No more major vessels were built by the yard until 1940. Three new passenger vessels for the coast service of CN Steamships were ordered in 1928 from British yards because the Prince Rupert facility was not considered adequately equipped or staffed to build them.

During the early 1920s the Vancouver maritime community, supported by Ballantyne, the federal Minister of Marine, Fisheries and Naval Affairs, repeatedly pressed for the dry dock at Prince Rupert to be brought south to Vancouver. This pressure abated when Vancouver's own federally subsidized dry dock was completed in 1925.

Federal funding provided the port with two new facilities in the 1920s, though traffic projections could hardly have justified either now that the rail line to the port had been reduced to branch line status. The first new facility was Ocean Dock, completed in 1921. Built with treated wood pilings, the 258 m (860 ft.) dock face offered a water depth of 10.5 m (35 ft.). The new wharf included a 246 by 44 m wooden shed (819 by 147 ft.) for cargo assembly and storage, and adjacent trackage for 21 railcars. It would see very little use by deep-sea vessels until 1942. Concurrently, to serve the coastal trade and to accommodate the needs of fishing companies, the provincial government completed a 217.5 m (725 ft.) wharf and a 76.5 by 16.5 m shed (255 by 55 ft.) to supplement the CNR (ex GTP) wharf.

The Canadian Government Grain Elevator was the second facility provided to the port with federal funds. Completed at a cost of $1.2 million in 1926, the terminal offered 1.25 million bushels storage capacity, a 304 m (1,015 ft.) wooden dock with loading gallery, and a sacking shed. It was initially leased for two years to the Alberta Wheat Pool at a nominal rate and in 1928 this lease was renewed for a further five years. The first vessel loaded at the terminal in October 1926 and, by the end of the 1926/27 crop year on July 31, 1927, wheat throughput had reached 5,579,878 bushels. During the crop year that followed, the terminal handled 8 million bushels of wheat, but when the Alberta Wheat Pool completed their new terminal in Vancouver (1928) they clearly lost interest in Prince Rupert, relegating the facility to an "overflow" role. During the next 23 years the terminal handled only 10,487,576 million bushels and during 11 of those years no grain was directed to the "orphan" port. There were two reasons. There was no incentive for the CNR to haul grain the extra 307 km (192 miles) under the Crow rate and the Prairie Pools — in their capacity as agents for the Wheat Board — wanted the grain collected at their country elevators to be shipped through their lucrative ocean terminals at Vancouver. The terminal never became integrated into the movement of grain through the West Coast until the late seventies.

By 1929 Japan was Canada's third best customer, importing flour, pulp, salmon, lead and zinc, as well as more traditional lumber and grain. China, too, had become the country's fifth largest trading partner, exporting tea and silk, and importing lumber and wheat. Its very advantageous location with respect to the Orient should have greatly benefitted Prince Rupert, but vessel owners seemed unconvinced. They considered the port to be "off the beaten track" and demanded a premium if required to take on cargo there. Furthermore, though the Panama Canal had enormously expanded the reach of Vancouver's port facilities to the main transatlantic markets for Canadian goods, it offered little to the northern port.

While Vancouver's port underwent spectacular growth and development during the exuberant third decade of the twentieth century and was recognized as the fastest growing port on the Pacific Coast of North America, disillusionment and frustration characterized the situation in Prince Rupert. Though the CNR had doubled its revenues year after year and had even begun to repay the debts of its predecessors, it showed little or no interest in the Northern Gateway Port it had inherited and demoted it to the position of terminus of a little used branch line. In 1926 Sir Henry Thornton, head of the railway, visited Prince Rupert. He offered only hope to assuage the crushed dreams of the local citizens. He revisited in 1929, this time expressing a desire to see a railway hotel built and a large steamship company calling at Prince Rupert from the Orient. On that visit he admitted that the railway could move grain to Prince Rupert more cheaply than to any other Pacific port. Soon after that visit came the great Wall Street crash.

The Prince Rupert Board of Trade, in 1928, petitioned Ottawa to establish a Harbours Board for the port. The same year it sent a delegation to Victoria to plead for a rail line to be built north from Terrace to tap the Groundhog anthracite coal fields with a view to shipping this high quality coal through the port. Neither request received support from the respective governments.

Spirits rose in Prince Rupert three times during the decade. First came the spurt in activity at the shipyard with the orders from CGMM for two steel freighters. Concurrently, Ocean Dock was under construction and then, in mid-decade, the new grain elevator was completed. Each project raised hopes, but in each case stagnation followed the initial flurry of activity.

Reduced to a backwater at the end of a branch line and lacking political clout, the city, which had been established with such high expectations, shrank to a population of 5,000, primarily dependent on fishing for their living.

A Visual Record of the Gateway Ports and the Men Who Moved the Cargoes 1843 to 1918

City of Vancouver Archives A-6-155.2 and A-6-198

THE GATEWAYS FROM 1843 TO 1918

Victoria, the First Gateway

The seminal influences in the establishment and development of what became British Columbia were the Royal Navy and the Hudson's Bay Company. Britain's decision to establish and maintain a strong naval presence at Esquimalt was a clear expression of her determination to preserve a sector of North America's west coast from becoming absorbed into the aggressively expansionist United States or being encroached upon from the north by Imperial Russia.

The decision to relocate the HBC headquarters from Fort Vancouver on the Columbia River to Fort Victoria, instead of to the already established Fort Langley was significant. It reflected the HBC's emphasis on North Coast trade, the better ability of the new fort to resist attack from the south, the problems associated with river navigation, and the HBC's view of the immense difficulty in accessing the interior land mass of the mainland.

As a Gateway Port, Victoria benefited initially from the reluctance of deep-sea vessel sailing masters

VICTORIA HARBOUR

PLATE 1 *A panorama of Victoria's Inner Harbour in the early 1860s taken from Old Songhees Village, now Victoria West, showing wharves and warehouses along Wharf Street and the first bridge spanning James Bay. The very large building is the HBC warehouse. The HBC side-wheel steamer* Beaver *is berthed and the screw steamer* Otter *is anchored with her bow pointing toward the site where the Parliament Buildings were later built.*

to navigate the treacherous shallows at the Fraser River's mouth. The city grew in wealth and political influence, especially during the peak years of the Fraser and Cariboo gold rushes, so that when the island and mainland colonies were combined in 1866, Victoria was able to snatch the prize of Capital of B.C. from New Westminster.

In its gateway role, Victoria at first served only to distribute trade goods received from Britain in the HBC's annual supply vessel to points on the coast between Puget Sound and the Stikine River. Though there was some trade with the Sandwich Islands, California and Australia, the primary market for colonial exports of furs, forest products and salted salmon was in Britain.

Between 1858 and 1900 the Fraser, Cariboo, Cassiar, and Klondike gold rushes gave major impetus to the port's growth and development. Each gold rush caused a relatively short period of frantic activity. However, despite the steep peaks and deep valleys of economic activity, new long term industries developed, including shipbuilding and sawmilling. Indeed, as early as 1853, nineteen vessels sailed from Victoria loaded with lumber, seventeen of them destined for booming San Francisco and, by the late 1860s more than half the steamers trading in B.C. waters had been built in Victoria.

From the beginning, Victoria viewed itself as the entry gateway for trade goods being distributed to coastal and inland B.C. plus the Alaska Panhandle, as well as the sole loading port for colonial products sold to overseas markets.

The monopoly held since 1600 by the East India Company on all British trade with south and east Asia thwarted early HBC attempts to engage in transpacific trade. Late in the nineteenth century, these markets finally became available, as did Atlantic markets after World War I. However, by that time Victoria had lost its role as primary port for overseas trade and, thereafter, was mostly confined to loading vessels with the products of the forests of southern Vancouver Island.

Apart from intermittent, very modest shipments of prairie grain between 1928 and 1976, Victoria never became a true Canadian Gateway Port. It did, however, serve as the primary gateway for coastal and mainland B.C. for half a century.

B.C. Archives A 03114

PLATE 2 *Sailing vessels and the two HBC steamers* Beaver *and* Otter *tied to iron rings on Wharf Street in the Inner Harbour circa 1875.*

PLATE 3 *Victoria Harbour circa 1880. The HBC warehouse dominates the centre of the picture with the customs office on the right.*

PLATE 4 *The James Bay Bridge circa 1875. To the right of the bridge is the mudflat, future site of the Empress Hotel. The foreground was later developed into the grounds in front of the Parliament Buildings.*

City of Vancouver Archives SGN 909, 910, 911, 912

B.C. Archives A 03848

PLATE 5 *Wharf Street wharves in the Inner Harbour in the late 1880s. To the right of the sailing barque are the side-wheelers* Amelia *and* Olympian. *The* Amelia *operated a service to communities on the east coast of Vancouver Island and the Gulf Islands, while the* Olympian *connected ports on Puget Sound with Victoria.*

PLATE 6 *Panorama of the Victoria waterfront in 1898 showing developments on the Inner Harbour and James Bay and, in the foreground, the spire atop the dome of the newly completed first stage of the present Parliament Buildings (seen superimposed on the south end of the causeway).*

PLATE 7 *Inner Harbour wharves and the causeway across James Bay under construction in 1902. The dredge* King Edward *was brought from the Fraser River to deepen Victoria Harbour and fill in the mudflat east of the causeway to prepare for building the Empress Hotel.*

PLATE 8 *Victoria Harbour as seen from the Empress Hotel in 1912.*

PLATE 9 *The Inner Harbour wharves in 1920 as seen from the completed Parliament Buildings, showing the B.C. Coast Service wharf in the foreground and the Grand Trunk Pacific wharf centre right.*

HUDSON'S BAY COMPANY VESSELS

To trade on the Northwest Pacific Coast the HBC acquired and operated a total of 24 vessels between 1824 and 1883. These wooden vessels ranged in size from 30 to 680 tons and included sailing vessels of many types, four side-wheel steamers, one stern-wheel steamer and a screw-propelled steamer. In addition, the company sent at least one supply ship annually from Britain to the Pacific Northwest. This vessel returned with the raw products the company collected through trade including furs, salted salmon, and products of the local forests. On occasion, the returning vessel would call at the Sandwich Islands or California ports to discharge cargo.

By far the best known and most useful of the coastal trader and supply vessels were the *Beaver* and the *Otter*.

C. Gentile photo, City of Vancouver Archives Bo P204

PLATE 10 *The sail and/or steam powered side-wheeler* Beaver *served the HBC as a supply and trading vessel on the coast from 1837 to 1857. This 100 ft. 9 inch vessel was primarily operated as a steamer with a crew of 31, including 4 stokers and 13 woodcutters. Between 1858 and 1862 she operated between Victoria and the mainland, moving miners and supplies during the peak gold rush years. The Royal Navy chartered her for use between 1862 and 1870 and substantially altered and upgraded her upper works for service as a hydrographic survey vessel. She is seen in this role in this picture.*

PLATE 11 *Shipbuilding and repair developed early as a major industry in Victoria. Here the* Beaver *is seen on Cook's Ways in Victoria Harbour for repairs and maintenance, after her return to commercial work from service with the Royal Navy.*

PLATE 12 Otter, *the second steamer built in the U.K. for service with the HBC. This vessel, at 125 feet, was substantially larger than the* Beaver *and equipped with a single screw for propulsion, the first of this type on the North Coast. She operated successfully on the coast between 1853 and 1883 and was later converted to a barge. She is seen here on the mid-coast near Bella Bella circa 1880.*

B.C. Archives A 00104

PLATE 13 Otter *berthed in Victoria's Inner Harbour.*

B.C. Archives C09493

PLATE 14 *The HBC barque* Prince Rupert *at anchor in Victoria's Inner Harbour. This vessel served as one of the HBC annual supply ships during the period 1875–1884. These vessels sailed direct from Britain to Victoria via Cape Horn, their voyage taking anywhere from 105 to 170 days.*

PLATE 15 *The barquentine* Titania *in Victoria Harbour. On the right are the first Parliament Buildings (the "Bird Cages"), which were completed in 1869. The* Titania, *a fast clipper ship, operated for the HBC between Victoria and Britain from 1886 to 1892. She made that voyage in a record time of 105 days in 1889 and that same year became the first vessel to arrive in Vancouver with cargo direct from the U.K., returning loaded with canned salmon. Her voyage in 1892 marked the last of the annual supply services operated by the HBC since 1823.*

THE ROYAL NAVY AT ESQUIMALT

The presence of the Royal Navy (RN) on the west coast of North America starts, of course, with Cook's visit to Nootka in 1778 and Vancouver's survey of the coast from Puget Sound to Cook Inlet.

Officers of HMS *Racoon* raised the Union Jack over Fort Astoria at the mouth of the Columbia River and declared possession of the tributary country for Britain during the second year of the War of 1812.

In 1842 HMS *Pandora* surveyed Esquimalt Harbour, adjacent to the smaller and shallower Victoria Harbour, and determined it suitable for a major Royal Navy base. Four years later, four RN warships maintained a presence at Esquimalt to discourage U.S. ambitions during the Oregon Boundary dispute. During her three-year stay (1851–1854) the crew of HMS *Thetis* conducted marine surveys and built the first road between Esquimalt and Victoria, known at present as Old Esquimalt Road.

During the Crimean War (1854–1856) funding was provided by the RN to the colonial government to build hospital facilities at Esquimalt in preparation for a planned attack on the Russians (which never materialized).

After 1865, Esquimalt replaced Valparaiso as the primary western Pacific establishment for the RN. As such it became home for a squadron of 15 vessels, including a frigate as flagship. The crews of these vessels created a major market for the produce of local and Fraser Valley farms, as well as interior cattle ranches. This gave a substantial economic boost to the infant colonies. Later, as the RN converted to steam propulsion, their vessels became a major market for Nanaimo coal.

By the 1880s the RN presence was reduced to six vessels and in 1905 their Pacific Command was terminated and the Esquimalt base turned over to the Canadian Government. Between 1846 and 1905 a total of 130 Royal Navy vessels had served at the Esquimalt base.

City of Vancouver Archives Out P915

PLATE 16 *Royal Navy warships anchored in Esquimalt Harbour in 1868.*

PLATE 17 *Early development of shore-side facilities for the new, permanent naval base.*

PLATE 18 *Cannon and stacks of cannon balls stored among the buildings of the new naval base at Esquimalt circa 1867.*

ESQUIMALT DRY DOCKS

The first graving dock at Esquimalt was completed in 1887 at a cost to the federal government of $1.18 million. A major stimulus to its construction involved satisfying the need of locally based Royal Navy vessels that were being forced to use Seattle dry dock facilities. Although a provincial government initiative, the estimated cost of the project had been met by grants from the Imperial and Dominion governments. It soon became evident that these grants were far below the amount needed to complete the facility and this brought on a political crisis in the province. "Mainlanders," always suspicious of "Islanders," wanted funds spent on their planned roads and trails and would not tolerate provincial funds being used to complete the island dry dock. Eventually the matter was resolved when the Dominion Government took over and completed the project.

During its first seven years of operation the new dry dock served a total of 94 vessels, 70 of them Royal Navy warships.

This facility is part of HMC Dockyard and is the oldest continuously operated dry dock on the west coast of North America. It is presently used for dry-docking Canada's submarines.

The second, very much larger graving dock at Esquimalt was completed by the federal government in 1927 at a cost of $6 million. Its continuing ability to service very large vessels makes this marine facility a major asset on the Pacific Coast.

B.C. Archives F 08452

PLATE 19 *The sloop HMS* Cormorant *was the first vessel in the new dry dock in 1887.*

PLATE 20 Islander *in the original dry dock at Esquimalt. This 240 ft. passenger vessel was built in Scotland for the Canadian Pacific Navigation Company in 1888 for service between Victoria and Vancouver, as well as Puget Sound ports. In 1890 she was placed on North Coast service. This service proved very popular with excursion passengers and was extended in 1892 to Wrangell, Juneau, and Sitka. Islander is, accordingly, the acknowledged forerunner of the popular Alaska Cruise business — though her stateroom capacity for only 111 passengers pales in comparison with the current behemoths!*

PLATE 21 *RMS* Empress of Canada *in the second, very much larger graving dock at Skinner's Cove in Esquimalt Harbour. This facility was completed in 1927 and for many years was the largest dry dock on the Pacific Rim. Early in World War II it accommodated the liner* Queen Elizabeth.

THE DEVELOPMENT OF VICTORIA'S OUTER HARBOUR

At first, Victoria's constricted and shallow Inner Harbour with its wharves and warehouses was adequate to service the HBC's annual supply vessels, its coastal trading and supply fleet, and other marine related activities including the local sealing fleet. These facilities were expanded substantially to accommodate the great surge in traffic to the mainland during the Fraser and Cariboo gold rushes.

By the mid-eighties it was evident that new deep-water wharves must be developed, in order to remain competitive with the new developments on Burrard Inlet and to efficiently handle newer vessels with larger cargo capacity and deeper draft, including the new Empress liners. In response, R.P. Rithet, local merchant, entrepreneur and politician, created a company to build "Rithet's Wharves" at Shoal Beach in the outer harbour in the early 1890s. Thereafter, use of the Inner Harbour became confined to relatively small and manoeuvrable passenger ferries. New berthing facilities were built there and the original wharves along Wharf Street gradually disappeared.

The wharves in the Outer Harbour needed protection from periodic storms. This, together with the anticipation of a massive increase in overseas trade after the opening of the Panama Canal, convinced the federal government to upgrade the harbour. For a total expenditure of $5 million a 2,500 ft. breakwater at Ogden Point was completed in 1916, as well as two piers and a large cargo warehouse just inside the breakwater, completed two years later. Ironically, despite the substantial new deep water facility, 1918 was the last year that Victoria surpassed Vancouver in cargo tonnage throughput. Its steep decline from the dominant position as first western gateway began with the arrival of the CPR at Port Moody in 1886 and by 1918 its increasingly limited gateway role was over.

A private company, enthusiastically supported by the city, built a small grain elevator in 1928 on the Outer Harbour near Rithet's Wharves. It is remembered by many as "Victoria's White Elephant."

Rithet's Wharves and the grain terminal were demolished in the seventies to make way for a new Coast Guard Base. The Ogden Point Pier complex was administered by the CNR between 1928 and 1978 and was used to move regional cargo — mostly export forest products. By the mid-eighties, virtually all cargo handling ceased and the piers were upgraded and adapted for use by vessels in the Alaska cruise business.

PLATE 22 *Rithet's Wharves in the Outer Harbour circa 1891.*

PLATE 23 *RMS* Empress of India *berthed at Rithet's Wharf in 1901.*

PLATE 24 *The Ogden Point Pier complex and the Grain Terminal from the breakwater in Victoria's Outer Harbour in 1949.*

PLATE 25 *The first vessel to load grain from the Panama Pacific Grain Terminal in early 1929. The City of Victoria granted a very favourable lease on the site and guaranteed bonds covering five-eighths of the cost of this one-million-bushel capacity terminal. Over 48 years it functioned intermittently under four operators and moved a grand total of 3.4 million tonnes of grain, which arrived from the mainland on a CN rail barge. It ceased operation in 1976 and was demolished in 1978.*

New Westminster from 1859 to 1918

The Port of Queensborough was established by official proclamation on February 14, 1859, at the beginning of the interior gold rush period. It was at once perceived by the Victoria business community to be a threat to their cherished position as the primary port for both coastal and interior British Columbia. Accordingly, the Victoria dominated colonial government took steps to thwart the aspirations of the newly incorporated (1860) City of New Westminster to become the mainland port for deep-sea commerce. The hazards to navigation on the river for deep draft vessels posed an even greater challenge for the nascent port.

For its first 60 years, New Westminster had limited success in attracting deep-sea traffic to its wharves. However, as it became the location of large sawmills and many salmon canneries, the transfer point for interior traffic, and the mercantile centre for the burgeoning Fraser Valley agriculture communities, the port prospered by focussing on river traffic. It became the base for a fleet of shallow draft, steam powered paddle-wheelers which dominated river traffic, while the Victoria based coastal vessels of the HBC fleet dominated traffic across the Gulf of Georgia. Finally, in 1883 the leading New Westminster operator, the Pioneer Line, amalgamated with the HBC fleet to form the Canadian Pacific

Navigation Company. This company then became the dominant operator on both segments of the water route from Victoria to Yale.

River traffic peaked during the building of the CPR. On completion of that line, the Cities of Vancouver and New Westminster worked together, at first, to resist Victoria's continuing political dominance.

After confederation, federal funds became available to improve river navigation through dredging and snag removal programs and through construction of channel control works. These federally sponsored programs continued for over a century.

Some deep sea vessels risked the 14 ft. channel to load cargoes of lumber or canned salmon at riverside wharves, but by 1890 a pattern had developed of local sawmills barging their product to Vancouver for loading to deep-draft vessels. This was not accepted gracefully by New Westminster port boosters and thus began the rivalry, at times bitter, between the two southern mainland ports which would last until they were amalgamated in 2008.

Rail first arrived in New Westminster as a branch line from the CPR at Port Moody in 1886. Five years later, a Great Northern Railway subsidiary reached the south bank of the Fraser River and finally entered the city when the Fraser rail bridge was completed by the Province in 1904. In 1915 the Canadian Northern Railway used this bridge to cross the Fraser enroute to Vancouver.

B.C. Archives B 06377

PLATE 26 *This barque is considered to be the first deep-sea vessel to load cargo at New Westminster. It has been variously identified as the* D.L. Clinch, Vickeray, Island Queen, *and* N.C. Perkins. *Date of the picture is September 30, 1859. Note the stern-wheeler pulled ashore for repair and the bundles of cedar shakes at the lower left of the picture.*

PLATE 27 *The New Westminster waterfront and Government House in 1863.*

PLATE 28 *First waterfront developments at New Westminster, mid-1860s.*

PLATE 29 *The stern-wheeler* Onward *at Emory's Bar on the Fraser River in 1867. This 120 foot vessel was built in Victoria in 1865 for Captain William Irving's Pioneer Line.*

PLATE 30 *The steamboat* R.P. Rithet *at Yale in 1882. This new and much larger (177 feet) stern-wheeler was also built in Victoria for the Pioneer Line which amalgamated with the HBC fleet in 1883 to form the Canadian Pacific Navigation Company.*

PLATE 31 Samson, *the first snag boat built in 1884 for the federal Department of Public Works and tasked with removing floating debris and river hazards, and maintaining navigation markers. This vessel was succeeded by vessels named* Samson II to V, *all acquired and operated by the DPW over a total period of 86 years.*

PLATE 32 Thermopylae *loading lumber at Brunette Sawmill at Sapperton on March 27, 1894. This clipper barque was built in Aberdeen in 1868 and achieved fame as the winner of a race from Shanghai to London with* Cutty Sark *in 1872.*

PLATE 33 *Loading tall ships at the wharf of Brunette Sawmill Company in 1895.*

PLATE 34 *Tall ships berthed at salmon canneries on the river near Steveston in 1898.*
Between 1880 and 1950 a total of 150 salmon canneries operated at points along the B.C.
coast between the Fraser and Nass Rivers, peaking at 90 at one time in the 1920s.

PLATE 35 *The Malcolm and Windsor Cannery at Steveston in 1900. This cannery was later renamed the Gulf of Georgia Cannery.*

PLATE 36 *The first CPR passenger train to arrive at the waterfront in New Westminster from Port Moody in November 1886.*

PLATE 37 *New Westminster waterfront in the 1890s.*

PLATE 38 *The new road-rail bridge across the Fraser at New Westminster opened on July 23, 1904. This allowed the Vancouver, Westminster and Yukon subsidiary of the Great Northern Railroad to extend service into Vancouver from the south.*

PLATE 39 *The New Westminster downtown waterfront in 1904.*

PLATE 40 *The southern waterfront in 1905, including the Royal City Planing mills, rebuilt after the 1898 fire.*

PLATE 41 *The dredge* King Edward VII *was acquired by the federal Department of Public Works in 1901 to improve the navigable channel on the lower Fraser River. It was supplemented after WWI by the ex-German bucket dredge,* Fruhling, *which had operated on the Kiel Canal. Early in its more than half a century of service,* King Edward *undertook extensive dredging of Victoria's Inner Harbour, concurrent with the construction of the causeway across James Bay.*

Vancouver from 1867 to 1918

BURRARD INLET BEFORE 1886

Five years after the proclamation that created the new colony of British Columbia the first water powered sawmill began operation on the north shore of Burrard Inlet and, in November 1864, the first vessel sailed from that mill loaded with forest products destined for Australia. A second mill on the south shore began production in 1867 and became the focus around which the tiny community of Granville developed.

Marine activity on the inlet for the next two decades depended almost exclusively on the export production of these two mills and a small fish processor, Spratt's Oilery, which was located west of the south shore sawmill.

David Withrow photo, City of Vancouver Archives Mi P43

PLATE 42 *Tall ships at Sewell P. Moody's mill at Moodyville on Burrard Inlet's north shore in 1872.*

PLATE 43 *A group of First Nations longshoremen on the Moodyville Sawmill dock in 1889.*

PLATE 44 *The Moodyville Sawmill in 1897: note the steam tug with the tall ships at the wharf.*

Norman Caple photo, City of Vancouver Archives Mi P26

PLATE 45 *Hastings Mill on the south shore of the inlet. The site is now occupied by Centerm. This mill commenced production in 1867 and finally ceased operation in the late 1920s.*

City of Vancouver Archives Mi P47

PLATE 46 *The slow and very labour intensive business of loading lumber on a vessel through ports in the bow (and/or stern). These vessels are loading at Hastings Mill in 1890.*

PLATE 47 *"B.C. Toothpicks" being loaded on flatcars at Hastings Mill in 1893. These timbers measured 36 inches x 36 inches x 60 feet in length.*

PLATE 48 *Loading tall ships through stern ports at Hastings Mill in 1906. At least there was no air pollution from these vessels.*

PLATE 49 *Spratt's Oilery in 1884. Joseph Spratt, a redoubtable Victoria entrepreneur, established this plant at a site just west of the foot of present day Burrard Street — to convert herring, caught in the Inlet by dynamiting, into marketable oil and grease products. His facility was a refuge for citizens of Vancouver fleeing the Great Fire of 1886. When it burned later that same year, the fire became the first fought by the new Vancouver Fire Department.*

BUILDING THE CORRIDOR TO THE SOUTHERN GATEWAY PORTS

The Port of Vancouver owes its development and success to two massive world scale projects, the Canadian Pacific Railroad and the Panama Canal. Both posed enormous engineering problems. Prime Minister Alexander Mackenzie spoke of B.C. as a "Land of superlative difficulties," none more problematic than trying to build a rail line to the coast across mountain ranges and deep canyons. The first wagon road into the central interior of B.C. was built by a small force of Royal Engineers and their contractors to provide access to the goldfields.

Frederick Dally photo, City of Vancouver Archives CVA 3-16

PLATE 50 *The Yale-Cariboo wagon road in the Fraser Canyon in 1867.*

PLATE 51 *Men working on the Cariboo wagon road in 1868.*

PLATE 52 *Newly constructed CPR tracks above the Cariboo Wagon Road in the Fraser Canyon 3 miles beyond Yale, 1880.*

PLATE 53 *CPR locomotive #365 in the Canyon during construction. It is hard to believe, but the CPR chose the "easier" route through the Canyon, leaving the Canadian Northern to build their line on the even more difficult terrain.*

PLATE 54 *The first through-train to Port Moody, July 4, 1886.*

PLATE 55 *The first official passenger train to arrive in Vancouver on May 23, 1887.*

PLATE 56 *Sir Richard McBride and a group of dignitaries cutting the first sod for the Canadian Northern Railway at Vancouver in 1910. McBride certainly favoured the Canadian Northern over the Grand Trunk Pacific, which was being built concurrently.*

PLATE 57 *Opening ceremonies for the north shore line of the Pacific Great Eastern Railway on January 1, 1914. The line was extended to Horseshoe Bay by July 1914.*

WATERFRONT DEVELOPMENTS ON BURRARD INLET, 1887 TO 1918

The decisions by the CPR to extend their line west along the south shore of the Inlet from Port Moody and to actively engage in transpacific trade transformed the little village of Granville. No longer restricted to exporting locally produced forest products, the shoreline on the inlet's south side under-went almost continuous development with rail yards, wharves, and ancillary facilities constructed to serve both passenger and cargo vessels, especially in the sector west of Hastings Mill.

PLATE 58 *Looking west along the new CPR wharf in 1887. Later the foreshore area was filled in.*

PLATE 59 *The first CPR station and wharf in 1887.*

PLATE 60 *RMS* Abyssinia *unloading tea at the CPR wharf in Vancouver in 1890.*

PLATE 61 *Arrival of RMS* Empress of India *April 28, 1891 with mail and passengers from Yokahama. She was soon joined in transpacific service by the* Empress of China *and the* Empress of Japan.

PLATE 62 *The* Empress of India *leaving harbour.*

PLATE 63 *Cargo handling on the CPR wharf in 1898.*

PLATE 64 *Looking east along the south shore of the inlet to the first CPR wharves, from Coal Harbour in 1890.*

PLATE 65 *The* Premier *and the* Yosemite *in Vancouver harbour in 1889.* Yosemite *was the largest of the stern-wheelers operated by the Canadian Pacific Navigation Company in south coastal services.* Premier *was a single-screw steamer, built in San Francisco in 1887 for the CPNC and renamed* Charmer *in 1894. She continued to operate with the B.C. Coast Service of the CPR until 1935.*

PLATE 66 *The Evans, Coleman and Evans wharf at the foot of Columbia St. in 1898. The foreshore out to the dock was later filled in.*

PLATE 67 *The B.C. Sugar Refinery built in 1890 on a site just east of Hastings Mill. This was the first major industrial development on the waterfront which was not based on forestry or fishing.*

PLATE 68 *A busy harbour in 1908; looking NE from the CPR wharves to Hastings Mill. Note the North Vancouver ferry crossing the Inlet.*

PLATE 69 *The dredge* Mastodon *was purchased in Scotland by the Dominion Government Department of Public Works to undertake a multi-year program of removing shoals and navigational hazards from what mariners considered the "indifferent entrance" to the harbour at first narrows.*

PLATE 70 *CPR piers A & B near the foot of Burrard Street in 1909.*

PLATE 71 *Looking west from the foot of Carrall Street at the CPR rail yard and wharves in 1911.*

PLATE 72 *The second CPR passenger station at the foot of Granville Street with adjacent extensive wharves and warehouses parallel to the shoreline and CPR Piers A and B a little further west.*

PLATE 73 *A Japanese freighter loading sacked grain at Pier B in 1911. Prior to 1917, grain shipments through the West Coast were very modest and virtually confined to Pacific Rim markets.*

PLATE 74 *The newly completed Great Northern Railway Pier at the foot of Campbell Avenue in 1915. The remains of this facility have recently been acquired by the Southern Railroad of B.C. and renamed the SRY Burrard Barge Terminal.*

PLATE 75 *Indian Reserve at the mouth of Seymour Creek in 1886.*

PLATE 76 *North Vancouver west of Lonsdale Avenue circa 1890.*

PLATE 77 *The Great Northern Cannery, formerly the Defiance Cannery, in West Vancouver in 1908.*

PLATE 78 *Wallace Shipyards in North Vancouver in 1910.*

PLATE 79 *SS* War Dog, *the first steel deep-sea freighter built in B.C. by Wallace Shipyards in 1917.*

PLATE 80 *Aerial photograph of the North Vancouver waterfront showing Burrard Dry Dock and Lonsdale Avenue in 1919.*

Prince Rupert from 1906 to 1918

The Grand Trunk Pacific/ National Transcontinental Railway was primarily a product of Prime Minister Laurier's determination to have a Liberal sponsored railway built from the Atlantic to the Pacific Coast of Canada to compete with the well-established, Tory favoured, Canadian Pacific Railway. He had strong support from the Grand Trunk Railroad general manager Charles M. Hays who was able to convince his reluctant London directors to build the section of the line from Winnipeg to a new port on the Pacific Coast.

Despite the euphoria surrounding the development of the new port, culminating in the arrival of the first train in Prince Rupert on April 8, 1914, the infant terminal city was destined to be denied growth or development for the next seven decades.

B.C. Archives B 02019

PLATE 81 *Driving the first piles for the first wharf at Prince Rupert, June 8, 1906.*

PLATE 82 *By February 1907, several buildings had been completed adjacent to the new dock at the foot of Centre Street. From here Prince Rupert's first street extended up the slope to approximately the present intersection of Second Avenue and Sixth Street.*

PLATE 83 *An early 1908 view of the expanding Grand Trunk Pacific Docks.*

PLATE 84 *A crowd meeting one of the fleet of Skeena River stern-wheelers at the GTP dock on May 25, 1908.*

PLATE 85 *Further development of the GTP wharves and the second freight shed, as completed by late 1908.*

PLATE 86 *The Grand Trunk Pacific Hotel and wharf photographed from the harbour in 1908.*

PLATE 87 *Unloading rail for the Grand Trunk Pacific line being built east from Prince Rupert.*

PLATE 88 *Preparing to offload the first train at a temporary barge slip near the GTP wharf in late 1909.*

PLATE 89 *The first train set on the first tracks laid at the northeast end of the developing rail yard in late 1909.*

PLATE 90 *Sir Wilfrid Laurier leaving the new* Prince George *with the city's first mayor, Alfred Stork, August 22, 1910.*

PLATE 91 *Riverboats* Skeena, Operator *and* Conveyor *moored at Prince Rupert in 1910. River steamers had been operated on the Skeena by the HBC since 1891, replacing the canoe brigades that had been supplying their post at Hazelton from Port Simpson. During the construction of the Grand Trunk Pacific Railroad, the railway and its contractors operated several vessels to supply their construction camps along the last 180 miles of the river.* Operator *and* Conveyor *were owned and operated by railway contractors Foley Welch and Stewart. The smaller* Skeena *was used by P. Burns and Co. to supply meat to the construction crews.*

PLATE 92 *A visit to Prince Rupert by Charles M. Hays (third from left) and other GTP officials on June 7, 1911. Hays returned for a last visit August 30, 1911.*

PLATE 93 *The arrival of Premier Richard McBride and Attorney General (later Premier) Bowser on the* Princess May, *July 15, 1912. The Premier officially opened the new Provincial Government wharf on July 16, 1912.*

PLATE 94 *Wharves for fish plants were soon established on the harbour. At first, they were located southwest of the GTP wharves, but were later relocated north of the Provincial Government wharf and shed.*

PLATE 95 *The North Pacific Cannery in 1910. Fishing very soon became the main economic support of the community.*

PLATE 96 *After constructing several temporary rail barge slips, the Grand Trunk Pacific selected a site at in the harbour at Pillsbury Point for this permanent structure to serve the port's first AquaTrain operation. Pulp from B.C.'s first pulp mill at Swanson Bay was stowed there in box cars and carried to Prince Rupert on a nine-car rail barge towed by the tug* Francis Cutting.

PLATE 97 *A busy waterfront in 1913.*

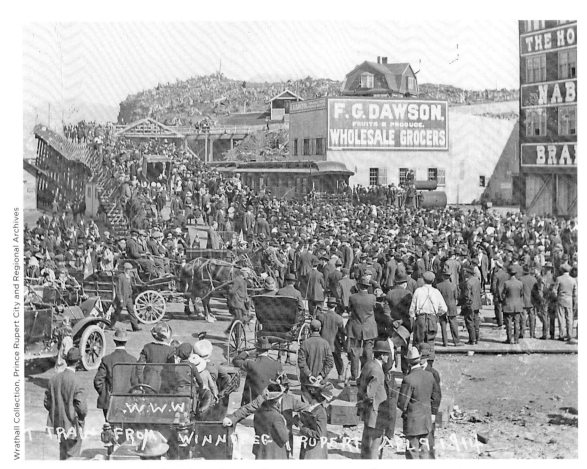

PLATE 98 *Arrival of the first through train from Winnipeg, April 8, 1914.*

PLATE 99 *During World War I, spruce was in great demand in Britain for use in aeroplane construction. H.R. MacMillan, then chief forester in B.C., played a major role in expediting its acquisition and shipment through Prince Rupert.*

PLATE 100 *The Grand Trunk vessel* Prince George *is seen here in Prince Rupert harbour in August 1914, during her short and curious career as a hospital ship. The* Prince George's *conversion and the British Columbia government's acquisition of two submarines from a Seattle shipyard for $1.15 million cash were part of the local panic response to the reported presence of the German cruiser* Leipzig *off the California coast at the beginning of World War I.*

PLATE 101 *View of the Grand Trunk Pacific shipyard and dry dock development October 9, 1916.*

PLATE 102 *On October 21, 1916 the armed merchant cruiser HMS* Orbita *became the first large vessel accommodated in the new floating dry dock.*

PLATE 103 *SS* Prince George *in the Prince Rupert Dry Dock, March 7, 1917.*

CHAPTER FOUR

The Depression Years — 1930 to 1938

The enormous expansion of world trade during the third decade of the twentieth century brought prosperity to Canada. Living standards improved greatly in the world's fastest growing economy, albeit an economy based primarily on production of export commodities. Nations had been sobered by the slaughter of the Great War followed so soon by the devastating 1919 influenza pandemic. Peace, however tenuous in places, reigned worldwide, allowing trade to flourish.

It is a sad truth that neither individuals nor nations seem able to cope well with prolonged prosperity. Undisciplined and unregulated greed, often marketed as "vision," and associated with easy credit led to the stock market crash of October 1929. That event signalled an abrupt end to the spectacular growth of the "Roaring Twenties." The long and very painful descent of the world's major stock markets took three and a half years to reach bottom and by then stock averages had lost 89 percent of their 1929 values. Recovery would be even slower. Greed was replaced by fear; irrational exuberance was replaced by despondency.

World trade shrank by two-thirds in the global slowdown from 1929 to 1934 as economic nationalism manifested by protectionism and "beggar thy neighbour" policies became the order of the day. Canada's largest trading partner led the way, on average doubling tariffs on 20,000 items in accordance with the infamous Smoot-Hawley *Tariff Act* passed by Congress in mid-1930. Canada and many other countries retaliated, building their own tariff walls, but with an economy so dependent on commodity exports, especially to the United States (U.S.) market, Canadians suffered disproportionately. Canada's Gross National Product fell over 40 percent between 1929 and 1930. Wages fell, and by 1933 — generally accepted as the deepest point of the depression — unemployment in Canada had reached 27 percent.

Some relief for Canada followed the Imperial Economic Conference held in Ottawa in 1932. As a result of deliberations by representatives from the British Commonwealth and Empire, a system of preferential trade agreements among the member states was established. The United Kingdom (U.K.) market, especially, began to absorb a great deal of the exports which Canada had formerly traded with the U.S. This Commonwealth link played a vital role in enabling Canada to stabilize its balance of payments. Whole markets switched to Commonwealth and Empire sources as it would be five years before the U.S. was amenable to renegotiation of some of the harsher elements of her trade restrictions on imports from Canada.

As if tariff walls, non-tariff barriers, trade embargoes, boycotts, preferences, and foreign exchange problems were not causing enough global misery, new sources of turbulence arose with the arrival of expansionist policies and militarism in Japan, Italy, and Germany during this unhappy decade. Japan forcibly annexed Manchuria in 1931 and then continued a progressive policy of aggression against a weak China which led to all-out war in 1937. Mussolini's Italy invaded a defenceless Ethiopia in 1935 and the League of Nations proved powerless to stop him. Hitler rose to power in Germany in 1933 and five years later started his takeover of Europe by annexing Austria. Both Germany and Russia meddled in the tragedy of the Spanish Civil War from 1936–1939. The world drifted inexorably into World War II, starting in Europe in September 1939 and then spreading to the Pacific and Far East in December 1941.

The onset of the depression found Canadian governments at all levels in debt from excessive infrastructure expansion. The federal government assumed debt of over two billion dollars in creating the Canadian National Railway from its bankrupt antecedents. In British Columbia (B.C.) the builders of the Pacific Great Eastern Railway defaulted on their government guaranteed bonds, so that in 1918 the province inherited this albatross, which soon became the "Province's Greatest Expense." Still in power in 1929, Mackenzie King exuded confidence that the crisis would soon pass and so, doing nothing, lost the summer election in 1930 to R. B. Bennett. Though fumbling at first, Bennett eventually tried to emulate the "New Deal" programs of Roosevelt in the U.S., but the provinces challenged Ottawa's right to implement plans that might infringe on their constitutional turf. By the time King was re-elected in October 1935, recovery was underway, although it would be 1939 before the Canadian economy returned to 1929 levels.

THE ADMINISTRATION OF NATIONAL PORTS

Vancouver's Harbour Commission was not alone in receiving loans from Ottawa for port development. By 1929, $150 million had been made available to Harbour Commissions in Montreal, Quebec City, St John and Halifax, as well as Vancouver — and on similar terms. There were, however, problems with the loans and with some port administrations. Only Vancouver and Montreal were honouring their obligation to pay interest on the loans and Vancouver alone had demonstrated intent to repay the loans by establishing and maintaining a sinking fund. In addition, some Commissions were making commitments to new and costly projects without prior approval of the Minister. There was the perception of inappropriate and incompetent political appointments to Harbour Commissions and this was causing irritation and frustration in maritime communities. Furthermore, overbuilding of facilities — clearly a waste of taxpayer's money — had led some eastern ports into serious financial difficulties and given rise to unseemly competition between them.

Recognizing the mounting problems, the new R. B. Bennett government, in early 1931, appointed Sir Alexander Gibb, a highly respected British engineer and port administrator, to conduct an inquiry. Gibb studied the existing Harbour Commission system in Canada with emphasis on assessing efficiency, needs, and management of each Commission port.

As with the railroads, there had been overbuilding during the boom years, followed by fierce competition, bankruptcies, and government bailouts and takeovers in leaner times.

Gibb reported to Parliament on April 6, 1932. Among his general observations and conclusions he stressed that:

- Canadian ports were vital units in the national transportation system.
- National ports must serve more than local interests.
- Almost all Canadian ports were federal government property.
- National ports have needed, and will continue to need, subsidization from the federal treasury. Their operation should not be measured solely on the usual criteria of business and economics.
- Federal subsidization required close central control.
- The construction of facilities in Canadian ports had reached or exceeded present needs.

Accordingly, he recommended that all 14 existing Harbour Commissions be abolished and be replaced with a harbour manager in each port. The harbour manager would be directly responsible to a central board in Ottawa that in turn would be directly responsible to the Minister of Transport. Gibb also held that the control of port affairs should be non-political, suggesting that existing harbour commissions were "official organizations for the control of patronage" and had a "stronger political than business outlook."

Among Gibb's recommendations for Vancouver were:

- That there be no further additions to grain terminals, as the port's existing plant could handle 150 million bushels annually, well in excess of available traffic.
- That track storage yards needed expansion.
- That grain traffic should carry its fair share of the cost of the port's operation.
- That all sawmills should be moved out of Burrard Inlet and False Creek.
- That the Harbour Commission railway should be abandoned in favour of a cooperative agreement between the CPR, CNR, and Great Northern railways.
- That Vancouver port capital should be written down by $7 million to a manageable $15 million.
- That the existing design of the inoperable second narrows bridge constituted a serious menace to navigation and should not be used in its reconstruction.
- That a first narrows bridge crossing was not needed at the present time.

For New Westminster and North Fraser ports Gibb concluded and recommended:

- That the ports of Vancouver, North Fraser, and New Westminster be merged into one port authority.
- That the federal government had spent approximately $7 million on jetties and training works to improve the navigable main and north arm channels of the Fraser River, in addition to the costly annual programs of dredging, reclamation, and other works.

- That there was nothing in the Canadian Constitution that obliged the federal government to fund projects to provide free access from the open sea to New Westminster, or any other port in the Dominion.
- That Fraser traffic was subsidized, as neither shipping, nor traffic had contributed to the cost of works carried out to make the Fraser River channel navigable.
- That, as New Westminster traffic was 70 percent lumber, a new large lumber assembly wharf should be established, which would handle product from both the existing mills on the river plus those to be moved out of Burrard Inlet and False Creek.
- That existing competition between Vancouver and New Westminster was artificial and only made possible by extensive and continual federal outlays.

It is not difficult to imagine the vigorous opposition to much of this report from New Westminster, whose three-member Harbour Commission, unlike Vancouver's, included a municipal representative.

Gibb's prime recommendation was for centralizing the administration of Canada's national harbours. On the West Coast he carried this centralization theme further with the advice that Vancouver "*should not be handicapped or prejudiced by subsidized competition*" and that "*if Vancouver is to attain the position that is planned for it, it can only do so if it be protected from establishment of a competitive port further north, which could only exist on direct or indirect subsidization.*" Gibb suggested no time limit for these recommendations. Clearly, they were directed at New Westminster and Prince Rupert, respectively. Though unquestionably music to Vancouver ears, they created discord in the other two ports. New Westminster had the political clout to fight Gibb's recommendation. Prince Rupert did not. This second Gateway Port's development was, unquestionably, held back for the next four decades by Vancouver's and Ottawa's enthusiastic acceptance of the latter recommendation.

Gibb's report was shelved by the Bennett government, and then resurrected by C. D. Howe, the newly appointed Minister of Marine in the King government that replaced Bennett in the October 1935 election. Not all Gibb's recommendations were accepted, but in 1936 a new National Harbours Board (NHB) was created by an act of parliament. This act abolished the Harbour Commissions of Montreal, Vancouver, Quebec City, Halifax and St. John, and re-established them as port authorities. It left the New Westminster Harbour Commission intact. Under the new act, each of the port authorities was to have a local advisory committee and a port manager who reported directly to the Ottawa based central administration, which was supervised by three appointed commissioners. Specialized services such as port engineering would be provided from this central body to each NHB port as required. The head office would report to Parliament through the Minister of Marine.

In succeeding years, there were a number of additions to the original complement of five NHB ports including the tenth, Prince Rupert, in 1972.

The NHB was set up to centrally control, administer, and provide specialized professional services to Canada's major public ports. Established in the middle of the Great Depression in response to past excesses, it was guided for at least two decades, by a policy of retrenchment rather than development of the ports under its jurisdiction. It was perceived in the west to be strongly influenced by political pressures from St. Lawrence and Maritime interests, while neglectful of the needs and aspirations of West Coast ports. The often politicized Ottawa bureaucracy exercised such excessively rigid control over capital expenditures that they tended to stifle initiative. Under the *National Harbours Board Act*, the new Vancouver Port Authority was restricted to a spending limit of $10,000 without prior approval from NHB headquarters in Ottawa. This ludicrously tight rein, established in mid depression, caused much local frustration and tedious delays in accomplishing worthwhile goals.

Though flawed, and most certainly not free of political influence, the NHB functioned to administer the major public ports of Canada until it was replaced in 1983 by the new "National Ports Policy," which began breaking with the long Canadian tradition of public ownership, investment and management of all ports and harbours.

LOCAL PORT ADMINISTRATION
AT VANCOUVER AND NEW WESTMINSTER

Federal legislation passed in 1913 had created Harbour Commissions to administer several Canadian ports including Vancouver and New Westminster. Vancouver's port included Burrard Inlet, English Bay, and False Creek. Prior to this, there had been no central administration or overall planning and development depended solely on the private sector. The new Vancouver Harbour Commission (VHC) was tasked to act as trustee for all foreshore crown lands not in dispute with the CPR.

Since Confederation, very substantial public funds had been provided for navigational aids, marine surveys, and improvements to the entry channel into Burrard Inlet at first narrows. In New Westminster, this funding source covered the cost of annual river dredging and snag removal programs, as well as expensive attempts to confine the lower river into a narrower, deeper, and faster flowing stream with a more easily maintainable navigation channel. The port was not expected to use its revenues to repay Ottawa for these continuing expenditures.

With funding provided by Ottawa in response to local importuning voiced through their Member of Parliament, H. H. Stevens, the new VHC proceeded to build a fine new Government Pier (later known as Lapointe Pier) as well as Dominion No.1 grain elevator, Vancouver's first.

Then, to enable Commission ports to further develop the infrastructure needed to capitalize on the booming post-war maritime trade, Ottawa passed legislation, in mid-1919, to provide loans to Harbour Commissions for works approved by the Minister of Marine. These loans were to be secured by debentures issued by the borrowing Commission. They were to pay 5 percent interest and were issued on a commitment by each Commission to provide for repayment by making annual contributions to a sinking fund.

Over the next 10 years the VHC tapped this source of funding to build Ballantyne Pier, grain elevators and jetties, a lumber assembly wharf, a waterfront railway, and to acquire and begin development of the Hastings Mill site. The Commissioners deemed these and other lesser facilities necessary to cope with the seemingly limitless growth of the port's traffic.

VANCOUVER IN THE THIRTIES

In 1929 the port handled 4.9 million tonnes (5.4 million tons) of foreign import and export cargoes, a spectacular increase over the 1.2 million tons over the docks in 1921. Export commodities made up two-thirds of this movement as measured by weight with wheat dominating at 55 percent and lumber next at 17 percent. Vancouver led all Canadian ports in the movement of export cargo. This great surge in traffic had been made possible by the investment of substantial amounts of both public and private capital in a variety of new port facilities. This was especially the case for the specialized terminals required to handle the rapid post-war growth in grain throughput, made possible when the Panama Canal shortcut to Atlantic markets became available. Though certainly not clear at the time, the pattern of terminal development in place at the end of 1929 would remain largely unchanged for the next 20 years.

The severe contraction in world trade during the thirties inhibited further growth and development, but both wheat and lumber, the port's two main exports, were still in demand worldwide, albeit at very low prices. Average annual throughput tonnage for the decade was only 7.5 percent less than the average for the period 1925–1929. Lumber exports fell off precipitously at first, then, as the British preferential tariff took effect, they recovered and surpassed all previous records during the latter half of the decade. Grain, on the other hand, held up well at first, but successive droughts resulted in crop failures and the formerly large surplus stocks were disposed of by mid-decade. Consequently, the total grain movement for the three years 1937–1939 fell below 2 million tons, slightly less than the tonnage of lumber shipped over the same time period.

Though Vancouver's terminals handled 95 percent of the grain exported from the West Coast during the 1930s, the port's share of the growing lumber exports from B.C. fell during the decade from 55 percent to about one-third, as New Westminster and Vancouver Island ports played an increasing role. Exports of canned salmon held steady over the decade, while flour shipments decreased by two-thirds. When Consolidated Mining and Smelting acquired a controlling interest in New Westminster's Pacific Coast Terminals in 1935 most export shipments of metals and fertilizers moved there from Vancouver.

Trade patterns for Canadian exports shifted during the 1930s with U.S. markets closed by tariff walls and replaced by a strong shift to the U.K. and other Commonwealth countries. A huge excess of shipping drove rates to a quarter of those quoted in 1929 and with bunker fuel selling for $1.50 a barrel the long haul to markets in Europe, the Antipodes, or even South Africa became economically feasible. Orient trade, however, suffered as a result of Japan's aggression against China, which started with the "Manchuria Incident" in 1931 and led inexorably to full scale war with China in 1937.

WATERFRONT DEVELOPMENTS

In mid-1929 Parliament authorized a further $10 million loan to the VHC to fund approved new facilities. Plans included storage additions to all three Commission grain elevators and development of the recently acquired Hastings Mill site. A grand new Ocean Pier was to be the centrepiece for the site of the demolished mill and in addition fishermen's wharves, a cold storage plant, wharves for coastal vessels, a lumber assembly facility, storehouses, and office buildings were all under consideration. The stock market crash and associated economic collapse brought an abrupt end to many of these plans.

Storage additions to the VHC No. 1 elevator annex and to the VHC No. 3 terminal did proceed and when completed in 1932 the grain storage capacity of the port had increased from 14.4 to 17.8 million bushels. This compared favourably with Montreal's 15.2 million bushel capacity.

In 1930 the port could boast 24 piers capable of accommodating 62 vessels. With the uncertainty stemming from the global economic crisis it was deemed prudent to defer development at the valuable Hastings Mill site. In fact, it would be another 30 years before Centennial Pier opened on that site. Further development there resulted in Vancouver's first container handling facility in 1970.

The CNR pier and warehouse was mostly destroyed by fire on August 10, 1930 but was promptly rebuilt. Likewise, Canadian Pacific's Pier D was totally destroyed by fire in 1938, but it was not replaced. The Commission's plans for a fishermen's wharf and cold storage plant did proceed and, in addition, a tank farm for storing vegetable and fish oils was constructed on the south shore of the inlet. These tanks received edible vegetable oils for the first time in September 1933, the beginning of a new commodity for the port to handle.

For the most part, the depression years were a time of consolidating the spectacular growth spurt of the 1920s. Funds, both public and private, were scarce and most certainly not available for visionary projects.

WATERFRONT STRIFE

A potent mix of factors, superimposed on the general misery and high unemployment so prevalent during the great depression, led to the infamous "Battle of Ballantyne Pier" on June 18, 1935 — the blackest day in Vancouver's waterfront labour history.

The first waterfront union in B.C., the International Longshoremen's Association

(ILA), formed locals in Vancouver and Prince Rupert in 1910. Other locals soon followed and over the next decade the union succeeded in winning better wages and working conditions for their workers from a reluctant Shipping Federation, the organization that represented waterfront labour employers. In 1923, the Federation decided to break the union with a lockout and the use of non-union strike breakers whom they protected with armed guards. After two months of this intimidation the ILA collapsed and the Shipping Federation set up a new "company union" to represent only those dockworkers acceptable to their employers.

Though passive at first, the Vancouver and District Waterfront Workers Association (VDWWA) soon came into conflict with the Shipping Federation. In 1933 communist organizers gained influence in the affairs of the union and, with a different agenda, sought to encourage membership militancy and strike action. Local political and business leaders viewed this trend with alarm and claimed that waterfront unrest was part of an international communist conspiracy, though historians now agree on the substance and legitimacy of the waterfront workers grievances. Passions rose on both sides.

The spark that lit the conflagration came in May 1935, as a result of a strike by waterfront workers in Powell River who were trying to form a union. Strike breakers were employed by the company and, as a result, Vancouver longshoremen refused to handle "hot cargo" from Powell River. The Shipping Federation responded by locking out the union dockworkers and the war was on.

On June 18, 1935 union members and their supporters, variously estimated to number between 1,000 and 5,000, headed for Ballantyne Pier with the intent of dissuading strike breakers from unloading vessels. They were blocked from entering the Pier by several hundred federal, provincial and municipal police, many of them mounted on horses. When they refused to disperse they were attacked with tear gas and charged by mounted police who wielded clubs. In the ensuing battle, which lasted for three hours, at least 100 demonstrators and 40 police were injured, some seriously enough to be hospitalized. The strike and lockout continued until December 9 and ended with the VDWWA much weakened.

Though this demonstration of anger and frustration was broken, longshoremen continued to fight for the right to form an independent union and control the allocation of labour to waterfront employers. In 1944, Local 500 of the International Longshore and Warehouse Union (ILWU) was formed in Vancouver and, over the next decade, that independent union formed locals in most B.C. ports and assumed responsibility for representing the best interests of waterfront labour.

This most unfortunate episode left a legacy of bitterness and mistrust between waterfront labour and the employers. One consequence of this unhappy relationship would be the long held resistance to removing the "container clause" contained in the 1970 union contract; a clause that was at least partially responsible for the port's slow progress in developing its container business in the seventies and eighties.

HARBOUR NARROWS AND BRIDGES

Though new waterfront facility developments at the Southern Gateway during the 1930s were severely limited, the bridging projects needed to span Burrard Inlet, False Creek, and the Fraser River were undertaken with both public and private funding.

Road and rail access to the north shore was interrupted on September 19, 1930 when a barge collided with the second narrows bridge and one of its spans dropped into the harbour. The owners were eventually forced into bankruptcy and the VHC assumed responsibility for providing a crossing at that crucial point. There were radically differing ideas on how to achieve this. Some believed the narrows should be dammed, while others felt that the remains of the existing span could be used if a new lift span was placed in the centre of the channel. A Royal Commission staffed by eastern based engineers recommended in mid-1931 that a "ship channel" be constructed at the site along with the re-erection of the existing span in the same place. Ignoring the recommendation, the Harbour Commission elected to proceed with a new lift span for the existing bridge, located mid-channel rather than near the south shore, and proceeded to raise $1 million through a bond issue to cover the cost. The reconstructed bridge finally reopened June 18, 1934 and a year later the Harbour Commission's takeover of the bridge was made legal. The four-year loss of access to the north shore was a major contributing factor in forcing the North Vancouver City and District into receivership in 1933.

A plan to build a bridge across first narrows had been soundly defeated in a 1928 plebiscite, but the idea was revived in 1933 when British investors indicated an interest in providing the needed financing. The marine community, sensitive to the "indifferent entrance" to Burrard Inlet, insisted that any crossing at first narrows must be at a high level and with a span of at least 540 m (1,800 ft.) between towers. Their sensitivity on this issue related to the inadequacy of the existing navigation channel with its limited depth, currents, and shoals. In 1933 the channel was declared to be 450 m (1,500 ft.) wide at the 9 m (30 ft.) contour, but having the potential for 12 m (40 ft.) depth at low water.

In October 1936, C. D. Howe, Minister of Marine, accepted the proposal that Parthia Shoal and several other shoals be removed to create a 10.5 m (35 ft.) channel depth over its length and make the harbour entrance navigable at all tidal levels for the largest vessels using the port. Again, in 1939 the federal government acknowledged the urgent need for a program to remove several million cubic yards of material, but war intervened, postponing the award of a major dredging contract until 1953.

After long negotiation and some design compromises, the Lions Gate Bridge project went ahead, financed by British capital. It opened in November 1938 with a 465 m (1,550 ft.) centre span that cleared the water by 60 m (200 ft.). The Burrard Bridge spanned False Creek in 1932 and the provincially funded Pattullo Bridge crossed the Fraser River crossed at New Westminster in 1937.

GRAIN EXPORTS FROM VANCOUVER

In the early 1930s grain constituted 30 percent of Canadian exports by value. Figures for the routing of those exports (including wheat, barley, oats, rye and flax) during the 1930/31 crop year, show that 38.5 percent moved through five eastern Canadian ports, 32.3 percent via East Coast U.S. ports and 29.2 percent through the West Coast Canadian ports. Of this latter amount, 95 percent moved through Vancouver's terminals. Vancouver's hugely successful entry into handling the overseas export of Canadian grain was, at least in part, at the expense of winter shipments through the U.S. East Coast ports. With low ocean freight rates, growing markets in the Orient, and expansion of grain cultivation north and west in Alberta, the long term prospect for an increased share of grain movement through West Coast ports seemed assured.

With the new additions to VHC No. 1 annex and VHC No. 3 elevator completed in 1932 the port's grain storage capacity rose to 17.8 million bushels. During that calendar year, these terminals loaded out 104.7 million bushels of wheat, a new record that stood for the next two decades. Even though this movement dented the very large carryover stocks of Canadian wheat from prior years, prices were miserably low and prairie producers suffered severe economic hardship for the rest of the decade. Ironically, as prices began to improve, production collapsed due to recurring drought conditions over much of the growing area. Once the carryover surplus stocks from former bumper crops was disposed of, there remained very little new crop grain available for export, especially in the last three years of the decade.

The Central Selling Agency, which had been established by the Pools was an early victim of the collapse of grain prices. By January 1930, wheat prices had fallen below their initial offer to farmers and the Pools turned to their provincial governments for help. By 1931, with no price relief in sight, the provinces turned to Ottawa to provide at least a base price payment to farmers. The new Bennett government reluctantly succumbed to pressure from the Pools and their bankers, and provided a limited guarantee to cover the 1930/31 crop losses only. The demise of the Pool's Central Selling Agency soon followed, to be replaced by increasing federal government involvement, which led to the creation of the Canadian Wheat Board (CWB) in 1935. At first the CWB operated as a temporary and voluntary agency to which producers could sell and be guaranteed an initial price for wheat only. It soon developed into a permanent, compulsory, centralized marketing agency with total control over the purchase, delivery, storage, sale, and movement to export ports of wheat, barley, oats, and rye.

By 1930 four West Coast ports had functioning grain terminals. However, the Vancouver terminals firmly held a 95 percent share of the total movement of this commodity during the next decade. Indeed, the Victoria terminal was closed for four of those 10 years and Prince Rupert's for three.

In response to America's extremely high protectionist tariffs, the 1932 Imperial Economic Conference established a preference of six cents per bushel for wheat shipped from any port within the British Commonwealth. In retaliation U.S. railways cut their rates for Canadian grain movement to New York terminals. Canadian railways then countered by reducing their rates for grain bound for St. Lawrence or Maritime ports. That reduction coupled with a rate war in 1933 among Great Lakes ship-owners and the opening of a new outlet for export grain at Churchill (with a very low handling tariff) led to demands from Vancouver terminal operators, strongly backed by the B.C. Government, for reduced rail rates for west-bound grain. This was very vigorously opposed by those involved in the eastern movement, still upset by the shift of one-third of Canadian exports to the West Coast during the 1920s.

In summary, although production during the worst of the "dust bowl" years fell by nearly half, the Wheat Board was able at first to maintain a fair level of exports by drawing down surplus stocks carried over from prior years. However, with the 1937 crop less than half average and the surpluses gone, exports had to be drastically reduced. Vancouver terminals moved only 18.8 million bushels in calendar 1937, less than one-fifth the amount moved in the banner year 1932. Shipments in 1938 and 1939 were a little better, but during the next four war years very little export grain moved through the port's terminals.

NEW WESTMINSTER IN THE THIRTIES

Vessel calls at the river port had increased dramatically from 13 in 1921 to 248 in 1929. They were to double again to 509 by 1939. The increase during the thirties was largely a result of investments made by Pacific Coast Terminals (PCT), the CNR supported private company that had, in 1929, purchased and then expanded the facilities built by the Fraser River Dock and Stevedoring Company in 1925 on the city waterfront. These facilities now included a cold storage plant and the commodities handled included lumber, metals, fish, agricultural products, as well as general cargo. During the early years of the depression, however, markets for these products were devastated. This, coupled with labour unrest leading to prolonged strikes, resulted in PCT revenues that were insufficient to meet financing commitments, so the bondholders forced its sale in 1935. Consolidated Mining and Smelting (CM&S), owned by the CPR, acquired 55 percent of the company in a reorganization that saved the City of New Westminster from having to meet its guarantee of the unpaid interest on PCT debentures. With CM&S a majority shareholder, the company and the port benefitted from all the traffic it generated as a very large exporter of metals and fertilizer as well as importer of phosphate rock. Markets recovered by mid-decade and by 1936 the port recorded a peak throughput of 916,380 tonnes (1,008,019 tons). After the reorganization, PCT was profitable and by 1939 was in a position to upgrade and expand its facilities.

Though supposedly complete in 1928, the New Westminster Harbour Commission grain elevator required further investment before it could operate. Leased at first to the Fraser River Elevator Company and later to Searle Grain, the terminal moved only very modest amounts of export grain each year during the 1930–1939 period. Over that decade, it handled a total of 16 million bushels and most of that represented overflow from the Vancouver operations.

Ongoing programs to further define and deepen the navigable river channel continued to be an urgent priority as traffic, vessel size, and loaded draft increased. Annual removal of snags, as well as dredging programs to maintain at least a 7.5m (25 ft.) depth in the main channel were essential and, since confederation, these had been funded by Ottawa. The fifth in a series of snag boats for the river, the *Samson V*, was commissioned in 1937 and, further special projects involving substantial federal expenditures were undertaken in the continuing effort to confine the river between rock groins and jetties. These works were expected to speed the river's flow so that more of its silt load would be carried out to sea, thereby lessening the need for dredging to maintain the channel depth.

When the Pattullo Bridge was completed in November 1937 the combined road rail bridge across the river, built by the province in 1904 had its upper road level removed and its ownership transferred to the federal Department of Public Works. The fine new $4 million high-level road bridge had been a major plank in Premier "Duff" Pattullo's election platform in 1933. It had been opposed by Vancouver interests who favoured, instead, a planned low-level bridge at Ladner. That, of course, would have virtually eliminated marine traffic on the south channel of the river.

VICTORIA IN THE THIRTIES

Victoria's misguided initiative to participate in the grain export business very soon acquired the local sobriquet, "Our White Elephant." From its opening in the summer of 1928 to the end of the 1938/39 crop year, the terminal handled only 5,828,509 bushels of wheat and, during four of those years the terminal was effectively closed. By 1936 the City of Victoria, guarantor of bonds issued to build the terminal, foreclosed on the Panama Pacific Grain Company. The terminal limped along, sporadically used by several operators, until finally demolished in 1976.

During 1930, the federal government undertook some dredging and rock removal in the shallow inner harbour. The Ogden Point dock complex saw regular calls by the transpacific *Empress* liners of the CPR as well as freighters loading lumber.

The naval base at Esquimalt welcomed HMCS *Skeena* in 1931, the first of a new series of destroyers for the Royal Canadian Navy, built in Britain at a cost of $3.3 million each. The graving dock completed in 1927 was underutilized during the depression years, but was destined to become by far the port's most valuable non-military asset.

PRINCE RUPERT IN THE THIRTIES

Canada's second Pacific Gateway, with its superb natural harbour and the best connecting rail corridor to the interior of North America of any Pacific Coast port had been condemned to near oblivion as an out-port at the end of a little used branch line, after the CNR was created from its bankrupt antecedents. Harsh American protectionist policies countered by the British Commonwealth trade agreements resulted in the reorientation of Canadian exports during the thirties to the U.K. Japan's aggressive moves in the Far East increasingly limited trade across the Pacific. Prince Rupert's location, though 800 km (500 miles) closer to Asian ports, was 480 km (300 miles) further to Panama than Vancouver. This became a liability. Vessel owners demanded special inducement to pick up cargo destined for Europe at the northern port.

The port had only three major deep-sea marine installations in 1930, the Ocean Dock, the shipyard and dry dock, and the grain terminal. Of these facilities, the latter, completed in 1926, had started off fairly well. Leased to Alberta Wheat Pool, it had handled eight million bushels of wheat during the 1927/28 crop year, 8 percent of the West Coast movement for that 12-month period. That modest level of throughput, however, set the record for the next 24 years. With completion of its large terminal in Vancouver, the Alberta Wheat Pool consigned the Prince Rupert terminal to an overflow role. That role would be its lot for the next 50 years, only to be sparingly used — and not always then even — when Vancouver terminals could not meet Wheat Board export commitments. Between 1930 and 1939 the terminal handled only 6.6 million bushels and for three of those years it was closed.

The shipyard and dry dock, managed by CNR, kept moderately busy early in the decade with work on fishing vessels, CN owned and other coastal ships, as well as refits and repairs to Canadian Government Merchant Marine vessels. At times it was the largest employer in the city with up to 250 employees. Later in the depression years, however, with the final disposal of the CGMM fleet, work became very scarce and Ottawa grumbled at paying a $76,970 annual subsidy to keep the facility open. That amount, however, paled alongside the $247,500 yearly subsidy to St. John Dry Dock and Shipbuilding, or even the $112,500 to Burrard Dry Dock in Vancouver.

Japan's annexation of Manchuria in 1931 and its subsequent aggression against China, culminating in all-out war in 1937, was the final straw in condemning the port, built on the expectation of a busy trade with the Orient, to almost total somnolence. Ironically, subsequent Japanese adventures in the Pacific and South Asia would propel the port into a period of frantic activity early in the next decade.

Though certainly frustrated by the turn of fate that had left the aspiring port a backwater on the West Coast, Prince Rupert's remaining 5,000 citizens, with little or no political clout, focused on their viable fishing industry to survive the dark depression years.

CHAPTER FIVE

The War Years — 1939 to 1945

S adly, the "War to End All Wars" did no such thing. After the short span of 20 years modern warfare again ravaged Europe. The Western World had enjoyed a spectacular decade of booming "good times" and then endured an equal period of economic misery, the inevitable hangover from the "Roaring Twenties." During those depressed years, increasingly aggressive actions by dictators in Italy and Germany, as well as militarists in Japan and civil war in Spain, set the stage for a renewed outbreak of war, this time on a global scale and an almost unimaginable death toll of 60 million.

The exigencies of war transformed Canada and its depression related problems. For the next six years the country's economy was run on a wartime basis with ports, railways, and shipyards key components of the national war effort. The struggle to maintain the vital north Atlantic supply line to Britain affected both Western Gateways, while the long neglected northern "orphan" also became deeply involved in the primarily American war in the Pacific.

During World War I, German submarines sank 2,510 merchant ships, 60 percent of them British, before the Royal Navy inaugurated a convoy system in the spring of 1917. This bitter experience led to convoys being established very early in World War II, but despite the protection offered, 1,281 vessels were lost to submarines, mines, aircraft, and raiders by the end of 1940. Most of these losses were British flag ships and represented over one-fifth of her 1939 merchant fleet. By VE day 5,150 Allied ships totalling 21,570,720 tons had been sunk and 82 percent of these had been lost between 1939 and the end of 1942. Winston Churchill writes in the second volume of his series entitled, *The Second World War* that, "The only thing that ever frightened me during the war was the U boat peril."

Sea transport was the paramount war problem for the western Allies. Britain's supply lines were very nearly cut and, if the U boats had succeeded in strangling that unsinkable base, the eventual liberation of Europe from Nazi tyranny would have been virtually impossible.

The prime consequences for Canada's Pacific Gateways were twofold and both stemmed from the rapidly decreasing cargo carrying capacity of the free world's merchant fleets. That decrease was due to both vessel losses and to the one-third reduction in efficiency that was inherent in the convoy system. A program to build very large numbers of a standard steel cargo vessel was needed urgently and production on the scale required could only take place in the "New World." As obvious was the need to reduce shipping distance to the bare minimum, thereby limiting exposure to the perils of wartime passage and using available capacity to the maximum.

The distance from Vancouver to the United Kingdom (U.K.) via Panama is triple that from Atlantic ports such as Halifax or Sydney, so it was inevitable that by the end of 1940 few ships would be sent to pick up cargoes such as grain on the West Coast. This situation continued until late in the war when new built ships coupled with much reduced losses made vessels available for long voyages.

THE SOUTHERN GATEWAY

In 1914, deep-sea shipping out of Vancouver was confined to Canadian Pacific's transpacific service, Canadian Australasian's service to the Antipodes, calls by Blue Funnel Line and Harrison Line vessels, occasional steamship tramps to the U.K. via Cape Horn and a few sailing ships. Lumber was the main export commodity with 35 million board feet (approximately 48,000 tonnes) shipped from south coast B.C. ports that year to Australia, South America, China, and Japan plus a paltry 5 million board feet (7,000 tonnes) to Europe. There was no reefer service, no bulk grain export, no metal export, and a total of only 121 vessel calls for the year.

With shipping freely available after 1920, the port underwent a transformation with its new ability to serve markets on the United States (U.S.) Atlantic seaboard and Europe via the Panama Canal. By 1939, lumber exports from British Columbia (B.C.) ports had increased to a record 1.4 billion feet board measure (1.95 million tonnes) with about one-third of that amount loaded in Burrard Inlet and another quarter loaded at Fraser River wharves. Since 1922, however, grain moving through the new terminals on the Inlet had overtaken lumber as the leading commodity export in tonnage, with the sole exception of 1937. In 1928, the banner year for grain throughput, a total of 1,325 vessels loaded 5.1 million tonnes (5.6 million tons) of cargo in Burrard Inlet and, though grain exports were much reduced in the latter half of the 1930s, the port still loaded 1,049 vessels with 1.91 million tonnes (2.1 million tons) of cargo in 1939.

War renewed demand for materials and, despite severe disruption of normal import-export trade patterns, there was a very real need for the products of B.C.'s forests, farms, mines, and fisheries. The increasing scarcity of ships resulted in almost all prairie grain destined for overseas export being carried by rail to eastern Canadian and northeast U.S. ports for loading. Due to facility limitations at Canada's Atlantic coast ports, especially in winter, U.S. ports increased their share of Canadian grain exports from 14.4 percent in 1940 to 43 percent in 1943 — virtually all at the expense of B.C. ports.

Very little grain passed through Vancouver terminals between 1940 and 1943. The overland diversion to Atlantic ports put a very heavy burden on the already overtaxed railroads. Their normal equipment suppliers were now heavily engaged building such items as ships engines and tanks, resulting in difficulty replacing worn locomotives and rolling stock. As ships became available in 1944, grain exports through the West Coast picked up again and by crop year 1945/46 had reached 61 million bushels (1.66 million tonnes), the largest amount since the 1932/33 year.

With Britain cut off from her regular Baltic lumber suppliers, and with an urgent need for "airplane spruce" and plywood, the products of B.C.'s coastal forests were in great demand and those exports to the U.K. held up well through 1940 before settling to about half their 1939 level for the rest of the war.

New Westminster port facilities were little used during World War II. In 1943 only 89 deep-sea vessels called at the port.

THE DEFENSE OF THE SOUTHERN GATEWAY

For the first 27 months of World War II, the Pacific was a virtual non-combat zone. There was no powerful squadron of German cruisers loose in the North Pacific this time to create a near panic on the West Coast.

The Royal Canadian Navy (RCN) base at Esquimalt, 75 miles from Vancouver, was a legacy from the Royal Navy. Along with nearby fixed artillery installations it protected the southern entrance to the Strait of Georgia. The northern entrance to the Strait was protected by a fixed gun battery on Yorke Island in Johnstone Strait.

Very early in the war the four destroyers based at Esquimalt were transferred to Halifax to operate in the north Atlantic and, until the attack on Pearl Harbour, only a very few minor naval vessels were left on the West Coast. After December 7, 1941 the defense of the Canada's West Coast depended mainly on the U.S. Navy working with what the RCN could spare from its primary, very heavy, and crucial Atlantic anti-submarine commitments. In June 1942 the Navy's vessel muster on the West Coast consisted of three auxiliary cruisers, seven corvettes, thirteen minesweepers, and a number of smaller craft plus the fishermen's reserve fleet. Shore facilities were, however, considerably expanded and included rehabilitating the original graving dock at Esquimalt and returning it to service. The Navy assumed management of the Port of Vancouver, fortifying its entrances and controlling all vessel movements.

Fortunately for the West Coast, the main Japanese military thrust was directed at Southeast Asia and their occupation of two islands in the Aleutian Chain was primarily a diversion undertaken in their attempt to take Midway Island. A Japanese submarine did make its presence felt off the B.C. coast on June 20, 1942 when it torpedoed the *Fort Camosun*, the first "North Sands" freighter built in Victoria, at the entrance to the Strait of Juan de Fuca. The same day, the sub shelled the Estevan lighthouse, but without serious damage. During the war eight vessels, mostly tankers, were sunk off the California coast, but at no time were the ports of Vancouver or New Westminster under any direct threat of attack. The only convoy assembled on the West Coast was the one carrying Canadian and U.S. troops to reoccupy the island of Kiska in August 1943.

SHIPBUILDING IN VANCOUVER AND VICTORIA

The extensive port installations built at both Canada's Pacific Gateways during the boom years of the 1920s were assets that could not be fully exploited during the war, due to the increasingly desperate shortage of ships. Despite the early establishment of the convoy system on the north Atlantic, Britain alone had lost one-fifth of her merchant fleet to enemy action by the end of 1940. With new warship production an absolute priority it was impossible for British shipyards to replace lost merchant tonnage. Consequently, in October 1940 the British Merchant Shipbuilding Mission came to North America to investigate yards in the U.S. and Canada. Their intent was to place orders for a large number of freighters of a single basic design — the relatively simple and easy to build "North Sands" general cargo vessel of 10,000 dead weight tons. The first order was for 60 vessels to be built in U.S. yards (and paid for in sterling) plus another 26 of the same type to be built in Canadian yards.

Concurrently, the Canadian Government placed orders for vessels of the same basic design and the U.S. Maritime Commission followed with a slightly modified variant, the famous "Liberty" ship. Vessels built in Canada were given names with the prefix *Fort* or *Park* and the first vessel completed on the West Coast, the *Fort St. James* was delivered by Burrard Dry Dock in North Vancouver in early 1942. Existing West Coast yards underwent rapid expansion and new yards were built. In April 1941, the federal government set up Wartime Merchant Shipping Ltd with H. R. MacMillan as president to coordinate, supervise, expand and expedite the construction of large numbers of this Standard Steel Freighter. The result of this enormous Canadian effort was the construction of 354 ships of the "North Sands" type in the nation's yards. Thirty-three were completed as stores or maintenance ships for the Royal Navy's fleet train in the Pacific. Primarily due to more favourable climatic conditions on the West Coast, a total of 255 of these vessels were built on 22 berths in seven B.C. yards. Of that number, 220 were completed in four large yards in Vancouver. It is worth noting that on a per capita basis Canada's production of merchant ships during the war substantially surpassed the much vaunted 2,710 "Liberty" ships completed by U.S. yards.

In addition to the *Forts* and *Parks*, a number of smaller cargo vessels and tankers were built in Canadian yards, and conversions and repairs were undertaken on existing tonnage. The navy was expanding very rapidly and hundreds of warships, ranging from destroyers and frigates to the smaller corvettes, minesweepers and patrol craft, as well as tugs, landing craft and other auxiliary vessels were required. Most of these vessels were built in yards on the Great Lakes and St. Lawrence waterway, or on the Atlantic coast. By mid-1943, 57,000 Canadian workers were employed in building merchant ships, while another 28,000 were engaged in construction of naval craft. At the construction peak, the four Vancouver area shipyards alone employed 25,000 men and women building "North Sands" type freighters. Another 5,000 local workers were engaged in making components for the new ships, including winches, boilers, shafting, and masts. Compared to pre-war rates, shipyard wages in 1940 of 90 cents per hour for skilled workers and 67.5 cents for unskilled were considered a bonanza. These rates were increased by 10 cents per hour in 1942 and employees working 48 hour weeks were paid for 50 hours. All shipyards provided training programs in riveting, welding, and other necessary skills.

War's mass destruction thus proved a bonanza for shipbuilding. For Vancouver especially, this activity more than made up for the considerable reduction in waterfront employment at the underutilized port facilities. Indeed, one of the port's major facilities, Lapointe Pier, was leased to Burrard Dry Dock in 1943 to convert 23 US-built escort aircraft carriers for use in the Royal Navy and the RCN. Both Burrard Dry Dock and North Vancouver Ship Repair yards added new floating dry docks in 1941 and 1942.

The worst wartime disaster on the Vancouver waterfront occurred on March 6, 1945 when the Vancouver built freighter *Greenhill Park* was shattered by a series of explosions while loading at Pier B-C. Eight men were killed and another 19 injured, and much damage was done to structures in the vicinity. The shattered vessel was later repaired and went to sea again in June 1946.

THE NORTHERN GATEWAY

Prince Rupert — the focus of so much enthusiasm in the century's first decade, before being left virtually dormant and all but abandoned for the next 30 years — at last achieved temporary recognition for the role it could play as a land-sea interface in the struggle against Japanese aggression in the Pacific. The port offered:

- A superb natural harbour widely recognized to be one of the three best on the planet
- Strategic value as the western terminus of the most northerly transcontinental railroad in North America
- An ideal base for the operation of naval and air forces in the Gulf of Alaska and Northwest Pacific
- A 20,000 ton floating dry dock equipped with repair and shipbuilding shops capable of building "North Sands" type cargo vessels or small warships.

By 1937 plans had been drawn for defending the West Coast in the event of war. For Prince Rupert these plans included the provision of anti-submarine nets, a signal station, vessel examination services, fixed artillery installations, local patrols by fishing craft, and auxiliary minesweepers. Before 1939 none of these naval plans for the port were implemented, though clearing of two sites for fixed artillery installations began in 1938. By November 1939 several medium and light guns were in place at Fort Barrett and Fort Frederick on opposite sides of the harbour entrance. These forts were manned by Canadian Army personnel. A start had been made on preparing the site for a seaplane base for the Royal Canadian Air Force at Seal Cove, although a long range patrol squadron did not become operational there until late in 1941.

Immediately after war was declared the Navy sent HMCS *Armentiers*, an old armed trawler, from Esquimalt to Prince Rupert to establish an examination service for the port. Several naval officers including a Naval Officer in Charge were posted to the port, taking over the quarters of the Royal Canadian Navy Volunteer Reserve division. Over the next 12 months a single line of anti-submarine nets were installed between Digby Island and Kaien Island to block the main harbour entrance. Metlakatla Pass was later closed with a log boom. Though the Navy's priorities were overwhelmingly directed to keeping the North Atlantic sea-lane to Britain open, development of Prince Rupert as a second naval establishment progressed through 1941. By mid-1942, barracks for 360 naval personnel had been built and minesweepers and patrol craft were based at the port. Plans were drawn up at Naval Headquarters to expand the base to support 18 warships. Few of these plans came to fruition. After the Battle of Midway in June 1942, the tide of war in the Pacific began to favour the Allies and the threat to the West Coast diminished accordingly. The number of RCN vessels based at the port peaked at ten, including three minesweepers and seven patrol craft in January 1945. A naval auxiliary group, the volunteer Fishermen's Reserve, which was made up of local fishing craft and their crews, conducted patrols off the west coast of the Queen Charlotte Islands (now Haida Gwaii) between 1942 and mid-1944.

The development of a strategic fuel oil reserve at the port did proceed. Three tanks holding 93,408 barrels of fuel were set into rock in Morse Creek basin with fuel lines laid onto the grain elevator dock. This installation was not, however, completed until the fall of 1944 and so saw little use during the war.

Certainly, the Navy's wartime presence in Prince Rupert was substantial, peaking at 804 personnel in January of 1945.

The U.S. military recognized the strategic value of Prince Rupert to the defense of Alaska very shortly after Pearl Harbour. It was obvious to them that using the northern port in place of any existing port in California, Oregon, or Washington would save time and reduce marine hazards, including the potential menace of enemy submarines off the coast. Thirty-five days after Pearl Harbour, the first U.S. military transport sailed from Prince Rupert to Alaska with men and supplies to bolster the very meager defenses of that enormous territory. By February 1942, the U.S. Army had decided to use Prince Rupert as their main embarkation base for troops, supplies and equipment for their Northwest Pacific Theatre of Operations. With the additional affront to U.S. pride caused by the Japanese occupation of Attu and Kiska in the Aleutian chain in June 1942, the strategic value of Prince Rupert increased exponentially as a base for mounting a recovery operation to regain the islands. With typical American gung-ho fervour a $16 million program of base development and port facility expansion was undertaken over the next two years at both Prince Rupert and nearby Port Edward on Porpoise Harbour. In Prince Rupert the U.S. Army extended the Ocean Dock and connected it to an enormous warehouse that straddled the CN rail yard. Barracks and administration offices were built in an area of the city later called Roosevelt

Hill. At Port Edward a large staging area consisting of 180 buildings was opened in March 1943 to accommodate the thousands of troops in transit through the port. Two wharves and 20 magazines for ammunition and bombs were constructed on Watson Island.

On July 17, 1944 the tragic explosion of 10,000 tons of ammunition at the Port Chicago annex to the Mare Island Navy Yard, in the San Francisco Bay area, killed 320 naval and civilian personnel and wounded another 390. The installation was destroyed and during the last year of the war the U.S. Navy turned to Port Edward's magazines and wharves on Watson Island to load vessels with over 100,000 tons of ammunition and bombs for the South Pacific Theatre.

At peak strength the U.S. sub port of embarkation at Prince Rupert reached 5,084 personnel. Between March 1943 and August 1945, 73,884 members of the military and related civilian workers embarked from the staging area to Alaska. During that period the outbound, waterborne, military-oriented cargo passing through the port totalled 1,019,684 tonnes (1,121,653 tons). Troop trains, ammunition trains, freight trains, and even an armoured train operating along the Skeena River put quite a strain on the old Grand Trunk line, which had had little use or maintenance since it was completed three decades earlier. For Prince Rupert, a major and lasting bonus from all the war related activity was the roughing-out of the highway along the Skeena, connecting the city to Terrace and the interior.

The role of the U.S. army in Prince Rupert during World War II was limited to the movement of troops, supplies, equipment, and ammunition for their Pacific Theatres of Operations. Defense of the port was a Canadian commitment, but included some assistance from the U.S., particularly in anti-aircraft defense.

The final eviction of the enemy from U.S. owned islands in the Aleutians in August 1943 and the shift of the Pacific war closer to the Japanese home islands reduced the strategic importance of Prince Rupert. The U.S. presence peaked in mid-1943 and, together with activity at Canadian army and air force installations, was substantially reduced during 1944.

Overseas exports of commercial cargoes from Prince Rupert during the war were negligible. The grain terminal loaded only two vessels with 392,000 bushels of wheat during the entire 1939–1945 period.

SHIPBUILDING IN PRINCE RUPERT IN WORLD WAR II

Prince Rupert's fully equipped shipyard and dry dock had, under CNR management, managed to stay open since the two CGMM vessels were completed in 1922. Indeed, at times it was the largest employer in the city. Repair and maintenance work (primarily on government owned vessels), plus some small boat and barge construction enabled the yard to keep a core group of skilled workers. After the mid-decade demise of the CGMM, activity reached a very low ebb, but soon after the outbreak of war the yard won contracts to build four Bangor class minesweepers for the RCN. These vessels were completed between

June 1941 and March 1942. While this program was underway, the yard prepared berths to construct the "North Sands" type standard steel freighter and, between mid–1942 and mid-1945, it delivered 13 of these vessels. In addition, Ottawa ordered a series of 15 "China Coaster" type small cargo vessels from West Coast yards, two of which were completed in Prince Rupert shortly after the war ended.

To provide manpower for this labour intensive work, hundreds of workers were brought to Prince Rupert from the Prairie Provinces and a federal agency, Wartime Housing, built several hundred, four- and six-bedroom "temporary" houses in the city to accommodate them. A few key personnel were "loaned" from British shipyards and major training programs for riveters and welders undertaken.

Of the vessels built during World War II, three were lost and a fourth heavily damaged. HMCS *Clayoquot*, the first minesweeper to be completed, was sunk by acoustic torpedo off Halifax on December 23, 1944 with a loss of eight lives. *Fort Stikine*, the first of the large steel freighters completed, was the focus of one of the worst merchant marine tragedies of the war. Loaded with ammunition and cotton she caught fire and eventually blew up on April 14, 1944, while docked in Bombay. Two explosions caused enormous damage to shore installations, as well as to eighteen other merchant ships and three warships, most of which were a total loss. At least 750 lives were lost and well over 3,000 injured in this tragedy. *Fort Mumford* was sunk in the Indian Ocean in May 1943 on her maiden voyage. She was carrying war supplies from Vancouver to Egypt when torpedoed by the Japanese Submarine *I 27*. The submarine surfaced and machine-gunned the escaping crew. Only one crew member survived this criminal act and was picked up later by an Arab dhow and taken to Aden. *Fort Perrot* was badly damaged by an E boat torpedo in the English Channel in July 1944.

In addition to new construction, the dry dock lifted and repaired 914 vessels of all types and the yard undertook maintenance and repair work to a further 2,513 vessels during the war years.

Prince Rupert's population increased from about 6,500 in 1939 to an estimated 23,000 in 1943, the combined result of shipyard activity and the tremendous, though transitory, build-up by the U.S. military. This put a great strain on public services, especially water supply, roads, and telephone services. The U.S. military helped to service their extensive construction programs and, after the war, the city received a $143,846 grant from the federal government to help cover war damage to its public service facilities.

With the end of the Pacific War in August 1945, Prince Rupert quickly returned to relative somnolence, depending again on fishing for its livelihood. The shipyard, which had supplied so much employment, was the first to close on the West Coast. Most of the temporary structures built by the American military were removed. The population, swollen by so many recent arrivals, rapidly shrank back to its pre-war level. The tracks from Prince Rupert to Red Pass Junction again became one of the many losing lines in the CN system, as through-trains to Prince Rupert reduced from a peak of six daily in 1943–1944 to five weekly.

World War II turned the long deferred dream of making Prince Rupert a major port into temporary reality, albeit three decades after its rail link to the rest of North America was completed and even though the activity was hardly related to trade with the Orient! It would be another 32 years, however, before Prince Rupert's port facilities would include a modern cargo terminal with permanent concrete dock face, able to berth two vessels, and including adequate backup area for cargo assembly and storage.

CHAPTER SIX

The Gateways 1946 to 1970 — New Markets for Bulk Commodities

CHANGED POST-WAR POWER BASES AND TRADE PATTERNS

World War II ended in victory for the Allied Powers in Europe on May 9, 1945 and in the Pacific on September 2, 1945. The titanic struggle brought, in its wake, tremendous political and economic change; change from which a resource rich western Canada and its Southern Gateway would become a major beneficiary over the next quarter-century.

For the next half-century world politics were dominated by the Cold War between the U.S.S.R. and its satellites and the United States (U.S.) and its allies over "spheres of influence." In East and Southeast Asia, the post-war industrialization of Japan, followed soon by South Korea, Taiwan, Hong Kong, Singapore, and eventually China, resulted in a massive shift in economic power from Occident to Orient.

The United Kingdom (U.K.), traditionally the major market for Canadian exports, declared war on Germany on September 3, 1939, precipitated by its treaty obligation to Poland. Despite emerging victorious almost six years later, the country was left, in the words of Winston Churchill, "in melancholy financial position." While standing alone against Nazi tyranny during 1940–1941, Britain had been forced to pay cash for desperately needed war supplies from the "arsenal of democracy." Only after her gold reserves had been transferred to Fort Knox and her North and South American investments sold off at bargain prices to American buyers to raise cash, was Lend-Lease offered by the U.S., who were determined to force the dismantling of the British Empire and its sterling bloc, thereby establishing the American dollar as the preeminent post-war global currency.

Britain emerged from the war with enormous external debt, many ruined cities, a deeply devalued currency, and the impending loss of her empire. The U.S. insisted on the termination of the Imperial Preference, which had greatly helped Canada ward off the adverse effects of U.S. protectionism during the thirties. In the quarter-century after the war, Britain and Europe would shrink in relative importance to Asia as the destination for Canadian exports through the West Coast ports.

The U.S., foolishly attacked by Japan at Pearl Harbour, mobilized her impressive physical and human resources to emerge from the war with enormous wealth and power. As a result, she had the ability to force her allies to comply with her vision of the post-war world order. Foremost in this vision was the ending of all vestiges of nineteenth-century-type European colonialism and the acceptance of the U.S. dollar as the new global reserve currency. Fiscal imperialism would replace the physical occupation of lesser nations.

Though initially succumbing to Stalin's wiles, the U.S. soon realized that they had been "taken in" by the Russian dictator and began providing strong support for erstwhile enemies Germany and Japan to create a bulwark against the spread of Communism in Europe and Asia. The ensuing struggle between these two superpowers for world hegemony dominated the world's politics for the next half-century.

The U.S.S.R. had suffered appalling human losses, as well as devastation to most of its European cities in its "Great Patriotic War" against Nazi Germany. Unquestionably, its military forces took the measure of the Wermacht and it expected immediate returns by being allowed to dominate all of Eastern Europe and spread its Communist doctrine into Western Europe and Asia. The day before the atomic bomb dropped on Hiroshima, the U.S.S.R. declared war on Japan and entered Manchuria with a very large and powerful army. This opportunistic stroke led to the establishment of a Communist government in North Korea and, five years later, the Stalin-inspired invasion of South Korea by its northern neighbor. Confrontation in both Asia and Europe between the "Free World," led by the U.S., and the U.S.S.R. with her satellites became the unfortunate norm for the next 50 years.

Japan, with most of its major cities and their industries devastated by conventional or atomic bombing, submitted meekly to Allied occupation and began rebuilding its industrial base and its merchant fleet. Thwarted in her aim to achieve power and influence through military conquest, Japan refocused on attaining prosperity through trade. After the signing of the Japan Peace Treaty in 1951, progress toward this trade objective gained momentum and Japan very quickly achieved recognition as a world class industrial and economic power. As a resource-poor nation, she had to purchase abroad large quantities of raw materials in order to manufacture a very wide range of high quality, export oriented products, from ships to grand pianos. Western Canada became a major supplier of many of these basic requirements. These exports at first consisted of food grains, but by 1954 Japan had regained her former position as Canada's third largest trading partner and dominated Canadian trade with the Far East.

The Korean War (1950–1953) left that unfortunate Cold War pawn devastated and solidly divided, but, as with Japan, strong U.S. support aimed at checking the spread of Communism led to the south half of the country following the Japanese model. It soon became an "Asian Tiger" with a very large appetite for imported raw materials and looked to Western Canada to supply many of these needs.

China had suffered incalculable loss in her long struggle against Japanese occupation. Then, with Japan defeated, civil war prolonged China's agony. This ended in 1949 with the overthrow of the corrupt, American-backed regime of Chiang Kai Shek by the Communist forces, led by Mao Tse Tung. Initially accepting assistance and advice from the U.S.S.R., Mao's xenophobic regime soon fell out with its overbearing mentor. Apart from food grain imports, China remained mostly closed to foreign trade until after the Mao's death in 1976. Then, under the pragmatic leadership of Deng Xiao Ping, China reopened to world trade. Within three decades the "Middle Kingdom" would become the ultimate "Asian Tiger" with a colossal appetite for raw materials and a tremendous effect on world trade patterns.

Canada emerged from World War II an industrial and maritime power, second only to the U.S. as an exporting nation. During the war, Canadian trade with Europe and Asia was totally disrupted. Except for food supplies to sustain the U.K. population, virtually all wartime exports were destined to support the military effort against Nazi Germany. Very few of these exports, other than lumber, moved through West Coast ports. Seaborne imports through either coast were negligible.

With the defeat (though not elimination) of the submarine menace in mid-1943 and the surge in merchant ship production in the U.S. and Canada, vessels became more freely available, so that grain started to move again through West Coast ports to the U.K. during the 1943/44 crop year. Within two years, grain exports via Panama had returned to pre-war levels. Overseas exports of lumber from British Columbia (B.C.) halved during the war years from their 1939 peak, returned more gradually to reach late 1930s levels by 1950. About one-third of those West Coast lumber exports were shipped to the U.K. and another third to the U.S. East Coast. A substantial proportion of these shipments were made through Vancouver Island ports, rather than through one of the Gateways. Other traditional B.C. exports such as canned salmon and apples had to wait until financially distressed Britain was able to pay for such luxury items.

Western Canadian overseas trade in the post-war period would be marked by a gradual shift from traditional markets in the U.K. and Europe to the rapidly expanding markets of East and Southeast Asia. These markets needed not only food grains and forest products, but also a wide range of basic raw materials to feed their rapidly expanding industries. This requirement had a profound effect on the development of the Pacific Gateways and their rail corridors — albeit confined, for the first three post-war decades, to lower mainland facilities. To successfully handle large volumes of new bulk products such as coal, sulphur, potash, phosphate rock and mineral concentrates, major public and private investments were needed to develop new, state-of-the-art terminals. These were initially located on the north shore of Burrard Inlet, replacing shipbuilding as the main activity.

Export tonnage through Canada's Southern Pacific Gateway increased by a factor of eight between 1946 and 1970, although imports remained fairly static. The ratio of exports to imports in 1946 stood at 55:45. By 1970 this ratio had shifted to 91:9, reflecting the massive surge in bulk commodity exports to Asia. Export tonnage tripled during the first 15 post-war years and tripled again over the next 10 years to reach 15.5 million tonnes (17 million tons) by 1970.

In 1946, grain and flour made up 76.5 percent and lumber 10.6 percent of export tonnage through the Southern Gateway, but by 1970, grain's relative proportion of total throughput had dropped to 38 percent of the export tonnage, which had increased eight times. Pulp and lumber stood at 7.3 percent, while coal, sulphur, and potash now constituted 53 percent of the total.

The justification for all three transcontinental railroad projects had been partly based on the prospects for lucrative trade with the Orient. Only the CPR, however, benefitted substantially from its land bridge, moving tea and silk from Asia to Europe. During the war years, the track and equipment of the two surviving railways saw very heavy use and required a great deal of war-deferred maintenance, as well as new rolling stock, and upgrade from steam to diesel-generated motive power. This particularly affected their western divisions, which had to cope with the new demands to efficiently move very large amounts of bulk commodities in unit trains to Pacific ports. The CNR, with its traditional Atlantic orientation, began to change focus to the Pacific and make substantial investments there to compete in earnest with the CPR, long dominant at "their" port in Vancouver.

In B.C. the first post-war quarter-century was a period of tremendous growth and development. From 1952–1972 a man with extraordinary drive and vision led the provincial government. Premier W.A.C. Bennett very actively fostered development of the province's resources, primarily by massively upgrading the province's highway, rail, power, and port infrastructure and creating an atmosphere that let business prosper in the province. He accomplished this with very little help from distant Ottawa and without plunging the province into excessive debt. His vision embraced the entire province. It was by no means confined to the Victoria-Vancouver axis.

Bennett's drive for economic development and use of provincial resources focused primarily on the forest, coal and power sectors, along with highway and rail projects, but the need to provide an adequate port infrastructure to cope with the enormous surge in western Canadian exports did not escape his attention. Though public ports were the federal government's responsibility, it was Bennett's perception that Ottawa was both tardy and negligent when it came to moving on projects needed on the Pacific Coast. He defied Ottawa's jurisdiction, and his actions prompted the National Harbours Board (NHB) to prepare the sites needed for port facilities in Vancouver and, eventually, in Prince Rupert.

Between 1952 and 1971, the Pacific Great Eastern Railway (PGE), so long a bad and expensive joke, was extended successively to Prince George, North Vancouver, Dawson Creek, Fort St. John, Mackenzie, Fort St. James and finally Fort Nelson. In 1969 work began on a line to Dease Lake, which was destined to be the first phase of the Bennett-Jamieson "Grand Plan" to provide rail access to northwestern B.C. and the Yukon. The subsequent collapse of this last great infrastructure initiative was a severe blow to the proponents of development of the Northern Corridor and Port of Prince Rupert. Additionally, the province became very effective in "persuading" shippers from the many new government licensed forest product mills in central and northern B.C. to ship via the provincially owned PGE. This influence, coupled with the painful delay in completing the Fairview Terminal in Prince Rupert, resulted in virtually all the overseas export product from these new mills moving through south coast ports.

THE SOUTHERN CORRIDOR AND VANCOUVER GATEWAY

Shipbuilding dominated waterfront activity in Vancouver during the war years. With government orders for freighters and naval vessels complete, some yards closed and others amalgamated in the face of much smaller order books for domestic, commercial, and pleasure vessels. The north shore of Burrard Inlet was particularly affected by this massive reduction in marine related activity, but it was replaced over the next quarter-century by the new and busy bulk and break-bulk terminals. Their location was made feasible by the new rail access. From the north, the PGE was extended into North Vancouver and from the southeast, access was much improved with the completion of the new CNR second narrows bridge and tunnel project.

On the south shore of the Inlet, the NHB developed Centennial Pier and later built an extension to accommodate Vancouver's first, very modest container facility.

The first part of the post-war period was characterized by a return to normal for the waterfront, coupled with moderate and stable growth. Then in the 1960s, under the twin stimuli of a renascent Japanese market and a dynamic provincial leadership, the Southern Gateway underwent a decade of spectacular growth and development akin to that of the 1920s.

LOCAL PORT ADMINISTRATION

In 1950 the assets of the Vancouver Port Authority (VPA) were valued at $25,090,000. They included four grain terminals, seventeen ocean berths, two coastwise berths, storage tanks, and 56 km (35 miles) of terminal railway lines. The port ran a net surplus annually during the fifties of between $500,000 and $1 million, in stark contrast to the very substantial annual deficits at most of the eastern ports administered by the NHB.

An issue with the CPR over jurisdiction of a key section of the waterfront had festered since the formation of the Vancouver Harbour Commission in 1913. This matter was finally resolved in 1966 with a Memorandum of Agreement that gave the CPR the waterfront west from Burrard Street to Cardero Street and gave the VPA that portion east to Dunlevy, with the exception of the CNR dock at the foot of Main Street. The VPA purchased Pier B-C for $3,741,000 with a leaseback to the CPR for 20 years and promised to give the CPR first opportunity to lease a planned new deep-sea berthing facility to be built between Pier B-C and Western Water Terminals (formerly the Union SS Wharf). This agreement resolved 33 years of bickering over jurisdiction in the prime section of the Vancouver waterfront.

In 1962 access to the waterfront facilities between the new Centennial Pier and Terminal Dock was significantly improved on completion by the VPA of a $1 million program of overhead ramp construction at the foot of both Heatley and Renfrew Streets. Stimulated by the threat of provincial government interference in port development, the VPA hastily extended the limits of the port south to Boundary Bay, thereby increasing its area of jurisdiction from 127 to 500 square kilometers (49 to 193 square miles).

Late in 1970, the VPA announced plans for a $5 million general cargo complex in North Vancouver on reclaimed land between Neptune Terminal and Lynn Creek. When completed, this 22.2 ha (55 acre) parcel would be leased to Seaboard Terminals.

Though, ostensibly these moves were made by the VPA, under the *National Harbours Board Act* of 1936, the veneer of local authority continued to be pitifully thin. Any expenditures over $10,000 required detailed and lengthy examination as well as approval by the established bureaucracy in Ottawa. This painfully short leash would continue until the passage of the *Canada Ports Act* in 1983.

THE RAIL LINES SERVING SOUTHERN GATEWAY FACILITIES

During the depression and the immediate post-war period, the CNR's primary focus had been on Canada's transatlantic trade, then quadruple its transpacific trade. With the Japan Peace Treaty in 1951 this ratio began to change, though at first the CPR and Vancouver were the prime beneficiaries.

In response to the surge in exports of Asia-bound bulk commodities that soon followed, specialized new terminals were built on the north shore of Burrard Inlet and these required much better rail access. This would be provided by the CNR and by the provincially owned PGE.

Recognizing the new trend in the direction of Canadian overseas trade and its relatively weak position on the West Coast, the CNR took steps to increase its presence at the Southern Gateway. These steps began in 1952 with the purchase of the second narrows bridge and the harbour terminal railway from the National Harbours Board. With the latter acquisition the railway could at last reach the south shore of Burrard Inlet without having to interchange to another line.

Over the next 15 years, the CNR spent $34 million upgrading access to the north shore by constructing a two-mile tunnel and a new rail bridge, in addition to expanding their Port Mann yard in Surrey, and developing new yard facilities on the north shore. The new bridge and tunnel opened May 6, 1969 and the old bridge was demolished the following year.

The Pacific Great Eastern Railway completed its line from Squamish into North Vancouver in 1956. This greatly facilitated the flow south of the products from the rapidly expanding industries of central and northeast B.C., for export over the wharves of the new north shore facilities.

Rail access to the new Westshore Terminal at Roberts Bank was provided by a new 38.6

km (24 mile) line constructed by the B.C. Harbours Board during 1968–1969. This line was built by the province to assure fair and open rail access to the new terminal, and gave joint running rights to the CPR, CNR, and Burlington Northern Railways.

FIRST NARROWS

Problems related to the "indifferent entrance" to Burrard Inlet at first narrows continued to concern the local maritime community. The rapidly increasing size of vessels using the port prompted the local Harbours Improvement Committee to act. They identified and highlighted for remedial action, "the crooked approach and narrow entrance with its strong tidal currents and shoal patches." Ottawa responded with a fourth dredging program in 1954 and a fifth program in 1969–1970. This latter program cost $2.89 million and removed 2.8 million cubic metres (3.7 million cubic yards) of material to create a channel into the inlet 300 m (1,000 ft.) wide at the 15 m (50 ft.) contour.

Another Ottawa financed initiative that provided indirect, but very real benefit to Vancouver, was the successful removal of Ripple Rock in Seymour narrows at the head of the Gulf of Georgia, on April 5, 1958. At a cost of $2,639,878 a true mining approach to the problem — using 1,124 tonnes (1,237 tons) of high explosive — succeeded where previous wartime attempts costing over $1 million had failed.

THE NEW BULK TERMINALS

To accommodate the tremendous increase in dry bulk commodity exports, six new terminals were constructed at the Southern Gateways between 1959 and 1970, a decade of port growth and development reminiscent of the "Roaring Twenties." Four of these were located on Burrard Inlet and one each at Roberts Bank and on the south bank of the Fraser River, opposite the City of New Westminster. Two handled only dry bulk commodities, two both dry and liquid bulk, and two offered facilities able to store and load dry bulk, liquid bulk, break-bulk and general cargo.

Pacific Coast Bulk Terminals

Initial export coal shipments from Canmore, Alberta mines were directed to loading facilities in Seattle. With the addition of coal shipments to Japan from the Crow's Nest Pass Coal Company, the Seattle facility moved 160,669 tons of Canadian coal onto vessels bound for Japan in 1959.

Several Vancouver firms considered options to remedy this unwanted diversion of a Canadian bulk commodity to a cross-border export facility. A number of sites east of second narrows on the south shore of Burrard Inlet were examined. Eventually a site was chosen at Port Moody and, by late 1959, the first stage of a bulk loading facility designed to handle coal, sulphur, potash, and bulk liquids was completed. Operated by Pacific Coast Terminals (PCT) of New Westminster, the new development would be known as Pacific Coast Bulk

Terminals. As a subsidiary of PCT it was indirectly linked to the CPR through Cominco's ownership interest in PCT.

Over the next decade, Pacific Coast Bulk Terminals undertook a number of expansion projects and by 1967 had invested $17 million in the terminal. Early shipments of coal from Kaiser's mines at Michel used the Port Moody Terminal pending completion of the much larger facility at Roberts Bank. In 1969 the water depth at the dock face was increased by dredging from 9.9 to 13.5 m (33 to 45 ft.) to accommodate the ever larger ships calling for coal and sulphur.

Vancouver Wharves

While Pacific Coast Bulk Terminals was completing their facility at the eastern extremity of Burrard Inlet, a long established London terminal operator, Samuel William & Sons Ltd., acquired a site for a major development on the north shore opposite Stanley Park. A $2 million first phase investment created 16 ha (40 acres) of land reclaimed by dredging and faced with a 210 m (700 ft.) wharf with 10.8 m (36 ft.) of water at low tide. To be known as Vancouver Wharves and served by both the PGE and the CNR, the company objective was to develop a terminal suited to handling goods that needed a very large assembly area, goods such as sulphur, metal concentrates, bulk liquids, chemicals, automobiles, lumber and general cargo.

On May 8, 1960 the *Dona Ourania* became the first vessel to load at the terminal, taking on 2,700 tons of metal concentrates destined for Japanese buyers. The terminal was officially opened by Lieutenant Governor Ross in August 1960 and then underwent almost continuous expansion to docks, land area, and storage and loading facilities over the next decade.

Two of the next three bulk terminals within the VPA's jurisdiction had their leased sites prepared for them by the National Harbours Board. This arrangement was not welcomed by the owners of Pacific Coast Bulk Terminals at Port Moody.

Neptune Terminals

Over many millennia, the three mountain streams emptying into Burrard Inlet carried down sand, gravel, and boulders which formed extensive deposits along the north shore between first and second narrows. Beginning in 1966, the NHB contracted the dredging of 2.45 million cubic metres (3.2 million cubic yards) of these deposits immediately west of Lynn Creek to create a 52.5 ha (130 acre) development site faced with 1,500 m (5,000 ft.) of interlocking sheet steel piling at a cost of $5 million.

A new entity, Neptune Terminals, owned by the Webster family of Montreal, leased the western 28 ha (70 acres) of the new site from the NHB and optioned the remaining 24 ha (60 acres). Neptune developed their leased site with a loop track, potash shed, one train loading and two train unloading stations, phosphate rock silos, three berths, and dual quadrant ship loaders capable of loading vessels at 4,000 tons per hour. Subsequent dredging provided one berth able to accommodate vessels of 125,000 ton capacity and the other two berths, vessels up to 65,000 tons.

In December 1968 the first vessels to use the facility unloaded salt and phosphate rock. Federal Grain, owner and operator of the Pacific Elevator complex on the south shore, purchased Neptune in March 1969 and continued its development. The first unit train carrying potash arrived on the north shore via the newly opened tunnel and bridge on May 6, 1969 and the first 41 car, CNR unit train of coal from Luscar's Cardinal River Mine in Alberta arrived at Port Mann on February 23, 1970 for eventual shipment to the "Japan Three" over Neptune's facility.

The terminal officially opened on September 9, 1970 and, subsequently, onsite facilities were further developed to handle a range of commodities that eventually included coal, potash, fertilizers, methanol and agricultural product exports plus salt and phosphate rock imports.

Saskatchewan Wheat Pool Elevator

In response to the continuing westward shift in the direction of prairie grain exports resulting from massive wheat sales to China and the U.S.S.R. in the 1960s, Saskatchewan Wheat Pool decided to build a modern terminal of their own. They leased a site from the NHB immediately west of Neptune's developing terminal and built a 5.3 million bushel capacity elevator there, costing $20,418,000. It opened officially on June 14, 1968. It gave the port a much needed boost in its ability to efficiently handle the increasing west-bound grain volumes. Its location on the north shore was, of course, facilitated by the soon to be completed, and much improved, CNR rail access.

Westshore Terminal at Roberts Bank

Premier Bennett was frustrated by his perception of disinterest on the part of the NHB and its political masters to the needs of B.C. and Western Canada resource exporters. To counter this, he established a new Crown Corporation, the B.C. Harbours Board, on March 7, 1968, "to develop and encourage the development of harbour facilities in the province, to provide access to and from harbour facilities, and to assist and promote the industrial development of the province in conjunction with harbour development…" While its mandate was very broad, the Board initially focused on developing a "superport" at Roberts Bank to serve exports from Kaiser Resources' massive Elk Valley Coal development. To this end, the new Board's first act was to expropriate 1,619 ha (4,000 acres) of prime farm land backing the proposed Robert Bank port site. Provincial planners of a very large coal terminal had determined this land to be the key to the whole development.

The NHB had, in fact, not ignored the potential for port development outside Burrard Inlet and had moved decisively to counter any threat to its control over future port developments. In late 1966 the harbour limits of the Vancouver Port Authority had been extended south to the U.S. border. This extension included the transfer of the Fraser River Harbour Commission's seaward port limits in the Gulf of Georgia to the VPA. With this action, the VPA's limits of jurisdiction were increased from 127 to 500 square kilometers (49 to 193 square miles). Following this expansion, the NHB studied sites at Sturgeon Bank, Roberts Bank, and Boundary Bay and in April 1968 the federal government announced plans to build a $50 million "superport" at Roberts Bank over a thirty-year period.

This very long time schedule was totally unacceptable to Premier Bennett who demanded and then received assurance from Minister Hellyer that the federal government would discharge in full its responsibility at Roberts Bank and be ready in time for the first shipments of Elk Valley coal to Japan, under Kaiser Coal's first contract for 3.5 million tons per year for 15 years.

Dredging 4.6 million cubic metres (6 million cubic yards) of sand to create a 20 ha (50 acre) "island" with a 4.8 km (3 mile) causeway shore connection began in July 1968. A further 460,000 cubic metres (600,000 cubic yards) of gravel and rock was required to protect the outer slopes. The finished island was leased to Westshore Terminals and provided with car unloading, stacking, reclaiming, and loading equipment. Depth at the dock face measured 19.5 m (65 ft.) at low water. The first unit train comprising 88 cars carrying 9,000 tons of coal arrived at the new terminal April 30, 1970.

The *Snow White*, a remarkable name for a collier, lifted the first cargo of 24,289 tons of metallurgical coal from the terminal on May 4, 1970 and on June 15 Westshore Terminal was officially opened by Prime Minister Trudeau and Premier Bennett. By the end of 1970, the new terminal had loaded 33 vessels with 1.4 million tons of coal. The following year throughput increased to 3.9 million tons and by 1979 to 10.2 million tons, as more coal sources were tapped in southeastern B.C.

THE BIRTHPLACE OF SHIP BORNE CONTAINERS

The term "Intermodalism" may be defined as the movement of shipments in containers, using the transportation modes of ship to (or from) rail or road vehicles in sequence. With the cooperation of the involved modes of transport a container can be moved from the terminal nearest the shipper to the terminal nearest its destination at a single rate and on one billing. Simplicity, efficiency, and speed are the hallmarks of such a seamless movement. The overall movement is seen as a whole rather than a series of separate moves.

The movement of valuable tea and silk cargoes from Asia to Europe by the CPR, commencing in the last decade of the nineteenth century, involved an integrated system of ships and rail to transport this cargo across two oceans and a land bridge continent. Perhaps this movement could be described as "early intermodal," albeit without containers.

The world's first fully integrated, containerized, sea borne freight service utilizing a specially designed cellular vessel was the one inaugurated by the White Pass & Yukon Route in late 1955 to move "boxed" cargo from Vancouver to Yukon points via the Port of Skagway,

Alaska. The vessel, modified railcars, and a truck fleet were all owned and controlled by this Vancouver based company. In the early fifties, they defined a need to develop a new and better system of freight handling to minimize the costs, damage, and delays inherent in the multiple transfers of freight between ship, rail, and truck and, in addition, be totally under the control of the company from Vancouver to Dawson, Yukon Territory. By 1955 the company had built 550 containers, each 8 x 8 x 7 feet long and had modified their narrow gauge flat cars to each carry three of these. To move these containers from Vancouver to Skagway the company ordered a specially designed vessel, the 4000-ton *Clifford J. Rogers*, from Vickers Shipyard in Montreal. The plan of the vessel included "cells" to hold 165 containers that were stowed below decks. More containers were carried as deck cargo. This vessel, the prototype of all cellular container ships anywhere, sailed from Vancouver with cargo destined for the Yukon via Skagway, on November 26, 1955. The ship and its containers, coupled with the company's specially adapted railcars and truck fleet, constituted the world's first fully integrated, intermodal, containerized freight system. The company took over the site of the old West Indies Dock on the north shore where they built their "Asbestos Wharf" to serve as the southern terminus.

White Pass later increased the size of their steel framed aluminum containers to 8 x 8 x 25 ft. 3 inches for carriage in two new purpose built vessels, the 6,000 ton *Frank H. Brown* and the *Klondike*, delivered in 1965 and 1969 respectively. Containers were moved to shipside by straddle carriers and loaded with the ship's Munckloader gantry crane. The new vessels stowed 200 containers below deck and carried another 58 as deck cargo. A few containers were temperature controlled and a substantial number were insulated.

Five months after the *Clifford J. Rogers* inaugurated container service from Vancouver to Skagway, a slightly modified tanker, the *Ideal X*, entered domestic service on the east coast of the U.S. carrying, on a "spar" deck, 58 highway trailers, which had been detached from their running gear and loaded by dockside cranes. These trailers carried the name Sea-Land Service. The next development for this U.S. domestic service involved converting a conventional C2 cargo vessel to a dedicated container carrying vessel with cellular holds for 35 ft. containers stacked four high, with additional containers on deck stacked two high, for a total carrying capacity of 266 "boxes." This vessel, the *Gateway City*, sailed from Newark to Miami and Houston on October 4, 1957. The containers were loaded and unloaded by the vessel's own gantry cranes and were specially designed for weight bearing to allow stacking. They were equipped with a newly patented "twist lock" device in all eight corner castings. When manually thrown this device vertically unified the containers carried on deck.

From these rather humble beginnings by White Pass and later Sea-Land, the revolution in cargo handling for world trade developed and must surely be considered equal in significance to the revolutionary conversion of ships from wooden to steel hulls, or from sail to steam.

The evolution of container vessels necessitated the parallel development of specialized terminals in major world ports. With general cargo increasingly consigned to move in standard sized metal boxes, the role of traditional piers rapidly diminished. The new terminals had to be designed to quickly and efficiently handle the boxed cargoes that would soon dominate world trade. They needed to provide adequate backup land adjacent to their berths to temporarily store and assemble incoming and outgoing containers, pending transfer to their next transportation mode. Staff required extensive training in new technology and in the operation of specialized and expensive equipment. Successful terminals had easy access for both rail and road carriers.

The very substantial investment required to create an efficient container terminal combined with the operators' desire to minimize the number of port calls for their expensive vessels meant that these terminals would be confined to relatively few of the world's major ports.

Vancouver was slower than its major U.S. West Coast competitors to move on this front and Prince Rupert would wait another four decades before opening its first container terminal.

Centennial Pier

Named to honour the centenary of British Columbia's birth and built on the site of the historic Hastings Mill, Centennial Pier was completed by the NHB in 1959 at a cost of $8 million. It was officially opened on July 15, 1960. As initially developed, it offered four berths equipped with four travelling cranes and storage facilities on 15 acres of backup land. This mixed general cargo, break-bulk, and bulk facility underwent a $2 million expansion program between 1965 and 1967 that added storage and a 300 ton heavy lift crane. Centennial would eventually become the site of the VPA's first timid and tardy concession to the container revolution that was so rapidly changing cargo handling worldwide.

The last half of the 1960s saw the universal acceptance of Sea-Land's "twist lock" system and the twenty-foot standard size "box," as well as a rapid increase in the size and number of container-carrying vessels and the development in many world ports, including the U.S. West Coast, of specialized terminals dedicated to handling container ships efficiently.

The Port of Montreal assembled Canada's first container crane in late 1968 and in November of that year the CNR moved 200 containers — inbound from the UK — from Montreal to Toronto in a dedicated "container train." In Vancouver, the first semi container vessels discharged their boxed cargo using either their own gear or conventional dockside cranes. Japan Canada service was inaugurated when the *King's Reach* offloaded 10 twenty-foot containers destined for Montreal and Toronto at the Canadian Pacific wharf on December 17, 1967.

In the Pacific Northwest it was Seattle, not Vancouver, with its pioneer White Pass container operation, which led the way in specialized terminal development. Local ownership, financing, and operation of that port allowed rapid response to perceived opportunities. In the early sixties the Port of Seattle spent an initial $8 million at pier 46 to accommodate container traffic to Alaska and then aggressively followed that first commitment with expansion of the terminal to serve international container traffic. By 1978 the port boasted

17 container cranes compared to three in Vancouver and was handling 600,000 boxes annually, six times the Vancouver total.

Seattle's aggressive approach to container terminal development was in marked contrast to that taken by the Ottawa controlled VPA. Lack of adequate terminal facilities coupled with the unwillingness of vessel owners to divert to Vancouver if carrying less than 200 containers for the slowly developing Canadian market, resulted in a substantial percentage of Canada-bound containers being offloaded in Seattle and trucked north to their destination. This represented a serious loss to the port of Vancouver.

The NHB responded by adding 15 paved acres to Centennial Pier and purchasing a single Starporter crane to serve the new "Berth Six" for a total cost of $5 million. This new, very modest facility opened on June 1, 1970 in time for the arrival of the 738 TEU capacity *Golden Arrow* of the "Japan Six" line. It would be another five years before Vancouver could boast a specialized container terminal — and that several months behind a newly opened container facility on the Fraser River.

THE GRAIN TERMINALS

For the first 5 post-war years, the average annual export of grain through West Coast terminals totalled 1.5 million tons, approximately the same as the average for the decade of the thirties. Most cargoes were still destined for the U.K. or Europe.

Convinced of discrimination by the Canadian Wheat Board in favour of the eastern shipping route, Vancouver's marine community submitted a brief to the Minister of Trade and Commerce in 1948 demanding that a larger share of grain exports be directed through the Pacific Coast.

A number of bumper crops on the Canadian Plains in the fifties and sixties resulted in huge surplus stock carryovers. The Canadian Wheat Board's mandate to move these crops was made more difficult by politically inspired farm incentive programs in the US with high support prices, and their subsequent disposal of the resulting huge surpluses at a loss. Furthermore, the technical revolution in agricultural practices had greatly increased production worldwide. The Wheat Board and the federal government responded by devising a program of direct sales to buyers coupled with long term supply purchasing arrangements on credit terms, first to China in 1961 and two years later to the U.S.S.R. The destination of most of the grain sold under these multi-million ton sales agreements required that it be moved through West Coast terminals. As a result of these huge sales, Vancouver terminal throughput averaged 5 million tons per year between crop years 1965/66 and 1969/70, more than tripling the average of the first five post-war years.

Coping with this very substantial increase in throughput stressed a Canadian grain handling and transportation system that had hardly changed in four decades. The size of vessels reporting to Vancouver for grain loading was rapidly increasing and this created even more problems. In 1956 the *Mparmpa Christos* set a record for the port, loading 13,800 tons of wheat. Six years later the *Sonic* spent a total of 28 days in port, including 17 days loading at multiple terminals, to take on board 44,000 tons. Then in 1967 the *Sigsilver* took on 84,000 tons of wheat, though the British captain indicated the ship would not return to Vancouver due to the length of time and multiple berth transfers needed to fill his vessel.

In response to seeing more and more Saskatchewan produced grain moving west, the Saskatchewan Wheat Pool formed a West Coast division in 1957 and leased the recently refurbished and upgraded No. 2 elevator from the NHB. In 1964 the Pool started to plan for a new terminal in the port and, as previously outlined, this terminal, situated on the north shore next to Neptune's developing bulk terminal, opened in 1968.

The NHB increased the storage capacity of its No. 3 terminal by 1 million bushels at a cost of $728,500 in 1959 and, in 1967 sold this 3.25 million bushel capacity terminal to United Grain Growers for $3.5 million, although they retained the title to the land, water lots, and No. 3 jetty. After a major fire in May 1952, this terminal's dock had been replaced by the NHB at a cost of $1 million.

Another waterfront fire in 1958 destroyed the NHB No.1 jetty used by the Pacific Elevator and the adjacent NHB No.1 elevator plus its annex. This fire resulted in a number of vessels waiting long periods for loading berths at the port. The NHB replaced that jetty at a cost of $429,947.

The old Dominion No. 1 terminal ("Stevens Folly"), and its No.1 annex were sold by the NHB in 1968 to Pacific Elevators, a subsidiary of Federal Grain, after substantial upgrades and renovations costing $1.3 million. The sale included a long lease on the water lot. At the time of that sale Pacific Elevators also controlled, albeit for a short time, the Burrard Terminal in North Vancouver, the old Columbia elevator, and the terminals in Victoria and New Westminster.

Alberta Wheat Pool spent $2 million in 1955 expanding their workhouse and cleaning facilities, as well as adding 2 million bushels of storage space to the existing 5.3 million bushel capacity. The Pool then embarked on a second major program in 1969 that included a berth extension, gallery replacement, and dredging at the dock face to provide 13.5 m (45 ft.) of water at low tide. The upgraded loading facilities could now move grain to a berthed vessel at a rate of 3,000 tons per hour.

Despite the opening of the new Saskpool terminal in 1968, the closure and subsequent demolition of the New Westminster terminal in 1970 resulted in no net gain in the number of terminals on the West Coast. However, the addition of the much larger new terminal plus additions and upgrades to the Alberta Wheat Pool, United Grain Growers, and Prince Rupert terminals resulted in an overall increase in West Coast storage capacity from 21 million bushels in 1946 to just over 29 million bushels by 1970. West Coast throughput, however, had increased more than 400 percent during that 25 year period and little use was being made of the Prince Rupert facility. It is not surprising that in Vancouver, serious delays were appearing in the movement of grain from rail to ship.

There was a flurry of excitement at Squamish in 1961 when a provincial cabinet member tried to promote the construction of a grain terminal there to handle grain shipped by the PGE from its recently extended lines into the Peace River growing area. There were no takers and nothing came of this questionable and undoubtedly politically inspired brainwave.

Flour had long been a major Canadian export commodity. By 1947 there were 178 operating mills in the country with the result that flour was third, after wheat and newsprint, among Canada's exports in that year. Flour exports through the Port of Vancouver started in 1920 and in 1925 Robin Hood Mills built the Terminal Dock and Warehouse facility on the south shore of the Inlet, primarily to handle flour exports. Until 1939 flour exports from the port averaged slightly over 100,000 tons annually. After the war, average yearly exports over the "flour dock" doubled and reached a peak of 469,662 tons in 1964 with large sales to the U.S.S.R. Much of the flour exported up to that point had gone to buyers in Asia, especially the Philippines, but in the early sixties these countries developed their own milling capacity. As a result, by 1970 flour exports had fallen to 9,440 tons and subsequently declined to zero.

THE SHIPYARDS

With the completion of wartime orders for new construction and vessel conversions, it was inevitable that there would be closures, as well as changes in ownership and location among the four large Vancouver yards that had completed 220 major vessels in four war years. Burrard Dry Dock's second yard on the south shore of the Inlet was the first to go. Then West Coast Shipbuilders' yard on False Creek was closed and eventually taken over by Allied Shipbuilders. They moved to a new facility on the north shore at the mouth of Seymour Creek in 1966. Finally, Pacific Dry Dock (formerly known as North Vancouver Ship Repairs) sold their yard with its two floating dry docks to Burrard in 1952 and Burrard closed this north shore facility a year later, moving the floating docks to their main yard.

In the first few post-war years, the industry survived on the conversion of ex-Navy corvettes, minesweepers, and patrol vessels to pleasure or commercial uses. Federal government orders for new destroyer escorts for the Navy and replacement vessels for the Department of Transport coupled with orders for tugs, barges, and fishing vessels kept the yards moderately busy through the fifties. Then, attracted by a federal government shipbuilding subsidy (designed to help eastern yards) that started out at 40 percent, the Province of B.C. began construction of a fleet of roll-on roll-off ferries in the early sixties. These replaced the outmoded services offered by the B.C. Coast Service of the CPR and the Black Ball Ferry Line. Until very recently, new vessel construction for B.C. Ferries constituted a core source of work for the surviving major yards.

Clearly, with their high cost structure, B.C. yards could not compete in world markets for new construction of deep-sea vessels. By 1969 Japan dominated world shipbuilding with over 50 percent of the world market for new vessels. Local yards survived on federal and provincial government orders for naval vessels, ferries, and coastguard ships plus orders from domestic industry and ship repair work. To accommodate repair work the Vancouver maritime community began to press Ottawa for a new "super dry dock" capable of lifting the ever larger vessels using the port.

PASSENGER VESSELS

In the immediate postwar period, the only regularly scheduled passenger liner calling at Vancouver was the *Aorangi* of the Canadian Australasian Line. The Canadian Pacific, long so dominant on the Pacific, lost most of their big passenger liners during the war and the sole survivor, the *Empress of Scotland (ex-Empress of Japan)* was not returned to her former Pacific service. The long established P&O line, together with the Orient Line entered passenger liner service on the Pacific in 1954 with the *Orsova* and *Orcades*, later adding the *Arcadia, Oronsay, Himalaya, Iberia, Chusan* and finally, the *Oriana* and *Canberra* in 1961. All these fine vessels called at Vancouver on their various round the world, or transpacific routes, but the service they offered eventually succumbed to the "advantages" of air travel, especially after jet aircraft were introduced. These vessels made use of Pier B-C which, in 1966, was sold by the CPR to the National Harbours Board and subsequently refurbished. The old Pier A, built in 1909 to accommodate the *Empress* liners was replaced by the CPR in 1967 with a barge slip.

Domestic passenger and freight services to Vancouver Island and B.C. coastal points originated with the vessels of the Hudson's Bay Company in 1827 and were continued by the Union Steamships from 1889, the B.C. Coast Service of the CPR from 1901, and the GTP/ CN Steamships starting in 1910. After the Second World War an aggressive new entrant, Northland Navigation, took over calling at the most lucrative points on the coast and thereby contributed to bringing an end in 1959 to 70 years of service by the Union Steamships Company. Northland acquired Union's wharf east of Pier B-C in 1953 (later sold to Western Water Terminals) and operated from there pending completion of their own Northland Pier the same year, the first new pier on the Vancouver waterfront in 30 years. This pier was extended in 1963 to accommodate the new *Northland Prince* built at Burrard Dry Dock.

The *Prince Rupert* continued in passenger and freight service for Canadian National Steamships until 1956 and, between 1955 and 1957, this company and the CPR's B.C. Coast Service jointly operated the old *Princess Norah* under the name *Queen of the North* on the coastal run north. They sold that vessel to Northland in 1958 and both companies retired from servicing points on the long B.C. coastline.

Service to Vancouver Island by the B.C. Coast Service and by Blackball Ferries ended in 1958 after a long strike convinced Premier Bennett to take advantage of the generous federal shipbuilding subsidy and create a government service. The B.C. Ferry Authority was accordingly established to build and operate a fleet of roll-off roll-on vessels and appropriate terminals to connect Vancouver Island and the Gulf Islands to the mainland, as well as later developing a service connecting Vancouver Island to Prince Rupert and mid-coast points. Northland Navigation carried on a subsidized service for a few more years, but the reduction in populated points on the coast, the vastly improved highway system, the extensive airline service offered by both large and small carriers, the introduction of government ferry service and finally, the loss of their federal subsidy in 1958, spelt the end to all but the passenger and vehicle ferry service offered by the B.C. Ferry Authority.

B.C. coastal and Alaska Panhandle seasonal cruising resumed after the war with the *Princess Kathleen and Princess Louise* of the B.C. Coast Service and the *Chilcotin* of Union Steamships. A new *Prince George* was built in Victoria for Canadian National Steamships and commenced service in June 1948. A Seattle company, Alaska Cruise Lines, established by Charles West, chartered Union's *Coquitlam* in 1951 for Alaska cruises and finally purchased that vessel and her sister ship *Chilcotin* (ex-*Camosun*) in 1958, renaming the two ships *Glacier Queen* and *Yukon Star*.

As the popularity of cruising to Alaska increased in the mid-sixties, another Seattle entrepreneur founded Princess Cruises, a company that took its name from its first chartered vessel, the *Princess Patricia*, which had been built in Scotland after the war for the B.C. Coast Service of the CPR. This vessel soon proved too small to meet the demand and, starting in 1967 larger vessels were chartered, including the *Italia* and *Spirit of London*. Later, the *Island Venture* and *Sea Venture* were acquired from a Norwegian operator and renamed the *Pacific Princess ("Love Boat")* and *Island Princess*. Soon Holland America, which had acquired West's Alaska Cruise Line, and Sitmar introduced ever larger ships to this popular cruise itinerary and virtually all these vessels operated from Vancouver's Pier B-C or Centennial Pier.

PETROCHEMICAL TERMINALS

In 1915 Imperial Oil opened their IOCO refinery, tank farm, and distribution centre on the north shore of the eastern extension of Burrard Inlet. Subsequently, several other major oil companies built facilities to receive and distribute petroleum products on the Inlet's south shoreline east of Second Narrows. With the arrival of Alberta crude via the newly completed Trans Mountain pipeline in 1953 these facilities were no longer dependant on ship borne oil imports, and with the completion of the pipeline's Westridge Terminal, exports began to replace imports. In fact the port's imports of oil fell from 1.2 million tons in 1952 to 6,000 tons in 1955 and, by 1957, a total of 53 tankers loaded at the new terminal. A new dock, built at Westridge in 1959, could handle tankers up to 45,000 tons and with further dredging had the potential to take vessels of 65,000 tons. In 1966 Westridge completed a $3 million program that enabled the terminal to handle propane.

NEW WESTMINSTER: 1946 TO 1970

LOCAL PORT ADMINISTRATION

With the passage of the *Harbour Commissions Act* in 1964, the New Westminster Harbour Commission became the Fraser River Harbour Commission (FRHC), effective January 20,

1965. This Act trumped the key recommendation of the Gibb Report (1932) that harbours in Canada should be administered centrally and which specifically recommended amalgamation of the ports of New Westminster and Vancouver. The decentralizing provisions of the new *Harbour Commissions Act* flowed from the recommendations of the Glassco Royal Commission (1962) on Government Organization, which decried "inappropriate central control" and insisted that "local managers be allowed to manage."

The Commission found itself freed from the threat of being combined with Vancouver and allowed much more freedom — under its new mandate — than its much larger, centrally controlled, NHB administered neighbour. Furthermore, it now had double the local representation of its predecessor.

The new freedom of action given the FRHC rankled the Vancouver marine establishment, some of whom tended to ridicule the river port and begrudge the amount Ottawa spent annually on dredging, river works and snag removal, even though the amount paled in comparison to the amount spent on maintaining a navigable passage to St. Lawrence River ports.

CHANNEL MAINTENANCE AND IMPROVEMENTS

In 1945 the New Westminster Harbour Commission extracted a promise from Ottawa to contribute $2.5 million toward a 15,000 ton lift floating dry dock for the port. The project never materialized, but the federal Department of Public Works did undertake to continue programs designed to upgrade and maintain a navigable channel from Sandheads at the river's mouth to New Westminster's docks. Between 1882 and 1949, federal government projects had installed 20 km of control works on the river to narrow the channel and increase the velocity of the flow, thereby reducing sediment deposition. More post-war programs culminated in the major $5 million "Trifurcation" project in the mid-sixties. With the increasing size of vessels calling at the port, the City of New Westminster and the Harbour Commission lobbied continuously for more dredge and snag boats to reduce the hazards of navigating the 40 km (25 mile) stretch of the south Fraser channel from the port's facilities to the open water of the Gulf. Their motto became "Thirty to the Gulf," implying the crucial need for a 9 m (30 ft.) minimum depth for that channel. By 1968 the channel was deemed to have a control depth of 9.3 m (31 ft.) and be capable of safely allowing the passage of a vessel 225 m (750 ft.) long. This could only be safely maintained, however, with ongoing programs of dredging and snag removal.

The Massey Tunnel, carrying Highway 99 under the south channel of the Fraser, was completed in 1959. Its design allowed for 12.3 m (41 ft.) of low water clearance for the navigation channel and so established an ultimate draft potential for river traffic on the south channel.

PORT TRAFFIC

Though the port's facilities were little used during the war, traffic returned to pre-war levels by 1947 and slowly increased over the next 25 years from 1 to 1.5 million tons annually.

Export commodities handled consisted of lumber, grain, canned salmon, apples, metals, and fertilizers over the berths of Pacific Coast Terminals, Searle Grain, and Canadian Western Lumber Company.

The Harbour Commission sought to entice traffic away from Vancouver by charging no cargo fees and keeping port taxes one-third lower than its neighbour port. With support from the City, Ottawa granted the Commission authority in 1952 to borrow funds to create new docking facilities on City property. This project, though bitterly opposed by the underutilized Pacific Coast Terminals, was completed in 1955 and added three rail-served berths to the port. A concurrent project created a causeway to Annacis Island to stimulate development by Grosvenor Estates.

The grain terminal was leased and operated from 1933 to 1956 by Searle Grain and later by closely related Pacific Elevators, as an overflow facility to their Vancouver operations. Except for two years when the terminal was closed (crop years 1957/58 and 1958/59), throughput ranged between 50,000 and 200,000 tonnes annually from 1946, until it was closed permanently in 1968 after developing a lean. It was demolished in 1970.

Lumber was the real mainstay of the port averaging 375–450 thousand tonnes annually. It was loaded both at mill docks and New Westminster waterfront facilities.

A NEW TERMINAL

Unwilling to be left out of the boom in new Vancouver terminal developments, the New Westminster Harbour Commission followed through on a plan initiated by Johnston Terminals to re-develop the old grain elevator site. Fraser Surrey Docks was built on a large parcel of Commission riverfront land on the south bank of the river and was designed initially to handle a wide range of both domestic and international bulk and break-bulk cargoes. It commenced operations in 1964, offering three general cargo berths, one bulk berth, and one transit shed.

PRINCE RUPERT: 1946 TO 1970

During this time period there had been a tremendous surge in the development of new terminal facilities at the Southern Gateway. Most of this this occurred in the sixties and was directly related to the rapidly expanding overseas markets for bulk commodities, especially coal, potash, and sulphur. Tonnage throughput more than quadrupled and by 1970 the Port of Vancouver, served by four railways from the north, east, and south, was handling 2,000 deep-sea vessels annually and had become one of the ten top ports in the world, in tonnage terms.

In stark contrast to the multiple and major developments in the lower mainland, the first quarter-century after the war saw very little progress toward use or development of the Northern Gateway port. The tremendous wartime surge in activity at the shipyard, dry dock, and waterfront facilities came to an abrupt halt at war's end. U.S. and Canadian military personnel quickly left and most of the extensive facilities built by the Americans, including the large waterfront warehouse, were dismantled. The net long term benefit to the port from all the area's frantic wartime construction consisted of a wooden extension to the Ocean Dock and transit shed, and a wooden wharf at Watson Island. Both were eventually destroyed by fire.

For the dispirited local citizens, whose numbers had shrunk from a peak of 23,000 to about 8,000, the one substantial, lasting benefit was the road connection to Terrace and the provincial road network that had been roughed out during the war years.

The planned port city, terminus of the second, and certainly the best rail corridor across B.C., would see little progress toward its promised destiny as a Gateway Port during the next 25 years. Ottawa and its wholly owned railway were undoubtedly influenced by the recommendation in Sir Alexander Gibb's 1932 report to Parliament that, "*if Vancouver is to attain the position that is planned for it, it can only do so if it be protected from the establishment of a competitive port further north, which could only exist on direct or indirect subsidization.*" Neither showed interest in responding positively to pleas from the very small population for assistance in developing even one modern facility on the rail accessible waterfront that they almost exclusively controlled. No time limit had ever been placed on Gibb's recommendation.

Shipbuilding at the Prince Rupert Shipyard and Dry Dock ceased after the final order by Wartime Shipping Ltd. for two China Coasters was completed; the yard and dry dock reverted to its pre-war role of repair and maintenance work, primarily for the local fishing fleet. Even with minimal staffing, the work available could not support this large facility and for a few years the federal Department of Public Works compensated its CNR operator for the losses. When this aid was terminated in March 1954, the CNR offered the entire complex for sale. The dry dock was sold to the Puget Sound Bridge and Dredging Co. of Seattle and the day in 1955 that it started its eventful tow south was indeed a bitter one for those pioneers devoted to the concept of the city as Canada's alternate Pacific Gateway. The rest of the yard with its ship shed, marine ways, pattern shop, powerhouse, machine shop, blacksmith shop, foundry, fabricating shop, and office building were dismantled, leaving a cleared site served by the original wooden dock.

The substantial wartime naval presence in Prince Rupert ended in 1945 and Naval Services Headquarters in Ottawa showed no interest in any ongoing plans for the port city. Former Premier "Duff" Pattullo supported local lobbying that resulted in the re-commissioning of the naval reserve unit, HMCS *Chatham*, in October 1946 utilizing the building of the former Fisheries Experimental Station. This unit had originally been formed in 1923, closed in 1926, and then re-commissioned in 1929. It was paid off again in 1939 when the entire ship's company went active and its quarters were turned over to the newly formed Fishermen's Reserve. The post-war re-commissioning lasted until 1964 when it fell victim to a government austerity program and was decommissioned for the third time.

One of the port's few terminal assets, the grain elevator, had handled only 24 million bushels of grain in the 25 years since its opening in 1926. Put in perspective, the port's current terminal has comfortably handled that amount in a single month. No vessels were assigned to load at the terminal during 12 of those first 25 years of its existence, including the first five post-war years. Commencing with the 1951/52 crop year, the Canadian Wheat Board directed very modest amounts of wheat or barley to the terminal and vessels loaded an average of 7 million bushels annually for the next five years. Average annual throughput increased slightly for the next 10 years and then, for the last five years of this period, fell back to below the earlier figure. For the 20-year-period between crop year 1951/52 and 1970/71 throughput averaged only 240,000 tonnes annually.

The terminal was subject to valid criticism because of its insufficient storage capacity, especially in view of the rapidly increasing size of the vessels loading grain. Lobbying by the local Chamber of Commerce succeeded in convincing the Department of Agriculture in Ottawa to add a one-million-bushel annex to the terminal, thereby increasing its capacity to 2.25 million bushels. This $2.5 million addition was completed in October of 1968, but the increased capacity did not result in any immediate increase in grain made available to the terminal.

This failure to make good use of the port's one major facility was particularly discouraging to local people in the light of the more than fourfold increase in grain shipments through the Southern Gateway during the 1946–1970 period. Clearly, it was only being used as an overload facility when Vancouver's terminals were operating at well past their capacity. Prince Rupert's elevator was the sole ocean terminal owned and operated by the Canadian Grain Commission, a federal agency whose primary concern involved licensing grain elevators and assuring the integrity of Canadian grain production and handling. Owning the terminal was an anomaly and to some extent an embarrassment to the Commission. The terminal suffered, too, from the less than amicable relationship between its owner and the Wheat Board that controlled the direction of grain movement to ports. This stemmed, at least in part, from a lingering resentment engendered when the Canadian Wheat Board was created in 1935 under a new Ministry, rather than under the Ministry of Agriculture that was responsible for the Canadian Grain Commission.

Sporadic local attempts by the Chamber of Commerce to persuade the Canadian Wheat Board to direct a larger and more even flow of grain to the newly enlarged terminal failed and, reluctantly, it became accepted as a fact that grain collected at a company's country elevator must be directed by the Board to the same company's ocean terminals. Though false, this became a mantra and reflected the position that as the Canadian Grain Commission had no country collecting system, the local elevator should be denied the right to receive anything but overflow amounts from the owners of the "prairie skyscraper" collecting systems, who wanted all the grain they collected, as agents for the Wheat Board, to be directed to their very lucrative ocean terminals, wherever these were located. Thus Prince Rupert could only really expect to receive grain that these terminals could not handle at peak periods in peak years. That this practice contravened the terms of the *Canadian Wheat Board Act* was not successfully exposed until the mid-seventies. Curiously, the policy did not seem to pertain elsewhere. The terminal at Churchill Manitoba for example, operated by the NHB, with no collecting system and only accessible by shipping for 88 days a year, received a remarkably consistent flow of grain each year.

Despite the surfeit of negatives, a few positive events began to materialize for the seemingly abandoned, but still aspiring community that had been thrown back to near total dependence on its fishing fleet in the immediate post-war period.

In 1947 the Celanese Corporation of America took over the Watson Island site and adjacent wooden wharf that had been created by the U.S. military for storing and transferring ammunition and supplies to their Pacific Theatre of Operations. The company's subsidiary, Columbia Cellulose Ltd., proceeded to build a high alpha dissolving sulfite pulp mill on the site and later expanded it, in two stages, to 600 tons per day. At first the mill's production was railed east, but in April 1953 the first overseas shipment of 500 tons left the Porpoise Harbour dock destined for France. In 1965 a new entity, Skeena Kraft — owned 60 percent by Columbia Cellulose and 40 percent by Svenska Cellulosa of Sweden — built a 750 ton per day bleached kraft pulp mill adjacent to the sulfite mill. Most of that mill's product was shipped overseas. The war built wooden wharf was destroyed by fire on February 14, 1967 and was replaced later that year with a more permanent concrete structure for the sole use of the two mills.

While the Columbia Cellulose mill in Prince Rupert was being developed, a new pulp mill was constructed near Ketchikan, Alaska, 145 km (90 miles) by water from Prince Rupert. This induced the CNR to build a rail barge terminal on the harbour near Pillsbury Point and commence a regular AquaTrain (railcar carrying barge) service to pass the Alaska mill's product through Prince Rupert and thence onward on its lines to the "lower forty-eight." That service continued from 1954 to 1974. Pending completion of the 48-mile light rail branch line from Terrace to Kitimat in late 1954, this rail barge also made twice weekly trips south, carrying equipment to Alcan construction sites and returning with the first aluminum ingots poured by the new smelter to be carried east by rail.

This was not the first AquaTrain service to be based in Prince Rupert. From 1917 to the early 1920s the Swanson Bay Pulp Mill, 185 km (115 miles) south of the city, had moved their product to the railhead at Prince Rupert in a nine-car barge, berthing at a terminal located at approximately the same waterfront site.

In 1962 the CNR inaugurated a second rail barge service, established to connect the southern terminus of the Alaska Railroad at Whittier to U.S. Midwest tracks via CN lines. This service started with a 35-car barge and has continued to the present with upgrades to the local terminal and substantially increased barge capacity.

There were further positive developments for the city in 1961. These included the completion of the Digby Island airport and a start by the federal Department of Public Works on a marine terminal for the new Alaska Marine Highway system that was building its first major vessel, the *Malaspina*, in Seattle. This new service linking Prince Rupert with southeastern Alaska commenced operation in February 1963.

The site of the former shipyard was leased by Prince Rupert Sawmills Ltd. and a new mill built with a capacity to produce 40 million board feet (approximately 55,000 tonnes) of export lumber annually. In 1961 the mill began shipping lumber to Japan over the old shipyard wharf. An average of one vessel per month loaded from the old wooden facility until the Workmen's Compensation Board condemned it as unsafe, and, effective January 1969, it was restricted to tying up log ships. Thereafter, the mill barged its product to Nanaimo for vessel loading, but after a short time the operation closed and the site was again cleared.

The development of an iron mine at Jedway on the west coast of the Queen Charlotte Islands (now Haida Gwaii) in 1962 and an iron and copper mine at Tasu Sound in 1967 brought vessels loaded there to Prince Rupert, though only to clear customs, prior to heading to Japan. The Jedway operation closed in 1969, but the Wesfrob mine at Tasu continued production until 1983.

The Ocean Dock, completed in 1921, had a face length of 258 m (860 ft.) and a rail-served transit shed 246 m long by 43.8 m wide (820 ft. x 146 ft.). The dock was extended during the war to 480 m (1,600 ft.) and the transit shed to 375 m (1,250 ft.). The western end of the facility was leased to Canadian Fishing Company in 1951 and was converted to a cannery and fish processing plant. That operation continued until destroyed by fire in 1972. During the 1960s deep-sea vessels tied up at the dock to load logs, many of which had been barged over from the Queen Charlottes. Beginning in 1967, copper concentrates from the Granisle Mine on Babine Lake were railed to Prince Rupert and stored in the transit shed, pending loading on vessels that were usually already in port loading pulp and logs. This movement, too, ended with the near total destruction of the dock and shed in the June 10, 1972 fire.

The popularity of Alaska cruising gained momentum in the post-war period and by the mid-sixties the principle operator, Princess Cruises, was expanding rapidly as it acquired new and larger purpose-built ships. Soon Holland America, P&O, Royal Viking, and Sitmar would enter this market, with Prince Rupert hosting their vessels as the obligatory foreign port of call required by the U.S. *Jones Act*. Ocean Dock was used to berth these vessels for as long as it was available.

The Department of Transport opened a substantial new Marine Headquarters Agency at Seal Cove on July 2, 1966. Two of their vessels, the *Alexander Mackenzie* and the *Skidegate* plus a large Sikorsky helicopter were based at Prince Rupert with responsibility for the supply and maintenance of all navigational aids, as well as search and rescue for the coast south to Port Hardy on Vancouver Island.

Waterborne passenger and freight service to points on the long and rugged B.C. coast entered a period of major change in the early post-war years. The advent of air service (on floats or wheels), the consolidation of cannery operations, provision of road access to some formerly isolated points, centralization of logging operations, and reduction in coastal mining operations all contributed to the gradual decline in marine services between B.C. coastal settlements, many of which subsequently disappeared. With the arrival of the new *Queen of Prince Rupert* on May 21, 1966, the B.C. Ferry Authority inaugurated a new type of automobile and passenger service connecting upper Vancouver Island to Prince Rupert with a call at Bella Bella.

By the mid-sixties freighters called at fairly frequent intervals at Watson Island to load pulp. Some then moved to Ocean Dock to load copper concentrates and finish with a deck load of logs. Sporadically, a freighter would be assigned by the Wheat Board to pick up grain at the elevator. Putting on a brave front, the Prince Rupert Chamber of Commerce proclaimed that over 100 deep-sea ships had cleared the port in 1964. Though true, this statement omitted to mention the fact that 26 of the 111 vessels that "cleared" the port that year had actually loaded their iron and copper concentrates on the Queen Charlottes, or loaded logs at Port Simpson. Of the annual tonnage ascribed to the port, only about one-third was loaded within its environs.

With the exception of the very modest and intermittent movement of grains, and late in the period some copper concentrates from Granisle, all other exports from the port were either generated locally or within a 100-mile radius of the port. Virtually the only imports were chemicals for the pulp mills and petroleum products. AquaTrain movements were simply a pass-through of railcars that had been loaded elsewhere.

THE LONG HARD ROAD TO DEVELOPMENT AND UTILIZATION OF THE PORT AND ITS CORRIDOR

Uncomfortably aware of the many new, large scale terminal developments in the lower mainland, as well as the rapidly expanding transpacific trade opportunities, Prince Rupert citizens had, by 1964, recovered from their long post-war shock and started to press for at least one modern terminal able to handle bulk, break-bulk and general cargo. It appeared crystal clear that Ottawa had little or no interest in assisting the creation of port facilities in Prince Rupert as long as Vancouver could handle all exports through the West Coast. Such a policy ignored the potential for prolonged total disruption of the fragile common access corridor to the Southern Gateways that could result from natural or manmade disasters. Furthermore, the citizens were well aware that their tiny population lacked political clout, especially when compared to Vancouver, New Westminster, or the eastern Canadian ports.

Prince Rupert did, however, have some powerful friends east of the Rockies. Premiers Manning of Alberta and Thatcher of Saskatchewan urged Prime Minister Pearson to give priority to port development in Prince Rupert. Both were well aware that the potential disruption of the single rail corridor to the Southern Gateway Ports posed a threat to their provincial economies. Their support and that of their successors never wavered and, without question, was noted in Ottawa. As discussed later, that support and related financial backing was the prime factor in developing the large grain terminal on Ridley Island, and it in turn was responsible for providing infrastructure to that large and valuable industrial site. Japanese industrialists, too, noted both the shorter transit across the Pacific from Prince Rupert and the fact that the northern port could easily accommodate the largest vessels planned, or realistically foreseen.

The B.C. government's position on port development in Prince Rupert was complicated by the political imperative to support the provincially owned Pacific Great Eastern Railway (PGE). By 1958 this line had been extended south to North Vancouver and north to Dawson Creek and was planning further extensions to Mackenzie, Fort St. James, and Fort Nelson. As the B.C. government was both the issuer of forest management licenses and the owner of the PGE, exporters of forest products destined for overseas markets and produced in areas tributary to the railroad were "encouraged" to use it exclusively. The CNR made little effort to compete, as long as they were given the lucrative long haul of forest products to eastern markets. On one occasion in 1970 a shipment of 2,000 tons of pulp from Prince George was directed to Prince Rupert for loading to a vessel at Ocean Dock. This was not repeated. The rapidly expanding forest products industries in central and north central B.C., seeing no prospect of a modern facility in Prince Rupert during the sixties and under pressure to utilize the PGE, made long term arrangements to move their overseas exports through the new specialized terminals being developed in Squamish and North Vancouver. It is interesting to note that the Prince Rupert Daily News anticipated this result when, in 1912 it fumed, in response to Premier McBride's substantial subsidies to the PGE's original backers, that building this line south from Prince George "would reduce by half the traffic this port has every reason to expect." The paper was half right — in fact it virtually eliminated it. Further, it might well have protested the very considerable involvement of Charles Hays in getting that line built!

As part of his primary aim to provide B.C. with the basic infrastructure needed to develop its resources, Bennett established the B.C. Harbours Board in 1968 "to develop and encourage the development of harbour facilities in the Province." The Board's activity was certainly not confined to the lower coast. Studies of port potential were undertaken at Stewart, Alice Arm, Kitimat, and Prince Rupert. With reference to Prince Rupert it focused on prodding Ottawa to get on with development, recognizing that while Kitimat terminals would be built as needed by industries choosing to locate there, Prince Rupert was destined to be a national port and should, therefore, be developed by the federal government.

In an attempt to resolve the conflicting interests between developing Prince Rupert as a major port and protecting the provincial railroad, the Premier stated in 1968 that, "If the CNR would sell their line west of Prince George to B.C., we would see to it that Prince Rupert had a port like no other." This offer was backed by the provincial ownership of Ridley Island and the adjacent area of Kaien Island, both prime sites for large scale marine facility development. Eventually, the matter of determining responsibility for developing the Northern Gateway was resolved in meetings between the Premier and the Minister of Transport, Don Jamieson in 1972.

In 1961, a subsidiary of Vancouver Wharves acquired waterfront property in Kitimat from Alcan for the purpose of developing a break-bulk and general cargo terminal. The statement of its president, D. Odhams, that "Kitimat is the correct port on the central B.C. coast in which to establish future terminals both from a geographic and cost viewpoint," was certainly not helpful to Prince Rupert's aspirations, though the company's plans were soon dropped. Kitimat later complained vociferously when the CNR established rate parity to either port for the movement of forest products, convinced that their location should benefit from the 48-mile shorter rail haul to tidewater.

In response to strong representations by the City, Art Laing, Minister of Northern Affairs and Natural Resources and the senior Liberal cabinet minister for B.C., avowed that "The federal government is prepared to undertake its full responsibility to see that services are made available here," whatever that meant. Minister of Transport Jack Pickersgill, in November 1966 stated that he and Laing had "been devoting all our spare time to consideration of Prince Rupert which we believe has the kind of future Sir Wilfrid Laurier envisaged for it in 1903." Although that bit of hyperbole was unimpressive, the Minister did visit Prince Rupert in 1967 and, after a tour of the waterfront, declared that he was "ashamed of its deplorable condition" and agreed that "we should just quit talking and get on with its development." His successor, Paul Hellyer promised to visit the city, but this never materialized. It would not be until Don Jamieson's five-year tenure as Minister of Transport (1968–1973) that real progress in providing a modern terminal for the port would supplant political hot air.

In 1964, the Port and Marine Committee of the Prince Rupert Chamber of Commerce suggested that the City consider requesting that a local Commission be created under the recently passed *Harbour Commissions Act* to replace the existing administration of the port as a public harbour by the Department of Transport in Ottawa. The City, however, had little or no waterfront property to contribute to harbour development and the CNR was not prepared to surrender any of theirs, or any foreshore rights. Furthermore, the City concluded that immediate revenues would be insufficient to assure the fiscal viability of a harbour commission and projections were too uncertain to be acceptable. Instead, the City chose to create a local Port and Industrial Development Commission in early 1966. Well aware that the CNR, which controlled most of the rail-accessible city waterfront had no interest in developing a terminal in the port, the local Commission directed its activity toward persuading Ottawa to place the port under the jurisdiction of the National Harbours Board. That goal was achieved on March 23, 1972 when Prince Rupert was proclaimed the tenth national port.

Back in 1950, Donald Gordon, newly appointed President of the CNR, had visited Prince Rupert announcing, "It may be that recent political developments in the Far East (the Korean War) have robbed you for the time being at least of an important trade potential." When Pacific trade really began to open up after the Japan Peace Treaty the following year, the CPR and Vancouver were initially the main beneficiaries. From 1952–1969 the CNR was deeply engaged in improving its presence at the Southern Gateway. It made clear its position that it would take no part in waterfront terminal development in Prince Rupert, though it monitored the port's aspirations, was aware of proposed plans for major investments by the forest industries between Prince George and Prince Rupert, and was closely involved with the Transport Ministry in periodically assessing the situation. In 1964, CNR President Gordon assured the City that "Whatever is good for Prince Rupert is good for the CNR." The railway had another reason to be interested in Prince Rupert, namely its desire not to see a major ocean terminal development in Kitimat which they would be called upon to serve, as this would necessitate a large expenditure to relocate and upgrade their light line to that port.

Any assessment of the situation in Prince Rupert in 1964–1965 would conclude that the keys to development were held by the CNR and the federal government, owners of almost all the rail-accessible foreshore. Increasing local impatience resulted in Roger Graham, CNR's Mountain Region Vice President, commissioning CBA Engineering in early 1965 to do a waterfront survey of its Prince Rupert properties and existing port facilities and to develop a plan that would realize the full potential of the harbour — with particular reference to the best use of CNR property. This report was completed and delivered to the CNR in October 1965 and subsequently received wide distribution. It provided a detailed inventory of harbour foreshore ownership, leases, and existing facilities and exposed the lack of overall planning in port development. To remedy this, the report proposed a pattern of orderly development and confirmed the position of the City's Industrial Development Commission that a port authority under the NHB could provide needed planning and guidance.

The authors showed excellent foresight in suggesting the northwest portion of Ridley Island and the adjacent part of Kaien Island as the best site for future bulk handling terminals, even though both locations were then owned by the province. Unhappily, however, they failed to recognize the value of the Fairview area south of the Fishermen's Cooperative Plant and designated it for fish processing. Their choice for a general cargo terminal was the old shipyard site.

The report proposed that two berths at the Rushbrook site with 6 ha (15 acres) of backup land would initially be adequate to handle lumber and mineral concentrates. The facility could later be expanded to four berths with 20 ha (50 acres) of backup land if existing oil storage facilities, warehouses, the yacht club, and almost all other existing structures were removed. If further general cargo facilities were needed, the report recommended that two berths be developed at the Ocean Dock site, despite the immediate proximity of the essential rail yard and lack of space for cargo assembly.

This study and report had a very substantial impact on events that followed. The inventory of existing foreshore, the recommendation of a port authority to guide development, and the designation of the northwest Ridley Island/southwest Kaien Island area as the best site for future bulk loading facilities were beneficial. However, the choice of the old shipyard/Cow Bay area for a general cargo development was most unfortunate, as was the relegation of the Fairview South area to fish processing plants.

For the next five years much time, money, and effort was wasted by the National Harbours Board and the local Port Development Commission, while clinging to the idea of creating an adequate general cargo facility at the Rushbrook site, in spite of its many obvious flaws that included space constraints, unattractive configuration, and central location on the city waterfront.

In 1966 eight local business and professional men formed a company, Western Wharves Ltd. Their primary purpose was to identify and see developed a better marine terminal location than the very limited site recommended in the CBA report. Shareholders contributed funds and a careful study of 10 potential sites in the area was undertaken. This study identified the present location of the Fairview terminal as superior to all others for developing a general cargo and forest product handling terminal. Several of the parcels that were needed to develop the site had complex ownership with the result that it took the company two years to complete the minimum leasing arrangements needed. Further funds were spent on detailed studies of the site and planning for its development. Intensive efforts were undertaken to market the proposed terminal to prospective shippers and to encourage major terminal operators elsewhere to take over the project, or at least become senior partners. Both Neptune Terminals and Star Bulk Shipping expressed considerable interest, but Neptune was in the process of being sold and Star Bulk Shipping chose instead to build at Squamish. The "chicken and egg" conundrum was a major hurdle for the local group. Without some guarantee of long term business it was difficult to arrange financing for the project. Potential shippers, on the other hand, insisted on seeing a facility underway before making commitments.

The City Committee persisted in their misguided support for the Rushbrook site, but Department of Transport and National Harbours Board personnel eventually admitted that the Fairview site was far better suited both for immediate and longer term development and, in 1970 they decided to "take out" Western Wharves. The company's leases and site studies were purchased (for less than cost) by the CNR with the clear understanding that Ottawa would proceed expeditiously to bring the terminal to fruition. The CNR subsequently turned the leases over to the National Harbours Board, which had assumed jurisdiction over the port in early 1972 and which then, painfully slowly, proceeded with the project.

It would be another seven years before the Fairview General Cargo Terminal became a reality. This was most unfortunate, as a great deal of business from the rapidly expanding forest products sector in central and north central B.C., which could have used a competing port in Prince Rupert, had by then directed their export business to the new terminals at Squamish and North Vancouver, under long term contracts.

A SURGE OF INTEREST IN POTENTIAL SITES FOR BULK TERMINALS

In the 1960s the owners of Japan's burgeoning steel mills realized that their country's limited coal resources would approach exhaustion by 1980. Needing to secure long term supplies of metallurgical coal from multiple stable sources they encouraged the development of large scale mining operations of accessible deposits elsewhere, especially in Australia, Canada, and the United States.

Such a large and expanding overseas market attracted keen interest in Western Canadian deposits of high quality coking coal and in the logistics of getting the export product to tidewater. Several large Canadian companies, usually partnered with Japanese buyers, investigated known areas of major coal deposits, especially in the Rocky Mountains of Alberta and B.C. First to produce for export in the early sixties were existing mines in southwestern Alberta. Their coal was moved over CPR tracks to the new Pacific Coast Bulk Terminal at Port Moody. Late in the decade, production from the much larger mines in southeastern B.C. moved over the same corridor to the new "super port" at Roberts Bank.

Coal deposits are, of course, not confined to the southern end of the Canadian Rockies. Two substantial deposits of metallurgical coal in west central Alberta were under development at the same time as the south east B.C. mines. Both were within reasonable distance of CNR lines and, therefore, stimulated considerable interest in the potential use of the Northern Rail Corridor to a new bulk loading facility in the Prince Rupert area.

During the period from 1967–1972 McIntyre Porcupine, developers of the Smoky River deposits in northwest Alberta, both alone and with potential partners, looked seriously at several port options including building a loading facility at Prince Rupert. Others also studied the area extensively with a view to developing a very large common-use bulk terminal.

The CNR commissioned study on Prince Rupert's harbour by CBA Engineering recommended Ridley Island and the adjacent part of Kaien Island as the most suitable site in the area for a bulk terminal. McIntyre Porcupine was clearly aware of this recommendation and in 1969–1970 obtained a "map reserve" on the provincially owned island and on Lelu and Kitson Islands. They worked both alone and with Neptune Terminals to develop the concept of a Prince Rupert facility for their projected exports. In addition to Ridley they assessed, with Neptune, the capacity of the Fairview site leased by Western Wharves and concluded that it could accommodate a loop track and storage for up to 5 million tonnes throughput per year. Western Wharves' directors did not actively pursue coal for the site, however, but did allow it to be examined by Carr & Donald Associates, Neptune's Toronto engineering firm.

After Neptune was sold to Federal Grain in March 1969, the new owners focused on the Lelu-Kitson Island area and by February 1970 had completed a detailed and elaborate "Norport" proposal for that potential site. McIntyre Porcupine, which had begun shipping through Neptune in North Vancouver, continued their interest in Ridley Island and by 1971 proposed an $18 million first phase development there, which could be expanded to handle 10 million tonnes annually.

The Alberta Government weighed in with the view that a terminal in Prince Rupert should precede the development at Roberts Bank, due to the need for an alternate route to the coast and the competition provided by a second port.

Publicly, the CNR was very quiet on the direction of coal from these deposits. They were aware of the increasing pressure by the Japanese for a new route to a new outlet on the north coast, but knew that this route would entail massive upgrading of their "north line."

The City of Prince Rupert's Port Development Commission chairman expressed the view in 1967 that "If Prince Rupert is to have bulk loading facilities, a private developer, not the federal government should be the builder. The federal government will not compete with private enterprise." This is certainly not the way it turned out! In 1969–1970 the City did move to incorporate Ridley Island into its boundaries and commissioned a report from CBA Engineering, which suggested a three phase development of the Island including two berths plus 42 ha (106 acres) of backup land that would cost $37.5 million. Concurrently, Port Edward incorporated Lelu and Kitson Islands into its boundaries.

On the occasion of Prime Minister Trudeau's visit to Prince Rupert in August 1970, the City made a special request for federal aid in providing services to Ridley Island for a potential coal terminal builder.

Others, too, were looking at the potential for coal terminal development to service Alberta exporters. Rocklen Development Corporation Ltd., backed by Swiss capital, undertook very extensive and detailed work on this between 1967 and 1971. They appointed an international engineering firm, Sir William Halcrow and Partners to examine both the Ridley Island and the Lelu-Kitson Island potential sites. Halcrow came out in favour of the latter site, also the subject of Federal Grain's "Norport" study, and proposed a Roberts Bank type of development with a long causeway over Lelu to Kitson and the potential to reclaim up to 1,400 ha (3,500 acres) on Flora Bank. Their total concept involved 76 million cubic metres (100 million cubic yards) of fill at a cost of $130 million. Theirs was indeed a detailed and carefully planned project, but it fell afoul of the Fisheries Department that feared damage to fish habitat. The project was officially blocked in January 1972.

Utah Mining Company spent $200,000 surveying and studying the De Horsey Bank area in 1967 for a bulk terminal development, again like Roberts Bank, but this too would have been blocked by the Fisheries Department.

Kitimat, too, was in the "act." The Vancouver Wharves' subsidiary there had acquired land and planned a facility to accommodate bulk coal, sulphur, potash, and mineral concentrates, as well as forest products. They planned a start in 1970, but failed to win initial contracts and sold their property to Eurocan.

By early 1972, the direction of coal produced at McIntyre's Smoky River and Luscar's Cardinal River deposits became fixed under long-term arrangements with Neptune Terminals in North Vancouver. The federal government took the position that no new coal terminals would be needed until 1980. It appeared that both the federal and provincial governments favoured Ridley Island for an eventual new terminal, as witnessed by the handover of the island from Crown Provincial to Crown Federal ownership on July 2, 1971, "for development as a port in the national interest." Furthermore, while blocking development of the Rocklen proposal at Flora Bank, the Federal Fisheries Department concluded that there were no contraindications from their standpoint to a bulk loading terminal at Ridley Island. Many hurdles, however, remained to be crossed during the next 13 years before the first newly mined coal from northeastern B.C. reached a new bulk terminal on the island.

OFFSHORE OIL EXPLORATION AND A POTENTIAL PIPELINE TERMINAL

The potential for trans-shipment of petroleum products through Prince Rupert and for oil and gas exploration in the Hecate sedimentary basin has aroused interest for a long time, though never on the same scale as more recent proposals for oil, petrochemical, or liquefied natural gas (LNG) terminals. The January 10, 1921 issue of the Prince Rupert Daily News suggested the possibility of a pipeline from the developing oil field at Norman Wells to Prince Rupert!

In 1966, local MLA Bill Murray suggested that a pipeline for oil and gas be built from new discoveries in the Peace region to Prince Rupert. Then in October 1967, there was an announcement of Japanese interest in an oil sands project near Fort McMurray with the extracted crude oil to be shipped by pipeline to Prince Rupert for export to Japan. Nothing came of this, probably due to the early experience of very high unit costs for the crude product extracted from the tar sands.

Since 1949 major oil companies have shown interest in the potential for large reserves of oil and gas along the B.C. coast, especially in Hecate Strait and Queen Charlotte Sound. Activity in pursuit of this interest has been sporadic due to intermittent provincial or federal government moratoriums imposed in response to public opinion. These, plus disputes between Ottawa and Victoria over the ownership of the offshore seabed on the North Coast have resulted in only one episode of drilling.

In 1961 Shell Oil obtained necessary federal oil and gas exploration permits and after several years of mapping and surveys, they commenced drilling a series of 14 holes off Vancouver Island's west coast and in Hecate Strait, during the period 1967 to 1969, using a new drilling platform built in Victoria on the shipyard ways just vacated by the *Queen of Prince Rupert*. Shell's permits were farmed out to Chevron Canada Resources in 1970 and Chevron continued to undertake seismic surveys until 1972. At that point the federal government decided not to approve any new exploration permits on the West Coast. Finally in 1989, following the *Exxon Valdez* oil spill in Prince William Sound, both federal and provincial governments placed a moratorium on further oil and gas exploration in Hecate Strait and Queen Charlotte Sound. A number of difficult issues need to be resolved before exploratory work can resume on this highly prospective area, which the Geological Survey of Canada estimates to potentially contain 10 times the resource offered by Hibernia.

Between 1975 and 1977, the Alyeska pipeline from Prudhoe Bay to Valdez was under construction and there was a flurry of interest in Prince Rupert as the port to unload the Alaska crude and ship it by a new pipeline to Edmonton, there to connect with lines able to carry the oil to refineries in North Central USA. Trans Mountain Pipeline and Koch Industries led a group of six companies investigating this proposition. By early 1977 their interest in a North Coast terminal had switched to Kitimat and then faded completely as other West Coast U.S. ports won the business.

CHAPTER SEVEN

The Gateways 1970 to 1985 —
A Tentative Response to the "Container Revolution"

This period was marked by very significant developments at both Northern and Southern Gateways. Specialized facilities to more appropriately accommodate the "container revolution" in international shipping were developed in both Vancouver and New Westminster. Existing Southern Gateway bulk and break-bulk terminals were upgraded and expanded, and new facilities were added. A magnificent new passenger terminal for cruise ships was nearing completion in 1985 at the Burrard Inlet site of the former Pier B-C. Two specialized terminals designed to receive autos were developed by the Fraser River Harbour Commission.

By the end of this period Prince Rupert finally had a modern general cargo facility with two berths plus a high throughput grain terminal and a modern coal shipping facility on Ridley Island.

To accommodate the westward movement of massive tonnages of bulk commodities in unit trains, very large projects costing nearly $2 billion were undertaken by the Canadian Pacific Railway (CPR), Canadian National Railways (CNR), and British Columbia Railway (BCR). In addition, the two transcontinental railways began to develop specialized facilities and equipment to efficiently meet the needs of the "container revolution."

Both Vancouver and Prince Rupert became Local Port Corporations, newly minted crown corporations under the *Canada Ports Corporation Act* of 1983 that replaced the National Harbours Board with Ports Canada.

THE ADMINISTRATION OF NATIONAL PORTS

The creation of the National Harbours Board (NHB) in 1936 flowed from the recommendations contained in the report of Sir Alexander Gibb, the British engineer who had been engaged by Parliament in 1932 to study Canadian ports, their efficiency, needs, and management. Gibb found problems akin to the "hangover" from excessive railroad building earlier in the century. A surfeit of optimism had resulted in construction projects that had led to gross overcapacity, fierce competition, bankruptcies, and calls for government bailout. Among his recommendations, Gibb proposed a merger of the New Westminster and Vancouver Harbour Commissions into what would become the Vancouver Port Authority under the new Act. With clear, albeit indirect, reference to Prince Rupert the report recommended that Vancouver *"should be protected from the establishment of a competitive port further north."*

Though unquestionably music to Vancouver ears, these two recommendations created discord in the other two ports. New Westminster had the political influence to block Gibb's recommendation that it be merged with Vancouver and continued as a Harbour Commission excluded from the jurisdiction of the new NHB. Prince Rupert had no such influence in the corridors of power. Unquestionably, this second Gateway Port's growth and development was held back for the next four decades by Ottawa and Vancouver's enthusiastic acceptance of Gibb's recommendation.

The NHB was set up to centrally control, administer, and provide specialized professional services to Canada's major public (national) ports. Established during the great economic depression of the 1930s in response to past excesses, it was guided, at least for its first two decades, by a policy of retrenchment, rather than development of the ports it controlled. It was by no means free of political influence and was perceived in the west to be strongly influenced by pressures from St Lawrence and Maritime interests, while neglectful of the needs and aspirations of West Coast ports. The frequently politicized Ottawa bureaucracy exercised excessively tight control over individual port capital expenditures to the point of stifling local initiative. The Board's annual revenues increased from $1.6 million in 1942 to $57.5 million 40 years later.

Government policy, which had long embraced public ownership, investment, and management of Canadian ports, began a long process of change in the late 1950s. There was increasing awareness that public ownership and especially public management was stifling initiative and jeopardizing Canada's competitiveness in world trade. The national ports were not alone in expressing frustration at their lack of freedom of action stemming from the rigid centralization of power in Ottawa.

Responding to pressures for new directions, the Diefenbaker government (1957–1963) appointed two Royal Commissions to study and make recommendations on the future of Canada's transportation systems and on government organization.

The MacPherson Royal Commission on Transportation (1959–1961), considering all forms of transportation in the country, emphasized in its report the need for less government control, more competition between modes, and deregulation wherever competition existed, in order for the Canadian transportation system to reach its potential efficiency.

The Royal Commission on Government Organization, under the leadership of J. Grant Glassco was appointed in 1960 with a mandate to inquire into the methods and organization of the departments and agencies of the federal government. The five volume report of the Commission, released in 1962–1963, recommended that government should "let the managers manage," that departments should be free of inappropriate central control, and should be allowed to devise management methods best suited to their needs. The main theme of the report was the dismantling of rigid central control over the day to day administration of government departments, allowing government agencies to operate more like businesses with only broad policies being imposed from above.

With special reference to the administration of the national ports, Glassco's recommendations were tantamount to a complete reversal of the centralizing policies advised by Gibb in 1932. Glassco deplored the "somewhat chaotic pattern" of divided responsibility that existed between the various government departments and agencies involved in the construction of harbour works and urged that local administration be established on the harbour commission model, not the NHB model.

New Westminster benefited substantially from the Glassco Report. Under the *Harbour Commissions Act* of 1964, the New Westminster Harbour Commission became the Fraser River Harbour Commission, continuing free of the threat of merger with Vancouver and with considerably more room to maneuver under its new mandate than its much larger, centrally controlled neighbour — to the chagrin of the latter!

Despite Glassco and MacPherson, there would be no easing of the tight central control of NHB Ports for a further 20 years. Under increasing pressure from these ports, the Trudeau administration promised, in 1975, to abolish the NHB. Two years later a new *Canada Ports Corporation Act (CPC Act)* received first reading in the House, but further passage of this bill proceeded at glacial speed. Finally, after a six-year gestation, the Act was passed in 1983.

This new legislation replaced the *National Harbours Board Act* of 1936 that had created the Vancouver Port Authority and later the Prince Rupert Port Authority (1975). Former NHB ports, including Vancouver and Prince Rupert, became Local Port Corporations (LPCs), each with their own Board of Directors. The new Vancouver Port Corporation's spending authority was eventually increased to $5 million, though the Prince Rupert Port Corporation was limited to $500,000.

The new National Ports Policy established under the *CPC Act* was an attempt to provide each newly created LPC with a higher degree of autonomy to manage and operate its port. The Act sought to provide accessibility and equitable treatment for moving goods and persons to users of Canadian ports and to become an effective instrument to support the achievement of Canadian International Trade objectives, as well as national, regional, and local economic and social objectives. Local Port Corporations became "landlord ports," leasing port property to tenants to operate.

Though certainly an improvement over the totally centralized, bureaucratic, and politicized NHB, the new environment under which the LPCs had to operate soon revealed that they were not free of political influence, or the meddling of Ottawa officials determined to retain and exercise tight control. Spending limits imposed on the LPCs and a government propensity to raid any surplus built up by a port, over and above the dividends the port paid annually to Ottawa, continued to be a major source of irritation. However, this flawed legislation governed Canada's major ports for the next 15 years until repealed in 1998 and replaced by the *Canada Marine Act*.

In line with a major Trudeau government initiative, the Minister of Transport directed that all port traffic would be stated in metric measurements effective January 1, 1978.

RAIL CORRIDOR DEVELOPMENTS

Between 1970 and 1985 tonnage exports of dry bulk commodities through the Southern Gateway continued to grow, led by a 400 percent increase in coal throughput, a doubling of sulphur and potash, and a 60 percent increase in grains. By mid-1985 the Northern Gateway could offer state-of-the-art facilities capable of moving 15–18 million tonnes of bulk grain and coal annually.

Though very large sums had been committed to construct new terminal facilities to handle these bulk commodities at both Gateway Ports, even larger and more costly projects had to be undertaken by the railways to move them to the export terminals.

The CPR moved its first 88-car unit train of coal to the new Westshore Terminal at Roberts Bank on April 30, 1970. To move that train the 1,120 km (700 miles) from the Kaiser Resources mines in southeastern British Columbia (B.C.) to the port, the railway had to supply substantially more motive power on a section in the Rogers Pass in the Selkirk Range with an adverse grade of 2.2 percent. As coal volumes increased over the succeeding decade, it became economically expedient for the railway to spend the estimated $600 million required to reduce that grade to an acceptable 1 percent, by constructing a new line through the pass. Work on this project commenced in 1983 and included driving two tunnels totaling 15.7 km (9.8 miles). The new 35 km (21.7 mile) line was 107 m (357 ft.) lower than the original line. It achieved the desired grade and reduction in required motive power and was then dedicated to the west-bound movement of heavy unit trains.

The CNR moved its first unit coal train from the west central Alberta mines to the north shore of Burrard Inlet via its new second narrows rail bridge in February 1970. With a 90 percent increase in traffic over its lines to the West Coast between 1968 and 1972, the railway embarked on a number of double tracking projects on key sections of the main line east of Jasper and east of Port Mann. Then, with the impending large increases in grain and coal flows to the new Prince Rupert terminals anticipated in the mid-eighties, the railway committed approximately $600 million to a major upgrade of its north line from Red Pass Junction to the coast. This work included replacing mainline track with 138-pound rail, creating new sidings, buying new train sets, and installing centralized traffic control over the line. This commitment reflected the view of the Mountain Region Vice President, Charles Armstrong who expressed in 1974 that the railway needed Prince Rupert to complement Vancouver, inasmuch as the rail lines to that Southern Gateway were nearing capacity.

A number of prairie farm organizations, concerned about the potential for prolonged disruption to traffic in the single rail corridor through the Fraser Canyon — then carrying over 90 percent of westward moving export grains to Vancouver terminals — pressed for a rail connection to link the main rail lines at Ashcroft with the British Columbia Railway line at Clinton. Such a link could circumvent the canyon in the event of prolonged blockage of both main lines. This issue became one of the topics considered by the Hall Royal

Commission on Grain Transportation and was thoroughly aired at the Vancouver hearings in October 1976. It received absolutely no support from the two national railways, based primarily on their distaste for trying to move long and heavy trains over the tight curves and multiple 2.2 percent grades of the provincial line from Clinton to the coast. With the new outlet at Prince Rupert able to handle at least a third of West Coast grain exports by 1985, interest in this matter faded.

Both of the federally regulated national railways carried an excessive burden of fuel and property taxes, the latter especially high in B.C. In addition, they faced the increasingly discouraging task of moving grain to the West Coast under a rate established in perpetuity in 1897, as well as the federal government's refusal to allow them to abandon thousands of miles of little used branch lines in the central plains. Furthermore, within the Port of Vancouver, rail access to Burrard Inlet terminals was jealously guarded by five different railways with jurisdictions split between federal and provincial governments. These frustrating and serious problems hampered efficiency in many ways and would take many more years to resolve.

Added to the very substantial commitments made during this period to expedite the movement of increasing tonnages of bulk commodities, the national railways were faced with the altogether new problem of handling containers. In 1977, Sea-Land became the first container shipping line to dispatch containers arriving in Los Angeles from Asia to the eastern states via the Southern Pacific Railway. APL Line soon followed, moving containers east from Seattle on Burlington Northern Lines. As traffic rapidly increased, low slung cars able to carry double-stacked containers were developed by Sea-Land and first used on Southern Pacific's lines out of Los Angeles.

Though provision of fully equipped port terminals for container traffic in Vancouver lagged far behind U.S. West Coast ports, numbers did increase from 35,000 TEU[4] in 1971 to 178,125 TEU in 1985. Dockside rail, heavily favoured by the container shipping lines, was installed at both Vancouver terminals — albeit constrained in extent by their space limitations — and intermodal terminals and "load out" centres were developed as close as possible to the waterfront for receiving and dispatching containers. Later, the lure of very much cheaper land prompted both railways to develop large intermodal terminals at more distant sites in the lower mainland, as well as at central distribution points across Canada and the U.S.

At first containers were moved east from Vancouver on flat cars, but as numbers increased it became clear that efficient operation required dedicated trains hauling containers double-stacked, on specially designed low slung cars. This necessitated major expenditures by both Canadian railways to increase the vertical clearance of many mainline tunnels, snow sheds, and bridges. Observation of the innovations in container handling by U.S. railroads gave impetus to these changes by CP and CN.

---

[4]Twenty Foot Equivalent Unit.

The PGE changed its name to British Columbia Railway in 1972 and later, as part of a major restructuring in 1984, the rail division was designated BC Rail, which then took over the B.C. Harbours Board railway line connecting three Class 1 railways to Roberts Bank. This provincially owned and regulated line undertook construction of a new 81 km (50.3 mile) branch line from Anzac to Tumbler Ridge in northeast B.C. to access the coal mines being developed there. Completion of this half billion dollar project enabled the railway to begin moving coal to Prince George in early 1984 for interchange to the CNR line and onward to the newly completed Ridley bulk terminal, a total distance of 987 km (614 miles).

VANCOUVER: 1970 TO 1985

LOCAL PORT ADMINISTRATION

Before World War II and in the immediate post-war period, the south shore of Burrard Inlet provided adequate sites for rail-accessible terminals suited to handling general cargo, grain, lumber, and overseas passenger vessels, as well as the extensive Vancouver based coastal marine services.

By the mid-sixties the local port administration undertook a number of mid to long range planning initiatives. These were stimulated by the continuing growth in the export of dry bulk commodities, the renewed growth in the seasonal Alaska cruise industry, the need for a local response to the "container revolution," and the recognition of increasing demand for public access to segments of the harbour shoreline.

Available sites on the south shore could not satisfy all these needs. The arrival of the PGE in North Vancouver in 1956 and the 1969 opening of the new and more reliable CNR bridge at second narrows enabled the development of several good sites on the north shore for bulk and break-bulk terminals. Furthermore, the 1967 expansion of the harbour limits to include Roberts Bank allowed for the development of a massive facility to handle coal exports there.

In 1966 a 5,000 square foot model of the harbour was ordered by the Vancouver Port Authority (VPA) and installed at Ballantyne Pier. Then in the early seventies, the Port of Vancouver Development Committee, funded by the NHB, studied the existing waterfront and its future potential, and then advised the VPA on the best use of available sites for new waterfront facilities.

A Central Waterfront Committee was established in 1978 and tasked with planning the future of the portion of the south shore between Coal Harbour and Centennial Pier with a view to blending industrial, commercial, public, and private developments. One of this committee's prime recommendations was the development of a combined convention centre and passenger terminal at the former Pier B-C site.

By 1981, the VPA had Ottawa approval for planned projects totaling $51.5 million. This amount included expenditures of $35.1 million at Roberts Bank, $3.3 million for expansion at Lynnterm, $11.7 million for Vanterm upgrades, $1 million to rebuild the Burrard viaduct, and $430,000 for a 30-year master plan for the port. These programs would soon be expanded to $80 million over five years with over half that amount to be spent at Roberts Bank.

SOUTHERN GATEWAY BRIDGES

The inherent fragility of the main rail corridor to the Vancouver waterfront was underlined by prolonged disruptions in service to the Burrard Inlet terminals resulting from extensive damage to the port's two key bridges caused by vessel collision. The federal Department of Public Works Bridge across the Fraser River at New Westminster, built by the province in 1904, and serving all the rail lines into Vancouver except the CPR, was knocked out by a runaway barge in December 26, 1975 and not reopened until April 21, 1976. Between 1951 and 1983 this bridge received a total of 44 hits from river traffic and, although most of these collisions caused little damage, several caused damage that required very inconvenient rerouting of rail traffic for prolonged periods. In addition to damage from collisions, fire damage to the centre span on May 29, 1982 required a month's closure for repairs. The venerable bridge continues to constitute a veritable Achilles Heel to reliable rail service to Burrard Inlet terminals.

The original second narrows bridge was involved in 16 accidents between its opening in 1925 and the demolition of its main span in September 1930. It was rebuilt and reopened in June 1934. Greater care in the operation of vessels transiting the narrows later reduced the frequency of collisions and finally the old bridge was replaced in 1969 by the new CNR bridge. This new bridge, in turn, was severely damaged on October 12, 1979 when it was hit by the *Japan Erica*. Repairs cost $10 million and the bridge was out of service until March 5, 1980, a disruption that cost the north shore terminals dearly. Especially hard hit were the Pioneer grain terminal, which had just reopened, and the recently completed Fibreco woodchip terminal.

CONTAINER TERMINAL DEVELOPMENTS

Vancouver opened its first specialized facility on June 1, 1970 at the newly created Berth Six on Centennial Pier. Equipped with one container crane and operated by Empire Stevedoring, it served vessels with a capacity of 700–1,000 TEU.

During 1971 the facility handled a total of 28,000 containers, while another 17,000 were accommodated in the port using mobile dockside cranes or the vessels' own gear. A record was set in July 1971 when the specialized facility moved 2,763 containers in 12 days!

The "container revolution" was rapidly gaining momentum, as manifested by the number and size of the specialized vessels operating worldwide. By 1971 there were 160 "boxships" operating in international trade with another 100 vessels under construction. Early cellular vessels could carry only 700–1,000 containers, but by 1985 vessels designed to carry 3,000 units were under construction. This increase in size created the need to expand

and re-equip the early container terminals. Furthermore, the railways serving the terminals had to adapt by designing and acquiring new railcars and by modifying and expanding their terminal rail yards.

Port labour was quick to realize that containerization would result in a substantially reduced demand for waterfront employment. The ILWU in Vancouver responded by negotiating a "container clause" in their 1970 contract with the B.C. Maritime Employers Association. This clause gave ILWU members the exclusive right to de-stuff import containers with contents destined for multiple local consignees. As a result, companies found it cheaper to have their boxed imports off-loaded at Puget Sound terminals and trucked north to be de-stuffed by their own employees, or agents. This clause soured labour-management relations at Vancouver's embryo container terminals and, unquestionably, was a major factor in retarding the growth of boxed traffic — to the substantial benefit of Seattle and Tacoma. The clause remained in effect until January 1988.

Despite the late entry of the poorly located facility at Centennial with its single crane, the reluctance of vessel owners to divert to Vancouver for less than 200 containers, and the contentious "container clause," growth in container traffic was impressive. It doubled between 1971 and 1976 and then, with a second terminal available, doubled again by 1985 to 178,175 TEU.

In September 1972 the Vancouver Port Authority received approval from Ottawa to proceed with a plan to create a combined general cargo, ro-ro (roll on roll off), and container terminal at a site between the United Grain Growers elevator and Lapointe Pier. This new terminal, named Vanterm opened in mid-1975, offering two 277.5 m (925 ft.) berths for container vessels, 30.75 hectares (76 acres) of backup land, a ro-ro berth and 438 m (1,460 ft.) of general cargo berthing space. The container berths were equipped with two rail-mounted container cranes. The new terminal, costing $30 million, was leased to Empire Stevedoring for operation. Casco Terminals, a subsidiary of Canadian Stevedoring, then took over the operation of all of Centennial pier, including its small, one crane container facility and the adjacent Ballantyne Pier. Both Vanterm and Centennial (renamed Centerm in 1977) retained substantial capacity to handle bulk and break-bulk cargoes.

Though container movement through the two terminals continued to grow, reaching 151,551 TEU in 1984, there was still a very substantial number of locally destined containers being off-loaded in Seattle and Tacoma. Canadian Customs reported that in 1984 a total of 79,597 TEU destined for Canadian points were landed at U.S. West Coast ports, while only 3,367 TEU were unloaded in Vancouver for onward movement to the U.S. This was in marked contrast to the situation at the East Coast where Canadian terminals unloaded a very large number of containers destined for the U.S. This 1984 figure represented a loss of one-third of Vancouver-bound boxes to Puget Sound terminals and was, unfortunately, typical of the first 15 years of the port's container operations.

Sixteen hundred containers unloaded at Vanterm in 1984 were railed to Chicago, but aggressive attempts to secure more of this business were initially inhibited by fear that Burlington Northern and Union Pacific would retaliate.

To accommodate growth over this period a third crane was added at Vanterm in 1983 and a second at Centerm in 1984. The 300-ton heavy lift crane at Centerm was removed to make way for the new container crane. The old Terminal Dock, built by Robin Hood Flour in 1924, was declared unsafe by the Workmen's Compensation Board in 1983 and subsequently demolished. Its solid ground was used to store containers.

BULK TERMINALS

In the immediate post-war period, grain and lumber continued to dominate exports from the port's facilities, most of which dated from the 1920s or earlier. Apart from the grain terminals, modern specialized bulk or break-bulk facilities did not exist. Imports still constituted nearly half of total port tonnage.

Twenty-five years later, the port picture had changed dramatically. Exports now constituted 90 percent of the port's tonnage throughput and the new export commodities of coal, sulphur, and potash had, collectively, far overtaken grain. By 1985 grain had been reduced to 16 percent of the massively increased total tonnage exports, in marked contrast to its overwhelming 76.5 percent dominance 40 years earlier. To accommodate these new commodities as well as increasing grain volumes, six specialized bulk handling facilities were completed in the lower mainland by 1970. Two more would be completed in 1979, including a rebuilt, enlarged, and thoroughly modernized grain terminal on the north shore. In addition three break-bulk facilities, designed to handle forest products with maximum efficiency, were completed between 1971 and 1976.

Facilities to handle the import and export of petroleum products remained confined to terminals in the eastern reaches of Burrard Inlet past second narrows and were expanded and upgraded as needed.

Pacific Coast Bulk Terminals

Vancouver's first bulk terminal opened in 1959 and underwent a major expansion in 1967. By then its two berths and ship loaders were handling coal, sulphur, and woodchips. The terminal shared port sulphur exports which, between 1970 and 1979 averaged 3 million tonnes per year, with Vancouver Wharves. By 1985 total sulphur exports had reached 6.1 million tonnes.

Coal exports came, at first, from relatively small southwest Alberta producers. In 1968, initial coal production from Kaiser Resources operations in southeast B.C. was moved over the Port Moody facility, pending completion of Westshore terminal. Pacific Coast Bulk Terminals had strongly objected to the B.C. government's enthusiastic promotion of the new coal terminal at Roberts Bank, convinced that it could handle foreseeable coal exports up to at least 5 million tonnes annually.

Pacific Coast's terminal site did not allow for a loop track and coal throughput declined from a peak of 1.4 million tonnes in 1977, as the terminal could not match the efficiencies of its new competitors at Westshore and Neptune. Sultran, the logistics service company owned by the sulphur producers, purchased the terminal from Cominco in 1981 and the new owner chose to phase out coal handling, refusing to accept future overflow shipments from Westshore. Reverting to the name of its original parent, Pacific Coast Terminals, the operation focused on handling sulphur and ethylene glycol.

Vancouver Wharves

From the time of its official opening in August 1960, this privately owned and operated terminal underwent almost continuous expansion to its land base, berths, railcar and ship loading and unloading equipment, and storage facilities. In addition to handling lumber, pulp, plywood and scrap steel, the terminal started handling sulphur in 1962 and potash later that year. Storage for metal concentrates was added in 1971. Eventually sulphur, potash, and metal concentrates would dominate export tonnage at this terminal. From 1965–1968 phosphate rock imports were unloaded at the terminal, but this business moved to Neptune when it was completed late in 1968.

The terminal was provided with a rail barge slip, a facility that was much used during disruptions to rail service over the second narrows bridge, and especially during the long outage from October 12, 1979 to March 5, 1980.

Vancouver Wharves became the sole independently owned bulk terminal in the port, after Sultran took over Pacific Coast Bulk Terminals and Neptune had been sold to a consortium of its customers. The terminal was sold by its British owners to the Norwegian shipping company Stolt-Nielsen in 1982.

Neptune Terminal

In 1970 this new, state-of-the-art bulk terminal focused primarily on the efficient handling of coal and potash exports, as well as the import of phosphate rock and salt. Export commodities, arriving by unit trains onto the terminal's loop track were unloaded to storage, or when possible, directly onto a berthed vessel. Substantial sums were spent on dust control equipment to calm fears in the adjacent residential community.

The new owners, Federal Grain, decided late in 1971 to conduct an experiment in moving grain over their dry bulk facility, using essentially the same equipment and operating procedures used for potash. A shipment of 279,000 bushels (7,600 tonnes) of wheat, processed to export standards at the government elevator in Saskatoon, arrived at the terminal for "direct hit" loading onto the berthed grain carrier *Mari Chandris*. Though this experiment was a success, it was not repeated. The ILWU insisted that grain loading required the traditional six-member gang per hatch, regardless of the loading method used. Furthermore, owners of the port's conventional and profitable grain elevators were not willing to lose the benefits of oceanside grain processing; neither were they prepared to tolerate any avoidable reduction in their terminal throughputs. When terminal owner Federal Grain sold their Pacific Elevator complex to the Pools in 1972 they agreed to stay out of future grain movement through the port.

The terminal was a major victim of the almost five-month disruption in rail service to the north shore as a result of a vessel collision causing extensive damage to the second narrows rail bridge on October 12, 1979. Stressed financially, the company arranged a loan from the Alberta Government in 1980 and, in return, used some of the funds to equip the terminal for handling agri-products. The loan was later repaid in full.

Coal sourced from the mines of Luscar, McIntyre, and Consolidation Coal in west central Alberta moved to the terminal in CNR unit trains. Total throughput of coal alone reached a record 4.1 million tonnes in 1982. That year the terminal was acquired by a number of its major customers including coal shippers, Canpotex, the marketing arm of the potash producers, and other terminal users. Following their purchase, they invested $12 million on upgrades to the facility.

Roberts Bank and Westshore Terminals

Initially, the Roberts Bank development consisted of a 20 hectare (50 acre) "island" and a narrow 4.8 km (3 mile) causeway, created from dredged seafloor material and served by a 37 km (23 mile) rail line supplied by the B.C. Harbours Board. The island was leased by the VPA to Westshore Terminals, a new company owned by Kaiser Resources and Japanese coal buyers. At the time of its opening in mid-1970 the terminal had an annual throughput capacity of about 5 million tonnes of coal. Additional equipment added over the next few years doubled that capacity and in its fifth full year of operation, the terminal loaded out 8.3 million tonnes of metallurgical and thermal coal.

The success of the new terminal prompted interest by others seeking to develop facilities for moving large quantities of dry bulk materials. Trimac proposed a plan for a $25 million multi-commodity bulk terminal capable of handling 18 million tonnes per year on an extension to the Westshore site. When the VPA proposed preparing a series of 20 hectare parcels for lease, Westshore agreed to option the first prospective site and Trimac the second.

Extension to the original island was, however, delayed for several years by a difference of opinion between the Government of Canada and the Province of British Columbia over ownership of the seabed at Roberts Bank. This stemmed from the larger issue of whether or not the Strait of Georgia constituted "inland waters." Though failing to resolve the basic issue, an interim agreement was reached in 1980 whereby B.C. donated 60.7 hectares (150 acres) of seafloor to the VPA/NHB for the purpose of further terminal development, without prejudice to its position on ownership of the rest of the seabed in the Strait.

By 1979 the Westshore facility had surpassed its rated 10-million-tonne capacity, moving mostly metallurgical coal from the southeast B.C. mines of Kaiser Resources and Fording Coal. Though VPA and Westshore's plans to double the terminal's capacity were well advanced, action on these plans had to await resolution of the federal-provincial squabble. In 1981 the VPA predicted that coal volumes for shipment through the port would grow to between 39 and 50 million tonnes by 1990, with most of that growth in thermal coal exports. As a result of that prediction, the VPA shelved any idea of handling other dry bulk commodities such as potash and sulphur at Roberts Bank. Trimac abandoned its interest there.

The port authority embarked on a $48 million site expansion program in 1981 and, by 1984, the original 20 hectare island (Pod 1) had been expanded to 80 hectares (Pods 2–4) and the causeway widened. A second deep-water berth was provided, capable of handling vessels up to 250,000 tonnes. Concurrently, Westshore undertook a three-year, $130 million, phased expansion to their coal terminal, after doubling their land base by negotiating a new lease with the VPA on 20 hectares (Pod 2) of the newly expanded island. By 1984, having completed a program that included extensive re-equipping and upgrading of the terminal and the addition of a second berth, Westshore could comfortably accommodate an annual coal throughput of 22 million tonnes. With this extra capacity the terminal could serve new customers, including those formerly served by Pacific Coast Bulk Terminals at Port Moody, as that terminal's new owner, Sultran, had begun phasing out coal handling in 1983.

In 1979 Kaiser Resources, Westshore's majority owner and largest customer, was acquired by British Columbia Resources Investment Corporation (BCRIC) and renamed B.C. Coal, later changed to Westar Mining. The new owner bought out the Japanese minority interest in the terminal in 1985 and then sold the wholly owned terminal shares to Westar Industries, a BCRIC subsidiary, for $115 million in preferred shares.

Fibreco Terminal

This forest product terminal was developed as a bulk woodchip handling facility and constructed at a cost of $16 million on a 9.3 hectare (23 acre) site on the north shore, directly opposite Canada Place. The terminal was built for Fibreco Export Ltd., a coalition that included over 40 interior and coastal sawmills. Soon after it opened in May 1979, its supply of woodchips was drastically reduced for nearly five months by a combination of the disruption in rail service from the east, due to the collapse of the second narrows bridge, and a concurrent BC Rail strike halting incoming rail from the west.

THREE NEW BREAK-BULK TERMINALS

Three terminals designed primarily for maximum efficiency in handling forest products opened at lower mainland sites between 1971 and 1976. These specialized terminals were developed in response to the huge expansion of the B.C. forest industry, particularly in the interior of the province, under the prodding of Premier W.A.C. Bennett's administration in Victoria.

Seaboard International Terminal

The first new break-bulk terminal to be completed was located on the remainder of the 52.6 hectare (130 acre) north shore site developed from dredged material by the VPA/NHB between 1966 and 1968. Neptune Terminals had leased the western portion of the site and had an option on the remaining 22.3 hectares (55 acres), but declined to exercise it. That parcel was then leased to Seaboard International Terminals Inc. for development into a world class forest products export terminal. It is interesting to note that the first Burrard Inlet sawmills were located at or near this site more than a century earlier.

Seaboard had been formed in 1928 by a consortium of lumber mills with the primary aim of competing more effectively with the huge MacMillan organization in the sale and transportation of lumber to the U.S. Atlantic coast and overseas markets. Later, plywood producers joined the consortium. In the mid-sixties Seaboard studied better ways of handling and shipping lumber, and concluded that using specialized bulk carriers loading at one, or at the most two, dock assembly terminals was the path to greater efficiency. Clearly, the day of the traditional lumber carrier loading from multiple sawmill docks, or even from general cargo piers, was coming to an end.

Rejecting Roberts Bank as an option, the Seaboard consortium settled on the Lynn Creek site adjacent to Neptune and negotiated a 20-year lease with the VPA. The site was then developed with heavy paving, rail lines, covered storage for plywood, a barge ramp, and berths for three vessels. When completed the terminal was recognized as the largest wood products assembly and loading facility in the world. The new terminal received lumber by rail, truck, and barge and loaded its first vessel with packaged lumber and plywood in mid-1971.

Squamish Terminals

In 1965 Cattermole Timber leased a potential forest products terminal site at Squamish from the PGE Railway. They were later joined by Star Bulk Shipping, a large Norwegian company and a leader in operating vessels specially designed for efficiently loading and stowing pulp and other forest products. Star Bulk had looked at other potential sites to develop their own terminal, including Fairview in Prince Rupert but, recognizing the political imperative in B.C. that interior mills ship their products over the provincially owned BC Rail (ex-PGE), they chose to work with, and later buy out, Cattermole's interest at Squamish.

The site was developed at a cost of $6 million and equipped with a single wooden berth and a shed to hold pulp. It loaded its first vessel in late 1972.

Lynnterm

Before the Seaboard Terminal was completed, the VPA proposed the preparation of a second site on the east side of the mouth of Lynn Creek for a general cargo facility. Approval from Ottawa was received late in 1973 and site construction completed in 1976. Developed at a cost of $26 million, Lynnterm offered 27 hectares (67 acres) for cargo assembly, including covered storage, rail access, and three berths. It was operated by Western Stevedoring (partly owned by Seaboard) who equipped the terminal to efficiently handle forest products, steel, general and project cargoes.

THE GRAIN TERMINALS

During the thirties and the first five post-war years, the combined throughput of Vancouver's grain terminals averaged only about 1.5 million tons annually. This amounted to a very leisurely 3.2 times turnover of their licensed storage capacity. In response to a series of bumper crops and the huge new markets opening in Asia, there had been a 48 percent increase in the port's terminal capacity by 1975. Grain shipments between 1970 and 1975 averaged 6.6 million tons with a resulting turnover increase to 11 times annually, despite the substantial capacity additions. By crop year 1985/86 throughput had grown to 10.8 million tonnes, but turnover had dropped to 8.5 times due to a further 28 percent increase in capacity since 1975.

The traditional 60:40 split between grain moving east versus grain sent west had reached 55:45 by 1975 and by 1985 was well on its way to a complete reversal. This reversal finally took place, despite the fact that the eastern ship loading terminals had five times the capacity of those on the West Coast.

By the 1970s, the enormous increase in demand to move export grain from farm to ship through the western corridors exposed multiple inefficiencies in a grain handling and transportation system that had seen little change in four decades.

The railways were exceedingly unhappy at being obligated to move grain to the coast from thousands of collecting points, over a spider web of prairie branch lines that they were expected to maintain and serve, for a permanently fixed rate (the Crow rate) that the CPR agreed to charge in 1897 — a rate foisted on the CNR in 1925.

The Crow rate had been an important factor in reducing costs and keeping export markets available to farmers located much farther from ocean terminals than in other major grain exporting countries. In time, however, as with most subsidized enterprises, it produced crippling distortions. Protected by the "Holy Crow," there was little or no incentive to diversify crops, or consolidate tiny family farms into larger and more viable units, and there was a clear disincentive to process grain because it would then not be covered under the rates.

For the railways, the Crow rate structure had become a nightmare. Inflation had long since destroyed the basis for a permanently fixed tariff and the rate provided inadequate revenue to maintain branch line tracks, or repair or replace rolling stock used in grain carriage. Government responded to the issue with Band Aid solutions that included purchasing thousands of new hopper cars, providing grants to repair old boxcars, and funding to maintain deteriorating branch lines.

Despite the very large increase in the amount of grain moving through Vancouver, it was starting to lose its long dominance as the leading dry bulk tonnage export item to the surging exports of coal, potash, sulphur, and forest products. Producers of these commodities believed that they were being asked to pay excessive rail rates to make up the railway's losses on moving grain. The CNR president admitted as much when he stated in 1981 that for the two railways the combined losses resulting from the Crow rate on grain would be approximately $2 billion over five years.

The railways received no comfort or support from the ocean terminal operators or their labour force. It was a most unfortunate fact that each component involved in moving grain from farm to ship operated independently and was neither interested, nor concerned about the viability of the other players. It was well described as a "fractious industry." The ocean terminals operated on a 5-day work week, while receiving loaded cars from the railroads seven days a week, a classic example of inefficient use of resources. When, as a result of delayed unloading, car shortages loomed, there was always the benevolent taxpayer to pay for thousands more, especially if the car manufacturers were located in ridings held by the government of the day.

Labour management relations at the Vancouver terminals during the early seventies had been described by federal Labour Minister Munro as "poisoned." Between 1972 and 1975, sixteen percent of working days at the terminals were lost due to labour management disputes.

The inevitable result of these and other problems was long delays in loading grain vessels, a persistent feature of the 1970s at the port. As many as 30 vessels at a time could be seen swinging at anchor in English Bay, the Gulf Islands, or Royal Roads in Victoria, while awaiting a loading berth. It was not uncommon for a vessel to wait four to six weeks before reaching the first of several berths to load its grain cargo. In the 1973/74 crop year, for example, the Canadian Wheat Board paid over $17 million in demurrage charges to owners of waiting vessels, a direct charge against the amount farmers would receive for their grain. On only 18 out of 248 working days that year were no vessels at anchor waiting for a berth to load grain in Vancouver. Consequently, the Chinese buyers were obliged to send vessels to the East Coast to load 40 percent of their grain purchases that year. Producers of farm specialty crops visiting Japan on marketing trips were repeatedly told, "Vancouver is the worst port in the world," with regard to service delays and disruptions. They were urged to ship their products through Seattle.

Larger vessels fared especially poorly. One very large vessel, the *Amoco Cairo*, spent 78 days in the port and was forced to move 11 times to load 129,712 tons of wheat in early 1975. A year later, the *Aimee* spent 40 days in the port to complete loading 67,500 tons.

Despite the multiple and deep rooted problems plaguing grain movement through the Vancouver terminals, their owners successfully influenced the Wheat Board to continue its unwise dependence on the single rail corridor to the Southern Gateway. Prince Rupert's recently enlarged and upgraded terminal frequently sat idle, though full and thus unable to unload more cars, while many waiting vessels collected barnacles at southern anchorages. At best, only about one quarter of the Prince Rupert terminal's throughput capability was used during most of the 1970s.

Pressure to act to improve the situation came from many directions including farm organizations unaffiliated with the terminal owners, the railways, and overseas purchasers of Canadian grain. That southern anchorages were perpetually filled with vessels awaiting berths could not be hidden from the public. Submissions urging use of the Northern Corridor and gateway were strongly supported by the governments of the three grain producing provinces, as well as buyers in Beijing.

The *Western Grain Transportation Act*, passed on November 17, 1983, finally addressed the Crow rate issue. Thereafter, shipping costs for unprocessed grain were allowed to increase gradually, but were not allowed to exceed 10 percent of the world price. The federal government agreed to reimburse the railways for the balance of their costs. Ten years later the "Crow Benefit" was finally abolished and farmers were compensated with a onetime payment from Ottawa.

By 1980 several substantial changes had occurred in the southern grain terminal scene. Federal Grain sold the old Pacific Elevator, which had been combined with the NHB No. 1 terminal and its annex in 1968, to a consortium comprised of Alberta Wheat Pool, Saskatchewan Wheat Pool, and Manitoba Pool Elevators in 1972. The new owners subsequently spent $9 million to upgrade the facility. Stimulated by the Canadian Wheat Board's 1976 Storage Incentive Program, the other four grain terminals were also expanded, rebuilt, and/or modernized. The program guaranteed payment for 80–90 percent of all storage space to any Vancouver terminal adding substantial capacity. In response, the Alberta and Saskatchewan Wheat Pools each added a large annex to their terminals and UGG embarked on a three-year modernization program. The old and small Burrard Terminal on the north shore, which had been extensively damaged by explosion in 1975, was rebuilt by Pioneer Grain at a cost of $30 million and reopened in October 1979 as a substantially larger and fully modernized facility. Together, these new projects increased grain storage capacity in Vancouver by almost 40 percent.

Three small grain terminals were demolished. The New Westminster terminal, built on the south bank of the Fraser River in 1928 and not used since developing a lean in 1968, was removed to make way for the new container terminal adjacent to the Fraser Surrey dock complex. Next to go was the small, isolated, and badly located Victoria terminal. It ceased operating December 31, 1976 and was then demolished. Finally, in 1979 the idle NHB No. 2 terminal adjacent to Ballantyne Pier was removed.

In addition to the entrenched problems that inhibited the increasing amounts of grain from moving efficiently through the port, there were three prolonged rail service disruptions to the Burrard Inlet elevators between 1975 and 1982. Two of these involved damage to the Fraser River rail bridge at New Westminster and required rail traffic to be diverted to CPR tracks with inevitable delays. The third was even more serious, as it involved the rail bridge across second narrows to the north shore terminals and lasted almost five months. This disruption occurred on October 12, 1979; just two days after the rebuilt, enlarged, and modernized Burrard Terminal officially opened. It crippled the operations at both north shore terminals, then supplying almost 40 percent of the port's grain storage and handling capacity. The Canadian Wheat Board attempted to keep Saskpool's terminal operating during the outage, albeit at a much reduced level, by trucking 1,400 tonnes of grain each night over the highway bridge.

THE SHIPYARDS

The generous 40 percent federal subsidy available to Canadian shipyards, established in 1961, had been reduced to 17 percent by 1972 and 9 percent by 1980. It was eliminated altogether in 1985. During the 1970–1985 period, local yards relied almost entirely on domestic orders including new buildings and conversions for B.C. Ferries, Coast Guard icebreakers, arctic tugs and offshore supply vessels, as well as small vessels for coastal fisheries and forest product operations.

The wooden dry dock completed in 1925 with a 70 percent federal grant and installed at Burrard Dry Dock on the north shore had deteriorated and, by 1970 was capable of lifting only a quarter of the vessels visiting the port. The marine community lobbied Ottawa for substantial assistance to provide a much larger new facility for the port. A decision was finally reached in 1978, whereby the federal government promised to contribute $28.8 million toward the estimated $40 million cost. The Mitsubishi built dock arrived from Japan in August 1981 and was installed at Burrard Dry Dock. With support facilities the total cost had escalated to $63.3 million. Ottawa raised its contribution to $40.6 million, the province chipped in $1.5 million, and Burrard Yarrows borrowed the balance. (In the interests of harmony, Ottawa made a matching contribution of $40 million toward the cost of a new dock for Halifax!) The new Vancouver dry dock provided the port with the ability to service and repair vessels up to 75,000 tons dwt, as well as the potential for expansion as required.

PASSENGER VESSELS

The traditional passenger and freight service provided by an armada of Vancouver based vessels to so many isolated points along the B.C. coast had, by 1966, dwindled to the limited service provided by a single-vehicle passenger ferry, the *Queen of Prince Rupert* operating from Kelsey Bay to Prince Rupert with one stop at Bella Bella, and the subsidized passenger freight service of Northland Navigation that ended abruptly in 1976. B.C. Ferries added a second vessel, the *Queen of the North*, in 1980. That same year it completed a new terminal at Port Hardy and added a new service to the Queen Charlotte Islands (Haida Gwaii). In 1981 these two central and north coast services carried 105,000 passengers. With the exception of the activities of a few tug and barge companies, Vancouver no longer served as the base for services to coastal communities.

Port visits by conventional deep-sea liners of the P&O and Orient Lines, which began in 1954, lasted for only 20 years. At their peak frequency, one of these liners called at Vancouver every 2 weeks. For passenger travel over long distances, jet aircraft provided a new option and soon supplanted the more leisurely mode of deep-sea voyages. The last visit of one of these famous liners took place in September 1974.

The termination of visits by the deep-sea liners occurred at a time of ballooning interest in inside passage cruises to Alaska. The *Islander*, owned by the Canadian Pacific Navigation Company is recorded as having made the first "cruise" north in 1892. For the next 80 years, relatively small vessels were used in this seasonal service and were operated by the CPR's B.C. Coast Service, Canadian National Steamships, and Union Steamships. All were based at their owner's docks in Vancouver. As these companies retired from all coastal services, Seattle entrepreneurs acquired some of their vessels by charter or purchase and began marketing aggressively. This resulted in a rapid increase in the popularity of this leisure travel option. As demand increased, ever larger and more specialized vessels were acquired. By 1985 the newest purpose-built cruise vessels carried up to 1,200 passengers and were fully occupied all year on worldwide itineraries.

In 1974, the year the last P&O passenger liner called at Vancouver, the company bought Seattle owned Princess Cruises and then absorbed Sitmar Cruise Line to become — with Holland America and Royal Viking Line — the leading operators on the Alaska Cruise circuit. By this time, their new or extensively modernized vessels had replaced almost all the older and smaller ships. Virtually all these new, large, foreign flag cruise vessels operated out of Pier B-C or Ballantyne Pier and both passenger counts and annual sailings were increasing substantially each year. Between 1975 and 1985 sailings doubled to 180 and passenger numbers tripled to 267,472. When Pier B–C was demolished in 1981 all cruise vessels had to be accommodated at Ballantyne or Centennial cargo piers and the need to construct a modern passenger facility became urgent.

The prime recommendation of the Central Waterfront Committee established by the Vancouver Port Corporation (VPC) in 1978 was the development of a combined convention centre and passenger terminal at the soon to be demolished Pier B–C site. Concurrently, the federal, provincial, and municipal governments had begun planning for just such a project, but with the inclusion of a large waterfront hotel. In April 1982 the Government of Canada created a crown corporation, the Canada Harbour Place Corporation, to develop the Canada Place project. Construction at the former Pier B-C site commenced March 9, 1983 and made full use of the remaining concrete pilings from the old pier. Components of the project, considered at the time to be one of the largest integrated use waterfront redevelopments undertaken anywhere in the world, were completed on time and on budget between December 1985 and July 1987. The total cost came to $400 million and of that amount, $160 million represented private investment for hotel, office, and other commercial enterprises. The cruise vessel berthing and passenger handling component of the complex commenced operation April 28, 1986 in time for the opening of EXPO '86 and represented a $24 million investment by the VPC.

FRASER RIVER DEVELOPMENTS: 1970 TO 1985

Southeast of Vancouver, the New Westminster Harbour Commission, established by the federal government in 1913, was replaced by the Fraser River Harbour Commission (FRHC) in 1965. The new Commissioners focused on increasing the main channel depth, accumulating an extensive land base, and actively seeking the development of sites on the 270 km of river front under their jurisdiction.

Starting in 1982, the FRHC established a policy of placing surplus revenues from rentals and leases into a Land Acquisition and Harbour Development Fund. This wise policy led, over the years, to a property-rich port.

Between 1970 and 1975 two terminals were developed on the river to serve the auto import market and a fully equipped container terminal was built adjacent to the Fraser Surrey Dock complex.

THE RIVER CHANNEL

When B.C. joined Confederation the federal government assumed the cost of developing and maintaining a navigable Fraser River channel at least as far as New Westminster. Since 1892 the annual work of dredging and debris removal using specially designed, dedicated vessels had been supplemented by periodic major river control projects. These were designed to straighten and narrow the channel, thereby speeding the river flow and moving its silt deposits out into the deep waters of the Strait of Georgia. By 1949, twenty kilometers of these control works had been constructed and a further project, completed in 1969, added even more control works near New Westminster at a cost of $5 million.

The magnitude of the problem relates to the average annual deposition in the last 40 km (25 miles) of the river, estimated at three-quarters of its total sediment load, or approximately 3.8 million cubic meters.

For most of this period, annual dredging and more river control projects succeeded in maintaining the depth at 9.7 m (32 ft.) in the ship channel, a significant improvement over the 4.3 m (14 ft.) measured in 1899.

The greater loaded draft of the ever larger vessels engaged in international trade increased the pressure for further deepening of the main navigation channel. The Department of Public Works, at the behest of the Coast Guard, responded by commissioning studies to estimate the cost of the best way to achieve a 12.1 m (40 ft.) channel depth as far as New Westminster. The cost of submitted proposals ranged from $50 million in 1979 to $78 million in 1982 and $100 million in 1985. The Department of Public Works backed away from these expensive schemes, but in 1983 did reaffirm the commitment made a decade earlier to provide a channel depth of 10.6 m (35 ft.). However, persuading Ottawa to continue its century-old willingness to fund annual programs to maintain and increase the river channel depth was becoming increasingly difficult for the Commission, especially in the face of opposition from the Vancouver maritime establishment.

Removing floating debris from the Fraser River had been performed since 1884 by a series of five snag scows, all named *Samson*. These vessels were built and operated by the federal government for the benefit of river traffic and facilities. By the 1970s they were considered inefficient and excessively costly to operate and, in 1980, the last of the series, *Samson V* was retired. Their function was assumed by the Fraser Debris Trap located on the north shore of the river between Agassiz and Hope. This trap has been funded by federal, provincial, and regional bodies as well as the forest industry, albeit with varying levels of enthusiasm.

CONVENTIONAL FACILITIES AND PORT TRAFFIC: 1970 to 1985

For a century, deep-sea vessels transiting the lower reaches of the Fraser River berthed at wharves located parallel to the New Westminster City waterfront, or at sawmill and cannery wharves in the vicinity. From 1929 to 1964 the grain terminal operated alone on the south bank of the river opposite New Westminster. It was joined in 1964 by Fraser Surrey Docks and, soon after ceasing operations in 1968, it was demolished. The Fraser Surrey Dock complex was expanded during this period, serving first as a multipurpose terminal for handling general cargo, logs, lumber, pulp and steel. Later it added a well-equipped container terminal, built adjacent to the original terminal. This modern bulk, break-bulk, and container handling complex had excellent rail connections and plenty of land that could be developed relatively cheaply. During its first decade it became the dominant facility on the river for the export and import of break-bulk and general cargo.

Pacific Coast Terminals had been the mainstay of the port since 1929. Its berths, cold storage, and other facilities handled a wide range of commodities such as bagged fertilizers, lead and zinc concentrates, flour, pulp, canned fish, apples, lumber, and general cargo. By 1978 its limited land base, ageing facilities, and competition from across the river persuaded the company to sell its New Westminster riverfront property to the British Columbia Development Corporation for future development as New Westminster Quay. The last vessel to use the facility loaded bagged potash from the sole remaining berth in early 1982.

Since 1960 Pacific Coast Terminals had increasingly focused on its new bulk terminal at Port Moody, but soon after its New Westminster assets were sold, the company itself was taken over by its leading customer, Sultran, who wished to own and operate the Port Moody facility.

New Westminster missed the great boom in bulk commodity traffic that so greatly increased Vancouver's throughput in the sixties and seventies. Although the port was blessed with an abundance of riverfront land, the depth of the ship channel precluded access for the large vessels that were increasingly being used to carry bulk commodities.

Foreign cargo traffic on the river over the 1970–1985 period fluctuated between 1.5 and 2 million tons per year with a peak at 2,173,000 tons in 1974. That year, 448 deep-sea vessels called at port facilities. In the earlier years of this period exports far exceeded imports, but by the early eighties this had almost reached a balance, though now slightly in favour of imports.

THE AUTO TERMINALS

As the industrial bases of the war torn European economies recovered, automobiles exported from their modern factories began to flood into the North American market. Austin and Morris cars from the United Kingdom, Volkswagens from West Germany, Peugeot and Simca vehicles from France, and Sweden's Volvos arrived on slightly modified cargo vessels and unloaded at conventional docks such as Pier B-C in Vancouver. In the early sixties Japan, too, began introducing Datsuns and Toyotas into the Canadian Market. By the mid-sixties, vessels specially designed to carry up to 2,500 cars were under construction for Norwegian ship owners and, in May 1968, one vessel discharged 1,076 Volkswagens at Centennial Pier, the largest shipment yet to the port. Toyota built a fleet of numbered *Toyota Maru* vessels designed to carry the company's vehicles to overseas markets and return with a cargo of grain. The first of these vessels arrived in Vancouver in January 1969.

The arrival of ever larger capacity, specialized auto carriers created a need for terminals dedicated to receive, process, and distribute their cargo. The first of two lower mainland terminals was built for Canadian Motor Industries, the Canadian distributor for Toyota, at a site in Richmond at the foot of No. 6 Road. This riverfront property was developed with a single concrete berth and rail-served backup land sufficient to store 8,000 vehicles. Named Fraser Wharves, the terminal opened in 1971 and initially received 2,000 units on each voyage of the *Canada Maru*, a dedicated vessel. Its land base has since been expanded by owner Mitsui to 43.3 ha (107 acres), sufficient to store up to 14,000 vehicles shipped to the facility from Asian manufacturers on pure car carriers.

Two years after Fraser Wharves commenced operations in Richmond, the FRHC opened a second auto terminal on Annacis Island, initially operated by Nissan Canada. It too, has undergone several expansions including a second berth, added in 1983. The facility is currently operated by Wallenius Wilhelmsen Logistics and handles auto imports from Europe as well as Asia.

These two auto terminals presently handle over 400,000 cars annually, one-quarter of the overseas auto imports to Canada, and together they constitute North America's third largest specialized auto port.

THE CONTAINER TERMINAL

Though unable to benefit from the huge surge in the export of bulk commodities, the FRHC was not prepared to miss out on the new container handling business. In 1972 Ottawa gave the Commission authority to borrow $10.5 million from a commercial bank for the purpose of developing a container facility adjacent to the recently expanded Fraser Surrey Dock complex. Built at a cost of $12.5 million, the terminal opened for business in December 1974, offering two berths, two container cranes, and excellent rail connections with ample backup land. Despite its excellent land base and rail connections, many people, especially in the Vancouver port community considered the new terminal an unwise investment, in view of the ever increasing size and draft of newer container ships. However, if Vancouver had been more aggressive in providing first class facilities for container handling, the New Westminster terminal would not likely have been built.

At the time of its official opening it was the largest container terminal in Canada. Unfortunately for the Commission, the new facility failed to attract steady commitments from container vessel operators for its first 10 years and the cranes were primarily used as gantries to handle steel and other cargoes. By 1983, however, the terminal was able to woo the Columbus Container Line away from Vanterm with about 30 calls a year.

PRINCE RUPERT: 1970 TO 1985

The viability and future growth prospects for any export-oriented port depend largely on the extent of the hinterland that can be served by its rail links. Prince Rupert citizens were thus given good reason for hope in the early seventies when governments in both Victoria and Ottawa showed new interest in their "Grand Plan" for a rail infrastructure network in northwest B.C. with eventual extension into the Yukon and Alaska.

The Dease Lake extension of the PGE began construction in 1970 and the following year the B.C. government offered to take over the CNR north line. That offer was spurned, but subsequent amicable negotiations between Don Jamieson, federal Minister of Transport (1968–1973) and Premier Bennett, both men of vision, resulted in a plan for a network of rail lines and interchanges to be built and shared between the CNR and PGE. It was to include a connection from the Dease Lake extension of the PGE south to Terrace, as well as an extension north from Dease Lake to the Yukon and eventually Alaska. In mid-1973, the federal Minister of Transport, Jean Marchand, and his provincial counterpart announced a $325 million plan for rail, port, and resource access development that was designed to usher in a new period of economic growth for northwest B.C. Early in 1974, the CNR completed a preliminary survey for the planned link from the Dease Lake line to Terrace.

Unfortunately for Prince Rupert's port aspirations, this "Grand Plan" collapsed in 1977 when construction on the Dease Lake line was halted. It had been a seldom-seen example of cooperation between the visionary, but prickly Premier and a federal cabinet minister. Though the planned rail network never came to fruition, the more amicable atmosphere between Ottawa and Victoria did help to achieve three significant things for Prince Rupert. On July 2, 1971 the ownership of Ridley Island was transferred to the federal government by the Province of B.C., for port development in the national interest. Ottawa followed through with a proclamation on March 23, 1972 designating Prince Rupert as Canada's tenth national port, under the jurisdiction of the National Harbours Board and, on September 17, 1973 a sod turning ceremony marked the start of construction of the new, general cargo terminal at Fairview.

The cooperative spirit that had developed between Minister of Transport Jamieson and Premier Bennett did not survive their departure from their respective offices. In 1976 the British Columbia Development Corporation (BCDC), a provincial crown corporation, acquired a large parcel of harbour front land in Prince Rupert from the estate of Hector Cobb. This property included all the upland from Casey Point to the southern tip of Kaien Island, a distance of 5 km. This huge parcel had been purchased by Cobb from the Department of National Defence in 1957 for the proverbial song. The two ends of this waterfront property offered potential sites for grain or coal terminals. By threatening to proceed with their construction, BCDC exerted pressure on the federal government to act on the promised provision of infrastructure to Ridley Island to allow terminal development there.

In 1990, the port acquired the more valuable southern part of the property for potential development of a petrochemical terminal. More recent thinking has it designated for development as a second container terminal.

By 1985 Prince Rupert boasted three new terminals. None came easily. The Fairview site was indirectly acquired by the NHB from Western Wharves Ltd. in 1970 with the promise of early action on its development as a break-bulk and general cargo terminal. Unhappily, it was not completed until early 1977 and, by that time, most of the anticipated overseas forest product exports from central B.C. mills had been committed to Vancouver terminals under long term contracts. Site preparation for the grain terminal and infrastructure for Ridley Island commenced late in 1980, after eight years of intensive lobbying from Prince Rupert and the very strong support of the three prairie governments, especially Alberta. The coal terminal project finally commenced construction in March 1982, after great pressure to act had been exerted on Ottawa by the B.C. government and under a considerable cloud of suspicion with respect to its public-private ownership status. Both the Ridley terminals were built at a time of excessively high construction and financing costs with the result that their final cost far exceeded that originally anticipated.

With construction of the two terminals on Ridley Island underway in 1982 the Department of Transport committed $3.5 million to developing a vessel traffic management centre at Prince Rupert, as well as adding to navigational aids in the harbour approaches.

ADMINISTRATION OF THE PORT

Following the March 1972 designation of Prince Rupert as a national port, an officer in charge was appointed by the NHB and an office established in the city by September of that year. Bylaws and rates for the new port were established, all federal property leases were reviewed, and the current capability and future needs of the harbour were assessed. The NHB took over title to federally owned land and water lots in the port, extended the harbour limits, and accepted transfer by B.C. of certain provincial lands including Ridley Island.

In June 1975 the five-member Board of Directors of the Prince Rupert Port Authority met for the first time. Though charged with the administration and control of local port affairs, the Port Authority had miniscule spending authority, assuring that it would be kept on a very short leash by NHB head office in Ottawa.

Following the passage of the *Canada Ports Corporation Act* in 1983, the port was granted the status of a Local Port Corporation effective July 1, 1984. Though this Act supposedly granted each of the national ports more autonomy than before, the predilection for centralizing authority was still part of the mindset of the ex-NHB bureaucracy at Ports Canada's head office in Ottawa. Spending powers of the Prince Rupert Port Corporation were, however, now set at $500,000, a substantial improvement over that allowed the former Authority.

OCEAN DOCK

A spectacular fire on June 10, 1972 destroyed most of the rail-served wooden dock and all of its transit shed. The Oceanside Cannery, which had occupied the western end of the facility since 1951, was totally destroyed. It was replaced within a year by the New Oceanside Cannery, a much larger and more modern plant, built by Canfisco on the site of the recently vacated sawmill, which in turn had been built on the former shipyard site. The transit shed contained a substantial tonnage of copper concentrates from the Babine Lake mines that was awaiting shipment. Most of this valuable material was subsequently salvaged from the harbour bottom. Though 50 years old and out-dated in design, this dock with its transit shed had been the only general cargo facility the port had to offer, leaving only the dedicated grain elevator wharf and the new concrete pulp mill dock in Porpoise Harbour. It had seen a little use in the past decade, berthing vessels loading copper concentrates from the transit shed, as well as logs from bag booms in the water alongside the ship. It also served as the only tie-up berth available for large cruise vessels in the summer season.

After the fire, only 148 m (494 ft.) of the dock remained and by early 1977 the Port Authority had spent $500,000 repairing and resurfacing this otherwise useless remnant. The resulting truncated facility, with no shed or other shelter, offered little and therefore accomplished little.

FAIRVIEW GENERAL CARGO TERMINAL

In mid-1970 the CNR, on behalf of the NHB, acquired the leases and engineering studies done by Western Wharves Ltd. on the Fairview site. The civic minded local citizens who had financed Western Wharves to that point were assured that Ottawa would proceed expeditiously to develop a modern forest products and general cargo terminal at the site. The port's loss of the Ocean Dock in June 1972 did nothing, however, to speed the entrenched bureaucracy at NHB headquarters. Clearly, the project and the port's plight were far down on their list of priorities.

A sod turning ceremony finally took place on September 17, 1973 and construction proceeded painfully slowly. The two berth, concrete caisson wharf fronted 15 hectares (37 acres) of paved backup land, which had been created by adding rock fill to a rock shelf that extended out to deep water. The terminal was equipped with a small transfer shed and completed at a cost of $25.5 million. It loaded its first vessel on February 22, 1977. A 120 ton ro-ro barge ramp was installed two years later at a cost of $1.2 million.

Though slow at first, lumber throughput reached 496,823 tonnes by 1985. Most of this was the product of new mills established west of Prince George. A facility designed to handle specialty agricultural products and by-products was installed near the centre of the terminal by Arctic Grain in late 1979. This company was joined on the project the following year by Continental Grain, the resulting partnership operating as Conarc. The original concept was expanded and, by the time their terminal was complete, its cost had risen to $4.5 million. By 1985 this facility was shipping close to 150,000 tonnes annually.

Metal concentrates from Noranda's operations on Babine Lake and later from Equity Mines near Houston were stored in sheds at the south end of the terminal pending shipping. Throughput averaged about 50,000 tonnes annually between 1981 and 1994.

During 1980 and 1981 a sulphur pelletizing plant owned by Pacific Rim Sulphur Ltd. of Calgary operated on the terminal and shipped about 100,000 tonnes of prilled sulphur during each of those two years, but its operations were not profitable and were closed down.

Fairview Terminal at last gave the port an opportunity to offer an alternative export outlet to the many lumber and pulp mills that had developed during the sixties in B.C.'s central and northern interior. Its slow and stunted growth in forest product traffic was directly attributable to two factors. First, the producers of export forest products with operations within a reasonable distance of PGE lines were unquestionably encouraged by the B.C. government — the issuer of their forest management licenses — to utilize the provincially owned railway. The CNR made little effort to compete for this overseas export traffic as long as it received, from the PGE, loaded cars destined for the long rail-haul to eastern Canadian and U.S. markets. Second, the long delay in completing Fairview allowed Vancouver and Squamish terminals to tie down long term contracts for the lumber and pulp newly produced in north central B.C. Much of this could have been shipped through Prince Rupert if a facility had been available. By the time the terminal was operable, it had to rely heavily on the export production of mills west of Burns Lake.

THE GRAIN TERMINALS

Increased prairie grain production allowed export sales of Canadian wheat to double in the early seventies. This fact, coupled with a shift in sales to Pacific markets, created intolerable stresses in an already creaking grain handling system that had changed little in 50 years. This stress was particularly evident on the Pacific Coast where, by both tradition and the influence of the Vancouver terminals owners, the Canadian Wheat Board persisted in trying to funnel 95 percent of West Coast sales through the single rail corridor to the southern terminals. This policy led to excessively high vessel demurrage charges, lost sales (especially premium spot sales), and strained relations with valuable customers.

The addition of Saskpool's new north shore elevator in 1968 was countered by the closing of the New Westminster terminal in 1968, the loss due to explosion of the Burrard terminal in 1975, and the closure of the Victoria terminal in 1976. Clearly, Vancouver had insufficient capacity to function efficiently through the normal cycles of grain production, transportation, and marketing.

Despite these mounting problems, Prince Rupert's terminal remained grossly under-utilized and, between 1967 and 1977, saw no increase in its 4.8 percent share of West Coast exports. It was far from integrated into the West Coast movement and only received grain on a sporadic basis. By way of example, for 19 weeks in 1977 the terminal did not unload a single rail car. On occasion the terminal would be plugged with grain, but no vessel was sent from the many anchored in English Bay, Plumper Sound, and Royal Roads awaiting a loading berth. In 1974, nineteen out of thirty-four vessels that were finally directed to load at Prince Rupert had first collected barnacles for weeks at southern anchorages.

Observation of the growing problems in moving grain through the West Coast, coupled with the desire to see much greater use of the Northern Rail Corridor and port prompted the writer, in 1972, to embark on an in-depth study of the grain handling and transportation industry, and particularly the potential role of Prince Rupert in easing its chronic problems.

The ensuing struggle to overcome entrenched ignorance and stubborn resistance to the use of the northern port as an outlet for prairie grain would last for 10 years and involve many players.

Requests from Prince Rupert for better utilization of its best port facility had long been met by the excuse that the terminal had no affiliated country collecting system and, therefore, could only be used in an overflow role. On examination this excuse failed to satisfy. For many years, the NHB-operated elevator at Churchill, Manitoba, which also lacked any primary collecting system and was open to shipping only 88 days per year, had been consistently supplied with grain by the Wheat Board in amounts double that sent sporadically to Prince Rupert. Careful study of the *Canadian Wheat Board Act* revealed that Board grains passed from the ownership of the producer directly to the Board with the country elevator acting only as agent for the Board. This interpretation was supported by the fact that when a country elevator burned down, the loss of contained (Board) grain was borne by the Board and not by the elevator's owner. Furthermore, the Act clearly gave the Wheat Board full and absolute control over the movement of Board grains destined for overseas markets, so that they could be directed to the port where they could be most efficiently handled. It was, however, very clear that the owners of the country elevator systems had long influenced the Wheat Board to direct grain they collected to their own lucrative ocean terminals. This resulted in handsome returns for the Vancouver terminal owners, but the losses from vessel demurrage payments, lost sales, and unhappy customers had to be shouldered by the unwitting producer through reduced payments for Board grains.

With the question of responsibility for directing grain to ocean terminals clarified, it remained to expose the compounding inefficiencies of the existing system, identify opponents to change, and seek support from those who would benefit from integrating the alternate West Coast port and its underutilized rail corridor into the movement of overseas export grain.

Resistance could be expected from the existing elevator owners in Vancouver, from Thunder Bay and the politically powerful Seaway Lobby, and from the CPR. Support could be expected from informed producers, from the CNR, from the Alberta, Saskatchewan and Manitoba governments, and especially from major buyers of Canadian grain such as China.

A document entitled "The Case for Expanded Grain Facilities in Prince Rupert" was prepared and widely distributed in November 1975. It presented a careful analysis of the existing inadequacies apparent in the movement of grain through the West Coast and refuted the many misconceptions about the Northern Corridor and port, plus the specious arguments used to deny its use. It mocked the continued use of the Victoria elevator and presented a strong case for doubling the capacity of the existing terminal, as well as building a new large terminal at the northern port. Pointing to the folly of consigning 95 percent of Pacific Coast exports to one port served by one fragile rail corridor, the brief further made a strong case for integrating Prince Rupert into the system for moving grain west and for adding sufficient capacity to enable the port to handle one-third of that movement.

The distribution of the brief was timely. Burrard elevator had recently blown up, avalanches closed the CNR line in the Fraser Canyon for three weeks that winter, and a barge knocked out the Fraser Bridge at New Westminster for four months. Suddenly Prince Rupert's terminal was being assigned 600 loaded railcars a week.

The role of the federal government was complicated by disagreements between the Minister of Agriculture, Eugene Whelan, whose Canadian Grain Commission owned the Prince Rupert elevator, and the Minister in charge of the Wheat Board, Otto Lang. Whelan wanted to keep the existing elevator and upgrade its systems, while Lang wanted it sold to the trade.

The government of Alberta, for many years an outspoken supporter of port development at Prince Rupert, took a close interest in the proposal to help solve the growing grain movement crisis by utilizing and expanding facilities at the northern port. Deputy Minister Roth's visit to the port in 1975 confirmed Edmonton's support for the Prince Rupert proposals. Minister of Agriculture Whelan visited the port in February 1976 to announce that his department would spend $15 million on the existing elevator over the next two years and would not consider its sale. A year later his department offered to lease the terminal, but ten months later rejected all offers when it was clear the best offer had come from Cargill Grain, an American multinational and therefore politically unpalatable. In 1978 the Grain Commission actually spent $11.5 million on upgrading the facility, offered it for sale in 1979, and then rejected all offers. This vacillating course offered little beyond the expenditure on useful upgrades.

Pressures mounted after the Hall Royal Commission hearings on Grain Handling and Transportation held in Vancouver in October 1976. Among its recommendations released in May 1977 were several that were important to Prince Rupert, including the following:

- The Commission considers it likely that any further development of grain terminals will be outside Burrard Inlet.
- The Commission recommends a more aggressive role on handling and transportation by the CWB.
- The Commission recommends expansion, modernization and utilization of the Prince Rupert terminal.

Cargill Grain sent four of their senior executives to Prince Rupert in February 1976 and demonstrated by far the keenest interest in moving grain through the port. Their offer to lease the terminal had been rejected on political grounds and their later offer to lease a portion of the nearly completed Fairview terminal to build a new grain facility was likewise rejected. They then approached the BCDC with a plan to build at the latter's Casey Point site. This proposal stimulated interest from the Alberta Wheat Pool who engaged consultants in the fall of 1977 to confirm the suitability of that site for a terminal. Together, Cargill and the Alberta Pool approached Lang with a request for federal assistance from the Department of Regional Economic Expansion (DREE) to build a new terminal. There was ample precedent for federal assistance, examples of which included contributions from Ottawa to Bunge's terminal in Quebec City, upgrading of a Montreal elevator, and assistance with a new terminal at Windsor. Their request was rejected.

By early 1977, the entire grain industry was aware of the potential at Prince Rupert and many long held opinions were being revised. In October Esmond Jarvis was appointed Chief Commissioner of the Canadian Wheat Board and visited Prince Rupert in August 1978. Changes soon followed.

Grain began to flow on a consistent basis to the Prince Rupert terminal in 1978. Whereas between 1971 and 1977 the terminal handled an average of 530,000 tonnes annually, the throughput from 1978 to 1984 averaged 1.3 million tonnes annually, peaking in 1983 when 84 vessels loaded 1,620,650 tonnes. That figure constituted a record 12-month turnover of 27 times its storage capacity, more than triple the norm for the Vancouver terminals. Over its last seven years of operation, the terminal shipped more grain than in its first 51 years of lonely existence.

Premier Lougheed and Deputy Premier Horner of Alberta visited Prince Rupert in May 1978 and, thereafter, their potent support dominated the drive to make Prince Rupert a major outlet for prairie grain. They leaned heavily on the Alberta Wheat Pool to lead the formation of a consortium of six major grain companies (four Pool and two private) to take over the existing terminal and build a large new elevator in Prince Rupert. Their persuasion was combined with the offer of very substantial funding from the Province's Heritage Fund, but also carried the veiled threat to find another way to achieve their goal if the consortium failed to act. The BCDC also offered financing and project management for a new terminal, provided it was built on one of their two potential sites.

The Premiers of all three Prairie Provinces visited Prince Rupert in March 1979 to underline their support for the project.

Ottawa complicated these developing plans with the announcement in March 1978 that the NHB would spend $16.3 million over three years to provide access to Ridley Island, which had recently been given to them by the B.C. government and was their chosen site for a future coal terminal. It soon became evident that this sum was expected to be recovered through user charges paid by the first occupant of the island. The NHB then produced a "Master Plan" for Ridley Island and took the very strong position that if a grain terminal was to be built in Prince Rupert, it must be located on their island. This insistence caused consternation among the members of the nascent consortium who, with BCDC, countered that locating a grain terminal on Ridley would cost a great deal more and take at least an extra year to complete. There was also a strongly held perception that the NHB wanted the grain industry to pay for the provision of infrastructure to Ridley Island, thereby easing the way for the future coal terminal.

Negotiations between the consortium and the NHB in the early months of 1979 were an exercise in futility. The attitude of the NHB was, "This is our position; take it or leave it." For the consortium there were three primary issues: choice of site, ownership of the old terminal, and provision of infrastructure to the perimeter of the site selected.

The federal government changed on June 4, 1979 and with the change came a much more enthusiastic and supportive attitude toward the project. The new Minister of Transport, Don Mazankowski, called the writer to Ottawa to assume the role of chief negotiator with the consortium. On July 30, 1979 a Memorandum of Understanding (MoU) between the federal government and the consortium was signed, following successful renewed negotiations. The agreement provided for:

- The choice of site to be mutually agreed, after a comparative evaluation of each
- The sale of the old terminal for one dollar
- The provision of infrastructure to the perimeter of the site chosen
- A contribution of one-half the cost of site preparation for the terminal and half the cost of the support structure to the required dock.

The federal contribution was estimated at $42.5 million and this amount was approved by Treasury Board and Cabinet on January 28, 1980. None of this was to be recoverable.

On March 3, 1980 the government changed again and Jean Luc Pepin was appointed Minister of Transport by Prime Minister Trudeau. The NHB, determined to scupper the terms of the MoU signed with the consortium, influenced the new Minister to announce that the government was not committed to the expenditure of $42.5 million except on a cost recoverable basis. A whirlwind of pressure was brought to bear on Pepin from the opposition, the Prairie Premiers, and farm organizations. Gradually, the Minister's position softened. Alberta stepped up to the plate with a portion of the commitment and Ottawa finally allowed a grant of $22 million and reduced the amount of cost recovery to only $7.15 million to be repaid by way of throughput charges.

The consortium, in hard bargaining with Alberta, succeeded in getting non-equity funding for up to 80 percent of the project. Costs for the new terminal, originally estimated by the NHB at $80 million and by the consortium at $125 million, eventually reached $275 million by the time it was completed.

The Ridley Island site was finally chosen by the site selection committee, primarily because it offered more space for rail yard development and for future expansion. Site clearing began in September 1980. The road to the island from Highway 16 was built by the B.C. Highways Department and opened on September 28, 1982. The main contracts for the huge new elevator were awarded the same month.

The old terminal was turned over to the consortium for operation on February 1, 1980 and a contract awarded for a system of fendering to ease the strain of large ships on the old dock. In March 1985 the new, high throughput, state-of-the-art terminal with 210,000 tonne storage capacity loaded its first vessel and the old terminal was promptly closed.

The road to integrating an expanded capacity at Prince Rupert into the western movement of export grain had been long and frustrating. Resistance from powerful entities with vested interests in blocking the project had to be overcome. The management of the Wheat Pools was, at best, lukewarm, and to take action needed strong prodding from enlightened producer groups, as well as the governments of all three Prairie Provinces. From 1979 to 1984, the crucial years for the grain and coal terminal projects, the federal political scene was most unstable with four elections, each one changing the government in power. With each change the new government tended to cast a jaundiced eye on the actions of its predecessor. The NHB held true to its intransigent and arbitrary manner of conducting negotiations both with the grain consortium and the coal producers. In addition, this period was marked by very high inflation and exorbitant construction costs.

In retrospect it is remarkable that the grain and coal projects were finally completed. It did seem, however, that at the time the new grain terminal officially opened on May 16, 1985 most of the battles had been won and Prince Rupert was on its way to full integration in the overseas movement of this commodity.

THE OPTIONAL OUTLETS FOR NORTHEAST B.C. COAL

The first coal from the Luscar mine at Cardinal River reached Neptune's new terminal in North Vancouver in early 1970 and was soon followed by shipments from McIntyre's

Smoky River mine. With both these west central Alberta mines committed to the Southern Gateway port the substantial interest shown by several private concerns between 1965 and 1971 in the potential for bulk terminal development near Prince Rupert waned.

With all the metallurgical coal under export contracts in the late sixties now heading via the Fraser Canyon to Burrard Inlet or Roberts Bank, Japanese buyers advised the B.C. government that no further coal contracts would be awarded unless it moved to the coast by a different route. As large deposits were being identified in northeast B.C., a new route to a new terminal had to be found if this coal was to be marketed successfully.

In the dying days of the W.A.C. Bennett administration the provincial government, ever mindful of the need to nourish the PGE, began to make pronouncements that coal from the deposits in northeast B.C. would be shipped through a new loading facility at Squamish at the head of Howe Sound. Coal, too, from the Bowron deposit southeast of Prince George would follow the same route to Howe Sound if that deposit were developed. In October 1972 the federal Minister of the Environment, Jack Davis, blocked the Squamish proposal based on the damage it could cause to sport and commercial fisheries in Howe Sound.

Then, in January 1973, Bill Rathie, western member for the NHB opined that northeast coal would likely head to Roberts Bank! That view was soon contradicted by Jack Davis in May 1973 when he said northeast coal would go to Prince Rupert if the provincial railway could negotiate a master agreement with the CNR.

A new NDP government, elected in B.C. on August 30, 1972, was not about to be thwarted by the federal government denying the use of Squamish for a coal terminal. In early 1973 they received a report produced by Paish and Associate, which concluded that Britannia Beach on Howe Sound was a "highly feasible" site for a coal port. This report created a temporary furor, especially in Prince Rupert, where a year later city officials were still trying to obtain a copy. The report was alleged to demonstrate a saving of one dollar per tonne for coal shipped via Britannia versus Prince Rupert. Clearly it was an attempt to have northeast coal shipped exclusively by the British Columbia Railway. It failed.

By mid-1973 the federal government had available two studies, one economic and the other environmental, that clearly expressed preference for Prince Rupert as the best port for bulk terminal development. On June 23, 1973, Federal Transport Minister, Marchand, announced that preliminary studies would be undertaken at federal expense for a bulk terminal development on Ridley Island.

The B.C. Government, in mid-1975, weighed in with another bit of lunacy when a senior Cabinet member indicated that Port Simpson might be a better place for the terminal than Ridley Island.

On December 11, 1975 the government changed again. The new provincial government under Premier W. R. Bennett focused on a "Northern Development Strategy" to stimulate the depressed economy of northwestern B.C.

Denison Mines announced the signing of a letter of intent with Japanese buyers to supply

5 million tonnes of metallurgical coal annually from its Quintette property on September 25, 1976. Premier Bennett responded by designating Prince Rupert the provincial choice for a major coal port to serve the new northeast producers at an estimated cost of $50–60 million. An estimated additional $50 million would need to be spent by the CNR upgrading its north line from Prince George to Prince Rupert. Furthermore, Bennett expressed a firm resolve to persuade the Japanese to take an additional 5 million tonnes of northeast coal to justify the very heavy infrastructure costs required and also expressed the hope that Alberta production from the McIntyre and Luscar coal mines would be re-directed to the planned new northern ocean terminal from Neptune's Burrard Inlet facility. For their part, Neptune indicated their readiness to provide a common-use storage and loading facility on Ridley at an estimated cost of $50 million. They leased an appropriate site for $30,000 per year from the NHB and spent $0.5 million on a detailed study of that site.

Labour troubles on the Australian coal scene coupled with an oil crisis in 1977 increased interest in Canadian coal deposits and further stimulated a response to the perceived need for a new northern coal shipping facility.

The federal-provincial study to determine the most economic route for northeast coal and other bulk commodities from northern B.C. was completed in 1973, but was not released until May 1977. The report indicated that a terminal at Fairview had a modest advantage over Ridley for annual shipments under 5 million tonnes, but suggested the probability of much higher tonnages from the northeast mines once a terminal was available. Curiously, this report made the qualification that if northeast coal was destined to Europe it would be cheaper to move it through Vancouver, due to its 804 km (500 mile) advantage over Prince Rupert! This must have assumed that a vessel loaded at Ridley Island would first transit the Inside Passage to Vancouver and thence out to Cape Flattery. In fact, the extra distance direct from Prince Rupert to Panama is only 307 nautical miles (350 miles).

Finally, on March 7, 1978, the federal government announced that Ridley Island would be provided with road and rail links, built at a cost of $16.3 million over the next three years. This was expected to provide the basic infrastructure needed for the development of a coal terminal on the island and one or two grain elevators. There would be no further talk of northeast coal going to Squamish, Britannia, Kitimat, Port Simpson or Roberts Bank! (It is of interest to note, however, that in the fall of 1981 Pacific Coast Terminals at Port Moody loaded the first two shipments of northeast coal. They were trial shipments sent to Japan and Korea from BP's Sukunka deposit.)

THE DEVELOPMENT OF RIDLEY COAL TERMINAL

Bishop Ridley, no stranger to conflict, would have been appalled at the machinations, poisoned atmosphere, needless delays, and enormously inflated costs that plagued the development of the north coast coal terminal, even after its location had been widely accepted.

The federal funding announcement to provide road and rail links to Ridley Island was followed three months later with a $140,000 contract, awarded to CBA Engineering and Carr Donald Associates to prepare a "Master Plan" for the island. The route for road access was selected in consultation with the City.

There was interest aplenty in the proposed new coal terminal both from established operators and from the prospective producers. Neptune Terminals, which had a two-year option on a 150 acre site on Ridley and had already spent $350,000 on studies for a coal terminal, requested a renewal for a further two years. Vancouver Wharves too, no longer involved at Kitimat, expressed interest in developing the coal facility on Ridley. Denison, Teck, and British Petroleum, each exploring or developing deposits in northeast B.C., were very much involved and concerned that a terminal be available in time for their first shipments.

The provincial government, which had turned Ridley Island over to the federal government to develop as a national port in 1971 and which was making a huge investment in rail access infrastructure and townsite development, were very concerned that the NHB get on with the project without further delay or political maneuvering.

Early in 1979 the NHB set up a project coordinating committee "to initiate the logical sequence of events for implementation of the Ridley Island port expansion master plan." Concurrently, the NHB made it clear that they planned to recover the full amount of infrastructure investment through charges on commodity throughput.

The B.C. Government, in mid-1979, created the position of Provincial Coal Coordinator to facilitate the development and marketing of B.C. coal, with special emphasis on northeast production, and to monitor the progress of terminal development negotiations in Ottawa.

Despite the increasing pressures to get on with the development of a coal shipping facility on Ridley Island, the provision of infrastructure to the island had already been covered under the MoU signed July 30, 1979 following negotiations between six major grain companies and the federal government. That agreement provided not only for road access to the island, but also for a rail embankment with three operable tracks, water, power, telephone, and a natural gas line to the periphery of the site selected by the grain consortium. None of the cost to government of these commitments was to be recoverable. The Province of B.C. agreed to fulfill the federal commitment for road access and proceeded at once with the necessary engineering studies. The subsequent welshing by a later federal administration on the term of the MoU dealing with cost recovery has been dealt with in detail in the previous section on grain.

By November 1979, the Grain consortium had selected their site and the province had called for tenders to build the road at an estimated cost of $10 million. Denison and Teck, now deeply involved in the development of their properties, were becoming increasingly concerned about lack of progress on a shipping facility for their coal. Ongoing negotiations between the NHB and a number of parties interested in developing the terminal intensified, though the intensity was more in the direction of heat than light, for it was not until October 31, 1981, a further two years, that an unhappy "resolution" was reached.

By January 30, 1980 the cost to the federal government of their non-recoverable contribution to provide the Ridley infrastructure (including sharing the costs of site preparation for the terminal and the required support structures to reach its loading berth) had been established at $42.5 million. This expenditure had been approved by Cabinet. B.C. had agreed to build the access road and contribute an additional $4 million to widen the rail embankment to accommodate coal trains. C.B.A. Engineering was awarded a $685,000 contract for project management and construction supervision.

Then, on March 3, 1980 the federal government changed and by March 26 the new Transport Minister, Pepin, announced that the government was not committed to the $42.5 million infrastructure expenditure on a non-recoverable basis. He offered instead a $20 million grant with a further $13.8 million to be recoverable, plus another $4 million each to come from Alberta and B.C. By mid-1980, B.C. cancelled its previously agreed $4 million, but offered instead to go ahead and build the coal terminal. This offer was curtly rejected by the NHB, which had control of the island, given to it by the province 10 years earlier.

The province was now deeply involved in financing the costs of the new rail line from Anzac to Tumbler Ridge, as well as a major upgrade on the British Columbia Railway line from Anzac to Prince George. Eventually, the province provided slightly over half the total estimated $2.5 billion spent by all parties involved in the development of northeast coal. Little wonder that to be viable the project needed minimum sales of 10 million tonnes annually at a price well above the average world price for metallurgical coal. Optimism reigned, however, stoked by the apparent insatiable demand for coal by the Japanese steel industry.

On February 8, 1981 the Japanese signed a contract with Denison and Teck for 7.7 million tonnes per year for 15 years with delivery starting in October 1983. The initial price was set at $75 per tonne with escalation clauses.

The NHB now called for "full proposals" from parties interested in building the coal terminal, which they indicated would cost about $70 million. The NHB estimated their costs for infrastructure and site preparation for the coal facility at $35 million and proposed to recover this with a throughput charge, set initially at $3 per tonne with future escalation to $4. Teck and Denison protested strongly, believing it to be unfair that they alone should "subsidize all future producers by paying the entire costs of rail and port." Ottawa, however, was adamant that not a penny of federal money would subsidize coal export from B.C.

During February and March 1981, three-way negotiations took place between the NHB, Prince Rupert Grain, and the coal companies in an attempt to apportion the cost of infrastructure and site preparation on Ridley to each terminal. The coal companies' estimates for the cost of the required site preparation for their terminal were very much lower than the NHB's new estimate of $39 million, the amount on which the throughput charge was to be based. The NHB refused to provide them with a detailed breakdown of this estimate. Indicative of the acrimony surrounding these "negotiations" was the public statement by Bob Andras, former Liberal cabinet minister and then a senior vice president of

Teck Corporation, who deplored the atmosphere of "distrust and suspicion that plagued the negotiations."

Finally, on April 15, 1981 after a two-week deadline extension, five proposals were submitted to the NHB for development and operation of the coal terminal. Two were from consortia. The northeast coal producers estimated they could build a suitable common-use terminal for $70 million, a figure very close to the $67 million predicated by Vancouver Wharves in mid-1980 and the NHB's own estimate in January 1981.

In mid-June 1981, the NHB committee assessing the five proposals settled on a consortium made up of Federal Navigation and Commerce Ltd. of Montreal (Fed Nav), Gulf Canada Resources, Esso Resources, and Manalta Coal. "Final" negotiations began with this group to build the terminal, now estimated to cost $100 million. The three western companies soon dropped out of this consortium leaving the NHB to sign an agreement with Fed Nav alone on August 7, 1981, though Fed Nav had yet to conclude any agreement with Teck or Denison.

The two mine developers were very unhappy. They had wished to build the terminal themselves, controlling costs, and were quite prepared to allow future use by other shippers. They had accepted the $3 per tonne throughput charge, but were opposed to the NHB's proposed escalation of that charge. Their negotiations with the NHB had been, in their view, totally unsatisfactory and tantamount to serial ultimatums by this federal agency.

With the support of the B.C. Government the coal companies decided to look for a viable alternative to the NHB site. After a passing look at Kitimat they focused on the 32 hectare (80 acre) site owned by the BCDC on Kaien Island, immediately adjacent to Ridley Island.

Premier Bennett, in September 1981, threatened to build a coal terminal on that site if greater progress on the Ridley site was not soon evident. The province was very deeply involved financially and politically in the northeast coal project and was not about to see it fail for lack of a shipping facility caused by games being played in Ottawa and Montreal. British Columbia Railway was delaying tunnel contracts on the Anzac to Tumbler Ridge line pending resolution of the port matter.

By the fall of 1981, Fed Nav, alone after losing the other three members of its consortium, had clearly become much less optimistic about the coal terminal on Ridley Island. They also began to realize that despite owning the terminal, it was unlikely that significant amounts of coal would be carried to Japan in their own vessels.

With B.C. applying increasing pressure on Ottawa, the NHB, unwilling to call for new proposals, announced a new and quite incredible arrangement with Fed Nav on October 30, 1981.

A new company, Ridley Terminals Inc. (RTI) was incorporated under the *Canada Business Corporation Act* on December 19, 1981. Fed Nav would own 10 percent of the equity and the NHB the other 90 percent. RTI was to design, construct, and operate the terminal, now estimated to cost $230 million. The federal government would guarantee 80 percent ($184 million) of loans needed and the NHB and Fed Nav would guarantee the remainder. Fed Nav, controlled by the Pathe family of Montreal and good friends of the government in power, and especially of the NHB, was able to borrow its $23 million contribution from a chartered bank on the strength of this agreement and would never be at any risk. This was due to the fact that they were not only to receive a guaranteed 20 percent annual dividend, to accrue compounded annually if unpaid, but also had arranged a "Put" as part of the agreement, whereby the federal government had to buy them out in 1991, if they so requested, at a price reflecting their initial investment plus all unpaid compounded annual dividends. Fed Nav was to provide a management team and their interest could be bought out by the federal government at any time.

As a Crown Corporation, albeit with a minority partner, Ridley Terminals Inc. expected to be exempt from municipal taxation, but after years of dispute this exemption was denied.

If this lopsided public-private deal for the coal terminal project was not "conceived in iniquity," it certainly did nothing to enhance the less than sterling reputation of the NHB in B.C.

By December 1981, agreement had been reached between the coal companies and RTI over throughput charges, set at $3 per tonne until 1989 and thereafter at $3.35 until 1994. The rail tunnel contracts, on hold pending conclusion of the terminal issue, were awarded with the new 129 km (80 mile) line now expected to cost $315 million. RTI announced that construction of their terminal would commence early in 1982 and be completed by December 1, 1983 with costs now estimated to have risen from $230 to $275 million.

Early in 1982 there was a very strong protest by the Ironworkers Union against the award of a contract to Mitsubishi for the stacker reclaimers. The Japanese bid committed to only 53 percent Canadian content compared to 96 percent Canadian content from a competing bid by Stephens-Adamson. This soured labor relations on the project for some time.

Contracts to build the dock structures were awarded to Dillingham and Sceptre Dredging in the amount of $35 million, though it later transpired this was only a "target bid" and was subject to cost plus. Dillingham was also awarded a $7 million contract for the dumper foundation.

The new road across the back of Kaien Island and the bridge over the CNR tracks to connect the two islands was officially opened September 28, 1982. It cost approximately $10 million and was built by the B.C. Highways Ministry under a joint federal-provincial agreement. Also in September 1982, the CNR announced that they were spending $330 million to upgrade their 70-year-old "north line" and provide nine train sets to carry coal.

By spring 1983 Fed Nav's interest in the project was, again, waning. Their senior vice president admitted that their original interest rested on the long-term hope of carrying much of the coal on their own vessels. This was not going to happen. J. Auger of Ports Canada (which replaced the NHB in 1983) took over the chairmanship of RTI from L. Pathe of Fed Nav and the crown corporation took over management, a role previously assigned to Federal Marine Terminals, a subsidiary of Fed Nav. Auger predicted initial annual throughput of 8 million tonnes, growing in time to 12 million tonnes.

The outlook for western Canadian coal exports, especially from the high priced northeast mines, began to darken by September 1983. The Japanese began to press for price reductions on the grossly overpriced coal from Denison's and Teck's operations. Halvorsen Consultants predicted the closure of the Quintette and Bullmoose mines in a few years, due to massive over capacity of metallurgical coal production worldwide coupled with depressed Japanese steel markets.

By the time the first northeast coal was loaded aboard *Shoryu Maru* on January 7, 1984, the price under the long term contracts negotiated three years previously with the steel companies in Japan had escalated to $98 per tonne and the buyers were pressing for an immediate reduction to $84. The official grand opening on June 8, 1984 was marred by union protesters who blocked the road to Ridley Island forcing 10 busloads of dignitaries to walk 2–3 km to the ceremony. The demonstration was, at least in part, a protest against the non-union status of RTI.

Clearly, the magnificent new terminal had been grossly overbuilt relative to market conditions. It was also built at excessive cost, due in no small part to time constraints resulting from needless delays in getting the project underway. However, the operation of the facility was indeed a success and, by November 28, 1984 the new terminal set a record by loading 179,368 tonnes of coal on the *River Star* in 31 hours 10 minutes. Designed to handle 12–15 million tonnes annually, the terminal peaked at 7,190,454 tonnes in 1985 and would average only 6 million tonnes per year over its first 16 years of operation.

CRUISE VESSEL VISITS

Prince Rupert continued to host most Alaska-bound cruise vessels from the mid-sixties to the mid-eighties — two decades of very rapid market growth in that vacation itinerary. This period was marked by an almost complete transition from the traditional small coastal type vessels, which long served this route, to large purpose-built ships with a much greater passenger capacity.

Berthing for these ships in Prince Rupert was inadequate, especially after the disastrous 1972 fire that destroyed most of the 50-year-old Ocean Dock. The port spent $500,000 on minimal repairs to what remained of the dock and from 1978 charged cruise ship operators $3 per passenger (later raised to $4.50) to recoup that expenditure. This was not well accepted, especially as the facility was so inadequate. Larger vessels had to lighter their passengers ashore from anchorage in the harbour. To receive these passengers a very modest facility was constructed in 1984 on the foreshore near the CNR station, but it saw little use because, in 1985, amendments to U.S. legislation allowed the large cruise vessels to bypass Prince Rupert in favour of an extra port call in Alaska.

Attempts to entertain passengers ashore included bus tours, the Mount Hays ski lift, and the Museum, amongst others. After the Performing Arts Centre was completed in 1987, an excellent program was developed there for cruise passengers, but by then large vessel calls had virtually ceased.

Probably the chief reason for the near cessation of large cruise ship calls at Prince Rupert was that operators never wanted to call there in the first place, and only included the city in their itinerary to satisfy U.S. legislation for foreign-flagged cruise ships. Unquestionably, the magic word "Alaska" was the main marketing tool for cruise operators. Other factors contributing to their lack of interest in Prince Rupert were the NHB "Head Tax," the inadequate docking facilities, the perceived lack of tourist attractions, and the apparent apathy of some businesses in the community who, for example, refused to open for Sunday cruise ship passengers.

The loss of the large cruise liners was partially balanced by the beginning of visits by small exploration-type vessels able to use the truncated Ocean Dock. However, passenger counts, which had peaked at 28,000 in 1981, fell to an average of 21,000 between 1983 and 1985 and then collapsed to a nadir of 227 a decade later.

COASTAL SERVICES

The period from 1970 to 1985 included an episode of major upheaval in marine service to coastal communities. Dutch owned Northland Navigation abruptly withdrew service in 1976, following the termination of their federal subsidy. This left a number of isolated coastal points with totally inadequate service, or no service at all, unless by air. This was especially traumatic for the 6,000 residents of Queen Charlotte Islands (Haida Gwaii).

Over the next five years the Ferry Corporation stepped slowly into the breach, building new terminals at Port Hardy, Skidegate, and Prince Rupert and mobilizing a second vessel, the *Queen of the North*, for the northern services.

PORT TRAFFIC THROUGHPUT

Records show port throughput in the early seventies at 2–3 million tons per year. As a measure of port activity these figures are, however, misleading inasmuch as they include iron ore and copper concentrates loaded at Tasu on the Queen Charlotte Islands (Haida Gwaii), as well as logs loaded at Port Simpson. Commodities actually handled at the port of Prince Rupert averaged only about one-third of that total and consisted of pulp, grain, logs, mineral concentrates, and fish products. With the exception of grain and the mineral concentrates from Babine Lake these exports were produced locally.

Beginning in 1978, grain exports increased very substantially, averaging 1.3 million tonnes annually for the next seven years and constituting over half the port's throughput during that period. Concurrently, Fairview Terminal began to make a contribution, drawing most of its export commodities of lumber, agricultural by products, mineral concentrates, and sulphur from distant points of origin. In 1985 Fairview throughput reached 666,326 tonnes. Overseas pulp shipments from Watson Island pulp mills continued to average about 300,000 tonnes per year.

Completion of the coal terminal on Ridley Island brought a shift in dominance from grain to coal for the next 19 years. Coal shipments made up 61 percent of the total 169 million tonnes moved over the two Ridley terminals between 1984 and 2002.

The CNR AquaTrain that connected mainline trackage in the "lower forty-eight" to the Alaska Railroad at Whittier continued to move high-value general cargo, military supplies, and explosives on a regular eight-day cycle from its Prince Rupert terminal. In 1982, a new 55-railcar capacity barge was introduced to replace the 33-car barge that had started the service 20 years earlier.

By 1985 the port, at long last, had three modern terminals and had made a quantum leap in traffic throughput, reaching a new peak of 10.1 million tonnes in the year 1985.

PETROCHEMICAL AND NATURAL GAS TERMINAL PROPOSALS

Between 1969 and 1984 considerable interest was shown in the development of petrochemical and/or natural gas terminals in, or near Prince Rupert and several in-depth studies were undertaken.

In the spring of 1969, Canadian Industries Ltd. (CIL) approached Prince Rupert based Western Wharves Ltd. with a proposal to undertake a joint study of a development at Fairview designed to handle imports and exports of both liquid bulk and dry bagged chemical products. Preliminary site plans and cost estimates were prepared for a terminal to include a warehouse, a suitable dock and 12 tanks, of which three were to be stainless steel. By late August CIL indicated that they were preparing a proposal to Western Wharves, but by October their interest had waned.

Not until the early eighties was there a new interest in the import or export of petrochemical products through Prince Rupert. Then, from late 1980 to early 1984, and concurrent with the grain and coal terminal developments, a number of proposals for world class terminals were received from several sources and for several sites.

First on the scene was an American company, Carter Oil and Gas Ltd. who proposed a $2 billion LNG exporting facility on Ridley Island. This proposal was later expanded to include a $1.2 billion petrochemical plant alongside the LNG facility for a total estimated expenditure of $3.8 billion. Their proposal was soon followed by Dome Petroleum's announcement that they viewed the Prince Rupert area as ideal for an LNG exporting facility and had agreements in principle with five Japanese electrical utilities to ship 2.6 million tonnes of LNG annually for 20 years.

Clearly, the Dome proposal had the ear of the federal government whose National Energy Board had to rule on the amount of gas available for offshore export. Dome estimated their plant would require 200 hectares (500 acres) and selected a site at Grassy Point near Port Simpson. They began negotiations with the local Band Council with the aim of mitigating any adverse effects their project might have on the Port Simpson community.

By the summer of 1981, the Port of Prince Rupert was requesting authorization from the NHB to proceed with a $925,000 study for a $42 million liquid bulk terminal for a Ridley Island site. At the same time, the BCDC was proposing a dock to service a petrochemical plant on their 32 hectare (80 acre) property on Kaien Island adjacent to Ridley Island.

Late in 1981 the NHB, BCDC, Alberta Government, CNR and 16 Alberta energy firms met to consider developing a $100 million tank farm on the BCDC site with a capacity to ship $1.8 billion worth of petrochemicals annually. Then in February 1982, B.C., Alberta, and Ottawa announced the planned terminal would be built on either the Kaien site or on Ridley Island and would be ready for shipments by 1984. By June 1982 the Kaien site had been selected and Don Phillips, B.C. Cabinet Minister, announced that the terminal construction would commence late that year for completion in 1984.

Prince Rupert Terminals, a joint venture of Johnston Terminals of Vancouver and British interests and promoted by a former general manager of the Prince Rupert Port Corporation, entered the picture at this point. This group backed the development of an $80 million petrochemical tank farm in Prince Rupert with a throughput of at least 1 million tonnes annually by 1986, but Pacific Coast Bulk Terminals trumped this initiative with a plan to move export petrochemicals through their Port Moody site, which benefitted from an existing dock and shorter rail haul from commodity sources.

The prospects for a bulk liquid terminal for Prince Rupert darkened as product began to move through Port Moody, commodity supply sources dried up, and the B.C. Government failed to support their own proposal in the face of the better economics using Port Moody.

Dome actively pursued their LNG project during 1982–1983. They made substantial progress in their negotiations with the Port Simpson Band Council regarding the Grassy Point site and also with their application for export permits from the National Energy Board. They were less successful in raising financing for the project, or reaching an agreement with West Coast Transmission to provide a pipeline to the terminal, and were not strongly supported by the governments of Alberta or B.C. By early 1984, Dome was foundering under a $6.2 billion debt load to Canadian and international bankers and the prospective customers for the LNG in Japan were looking elsewhere for supply. By late 1984 their project was dead.

CHAPTER EIGHT

The Gateways 1985 to 2004 — Surging Growth in Containers and Cruise Passengers

During these two decades, the modest increase in Southern Gateway throughput of bulk commodities was comfortably handled by existing terminals, albeit with substantial expenditures on upgrades and expansions, as well as a number of changes in ownership. Bulk commodities still constituted over 80 percent of Vancouver's total tonnage throughput, but the areas of dramatic growth for the port during this period were cruise ship passenger visits, up 350 percent, and container handling, up 900 percent. To cope with these large increases the port opened a fine new cruise ship terminal in 1986 and a new container terminal at Roberts Bank in 1997.

The major rail lines serving British Columbia (B.C.) ports undertook several substantial programs during this period, including major expansion projects and additions to rail intermodal facilities at or close to the container terminals and key rail delivery points across Canada and the United States (U.S.).

The *Canada Marine Act* of 1998 further changed the way Canadian ports were to be administered, including the ports of Vancouver, Prince Rupert, and New Westminster.

Prince Rupert began this period equipped with modern facilities for handling forest products, general cargo, grains, and coal. The future at last looked bright and, by 1994, the port's throughput reached 13.8 million tonnes. Then, beginning in 1998, the port and its host city suffered a series of hammer blows that port staff appropriately labelled "A Perfect Storm." Activity slumped to its nadir in 2003, when total throughput was only 4.03 million tonnes. Gloom prevailed. The Port Authority could do little about the shrinkage in coal and grain exports, or the closure of the local pulp mill, but with help from all levels of government it was able to respond to the acute need for decent facilities to welcome cruise ship passengers. In addition, recognizing that the port's inability to handle containers was a contributing factor in the total collapse of forest product exports at Fairview in 2002, the Port Authority began planning to convert that terminal to a fully capable container handling facility.

THE ADMINISTRATION OF NATIONAL PORTS

Canada's national ports, including Vancouver and Prince Rupert, functioned as Local Port Corporations (LPCs) from the time they were created in 1983, until the repeal of the *Canada Ports Corporation Act* in June 1998. As Crown Corporations they had gained a modest measure of autonomy. They were, however, by no means free of political influences or the seldom-appreciated "benevolent" interference of an expensive central bureaucracy that had changed little from the NHB and which they were required to support financially. Spending limits imposed on both LPCs were a continuing source of frustration, as were periodic raids by Ottawa on any healthy surplus the ports might have been able to accumulate after paying annual dividends to Ottawa. Between 1986 and 1992 Vancouver alone had paid the federal government $51 million in dividends and $89 million in special levies, in addition to an annual assessment to help maintain Ports Canada's staff of 78 at its head office in Ottawa.

In response to mounting dissatisfaction, Doug Young, an energetic and determined Minister of Transport, reviewed Canada's port system and concluded that it was grossly overbuilt with 30 out of 300 "ports" handling 80 percent of the nation's waterborne cargo. He set out to overhaul and redefine the federal government's relationship to all these ports and, in December of 1995, announced a new National Marine Policy. To implement this policy, Bill C44, the *Canada Marine Act* was introduced in mid-1996, the first comprehensive piece of legislation covering all marine sectors in Canada. The new Act died on the Senate order paper with the election call of June 2, 1997 but was re-introduced with minor revisions and passed on June 11, 1998 by the successor Parliament. It became effective January 1, 1999.

The object of this new legislation was "to make the system of Canadian Ports competitive, efficient and commercially oriented." Major ports, including Vancouver, Prince Rupert, and Fraser Port became agents of the Crown rather than Crown Corporations. As Port Authorities, they were to manage their marine infrastructure and services in a commercial manner and be responsive to local needs and priorities. They were given greater autonomy under the new legislation than they had under the *CPC Act,* were no longer subject to periodic raiding of their treasuries by Ottawa, and did not have to pay "service fees" to support a central bureaucracy. Appointment of directors under the new Act was to be less political and no longer subject to post-election purges as before. Multilayered approvals for spending decisions were no longer required. The ports would pay dividends to the Crown but, as agents of the Crown, they would be exempt from taxation by local authorities. The primary goal and benefit of the legislation was local and regional control of port administration, rather than central control.

The new Port Authorities, established March 1, 1999, were not entirely free of centrally imposed restrictions. They were precluded from borrowing against their assets, from receiving money by way of any appropriation by Parliament, and from receiving the benefit of any government guarantee on their borrowing. Furthermore, each Port was assigned a limit on borrowing. For Vancouver Port Authority (VPA) this was set at $225 million, while Prince Rupert Port Authority was limited to $22 million. This cap engendered considerable frustration for the individual ports. It was perceived to be unnecessary for, if a port's borrowing was to be strictly commercial and without government guarantee, the lender would surely determine whether the loan was commercially sound.

In addition to the redesignation of Vancouver and Prince Rupert as Port Authorities, both the Fraser River Harbour Commission (FRHC) and the North Fraser Harbour Commission acquired a new status under the new Act, becoming the Fraser River Port Authority and the North Fraser Port Authority. The Fraser River Port Authority was given a one-time grant of $15 million in return for relieving Ottawa of the century old burden of dredging and containing the south-arm ship channel. Furthermore, both Fraser and North Fraser Port Authorities would now have to remit dividends to Ottawa.

The *Canada Marine Act* also redefined Ottawa's relationship with minor harbours across Canada. In B.C. a total of 72 small harbours were turned over to local control with a one-time grant to assist with their future maintenance.

THE SECURITY OF THE NATIONAL PORTS

Undoubtedly instances of nefarious waterfront activity have plagued ports from their earliest existence and providing Canadian ports with protection from criminal activity is not a new issue. A number of factors, however, caused this problem to escalate in the last quarter of the twentieth century. Among these, probably the most important were the extraordinarily rapid growth of containerization, the enormous expansion in world trade, and the potential for the use of containers in smuggling. A port facility handling bulk commodities such as coal or wheat offers little to interest organized crime. A container terminal, on the other hand, offers much greater scope for such mischief as theft, or the illegal entry of people, drugs, and weapons.

Traditionally Canada's national ports were patrolled by Ports Police, a unit of the NHB and its successor, the Canada Ports Corporation. This unit was disbanded with the winding up of the CPC December 31, 1998. At the port of Vancouver, responsibility for security on the waterfront was assumed by local police jurisdictions led by the Vancouver Police Department. A multiagency force, the Waterfront Organized Crime Unit was established consisting of the RCMP, local police, and customs officials. This unit was funded by the Vancouver Port Authority, Fraser River Port Authority, and the B.C. Government, after a one-time million dollar federal grant was given to the Vancouver Police Department. Press reports of infiltration of the ILWU by members of the Hells Angel Gang gave impetus to the new unit's activity.

Heightened concerns in the U.S. about waterfront security during Clinton's second term led to amendments to the *Merchant Marine Act*. U.S. ports were offered loan guarantees to improve fencing and gates, and to provide security cameras to cover sensitive areas of their facilities. Dock areas were to be restricted, photo identification required of people entering sensitive areas, and consideration given to background checks for all waterfront workers.

Following the terror attacks in Washington and New York on September 11, 2001 the issue of North American border and port security took on a very much higher profile. In response, the Canadian Senate Committee on National Security and Defence undertook extensive hearings between 2002 and 2004 and concluded that security at Canadian ports needed significant enhancement to combat terrorism, international crime, and illegal immigration. The committee recommended the development of a National Enforcement Strategy for Security at Canadian ports, support for a Universal Set of International Port Security Standards, and a National Screening System for port employees.

In response to these and other recommendations, the Government of Canada undertook a number of security initiatives, committing $930 million during the four years after 9/11 to the enhancement of national marine security. Included among the expenditures was the purchase of VACIS gamma ray screening units for examining the contents of containers, trucks, and railcars arriving at port terminals.

Marine Transportation Security Regulations were promulgated and became effective July 1, 2004. These regulations implemented the International Ship and Port Facility Security Code (ISPFS) that had been adopted by the International Maritime Organization (IMO) in December 2002. An attempt to implement a Marine Transportation Security Clearance Program involving background checks for all port workers met strong union resistance and a court challenge, and was consequently delayed.

THE RAILWAYS: 1985 TO 2004

This was indeed a period of tremendous change in North American railroading. One of the most significant side benefits of the "container revolution" was the focus it brought to bear on the inefficiency of the over regulated, over taxed and (in the U.S.) fragmented continental railroads. For more than a century, railroads in both Canada and the U.S. carried the burden of a politically inspired regulatory regimen and, especially in Canada, they were a mark for tax collectors at all three levels of government.

In the U.S. the *Staggers Act* of 1980 completed reforms initiated by the *Railway Revitalization and Regulatory Reform Act* of 1976. It replaced the rigid regulatory structure that had been in place since 1887 and that had led to the near strangling of rail transportation in the U.S. Two decades of rehabilitation, revitalization, and consolidation of U.S. lines followed. By the year 2000 these changes had produced four huge Class 1 lines, two based in the west and two in the east. Finally, a shipper could seamlessly move goods across the U.S. on a single carrier. By 1998 the merged Union Pacific-Southern Pacific and the Burlington Northern Santa Fe (BNSF) were moving all rail freight west of the Mississippi River. Without doubt, the major container ship operators, constantly analyzing different routes to achieve maximum economy and efficiency, provided much of the stimulus for these changes.

In Canada, shippers had been able to move goods from coast to coast on a single carrier since the first CPR train arrived in Port Moody in 1886 and failed or failing lines had long been consolidated into the Canadian National Railroad. However, in the early eighties, the country's two transcontinental railroads still faced substantial impediments — mandated by all three government levels — to their ability to provide economic and efficient service.

The most significant impediments were excessive fuel and property taxes (especially in B.C.), the notorious Crow rate for moving grain, regulatory restraints such as government refusal to allow little used branch lines to be abandoned, and inadequate capital cost allowances. The pressing need to ease or remove these burdens gained impetus with the passage of the Canada-U.S. Free Trade Agreement in 1988 and the expanded North American Free Trade Agreement (NAFTA) in 1994. These agreements reoriented the focus of both Canadian railways, as an increasing proportion of their business was now moving on a north south axis. With this change came direct competition with recently deregulated U.S. lines carrying a much lighter tax burden and, with their new combinations, able to provide very efficient service.

The *Western Grain Transportation Act* came into effect January 1, 1984 and replaced the 86-year-old statutory rate for moving grain with a "Crow Benefit," paid to the railways and initially set at $659 million per year. A decade later that benefit was terminated, cushioned by a one-time payout of $1.6 billion to producers and the establishment of a $300 million transition fund. Thereafter, producers bore the full cost of moving grain to export positions, subject only to federal overview.

The *National Transportation Act* of 1987 and the *Canada Transportation Act* of 1996 made changes to the long standing federal regulatory structure that encouraged massive main line capital investment by both the CPR and the CNR and spurred the creation of a vibrant short line industry on the prairies, developed from formerly unwanted branch lines.

Fuel and property taxes at all government levels, and especially in B.C., reached a point in 1992 where CN and CP were paying $225 million more than they would if operating in the U.S. In B.C., municipal taxes alone had escalated to $58.3 million. In 1995, measures taken by the provincial and other government levels finally brought this excessive tax burden down to a less onerous level, easing the railways' competitive disadvantage with U.S. lines.

To accommodate the movement of bulk commodities in unit trains both railways invested heavily in their B.C lines during the early to mid-eighties. Canadian Pacific expended $600 million on their grade easement project in the Rogers Pass and CN spent a similar amount upgrading their line from Edmonton to Prince Rupert in preparation for heavy grain and coal traffic.

Both railroads then had to procure appropriate equipment and adapt their main lines to efficiently carry an increasing number of containers. A new trend toward double stacking containers on specially designed railcars had been started by APL Lines in the U.S. in 1984 and within five years U.S. railroads were operating 250 double-stack trains weekly. The CP and CN had to make substantial modifications to tunnels and snow sheds to accommodate similar trains on their lines. CNR had the extra expense of modifying the federally owned rail bridge across the Fraser River at New Westminster at a cost of $15 million.

The CNR commenced a single-stack, weekly, nonstop service from Vancouver to Toronto in early 1988 using 60–65 flat cars to carry containers. It followed a year later with a modified double-stack service for Orient Overseas and Neptune container shipping lines. By 1991 this service had expanded to twice weekly. CP began double-stack service in 1992, promoting a "Maple Leaf" land bridge service to Europe with special incentives for through container traffic. Both lines offered service to Chicago from Vancouver, though CP was more successful, being able to offer single carrier service on a shorter and faster route than CN. As container numbers through the Vancouver terminals increased, it became necessary for the railways to develop intermodal terminals both in the Southern Gateway area and at key distribution centres across Canada and the U.S. Midwest. CN opened a $19 million facility adjacent to their Thornton yard at Port Mann in 1992, replacing two older yards on more valuable property in Vancouver. CP opened a $37 million intermodal facility in Pitt Meadows in 1999. With a view to capturing more container movement to the U.S. Midwest, CN opened a Gateway Intermodal Terminal in 1997 at Harvey, Illinois adjacent to facilities operated by the Illinois Central Railway and, in 2004 opened Super Terminal Memphis, a major rail/truck/barge intermodal facility on a mainline north-south axis in the U.S. This terminal was planned to be the most efficient in the world.

The massive revitalization and consolidation of American railroads that followed the *Staggers Act* undoubtedly influenced the Government of Canada to begin preparing in 1992 for the privatization of the CNR. This was accomplished in November 1995 and resulted in a dynamic, aggressive, and rejuvenated entity freed from the heavy shackles of politically inspired imperatives. Business oriented management now focused on network rationalization with emphasis on creating a core Atlantic to Pacific mainline and developing north-south traffic to and through Chicago. The new motto for the railway became "The Continent is Our Marketplace."

The CPR was equally determined to benefit from the expanded north-south trade opportunities flowing from the free trade agreements. By 1997 the CNR and CPR were the seventh and sixth largest rail operators in the U.S. Some of the major container shipping companies, dissatisfied with U.S. West Coast terminal operations, redirected their U.S. Midwest bound traffic to Vancouver terminals and Canadian rail lines.

In 1999 the CNR, the most improved railroad in North America, merged with the Illinois Central Railroad, the best performing Class 1 line in the U.S. This created a powerhouse able to offer single carrier service to many more points in North America and access to the Atlantic, Pacific, and Caribbean coasts. Concurrent long term marketing agreements with the Kansas City & Southern Railway provided the CNR with access to Kansas City, Dallas, and Mexico. The geographic reach of the CNR was greatly expanded and now exceeded that of any other North American railroad.

In 2000, the CNR attempted a second huge merger with the BNSF Railroad, but this was thwarted by the Surface Transportation Board in the U.S. and replaced with extensive cooperation and interline agreements between the two lines. By 2001 more than half of all CNR traffic was either to, or in the U.S.

With a clear time and distance advantage in carrying containers from Vancouver to Chicago over its own lines the CPR was able to secure contracts with a number of container shipping lines. Rival CNR began to address its relatively uncompetitive position with the purchase of the Wisconsin Central Railway in 2001 for US$1.2 billion in cash.

Closer to home, the CNR reached an agreement with the BC Railroad in early 1998 to create a more efficient rail system in north central B.C. by improving interchanges at Prince George and allowing reciprocal access to each other's lines. Loaded BC Rail cars reached Prince Rupert for the first time in the fall of 1998. Concurrently BC Rail, CNR, and Ridley Terminals reached agreement to lower their charges to the remaining, struggling coal producer in northeast B.C.

In 2003 the B.C. Government announced the sale of BC Rail operations to the CNR for $1.0 billion with the transfer effective July 15, 2004. The deal excluded the short line to Roberts Bank originally built by the B.C. Harbours Board. So ended the unhappy saga of this albatross that had burdened successive provincial administrations for nine decades. Promoted by Hays in order to connect his northern line with the burgeoning Port of Vancouver, BC Rail and its antecedents unquestionably stunted the development of the Northern Rail Corridor and its Gateway Port. Though the distances from Prince George to either Vancouver or Prince Rupert are virtually identical, the CN main line west is far superior in grades, curves, and track standards. This transaction must have a profound and beneficial effect on the long term development of the northern half of the province.

To increase the capacity and efficiency of movement through the Fraser-Thompson common rail corridor, CN and CP finalized a "directional running" agreement in late 1999 to share each other's lines over 248 km (155 miles) of their nearly parallel course. Despite this arrangement, by 2004 capacity constraints were beginning to appear on both main lines to the Southern Gateway Ports. CP, in particular, had reached capacity in several places west of Moose Jaw and, in 2004 spent $160 million to squeeze an extra four trains a day over their main line. U.S. lines in the west began reopening old abandoned routes and, indeed, the only mainline track with substantial spare capacity in western North America was the CN line from Red Pass Junction to Prince Rupert. This fact would have major consequences for the long neglected Northern Gateway Port.

GREATER VANCOUVER: 1985 TO 2004

Total export-import tonnage through the Port of Vancouver during this period increased from 56 to 73 million tonnes, but the two most significant events were the openings of Canada Place for cruise vessels in 1986 and the Deltaport container terminal in 1997.

Early in this period the Vancouver Port Corporation (VPC) began to actively redress the port's previously weak performance relative to its Puget Sound and California competitors in attracting container traffic. It engaged in more aggressive marketing both domestically and in Asia, and planned for more terminal capacity to cope with anticipated growth. These activities culminated in the 1991 decision to create a new terminal at Roberts Bank.

Between 1989 and 1998 the port embarked on a number of initiatives to help resolve the escalating problems of road and rail access to the south shore container terminals which were causing unacceptable traffic congestion and delays. The provincially funded Cassiar Connector project, completed in 1989, eased access to the eastern end of the south shore waterfront and an $11 million project, jointly funded by the VPC and the City of Vancouver in the late nineties, substantially eased problems with road access to Centerm and Vanterm. Waterfront roadways on the south shore were closed to public access in 2001.

In 1994 the Greater Vancouver Gateway Council was formed, a multimodal initiative aimed at making Vancouver the gateway of choice for North America. A major objective of this council was to determine the best way to resolve local infrastructure problems. By 2001 it had agreed on a regional plan for a Major Commercial Transportation System to include road, rail, and water links. Major components of the plan included a new South Fraser Perimeter Road, a new North Fraser Perimeter Road through New Westminster, and a new Fraser Road Bridge between Langley and Maple Ridge.

On the north shore the port, in 1992, purchased the site previously occupied by Versatile Pacific's shipyard. It also proposed a new terminal, Norterm, at the former White Pass and Yukon dock site, but that project was indefinitely deferred due to existing road and rail congestion.

LOCAL PORT ADMINISTRATION

The directors of Canada's largest and most prosperous port chafed under the limitations imposed on them as a Local Port Corporation operating under the Canada Ports Corporation Act of 1983. Central office approval was required for expenditures over $5 million and cabinet approval needed for projects over $10 million, for leases over 20 years, and for all property sales or purchases.

In 1993 the corporation commissioned Jonathan Seymour to study its relationship to Ports Canada and to the two Fraser Harbour Commissions. His subsequent report included a strong recommendation for the amalgamation of the Vancouver Port Corporation and the Fraser Harbour Commissions, under a new regional harbour commission structure free of ties to a central controlling agency. The result, he concluded, would be substantial savings on many fronts including marketing, boards of directors, losses due to unseemly competition for business, and payments to support a central head office. The Fraser River Harbour Commissioners were less than pleased and issued a strong rebuttal to Seymour's recommendations. It would be another 15 years before this logical merger of the three Southern Gateway Port entities took place.

On May 1, 1999 the VPC became the Vancouver Port Authority under the terms of the new *Canada Marine Act* with much greater spending authority and without the threat of raids on its surpluses, or required annual payments to support the central office in Ottawa. Despite commitments to the contrary, however, its new board of directors was locally perceived to be stacked with political appointees.

Though the *Canada Marine Act* lifted some of the Port Authority's burdens, there remained the twin issues of excessive local municipal taxation on privately owned port installations and the grossly uneven playing field in competing for container traffic with the heavily subsidized ports of Seattle and Tacoma. These issues had real potential to impede new developments and became major concerns for the VPA and terminal operators. Municipal taxes on Southern Gateway facilities increased an average 60 percent between 2001 and 2003. Clearly, some of the councils among the nine municipalities hosting port facilities considered them to be "easy pickings" for extra tax revenue. With the situation becoming increasingly untenable, the Province, in late 2003, introduced the "Ports Competitiveness Property Tax Initiative." This capped tax rates at existing rates for lower mainland terminal operators for five years and placed a ten year cap on new port facility investments. Local governments were compensated for the resulting revenue loss.

Resolving the problem of the uneven playing field created by the heavily subsidized U.S. port facilities was much more difficult, both for the Port Authority and especially for the heavily taxed B.C. container terminals. In 2001 the Seattle Port Authority collected USD $70 million from King County homeowners and businesses, whereas the VPA and its tenants that same year paid out CDN$55 million to local municipal governments. This disparity cancelled out any currency exchange benefit to the Vancouver terminal operators. In 2004, Deltaport paid CDN$5 per TEU in municipal taxation, whereas the Port of Tacoma received USD$5 and Seattle USD$20 per TEU by way of taxes collected.

In late 2002 the VPA made a number of specific recommendations to the federal panel that was reviewing the *Canada Marine Act* for the purpose of suggesting amendments to the federal government. Among items on Vancouver's wish list were removing the cap on commercial borrowing, acquiring the right to fully reinvest operating profits and retain proceeds from land sales for future investments, and removing the prohibition on public investment in port infrastructure. In response to a later, more specific request, the VPA's borrowing limit was raised by Order in Council to $510 million, effective January 29, 2005.

The Canada Harbour Place Corporation, a Federal Crown Corporation, became a subsidiary of the VPC in 1993 and was renamed the Canada Place Corporation. Ten years later the northern extension of Canada Place was completed and, in November 2004, the VPA moved its corporate offices to The Pointe in the expanded facility.

THE CONTAINER TERMINALS

Though the number of boxes moving over the port's berths tripled during the 15 years to 1984, Vancouver's container traffic growth continued to lag behind that at eastern Canadian and U.S. West Coast ports. Canadian Atlantic and St. Lawrence facilities benefitted from the movement of large numbers of containers destined for the U.S. In contrast, on the Pacific Coast in 1984 over a third of the boxes bound for or originating from Canadian points crossed the berths of U.S. terminals.

Ports in Puget Sound and Southern California aggressively developed and expanded well equipped terminals and the size of the U.S. market offered vessel operators economies of scale not yet available at Canada's Western Gateway. The centrally controlled VPC had taken a more timid approach to providing and expanding facilities and continued to have the embarrassing problem of the "container clause" in the union's contract with its employers.

So objectionable had that clause become to consignees that in 1986 it was estimated that half the containers off loaded in Puget Sound terminals and destined for Vancouver were taken from vessels also calling at Vancouver. Clearly, the consignees preferred to pay the $300 trucking cost to circumvent the greater cost of having ILWU members handle their container's contents.

A Federal Industrial Inquiry was convened in mid-1987 to examine the contentious clause that had been in the agreement between the union and the B.C. Maritime Employers Association since 1970. It recommended eliminating the clause with compensation for the union. Ottawa accepted this advice and the clause was removed effective January 1, 1988. A compensation package was agreed to and paid through a per-TEU assessment on container volumes exceeding 1987 levels.

Belatedly recognizing the importance of containers to the future of the port, the VPC began to take more aggressive measures to capture a greater share of this traffic. Though traditional bulk and break-bulk commodity exports continued to dominate total tonnage throughput in 1984, container traffic generated half the Port Corporation's revenue and provided 70 percent of the workload for the port labour force. The port's new marketing department initially focused its efforts in central and eastern Canada with a view to redirecting Asian traffic which, while destined there, was presently being off loaded at U.S. ports and carried east on U.S. rail lines. Later, it directed efforts at Asian shippers and in 1993 Vancouver became the first foreign port to establish an office in China. A new crane was ordered for each terminal in 1987 to supplement the existing five that had handled

280,777 TEU that year. Seattle, however, had seven terminals with 22 cranes that handled 1,026,000 TEU the same year.

In 1991 Vancouver's two terminals handled 383,563 TEU, although another 150,000 TEU destined for, or originating from Canada was still going through Puget Sound facilities. Vancouver had only a 6 percent share of total West Coast North America container traffic. Uncomfortably aware of this continuing loss of business to Seattle and Tacoma and desirous of capturing some of the Midwest U.S. market, the VPC announced a program of incentives to make the port more attractive to vessel operators. A 30 percent discount on wharfage charges was offered to vessels making Vancouver their first port of call. All lines were made eligible for a scaled volume discount and commodity based charges on boxed cargo were replaced with a per box tariff. COSCO, a regular visitor at the port with its container vessels for a decade, became the first transpacific carrier to respond to the incentives and commenced berthing at Vancouver on a 10-day-schedule with eight new 2,700 TEU box ships.

The race among the world's container lines to build ever larger vessels was matched by a near frantic effort between competing ports, especially in the U.S., to build bigger and more efficiently operated terminals. Serving these terminals with adequate road and rail connections to inland points was often the more taxing problem.

At the Burrard Inlet terminals, site development and equipment upgrades had occurred incrementally, but by 1988 it was clear that a quantum leap in capacity was necessary to meet growth projections over the next 10 years, which estimated that throughput would triple. Only a major project would suffice. The VPC at first proposed extending Centerm eastward, engulfing both Ballantyne Pier and the old Burlington Northern dock. To expand and equip the terminal on 21 hectares (52.5 acres) of new reclaimed land would have cost an estimated $200 million and would have increased the terminal's capacity to 750,000 TEU. This plan was abandoned three years later in favour of creating an altogether new terminal on already reclaimed land at Roberts Bank, while spending $44 million to redevelop and modernize Ballantyne Pier. The decision was motivated in part by the desire to avoid exacerbating the existing road and rail congestion on the Burrard Inlet waterfront. Furthermore, the new location offered a saving of 4 hours on each round trip for a container vessel, over terminals in Puget Sound or Burrard Inlet. The new terminal, Deltaport, opened officially June 25, 1997. As completed, it doubled the port's container handling capacity. Unhappy with frequent delays at congested California facilities, vessel operators were quick to make use of the new terminal.

The beneficial effects of the new and improved terminals were many and included: aggressive marketing, removal of the "container clause," installation of Electronic Data Interchange at the terminals, and availability of double-stack trains from both CN and CP. These benefits, combined with persisting congestion and delays at some of the U.S. West Coast ports, resulted in an average 12.5 percent annual growth in TEU handled by the Vancouver terminals between 1985 and 2004. That growth took the port's container throughput from 178,175 TEU in 1985 to 1,664,906 TEU in 2004. Projections of continuing growth to 4 million TEU by 2018 would soon require additional projects to double the port's existing capacity, rated in 2005 at 1.97 million TEU.

Centerm

At Centerm an $11 million expansion program completed in 1987 added 2.4 hectares (6 acres) and a second berth for container vessels. The terminal's original Starporter crane was rebuilt to increase its height and a third crane was added in 1989. The layout of the whole terminal changed and with 18 of its 22.6 hectares now devoted to container handling its capacity increased from 80,000 to 106,000 TEU per year. This project was the first phase of a planned eastward extension of the terminal that would have added 21 hectares (52.5 acres) to the terminal and increased capacity to 750,000 TEU, for an estimated cost of $200 million.

The plan for a major eastward extension was cancelled in favour of a new terminal at Roberts Bank. Centerm then underwent 10 years of piecemeal upgrades and minor expansions. A fourth crane was added in 1991 and, in 1993, one hectare (2.5 acres) of paved storage and 70.5 m (235 ft.) berth extension were added, costing $9 million.

Although only 43 percent of container traffic moved to or from the terminal by rail, a project to double trackage on the dock was undertaken in 1992 and this improved traffic flow considerably. Access for road traffic was also substantially improved for both Centerm and Vanterm, as a result of an $11 million overpass program, jointly financed by the port and city in 1997.

Another upgrade and expansion project — undertaken at a cost of $20 million between 1999 and 2001 — added a fifth crane and an extra 4 hectares (10 acres) of paved storage through an eastward extension of the terminal.

Ownership of the operation of Centerm changed twice between 1985 and 2004. Casco Terminals, which had operated the terminal since 1974, was sold to BCR Group in 1998 and merged into BCR Marine, along with Vancouver Wharves and Canadian Stevedoring. In early 2001 the VPA and BCR Marine developed a plan to inject $16 million into Centerm to increase its container handling capacity but, before this plan was activated, the parent BCR Group decided to sell Centerm along with the other two components of BC Marine. P&O Ports bought Casco Terminals for $105 million in 2003 and the following year signed a 50-year lease on Centerm with the VPA. They then began planning a $130 million project to increase the terminal's capacity to 720,000 TEU per year.

Vanterm

Early in this period (1985–2004), Vanterm handled 85 percent of the port's container traffic but, as Centerm dedicated more space and equipment to moving containers, this dominance was reduced, falling to 69 percent by 1996. Both Burrard Inlet terminals with their space-starved waterfront locations were hampered by road and rail access congestion and Vanterm, hemmed in between grain terminals, had little room to expand laterally. As the proportion of containers entering or leaving the terminal by rail increased (it increased to 57 percent in the year 2000), so did the need to increase on site trackage to allow a complete train to be marshalled. Satisfying this need on their limited sites continued to be a vexing problem for both terminals.

Labour disruptions were infrequent, but did include a 13-day ILWU strike in early 1994 and a 31-day stoppage by local truckers moving containers to and from the terminals in the summer of 1999. The latter led to prolonged dwell times for onsite containers, serious congestion problems, and very unhappy vessel operators, shippers, and consignees.

In 1996 Vanterm moved 426,000 TEU and was nearing capacity. New cranes were added in 1989 and 1993 and the east face of the terminal was strengthened to allow for a modest increase in trackage. An expansion project undertaken in 2000 extended the berth by 58 m (193 ft.) and added another crane. This extension enabled two vessels to be served simultaneously and provided an extra 0.5 hectares (1.2 acres) of paved working space. A larger project, completed in 2005 at a cost of $30 million, increased trackage on both east and west sides of the terminal and added extra storage space by removing some buildings. Two new cranes were also added, bringing the total to seven. When the project was completed the terminal's capacity reached a new rated level of 535,000 TEU.

Deltaport

The first development at Roberts Bank consisted of a 20 hectare (50 acre) "island" created by dredging sea floor material and served by a 5 km (3 mile) causeway that carried road, rail, and other infrastructure to the off-shore site. This "island," designated Pod 1, was leased to Westshore Terminals in 1970. An expansion project, completed in 1984 by the VPC, increased the size of the island to 80 hectares (200 acres) creating Pods 2–4 and, concurrently, widened the causeway. Westshore leased Pod 2, thereby doubling the area of their coal terminal to 40 hectares (100 acres), but Pods 3 and 4 lay idle until 1999 and 1994 respectively.

By 1991 it was apparent to the management and directors of the VPC that a quantum increase in the port's container terminal capacity would be needed within five years. Without this, VPC would likely suffer even greater loss to the aggressively expanding U.S. gateways and be unable to meet future domestic demand, or capture a portion of the massive Asian import business moving through U.S. ports to Midwest destinations. Given that Vancouver was then handling only 6 percent of North American West Coast container traffic, these goals seemed realistic.

The decision to build a new terminal at Roberts Bank, rather than expand the two Burrard Inlet terminals was based on the advantages this site offered. These included immediate availability, minimal road and rail traffic congestion, less cost and time to complete, and a transit time saving of 4 hours on a round trip over terminals in Puget Sound or Burrard Inlet.

Project Deltaport required the "layered" approval of the Canada Ports Corporation, the Treasury Board, Transport Canada and finally the Cabinet. This was finally forthcoming in the late summer of 1993. Construction took three years and the terminal was officially opened in June 1997. The $224 million cost of the project was shared between the VPC ($179 million) and the CNR, CPR, and terminal operator.

As completed, the new multimodal terminal offered a 625 m (2,060 ft.) dock face with water depth of 15.8 m (52 ft.), considered adequate to simultaneously berth two of the largest vessels then in service. Three container cranes were initially installed and a paved area provided to store 13,000 TEU. The intermodal yard provided four 1,414 m (3,500 ft.) tracks and was configured to enable two double-stack trains to be loaded at the same time. A fourth crane was added shortly after the terminal was completed, increasing its rated capacity to 600,000 TEU per annum.

The new terminal immediately attracted vessel operators including container lines new to the port. Boxes from Asia destined for the U.S. Midwest began to be diverted to Deltaport, due to congestion at U.S. Pacific ports. With three terminals now operating Vancouver's total container traffic rapidly increased from 724,154 TEU in 1997 to 1,163,118 TEU in 2000.

Continuing investment in all three Vancouver terminals, including major equipment additions and upgrades designed to increase productivity, barely kept up with demand. More capacity was urgently required. Between 1993 and 1998 the VPC worked with private developers to utilize the vacant Pod 3 at Roberts Bank by creating a bulk terminal to export agricultural products, but this initiative had failed.

It was then decided to expand Deltaport container terminal north onto the vacant site. This $43 million dollar project provided a substantial increase in the paved storage area and a doubling of the trackage in the intermodal yard to better accommodate the 70 percent of traffic served by rail. Two more cranes were added, bringing the total to six and on completion of this project late in 2000 the terminal's capacity was substantially increased.

Though the pace of growth was slower in the three years after the expansion project onto Pod 3, the VPA began developing plans for new and substantially larger projects to enable Deltaport to meet anticipated future demands. The first of these, the Deltaport Third Berth Project, was designed to lift the terminal's capacity to 1.8 million TEU by 2008 and the second proposed development, dubbed Terminal Two, would follow, taking capacity to 4 million TEU by 2012.

THE DRY BULK AND BREAK-BULK TERMINALS

Vancouver has been aptly called "The Port That Bulk Built." For 55 years after the departure of the barque *Ellen Lewis* in 1864, exports from the port overwhelmingly consisted of locally manufactured forest products. In the early 1920s prairie wheat began a meteoric rise to challenge, and finally pass, forest products as the dominant bulk export and this movement spurred a tremendous surge in the development of specialized terminal facilities in the port. Then, in the 1960s, the resurgent Japanese and, later, other Asian economies with huge appetites for basic commodities, led to the export tonnage dominance of coal, supplemented by sulphur, potash, and metal concentrates. Another round of construction took place to provide the specialized terminal facilities required to efficiently handle these bulk export products.

By 1985 growth in bulk and break-bulk traffic had slowed appreciably. While the annual throughput of containers moved increased by a factor of nine over the next 20 years, for an annual compound growth rate of 11.6 percent, break-bulk and dry bulk commodities grew by a far more modest 1.12 percent.

Though existing bulk and break-bulk terminals were able to handle the modest increases in exports experienced over this period, most increased their productivity by upgrading equipment or adding facilities to handle new commodities and several changed ownership.

Vancouver Wharves

Management purchased Vancouver Wharves in 1986 and then sold it to BCR Group in May 1993 for $15.5 million. BCR Group also assumed $60 million in liabilities. With this purchase BCR Group added the operation of the terminal to its prior ownership of most of the site. Before the sale, the owner managers had secured a long-term contract with Cominco Alaska to handle lead and zinc concentrates from their Red Dog Mine in Alaska. This new business necessitated the expenditure of $30 million to equip the terminal to adequately service the contract.

With the 1995 move by Canpotex to build a new terminal on the site of an abandoned coal terminal in Portland in partnership with Hall Buck Marine, shipments of potash through Vancouver Wharves began a steep decline and ended in mid-1998. To replace this traffic the new owners embarked on a major program to upgrade and modernize their sulphur handling facility, develop a dedicated agricultural products facility, and expand their pulp handling capacity. These projects were completed in early 2000 at a cost of $110 million. A long term contract with major sulphur exporters, Procor and Sultran drove the modernization of the sulphur handling facility, while another long term contract with Millar Western motivated the construction of a large new pulp shed.

The "ag-products" terminal, said to be the first purpose-built facility of its type in North America, was built in response to two factors; the huge increase in production of exportable specialty crops in the central plains, and Saskatchewan Wheat Pool and Cargill's loss of interest in building a bulk facility for grain and farm specialty products on Pod 3 at Roberts Bank.

With these major projects completed the main commodities handled by the terminal consisted of sulphur at approximately 50 percent of total throughput, metal concentrates at 25 percent, pulp at 15 percent, and specialty agricultural products at 10 percent.

In early 2002 the BCR Group announced their intention to sell all three components of BCR Marine, including Vancouver Wharves, to reduce their heavy debt load. No acceptable offer for the terminal had been received at the close of 2004.

Neptune Terminal

This large multi-product, user owned terminal on the north shore of Burrard Inlet encountered stiff opposition from the City of North Vancouver when, in 1989, it submitted plans to build a second large potash storage shed, the key to its plan to double potash throughput. The City wanted to block the project altogether, or at least force a reduction of its height. The VPC became involved in the issue and, learning from the recent, less than amicable, arbitrary resolution of the Elders Grain project on the south shore, established a Project Review Panel to study all aspects of the matter. Two years later the $30 million project was approved, albeit with some compromises, and was completed in late 1993. The new shed increased the terminal's potash storage capacity by 100,000 tons. Concurrently, the original shed was enlarged to a capacity of 130,000 tons, and reclaim and loading equipment were upgraded.

The main commodities handled by the terminal were export coal and potash. These were supplemented by imports of phosphate rock and exports of alfalfa pellets and canola oil. Total terminal throughput reached a peak of 11.4 million tonnes in 1998.

The first commodity handled by Neptune in 1967, even before its official opening, had been phosphate rock imported from Florida and this movement had continued over Berth No. 3 at the rate of about 1 million tonnes per year until mid-1999. With the termination of this business Neptune management decided to redevelop Berth No.3 to handle specialty agricultural products. That $17 million project included new conveyors and a new ship loader. The new "Agriberth" opened on May 9, 2001, a year after Vancouver Wharves had finished expanding and upgrading their facility to handle agri-products.

Seaboard and Lynnterm

Seaboard International Terminal, completed in 1971 by a consortium of forest product companies and operated by partly owned Western Stevedoring, initially handled only the production of member shippers. The terminal opened to non-members in 1974 and, along with neighbour Lynnterm, benefitted substantially from the tremendous surge in production of lumber, plywood, and oriented strand board at new plants in Alberta, in the latter half of the 1980s. By 1989 these plants were moving product through the West Coast at the rate of 1.7 million tonnes per year.

At Lynnterm a heavy lift (440 ton) crane was installed in 1992 for project cargoes, a third pulp shed was built in 1993 at a cost of $7.5 million to boost capacity, and a project was completed in 1994 that extended the dock to 900 m (3,000 ft.), allowing four vessels to berth and load simultaneously.

Forest product exports, especially lumber, began a long decline in the late 1990s and in 2002 Seaboard and Lynnterm combined under the name Lynnterm to create the world's largest forest products terminal. The combination boasted 59 hectares (147 acres) of heavy paved storage and assembly area, and seven berths ranging in draft from 12 to 15 m (40 to 50 ft.). In addition the terminal fine-tuned the ability to efficiently stuff and handle containers. By 2004, 64 percent of lumber and 43 percent of pulp was being boxed for shipment. Besides forest products, the terminal handled steel, project, and general cargoes.

With the continuing decline in forest product exports a feasibility study was undertaken in early 2003 to consider converting Lynnterm to a 350,000 TEU per year container terminal with potential for future doubling. No action followed for a number of reasons, not least of which was the rail and road access congestion on the north shore and the propensity of the North Vancouver administration to tax capital investments heavily. The taxation problem, at least, was resolved late in 2003 when the provincial government capped municipal taxation of port related property.

In 2005, Seaboard Shipping sold its half interest in Western Stevedoring, operator of Lynnterm, to Carrix of Seattle. A year later Carrix acquired the remaining interest. Carrix is a holding company for SSA Marine, one of the largest terminal operating companies in North America.

Pacific Coast Terminals

This Port Moody terminal expanded its ethylene glycol facility in 1992 and in 1997 spent $18 million on a new Krupp ship loader that had the capacity to load its primary export commodity, sulphur, at a rate of 5,000 tonnes per hour. To enable the terminal to handle larger vessels, the VPC dredged the terminal's turning basin in 1995 to increase its depth and turning radius.

Squamish Terminals

Throughput at the Squamish facility tripled during its first 15 years of operation. Anticipating further growth, two expansion projects were undertaken. A second berth, this time in concrete, with a 12 m (40 ft.) draft was completed in 1989 and the next year a third large warehouse was added for a total investment of $15 million. These two projects increased the terminal's capacity to 1 million tonnes annually.

The terminal operators successfully pursued business from new forest product mills in Alberta and by 1992 throughput had risen to 920,000 tonnes. Unfortunately for the terminal, the long BC Rail strike in 1993 resulted in the loss of some of this new business.

Westshore Terminals

After buying out the Japanese interests in Westshore Terminals for $31 million, the B.C. Resources Investment Corporation (BCRIC) became sole owner, through its subsidiary Westar Industries, in 1985. A decade later the Pattison Group acquired control of BCRIC. The failed conglomerate was reorganized and privatized and Westshore, the one viable unit, was spun off into an income trust. The Westshore Terminal Income Fund was created in 1997.

Coal throughput doubled between 1979 and 1989 and broke the 20 million tonne mark in 1989. It peaked in 1997 at 23.5 million tonnes and then levelled off to average 21 million tonnes per year, over the next seven years. A world record was set in May 1987 when the vessel *Hyundai Giant* lifted 239,084 tonnes of metallurgical coal in four days at the terminal.

A $30 million program to increase the efficiency of the terminal operations included a new dumper and was completed in 1991.

There were periodic, modest shipments of U.S. coal to Westshore from Wyoming's Powder River Basin as well as from small mines in Montana, Washington and Utah, though no long-term contracts have materialized to handle coal from these producers. They are in the difficult position of either having to ship overseas export coal through inadequate facilities at U.S. West Coast ports that are only capable of handling relatively small vessels, or absorbing the cost of a very long rail-haul to Roberts Bank, the only deep-water facility available.

On January 1, 2003, winds measured at 110 km per hour did extensive damage to the loading equipment at Berth Two of the terminal. One ship loader was swept into the sea and the other slammed against the side of a berthed vessel. Seven months later one ship loader had been rebuilt, but the other was not repairable and had to be replaced. While Berth Two was out of service, Berth One was able to handle most ship loading, although some coal had to be diverted to Neptune.

THE GRAIN TERMINALS

The Continuing Shift to the West Coast

For the first 50 years of grain movement through the West Coast, the fiction had been maintained that only grain produced west of an imaginary north-south line could be economically moved to a Pacific terminal for overseas export. This imaginary line was drawn through the tiny community of Scott, Saskatchewan, 80 km (50 miles) east of the Alberta border. The participants in the complex eastern movement of export grain with substantial investments in terminals and lake vessels were not at all eager to see that line moved eastward.

In 1973 the Canada Grains Council did an in-depth study of grain movement and estimated the total cost of moving wheat from Scott to Rotterdam using a weighted average for the years 1967 to 1972. This study demonstrated that it cost 53.9 cents per bushel through the West Coast, 60.2 cents direct from Thunder Bay, and 73.9 cents if railed to Maritime ports. Clearly, all production west of mid Saskatchewan could be more economically exported via the West Coast. However, a few years later Cargill Grain stated emphatically that the "Scott Line" had moved east to the Red River, implying that virtually all grain produced on the central plains and destined for overseas export could now be more cheaply moved through the West Coast.

Furthermore, during the sixties and seventies there was a shift to Asian markets from the traditional markets in Europe and these new buyers expected delivery at a West Coast port. Pacific terminals were able to offer year-round service and most had sufficient water depth at their berths to handle the ever larger vessels arriving for loading.

Thus, despite grumbling and accusations from eastern interests that the Wheat Board was showing favouritism to the West Coast, the inevitable trend to reversal of the long held 60:40 balance between eastern and western movement of overseas export grain continued.

The Canadian Wheat Board responded to accusations of favouritism in 1987 by releasing figures demonstrating that it cost $46.13 per tonne to move grain overseas via the eastern system, versus $28.25 per tonne through the two remaining West Coast ports.

In the 1985/86, the West Coast terminals at Vancouver and Prince Rupert handled over half of Canadian overseas grain exports for the first time and, between 1985 and 2004, they averaged 58.3 percent yearly with a peak of 69.3 percent in the bumper crop year, 1992.

Between 1985 and 2004 Vancouver's share of the west coast grain movement fluctuated between 70.3 percent in the 1988/89 crop year and 90 percent in the 2001/02 crop year. There had been no major additions to the Vancouver port since 1979 when storage capacity increased by 40 percent as a result of projects prompted by the Wheat Board's Storage Incentive Program. The new state-of-the-art, high throughput terminal at Prince Rupert, however, gave a very substantial boost to west coast capacity in 1985.

The Vancouver terminals averaged throughput of 11.5 million tonnes per year between 1985 and 2004 with a peak of 14.5 million tonnes in 1992. That year the Wheat Board created quite a stir by exporting 55,000 tonnes of barley through the port of Seattle. These throughput figures contrast with the average of 6.6 million tonnes per year handled between 1970 and 1975 and reflect both the shift in direction of movement from east to west and, of course, larger production.

Terminal Ownership Changes

There were several ownership changes involving three of the Vancouver terminals during this period. Alberta Wheat Pool and Manitoba Pool Elevators combined to form publicly owned Agricore in 1998 and three years later added United Grain Growers (UGG) to form Agricore United. The new TSE listed company owned 51 percent of the grain handling capacity in the port, as well as 44.9 percent of Prince Rupert Grain. The Competition Bureau considered this to be excessive dominance on the West Coast and directed Agricore United to divest either the former UGG terminal, which had undergone a second major modernization program in 1989, or sell its 70 percent interest in Pacific Elevators. Agricore United elected to sell the former UGG terminal and purchase the remaining 30 percent interest in Pacific Elevators from Saskpool.

Just prior to the formation of Agricore, Alberta Wheat Pool sold a half interest in their large Vancouver terminal to Cargill Grain. The facility, christened Cascadia at the time of its official opening June 11, 1998, then upgraded its galleries and conveyor systems.

Saskatchewan Wheat Pool also made the switch from a producer owned cooperative to a listed public trading entity in early 1998 and then commenced a $195 million program to construct 22 high throughput inland terminals, over the succeeding three-year period.

Drought caused low production in 2003/04 and this, together with a long, grain workers strike in Vancouver resulted in severe financial stress to both Agricore United and Saskatchewan Wheat Pool. This led to further consolidation and restructuring of terminal relationships three years later.

New Facilities to Handle Specialty Crops
In a series of moves between 1984 and 1997, the statutory Crow rate was first replaced with a Crow benefit paid to the railways and then this, too, was terminated. Producers were compensated with a onetime payout of $1.6 billion plus a $300 million Transition Fund. After 1997 producers had to meet the full cost of moving their grain to export positions, albeit under the protection of federal overview and regulation of rail rates. The vast spider web of rail branch lines to thousands of country elevators across the central plains continued to shrink and the face of prairie agriculture underwent accelerated change.

One of the most significant aspects of the "new" agriculture, which began in the seventies and gained momentum during the transportation and market upheavals of the eighties and nineties, was crop diversification. Prairie fields were no longer dominated by wheat. Crops such as canola, malting barley, alfalfa, mustard, lentils, and peas were increasingly grown in response to market demand and the need for better farming practices.

Existing facilities were modified and new terminals built on the West Coast to efficiently handle exports of the new wave of specialty crops. In 1999 Pacific Elevator, then jointly owned by Agricore and Saskatchewan Wheat Pool, completed a $20 million program which included a special ship loader purpose-built to handle specialty crop products. As already noted, Vancouver Wharves completed a substantial facility for specialty agricultural products in 2000 and Neptune followed with a similar project in 2001. At the Northern Gateway the pre-existing Conarc facility on Fairview Terminal was expanded and upgraded after the Prince Rupert Port Corporation takeover in 1998.

Bulk Grain for Roberts Bank?
The VPC completed a project in 1984 that quadrupled the size of the "island" at Roberts Bank and Westshore Terminals immediately moved to extend their lease to include an adjacent portion of the expanded site. The port subdivided the remainder into a northern half and southern half, designated Pods 3 and 4. In 1991 the port decided to build a new container terminal on Pod 4 and, three years later Deltaport commenced operations.

In 1993 Mercury International, a new entity formed and promoted by a former CEO of the Port Corporation and financially backed by Halifax interests, optioned a lease on Pod 3, the still vacant 26 hectare (65 acre) site on the north side of the "island" at Roberts Bank. Their plan was to develop a radically different type of bulk grain handling facility. This concept envisioned six concrete domes able to store up to 84,000 tonnes of grain, which had been pre-processed to export standards. This would be loaded to vessels at two berths on the west side of the terminal. Planning assumed that 40–60 percent of the grain received would be loaded directly to vessels from railcars. Under optimal conditions they expected the $120 million terminal could handle 8 million tonnes per year.

With scant support from the established grain industry, Mercury attempted to interest Canpotex in participating and bringing their substantial tonnage of potash exports to the proposed terminal for shipment overseas. Canpotex chose, instead, to move a portion of their exports through a new terminal they developed at Portland. After expending $1 million on engineering studies and a total of $230,000 for lease options over a two-year period, Mercury was denied a sixth extension of their lease option in June 1995 and dropped out of the picture. The port then began to seek other proposals for development of an agricultural products and fertilizer terminal for Pod 3.

A proposal made jointly by Cargill Grain and Saskatchewan Wheat Pool to develop a $175 million terminal for the site was selected by the port in February 1996, at least in part because these proponents originated 41 percent of the grain and oilseeds moving through the West Coast. After a one-year extension, the partners let their option on Pod 3 run out and, in February 1998, the Port Corporation again issued a request for proposals to develop the site. No acceptable submissions were forthcoming and in August of 1998 the port administration decided to reconsider the future of Pod 3 in its long term planning. The 2000 decision to extend Deltaport onto Pod 3 put an end to the idea of moving bulk grain over a terminal at Roberts Bank.

A Controversial Issue on the South Shore

An issue of considerable interest and significance arose in 1989 when Australian owned Elders Grain proposed building a small enclosed facility at the old Terminal Dock site on the south shore of Burrard Inlet. It was designed for the purpose of stuffing up to 40 containers a day with malting barley for export over the Vanterm or Centerm container terminals. The Vancouver City Council and the Board of Variance rejected the project; a challenge that was met by defiance from the VPC who authorized it to proceed. Elders Grain, unhappy with the controversy, dropped out and in 1990 Coastal Containers, a subsidiary of Canada Malting, took over the project. Their plan doubled the capacity of the project to 80 TEU per day and the project was completed at a cost of $3 million in 1991.

Attempts by City Council and planners to block this project were firmly resisted by the VPC. The issue at stake was the Port Corporation's right to retain in industrial use a waterfront site that a municipality desired for non-port related use. This issue arose for a second time in 1989 when the City of North Vancouver attempted to block Neptune's plans to build a second, large potash shed on their leased property. Compromise was eventually reached after a two year study by a Project Review Panel established by the port.

THE CRUISE TERMINALS

The popularity of seasonal cruising to Alaska continued unabated and passenger counts more than quadrupled from 267,472 in 1985 to a record 1,125,252 in the 2002 season, an annual compound growth rate of 10 percent. As the base for these vessels, Vancouver had a very lucrative near monopoly, but the rapid growth demanded continuing attention to providing acceptable terminal facilities.

The cruise terminal component of Canada Place opened on April 28, 1986, three days prior to the formal opening of EXPO '86. On busy weekends it was supplemented by Ballantyne Pier. On March 17, 1993 Canada Harbour Place Corporation, the federal crown corporation that developed Canada Place, became a subsidiary of the Vancouver Port Corporation with the new name Canada Place Corporation.

With the plan to extend Centerm to the east having been abandoned in 1992, the Port Corporation decided to redevelop Ballantyne into a more modern, multi-use facility that would include a single large pulp and general cargo warehouse plus an attached, but separate auxiliary cruise terminal. This major revitalization project for the 1923-built pier was undertaken at a cost of $49 million and it reopened May 12, 1995.

Continuing increases in passenger numbers resulted in a proposal from VLC Properties in 1994 to build a casino and third cruise terminal on the 19 hectare (47.5 acre) Port Corporation owned site just east of Canada Place. A later proponent suggested a public-private partnership to develop that site with a trade and convention centre and 1,000-room hotel. Neither proposal materialized.

With predictions that cruise vessel sailings would increase to 336 in 2000 with passenger counts over one million, the port elected to proceed with a major expansion to its Canada Place facility. This project provided a third berth and expanded passenger facilities in time for the 2003 cruise season for a total expenditure of $89 million.

By the time this project had been completed, Seattle had aggressively and successfully entered the Alaska cruise market. The events of September 11, 2001 gave a very powerful boost to their challenge to the long-held Vancouver monopoly. With only a single berth available in 2000, Seattle attracted 36 vessel calls and 120,000 passengers, a huge increase over the previous year's 6 calls and 6,615 passengers. By 2003 new and refurbished facilities hosted 99 vessel visits carrying 345,000 passengers. The impact on Vancouver was substantial with the passenger count for the 2003 season dropping by 15 percent to 953,376, the first significant reduction in 20 years.

Though the major entry of Seattle as a base for Alaska bound cruise vessels has been at substantial cost to Vancouver, other B.C. ports, including Victoria and Prince Rupert have benefited inasmuch as the foreign flag, Seattle based vessels must, by U.S. law, make at least one stop at a Canadian port before their return to Seattle.

SHIPBUILDING AND REPAIR FACILITIES

When the federal shipbuilding subsidy was terminated in 1985 local yards struggled to survive. After a number of closures, mergers, and takeovers the only functioning yards remaining by 1999 were Vancouver Shipyards and Allied Shipbuilders.

The fate of the fine floating dry dock, new in 1981, was of particular concern to the VPC. It had been installed at the pioneer Burrard Dry Dock site on the north shore at a total cost of $63.3 million, with two-thirds of that sum a direct grant from Ottawa, plus a small provincial contribution. In 1985 Burrard Dry Dock, recently amalgamated with Yarrows of Victoria, changed its name to Versatile Pacific Shipyards Inc. A continuing decline in business forced the financially distressed company to close the yard in March 1991, still owing $7.6 million on the bank loan, arranged 10 years prior to pay for its one-third share of the floating dry dock.

Versatile appealed to the federal government to allow the sale of the dry dock to willing Asian buyers, or alternatively buy it for the amount of the outstanding bank loan. To deal with this crisis a "Floating Dry Dock Task Force" was established. Negotiations led to an arrangement to save the facility whereby Ottawa contributed $8 million, Victoria $6 million and a new entity, the Vancouver Drydock Company, which was equally owned by Vancouver Shipyards and Allied Shipbuilders, agreed to contribute $1.8 million, to undertake long deferred maintenance work, and to operate the facility commencing January 1, 1992.

The floating dry dock remains the only functioning facility at the site of the former Wallace Shipyards-Burrard Dry Dock operations. It is indeed a facility provided to the Port of Vancouver almost entirely at the expense of Canadian taxpayers.

FRASER RIVER DEVELOPMENTS: 1985 TO 2004

The FRHC has been aptly described as "land rich and water depth poor." The Commission had jurisdiction over 270 km (162 miles) of river frontage and, due to its long established policy of acquiring useful parcels of backup land, had accumulated 567 hectares (1,417 acres) of sites with potential for port related activities. These properties were located in Surrey, Delta, and Richmond, were all served by uncongested road and rail links, and were made available for lease or co-development. Rivalry with Vancouver generally contributed to strong community support for port related activities on the river.

Despite these impressive assets, the Commission faced the chronic issue of persuading Ottawa to continue programs to maintain and deepen the navigable channel for deep-sea vessels through the final 40 km (25 miles) of the river. Depth limitations had precluded the development of bulk terminals during the sixties and seventies. All were developed on deeper saltwater sites in Burrard Inlet or at Roberts Bank.

LOCAL PORT ADMINISTRATION

The enthusiastic and opportunistic management of the FRHC actively sought business for their marine facilities and occupants for their expanded riverfront land base. They were rewarded by a doubling of international cargo traffic during the final five years of this period. This traffic, however, was dwarfed by domestic cargoes which consistently averaged 85 percent of the total business of what became known as Fraser Port.

In 1988 the Commission sent marketing teams to Asia and Europe and began an arrangement with Puget Sound terminals to barge import and export containers between the two ports. These initiatives and the concurrent plan to construct a large intermodal terminal adjacent to Fraser Surrey Docks triggered a strong reaction from the VPC and its Ottawa masters. The Canada Ports Corporation huffed about the dangers of misallocation of capital spending on the West Coast, clearly directed at the autonomous Fraser River Harbour Commission's efforts to use its container facility more effectively. The Vancouver Port Corporation insisted that all port activity at the Southern Gateway should be under its exclusive jurisdiction to avoid wasteful competition and better fight their Puget Sound rivals. That position clearly reflected Sir Alexander Gibb's recommendation in 1932. It had been strongly resented then and since by boosters of the river port who once looked on Burrard Inlet as their potential "Outer Harbour."

The FRHC produced a strong rebuttal to the 1993 report, prepared for the VPC by Jonathan Seymour, which stressed the benefits of a merger of the two river commissions into the VPC.

When the *Canada Marine Act* was passed in 1998, the two Fraser Commissions became the Fraser River Port Authority and the North Fraser Port Authority. As such they would now pay grants, in lieu of taxes, to their local communities and dividends to Ottawa. They retained their long enjoyed autonomy. Included in the legislation, however, was the immediate termination of the federal government's 107-year role in funding projects to maintain and deepen the navigable river channel. This was cushioned with a $15 million one-time grant to the newly created Fraser River Port Authority to assume that responsibility.

The North Fraser Port Authority held riverfront property on the relatively shallow north arm of the river and activities there focussed primarily on the storage and movement of large quantities of woodchips, sawdust, raw logs, and aggregate to domestic markets. In 2004 a total of 17.7 million tonnes of these commodities were handled by facilities under the jurisdiction of the North Fraser Port Authority.

THE NAVIGABLE CHANNEL

By 1985, one hundred and three years of federal government expenditures on projects to create and then maintain a navigable river waterway as far as New Westminster had succeeded in achieving a main channel depth of 9.6 m (32 ft.). However, with the loaded draft requirements of vessels prepared to use the port's facilities ever increasing, the Harbour Commissioners extracted a promise from Ottawa to further deepen the main channel. At this time the Coast Guard had taken back responsibility from the Department of Public Works for dredging the main navigation channel, while the FRHC continued their task of dredging access to berths and cleaning-up river debris west of Agassiz.

Between 1978 and 1985 a number of proposals had been submitted to Ottawa for works designed to reduce silt deposition in the navigable channel, thereby reducing annual dredging costs. These plans, ranging in estimated cost up to $100 million, were rejected as far too costly. Instead, between 1987 and 1991 a major dredging program removed 5 million cubic metres of sediment to achieve a working depth of 10.3 m (34 ft. 4 inches). The $13.6 million cost of that program was shared 60:40 between the Harbour Commission and the Canadian Coast Guard. A second major project, completed in 1993, created a training wall from Steveston to Sandheads at a cost of $16 million, mostly borne by the Coast Guard. That project was considered to have no net cost due to anticipated savings on future dredging.

Effective January 1,1999 the Fraser River Port Authority assumed full responsibility for maintaining the channel for deep-sea vessels to a guaranteed depth of 10.7 m (35 ft. 8 inches). By 2004 the Authority had spent an average of $3.5 million yearly on dredging, offset somewhat by sales of sand, and had succeeded in deepening the channel to 11.5 m (38 ft. 3 inches). This depth approached the maximum possible, the limiting factor being the crown of the George Massey Tunnel with its low water clearance of only 11.9 m (39 ft. 7 inches).

By this time, the final grant from Ottawa had been fully spent and both Fraser Authorities again petitioned Ottawa for help maintaining a navigable channel. They pointed to the U.S. where the Army Corps of Engineers maintained the Columbia River Channel and had recently received US$15 million to deepen it to 12.9 m (43 ft.).

Doing nothing was not an option given estimates that the river deposits 75 percent of an average annual 3.8 million cubic metres of silt in the lower reaches of its course and that, if dredging ceased, the channel would be impassable for all but the smallest vessels within six years.

FRASER SURREY DOCKS

The boom in terminal developments during the early 1960s had been confined to Vancouver. The FRHC, anxious to participate, responded positively to a suggested redevelopment plan for its riverfront property on the south bank of the river, then partially occupied by the little used grain elevator. As completed in 1964 the new terminal, Fraser Surrey Docks, was designed to handle a wide range of both domestic and international bulk and break-bulk cargoes and offered three general cargo berths, one bulk berth, and a transit shed. The terminal had excellent rail connections and an abundance of adjacent land available for expansion or use by port related enterprises.

From 1970 to 1985 the amount of international cargo handled fluctuated between 1.5 and 2 million tonnes per year with a peak of 2.2 million tonnes in 1974. For most of that period exports dominated, but by the early eighties imports began to exceed exports.

Determined not to miss participation in the developing "container revolution," the Commission added a two berth, container handling facility equipped with two cranes to the dock complex. With optimistic predictions this facility opened in December 1974, six months ahead of Vanterm.

Unhappily, neither the multi-use facility, nor the new container terminal prospered as hoped. Foreign cargo throughput remained stagnant in the 1980s at 1.5 to 1.8 million tonnes per year and reached a low point of 1.1 million tonnes in 1987. The new container cranes were used primarily to handle steel imports and attempts to attract container lines had little success.

In an attempt to attract container traffic by any means possible, the FRHC began, in 1981, to undertake a series of projects that included expanding their land base adjacent to Fraser Surrey Docks, adding another deep-sea berth and starting construction of an intermodal terminal. The intermodal yard was to be built on 16 hectares (40 acres) upstream from Fraser Surrey Docks at an estimated cost of $5.5 million. When it was clear in 1989 that the CNR was, indeed, going ahead with its planned large intermodal facility at Port Mann, the Commission delayed completion of their yard, though not before spending $2.6 million on the project. Two years later they granted a five-year lease to BNSF railway to complete a small intermodal yard on a portion of the site.

To the irritation of the Vancouver container terminal operators, Fraser Surrey inaugurated a feeder barge service in 1988 to move containers to and from Puget Sound terminals to connect with vessels not calling at Vancouver. This service, moving about 1,500 containers a month was discontinued in 1991, re-launched in 1993, and finally terminated in 1997.

In 1988 Fraser Surrey Docks was able to secure the financial support of the Government of Alberta, "for terminal development on the Fraser in the interests of Alberta shippers." This support consisted of a $9 million loan guarantee to enable the company to complete needed equipment and facility upgrades. Alberta had recently backed a loan to Neptune Terminals that had been repaid without a problem. This time, however, Fraser Surrey Docks was unable to meet its repayment obligations, the loan defaulted, and the Alberta Government took over Fraser Surrey, placing it under a new entity, Alberta Pacific Terminals Ltd. It was not long before the terminal was again in financial difficulty, aggravated by a warehouse fire and the accidental release of 9,100 litres of toxic lumber preservative chemicals into the river.

By 1992 the operation was again in deep financial trouble with debts of $40 million. Its main asset was its 20-year lease on the site from the Harbour Commission. The holding company was sold to Hong Kong investors to carry on business as APTL Terminals Ltd., with Fraser Surrey's debts settled at deep discounts and the Government of Alberta taking a $10 million loss.

At the time of the takeover the terminal consisted of a leased 48.6 hectare (121.5 acres) site, six berths, two container cranes, a barge slip and 22,300 square metres of warehousing. Management aggressively sought new business and the new owners made further substantial investments in the terminal. Container vessels of the d'Amico Line began bi-monthly calls in 1992 and the increasing depth of the ship channel began to attract interest from other shipping lines.

Between 1993 and 1997 a $19 million capital program was completed. This included a new deep-sea berth, on-dock rail lines, and a new pulp shed. In 2000 a modern container crane arrived from Korea to supplement the two, smaller, original Paceco cranes and the next year a dolphin berth was added for log ship tie-up.

By 1993 the port's fortunes were reviving. Within a decade international cargo tonnage doubled to 5.3 million tonnes. Growth in container traffic was spectacular, increasing from 13,343 TEU in 1996 to a peak of 372,844 TEU in 2005. The long delayed success of the 30-year-old container facility stimulated the Port Authority, together with Fraser Surrey Docks and a new company, IDC Distribution Services to unveil a $190 million program of expenditures on upgrades to the container terminal. These included two more cranes and a 7.5 hectare (19 acre) intermodal yard adjacent to the dock. When these projects were completed the terminal was expected to comfortably handle up to 415,000 TEU annually.

SURREY PROPERTIES

The Harbour Commission and its successor Port Authority had, over many years, acquired a substantial amount of land adjacent to the Fraser Surrey Dock complex. This was consolidated under the name Surrey Properties and offered prime rail served riverfront industrial sites for lease from a total of 143 hectares (353 acres). These sites attracted enterprises involved in the logistics of a wide range of export and import items, including steel, forest products and specialty agricultural products.

Westnav Container Services began stuffing export containers with specialty agricultural products in 1993 and further developed their facility to meet the logistic requirements of a wide range of commodities. By 2005, other tenants occupying sites leased from Surrey Properties included Westran Intermodal, Sylvan Distribution Centre, Titan Steel, and CT Steel. All enjoy easy access to Fraser Surrey Docks and excellent rail links to CN, CP and BNSF class one railways, as well as the local Southern Railway.

RICHMOND PROPERTIES

This 281 hectare (694 acre) riverfront property is situated on the north side of the river at the foot of No. 8 Road in Richmond. The former landfill site on a self-scouring bend in the river was acquired because of its high potential for a public-private, deep-sea terminal development.

Early tenants at the site were a large Hudson's Bay Company distribution centre and a huge auction mall for used cars. In 1999 the Fraser River Port Authority leased a 36 hectare (90 acre) waterfront parcel to Modalink Vancouver Gateway Distribution Hub, a new entity owned equally by the Vancouver Port Authority and the private Fraser Group Holdings. Modalink proceeded to develop the site at a cost of $35 million over the next three years and then the same two owners formed an operating entity, Coast 2000 Terminals to operate a rail, road, and barge served logistics terminal on 12 hectares (30 acres) of their leased site. Development of this terminal fit well into the strategy of both Port Authorities to foster the growth of "Short Sea Shipping" as a means to circumvent increasing road congestion on the lower mainland.

In addition to Coast 2000 Terminals, others engaged in the logistics business soon occupied more subleased sites on the Modalink development.

THE AUTO TERMINALS

Vehicle handling through the two Fraser River auto terminals reached 437,190 units in the year 2004. The original Fraser Wharves facility located on 43 hectares (107 acres) at the foot of No. 6 Road in Richmond, receives, services, and distributes vehicles imported by Toyota, Lexus, Mazda and Suzuki.

The larger Annacis Auto Terminals, located on 59 hectares (147 acres) of land leased from the Fraser River Port Authority at the eastern tip of Annacis Island, rebuilt its original berth in 1987 and upgraded its newer Berth Two in 1989. The terminal lands and distributes vehicles produced by Nissan, Honda, Mercedes, BMW, Hyundai, Kia, Subaru and Mitsubishi. For a time Western Star Trucks, produced in B.C., were exported from the terminal together with packaged lumber loaded on car carriers otherwise returning empty. Both terminals are equipped to service vehicles and load them to railcars or trucks for distribution throughout North America.

PRINCE RUPERT: 1985 TO 2004

For those who fervently believed in Prince Rupert's future as a major world port, this period began with considerable satisfaction over all that had recently been achieved and ended two decades later in near despair.

Port throughput had been fairly steady, averaging 11.3 million tonnes annually between 1986 and 1997 and had peaked at 13.8 million tonnes in 1994. A steady decline began in 1998, reaching a low point in 2003 of 4.03 million tonnes. Visits to the port by cruise vessels declined from 38 vessels carrying 20,621 passengers in 1985 to three vessels carrying 227 passengers 10 years later.

By 2003 the only commodities showing slight growth in throughput were modest exports of wood pellets over Fairview and logs from the harbour plus even more modest amounts of slack wax imports. All three of the port's modern terminals showed a drastic decline in total throughput.

In all the gloom, one bright spot did appear at the end of this time period with the return of visits by both large and small cruise vessels in 2004. This was a direct response to the port's provision of adequate facilities to welcome these vessels and their passengers.

LOCAL PORT ADMINISTRATION

Under the provisions of the *Canada Marine Act*, the Prince Rupert Port Authority succeeded the Prince Rupert Port Corporation, a crown corporation, effective May 1, 1999. With considerably increased autonomy it was directed to be efficient, competitive, and commercially oriented, while responsive to local needs and priorities. Before the changeover, the Port Corporation had successfully petitioned Ottawa to forgive $5 million of its outstanding $15 million long term debt and remove penalties from repayment of the balance.

No longer bound by a spending limit of $500,000 or the tedious and time consuming process of seeking multi-layered approvals for larger expenditures, it was nonetheless still tightly constricted by the new $22 million borrowing limit. Furthermore, the port could not look to Ottawa for a loan guarantee, nor could it accept funds from any parliamentary appropriation.

These limitations created a considerable problem in the planning for the conversion of Fairview Terminal to a container facility and required innovative solutions to allow that essential project to proceed.

RAILWAYS

The existence of the Pacific Great Eastern Railway and its renamed successor as an independent, provincially owned railway had long been recognized as a major factor in the retarded growth and development of the Northern Gateway Port and its corridor. Hopes that the port's hinterland drawing area would expand significantly rose with the Jamieson Bennett "Grand Plan" for rail development in northern B.C. in the early seventies. That project, which could have greatly benefitted Prince Rupert and indeed the economy of B.C. through resource developments, collapsed when the Dease Lake rail line was halted in 1977.

In 1998 the CNR and BC Rail did reach agreements that allowed reciprocal access to each other's lines and improved interchanges at Prince George. For the first time, BC Rail cars began to trickle in to Prince Rupert. Finally, in late 2003, the province sold the operations of BC Rail to the CNR, an interesting reversal of the position taken in 1971 when Premier Bennett offered to buy the north line of the CNR and turn Prince Rupert into a major world port.

Though the rail lines from Prince George to Vancouver or to Prince Rupert are virtually equal in length, the CNR north line is unquestionably superior in grades, curves and tracks, and is alone in its ability to carry long and heavy unit trains at economical speeds.

In the long term, the CNR takeover of the operation of north-south, intra-provincial line can only have a major beneficial effect on the growth and development of the Port of Prince Rupert.

FAIRVIEW TERMINAL

At Fairview there had been a steady annual increase in lumber throughput, reaching 566,000 tonnes by 1986. In addition, the terminal handled more modest amounts of mineral concentrates and agricultural products. With solid predictions for continuing growth in lumber exports the Port Corporation expanded the terminal by extending the dock face to 627 m (2,060 ft.) and increasing the storage area to 21.5 hectares (53 acres). Completed at a cost of $33 million the expansion was officially opened on June 14, 1990. Ironically, by that time lumber throughput had already peaked (at 834,694 tonnes in 1987) and was in a steady decline, reaching zero by 2002.

Despite the fading prospects for North Coast lumber exports, Kitimat port boosters convinced the provincial government, unpopular and in pre-election mode, to offer a $25 million grant toward the development there of a $60 million forest products terminal. To the relief of both Prince Rupert and the CNR this offer was abruptly withdrawn when the government changed in the 1991 election.

To compensate for the declining lumber traffic the port began a major effort to attract off-shore pulp exports from mills in north central B.C. and new mills in Alberta and Saskatchewan. Apart from shipments over the private dock of Skeena Cellulose at Watson Island, there had previously been only a single small shipment from Prince George Pulp and Paper (over the old Ocean Dock in 1970) and a few shipments totalling 100,505 tonnes between 1986 and 1993 (over Fairview Terminal), using the transit shed for temporary storage.

Aggressive marketing directed at new pulp producers east of the Rockies, in addition to the long established mills in central B.C., resulted in some increase in Fairview's pulp throughput. To secure this extra business the port built warehouses on the terminal in 1994 and 1998 at a cost of $4.5 million. Throughput peaked in 1998 at 114,242 tonnes and then collapsed to zero three years later, when specialized pulp carriers refused to call at the terminal for the modest tonnages available.

The failure of the initiative to move pulp through Fairview had two main causes. The first and most significant was aggressive competition for the new business from the established Southern Gateway terminal operators including Squamish Terminals, Lynnterm, Vancouver Wharves, and Fraser Surrey Docks, each of whom had spent very substantial sums to increase their pulp handling ability. The Province's continuing ownership of BC

Rail ensured that little of the pulp produced in central B.C. would move by CNR to Prince Rupert. The second significant cause was the very favourable cargo rate available to new pulp producers in Alberta and Saskatchewan when they stuffed their product into otherwise empty containers being returned to Vancouver terminals for shipment back overseas.

The Conarc facility on the terminal had been operated by Continental Grain since 1980 and, after a slow start, it gradually built up to a 1993 peak throughput of 237,892 tonnes of a wide variety of agricultural products. Faced with declining throughput over the next five years and the need to upgrade the facility, especially its inadequate ship loading equipment, Continental decided to turn the terminal over to the port for the sum of $1, effective January 1, 1998.

Under the new name, Agport, the port spent $2.9 million on a new ship loader rated at 900 tonnes per hour, a new dumper pit, and a general upgrade of all components. Delays in completing this program eliminated throughput entirely in 1999 and forestalled use of the terminal until late in 2000. By that time Vancouver Wharves had completed their new, large, dedicated agricultural products facility and Neptune was well on the way to completing its new facility at Berth Three. Furthermore, increasing amounts of specialty agricultural products were by then being stuffed into containers for shipment overseas at logistics enterprises in the lower mainland. As a result, Fairview's upgraded Agport moved only 427,253 tonnes between 2000 and 2005 for an unsatisfactory average of 71,209 tonnes per year. After 2001, throughput consisted solely of wood pellets.

In 1996 the port acquired two 30,000 barrel former Navy fuel storage tanks adjacent to Fairview Terminal from the Department of National Defence. These had been built in 1987 at a cost of $2.4 million. The port refurbished and adapted them to store petrochemical liquids or edible oils. They have been used since January 2000 to store shipments of slack wax imported from Asia by an Alberta chemical company and to transfer it to railcars. This traffic averages 15,750 tonnes annually.

There were also sporadic steel import cargoes through the terminal between 1998 and 2002 totalling 176,818 tonnes.

THE WESTVIEW SITE

In 1989–1990 the port acquired the site of the old grain terminal and adjacent upland from the federal government and the CNR, for $1.6 million, and optimistically named the new potential terminal site Westview. Though the elevator itself had been demolished in 1987 by the Prince Rupert Grain Consortium, the 309 m (1,030 ft.) wooden dock with its recently upgraded fendering system had been retained at the request of the port. The small, rail-served site offered the potential to be expanded to 5–6 hectares (12.5–15 acres) if it were filled out to the dock.

With the surge in the production of forest products in Alberta, the port considered the possibility of creating a facility at Westview to handle pulp exports, but in 1992 chose

Fairview instead. Since then it has seen some use by fish buyers. The on-dock sacking shed was destroyed by fire in 1996 necessitating substantial repairs to that end of the dock.

SKEENA CELLULOSE

After a long and very troubled history, which included massive provincial government bail-outs, the Watson Island pulp mill complex, the City's largest employer, finally ceased operations in 2001, ending 50 years of pulp exports averaging about 300,000 tonnes per year over their private dock in Porpoise Harbour. Two years later a new owner, New Skeena Forest Products, planned to overhaul the mill and recommence limited production with one line. This entity soon failed and went into receivership September 20, 2004.

Between July 2004 and March 2005, dredging removed 54,600 cubic metres of PCB contaminated marine sediments from Porpoise Bay, adjacent to the mill site, at a cost of $3 million, which was paid by the province from funds held back from the owners for such contingencies.

THE PRINCE RUPERT GRAIN TERMINALS

As if the collapse of Fairview's traffic and the closure of the pulp mill were not enough, throughput at the Ridley Island grain and coal terminals began to drastically decline during the last six years of this period, albeit for different reasons.

The opening of Prince Rupert's state-of-the-art grain terminal coincided with a period of drought on the Central Plains. As a result, the 1984 and 1985 crops were much diminished and this, coupled with very low carryovers, resulted in a substantial reduction in the amount available for overseas export and hence a rather inauspicious start for the new terminal. This strengthened the position of those who wanted to get rid of the old terminal and, on September 30, 1986 a final decision was made by the consortium to arrange for its demolition. Certainly, it could have been sold to a party or parties outside the consortium and could have served a useful function in the export of non-Board grains and agricultural by-products. The Canadian Wheat Board (CWB), too, wanted it kept available for the desirable extra storage capacity on the West Coast. The Consortium, however, was not prepared to maintain it and pay taxes on it on the basis of sporadic use and was adamant that it would not fall into the hands of an operator outside their group.

Crops recovered in 1986 and for the next 11 years Prince Rupert was fully integrated into the movement of export grain through the West Coast. The new terminal shipped 49,449,998 tonnes during that period for an average of 4.5 million tonnes yearly. During those years, the West Coast handled 60 percent of Canadian overseas grain exports with Prince Rupert's share being 26.9 percent of the West Coast movement and 16.2 percent of all Canadian overseas exports.

The new terminal reached a peak throughput of 5,547,916 tonnes in 1994 and that year a number of records were established. In the month of July 7,784 cars were unloaded and

733,862 tonnes of grain shipped. For a facility designed to handle 3.5 million tonnes annually, this was no small achievement and suggested that with a relatively modest expenditure the facility could comfortably move 7 million tonnes per year. Certainly, the terminal offered the cheapest and easiest site for capacity expansion on the West Coast if and when needed. No longer was Prince Rupert forced to accept the diminished role of "residual" port for grain export — the reluctantly used backup when the Vancouver terminals were unable to cope with export demands. Indeed, despite a very poor crop with low overseas exports in the 1988/89 crop year, the new terminal moved 29.5 percent of West Coast exports that year, a peak of considerable interest in view of the drastic drop to a low of 10.6 percent 10 years later.

Thunder Bay was very much aware of the new Prince Rupert terminal, complaining bitterly about it being "spoon fed" and, along with the St. Lawrence Seaway shippers, demanding a guarantee of a minimum of 7.5 million tonnes annually through their system. With a huge excess of capacity and substantial reduction in their share of total grain movement they were experiencing inevitable and unwelcome layoffs and shutdowns.

During 1993, a program of upgrading to cleaner batteries and sieve machines was undertaken at Prince Rupert Grain and new mooring buoys were placed to allow safer docking for vessels up to 280 m (933 ft.) long. Concurrently the storage silos underwent major repairs to remedy flaws and cracks in their concrete walls. Aware of the current initiative by Mercury International to create a "direct hit" type of grain terminal at Roberts Bank, Prince Rupert Grain, in 1993, examined the feasibility of linking a similar facility to their Ridley Island terminal and concluded it could be constructed for about $20 million.

Unfortunately, loss of port parity in rail rates coupled with a series of poor crops soon returned Prince Rupert's fine new facility to the role of poor relation to Vancouver's terminals. Prince Rupert Grain's run as an integrated unit in the West Coast grain export scene came to an abrupt end in the crop year 1998/99. Weather conditions reduced the amount of grain available for overseas export that year to only 21.2 million tonnes, but even though the West Coast still moved 55.8 percent of that amount, Prince Rupert's share fell to 10.6 percent at 1,254,800 tonnes, or 5.9 percent of total Canadian overseas exports.

The prime reason for this precipitous decline in grain shipments through the Northern Gateway's world class terminal lay in the final settlement of the "Crow Benefit" on August 1, 1995, which removed port parity for rail rates on grain moving to Prince Rupert or Vancouver. No longer obligated to equalize rates to the two Pacific ports, the CNR quickly pointed to the extra 313 km (196 miles) involved in hauling grain through their Northern Rail Corridor and demanded an extra $4.60 per tonne in compensation. The railway was initially unwilling to acknowledge, or to quantify, substantial compensating factors related to the northern route and its dedicated grain terminal rail yard which, at the very least, balanced costs for the extra distance. As a result, grain movement on the Northern Corridor came to a halt and Prince Rupert's terminal shut down during the summer of 1996. Without grain traffic on their grossly underutilized north line, the railway's position soon changed. At first they offered to halve the $4.60 per tonne surcharge if annual volumes directed to Prince Rupert Grain reached or exceeded 3.5 million tonnes. Then in early 1997 they reached an agreement with the CWB for a graduated system of rebates based on volumes directed to Prince Rupert. When annual tonnage exceeded 4.5 million tonnes rates would be the same as those to Vancouver.

For the first 3 crop years after the loss of rail rate parity, throughput at Prince Rupert Grain stayed well above the 3.5 million tonne figure, despite the summer shutdown in 1996. The CWB, strongly supportive of the new terminal, absorbed the additional rail charge. The Board recognized the substantially greater efficiency in ship turnaround that the modern, high throughput facility had over its Vancouver counterparts, especially for Panamax sized vessels. Happier ship owners and potentially reduced demurrage charges are, however, difficult to quantify.

Poor crops in 1998 and again from 2001 to 2004, coupled with producer pressure on the CWB to move their grain by the cheapest rail route resulted in much diminished exports. Prince Rupert Grain bore a disproportionate share of the reduction. For the 7 crop years from 1998/99 to 2004/05, annual throughput averaged only 2,234,191 tonnes, slightly less than half the previous 11 years. Clearly, when the supply of export grain was reduced, any extra rail charges would result in an asymmetrical reduction in shipment through Prince Rupert, over the Vancouver terminals.

During the crop year 2001/02, Prince Rupert Grain received only 1.25 million tonnes of grain for export, or only 10 percent of West Coast throughput. The next year the terminal was again closed for a short period, but a long strike at the Vancouver terminals resulted in a substantial diversion of grain to Prince Rupert so that, despite the poor 2002/03 crop, the terminal's share of West Coast shipments rose to 34 percent that crop year. Over the next two years, further concessions by the CNR on rail rates brought Prince Rupert Grain's share closer to its previous average of 27 percent of West Coast shipments, albeit on shrunken volume due to recurring poor crop yields.

THE COAL TERMINAL

The development of the northeast coal mines and related transportation infrastructure was enthusiastically promoted by the B.C. government in response to the apparently insatiable demands of the Japanese steel mills and their desire to diversify their sources for high quality metallurgical coal. Concerned with the potential for disruption to shipments through the Southern Rail Corridor, their buyers insisted that new purchases move to tidewater by a different rail route.

The predictions for northeast coal production made in the early eighties were excessive with some predictions emanating from Victoria suggesting production of 22 million tonnes per year by 1991.

Unhappily, by the time the new mines commenced production in late 1983 the outlook for world coal markets had darkened. The Japanese began to balk at the escalation clauses built into the contracts they had negotiated with the producers three years earlier and grudgingly took only the minimum required under those contracts. They could meet their metallurgical coal requirements at far less cost, elsewhere, and constantly badgered the operators of the Quintette and Bullmoose mines to reduce their costs of production.

In 1985 the Japanese mills were buying 43 percent of their metallurgical coal from Australia, 25 percent from Canada, and 22 percent from the U.S. With their steel industry in a slump, and the cost of metallurgical coal a major factor in steel production costs, they were clearly looking for the best coal at the best price from wherever they could buy it. Because of huge overproduction capacity worldwide, they had been able to lean hard on the southeast coal producers, so that their delivered price at Roberts Bank fell from $84 to $70, by mid-1985. The southeast producers felt they were being badly hurt by the new northeast producers who were getting much higher prices under long term contracts.

The Japanese buyers became increasingly vocal about the gross over pricing of coal delivered from the northeast mines under their contracts, and sought relief. The price of that coal was approaching $100 per tonne and not subject to review until 1988. Teck Cominco renegotiated their contract for coal from the Bullmoose Mine, reducing the price to $90 per tonne for a larger volume than in the original contract. Quintette held out for the full contract price. The Province of B.C., with $1.3 billion invested in the northeast coal project, reminded the Japanese very bluntly that there would be negative consequences if they reneged on their 1981 contracts.

The northeast coal mines struggled on against constant pressure to reduce their prices. By November 1987 the Japanese were offering $57.85 per tonne for Quintette coal when the contract called for $104. Quintette offered a reduction to $95 per tonne. Unable to reach agreement with the producers, the Japanese requested arbitration under the B.C. *International Commercial Arbitration Act*. Quintette resisted, but this went ahead and on May 29, 1990 a three-man arbitration panel ordered Quintette to substantially reduce their coal price and reimburse $46 million over-charged since April 1, 1987. The panel set a current price of $94.90 to be reduced to $84.40 by the third quarter of 1990 and followed by a further $1 per tonne reduction in each of the next two quarters. These prices were well below Quintette's cost of production and delivery. The company was also burdened with over $700 million in debt and was facing bankruptcy. The harassed coal producers sought and eventually received some concessions from the railways and from the terminal, on their freight and throughput charges. Ridley Terminals, in turn, was over $200 million in debt and could not be self-sustaining at 6 million tonnes annual throughput.

The two northeast mines, developed in the early 1980s, were planned on a grand scale with the expectation that high coal prices would continue into the future. Large open pits were designed along with huge coal preparation facilities. Quintette could not break even at the arbitrated price for minimal purchases under its contract and finally succumbed in August 2000, crushed under its debt burden and weak world markets, then offering only $41 per tonne.

The smaller Bullmoose operation was able to adapt somewhat to the new reality and continue to operate under its renegotiated contract until 2003 when its remaining reserves were depleted.

Ridley Terminals, designed to handle 12-15 million tonnes per year, achieved its peak coal throughput in 1985 when 7,190,454 tonnes of coal was loaded onto bulk carriers. This represented 29 percent of the total coal exports to overseas markets from B.C. that year. Between 1984 and 1999 coal shipments averaged 6 million tonnes per year. With the closure of Quintette in 2000 and Bullmoose in 2003 the dwindling coal throughput finally reached zero in 2004.

In 1992, in an attempt to diversify, the terminal management secured export consignments of petroleum coke from refineries in Alberta and, in the next 12 years, shipments of this commodity gradually increased, averaging 361,032 tonnes per year and reaching 581,935 tonnes in 2004. In 1997 Luscar Coal directed a total of 507,000 tonnes of their thermal coal through RTI to maintain their production in the face of a temporary shutdown at Neptune in Vancouver. That same year Manalta Coal predicted that by 2000 it would produce 1 million tonnes of export coal annually from seams in the Telkwa area, but subsequently backed away from the project in the face of continuing low prices.

Facing closure with the total cessation of coal shipments in 2003, the terminal managed to secure some business moving iron pellets from Minnesota and Michigan to export markets in Asia. This movement (487,922 tonnes during 2003–2004) together with continuing shipments of petroleum coke, kept the terminal operating, albeit with its finances in a parlous state. It survived on repeated bailouts from Ottawa, pending renewed coal exports expected from new mines developing in northeast B.C.

By 1990, the terminal's cumulative losses exceeded $70 million and the matter of the federal government buyout of the Fed Nav interest loomed. Under the terms of the original agreement that established RTI, Fed Nav could force the government to buy them out in 1991 with their initial investment paid in full, plus accrued and compounded annual dividends of 20 percent. The government had the option to buy out the Fed Nav interest at any time before 1991 and, by September 1985 some senior officials in Ports Canada wanted the Tory government to proceed at once to eliminate that interest.

The Commons Transport Committee investigated the original dubious deal with Fed Nav in early 1987 and recommended it be terminated forthwith. For whatever reason, this recommendation never reached Cabinet and nothing was done to terminate Fed Nav's very lucrative interest in this failing enterprise. In April 1991 Fed Nav exercised its "put" and was paid out $60 million, a very handsome return on a no risk investment of $23 million. Concurrently, the terminal's book value was written down to its estimated liquidation value of $25 million.

With the dissolution of the Canada Ports Corporation on November 1, 2000 its subsidiary, Ridley Terminals, became a crown corporation and in 2003 its workforce elected to form a local of the ILWU.

In May 2003 Transport Canada issued a Canada-wide request for proposals on the future of the terminal in an attempt to determine its options. Fearing that Ottawa might sell it to friendly private interests that would limit or dictate access to the terminal just as new northeast coal mines were about to enter production, the Province of B.C. began negotiations with Ottawa, in early 2005, with a view to taking over RTI as part of its Asia Pacific trade and gateway strategy.

RIDLEY ISLAND INDUSTRIAL SITE

Aware of their good fortune to control one of the few rail served land parcels located adjacent to deep tidewater on the B.C. coast that was suitable for major developments, the port staff continued efforts to attract new industries to this relatively flat 450 hectare (1,124 acre) island.

There was a transient flurry of interest in 1997 from a Texas firm proposing construction of a $250 million hot briquetted iron plant on the island, using B.C. coal and iron ore imported from South America.

A more promising prospect appeared when the Sulphur Corporation of Canada signed agreements with RTI and the port in 1999 for the construction of a facility to receive and export sulphur from producers in B.C., Alberta, and Saskatchewan utilizing RTI's ship loading equipment and dock. The plant would be situated on property RTI leased from the port and would utilize their ship loading equipment and dock to export up to 1 million tonnes of sulphur annually in molten or pelletized form. The $20 million project did proceed and was 80 percent complete when construction stalled due to legal issues between its Alberta backers. Under the terms of its agreement with Sulphur Corp., RTI took over the incomplete facility in 2002 and commenced efforts to interest a new producer or exporter of sulphur to complete the facility.

THE NEW CRUISE TERMINALS

The 1986 loss of the *Fairsky* — a new 1,200 passenger 43,692 ton vessel which had made nine calls at Prince Rupert in 1985 — to Skagway, seemed to many local citizens to signal the end of the City's historic participation in the summer cruise ship business. In 1984 a $100,000 study of the waterfront proposed a number of developments to include people oriented areas with both tourist and commercial facilities, along with a cruise ship dock. It further suggested renewing and developing the Cow Bay area, while preserving its unique waterfront character. The shoreline in front of the city's core consists almost entirely of the CNR rail yard and the railway offered to trade this for a new terminal facility on Ridley Island, provided by the city or the port. The port saw the rail yard as a potential site for a future container terminal, while the Chamber of Commerce envisioned people-oriented facilities including accommodation for cruise ships, charter boats, and float planes, as well as a large park and shopping area. However, the only result of discussions with the CNR on the future of this area was a 99-year lease granted to the City in 1987 on 1 acre around the Kwinitsa Station Museum. In return, the City replaced the old wooden ramp with a new road access to the railway station area.

As port calls by large cruise ships dwindled to near zero, a Seattle based company, Exploration Cruise Lines, entered the scene in 1985 with the concept of basing a small vessel at Prince Rupert for cruise operation to more "offbeat" places in Alaska. The local Visitors Bureau had been working on this idea for several years and their reward was the arrival of the Norwegian flagged *North Star* carrying 158 passengers on May 11, 1985. This small vessel was able to use the stub of the Ocean Dock to receive and discharge its passengers in Prince Rupert. Other small vessels with passenger capacities ranging from 12 to 250 soon followed and most used Prince Rupert as the base for their excursions to Alaska points. A total of 30 visits by these small vessels brought a total of 9,466 passengers to the city in 1988, a little over double the low of 4,468 two years earlier when large vessel calls ended.

Nothing, however, seems to come easily to Prince Rupert. Attempts to further develop the small ship cruise business ran into federally imposed drawbacks in 1988. Bill C52 imposed a tax on foreign flag vessels carrying less than 250 passengers and was clearly designed to benefit east coast operators. Strong protests from Prince Rupert resulted in a waiver being granted to the *North Star*, the first vessel affected, but the threat of this 25 percent duty on small cruise vessels with foreign flags remained. A further problem arose when the federal Department of Agriculture insisted that all garbage from a foreign flag ship must be incinerated. This forced ships operating from Prince Rupert to offload their garbage in Alaskan ports.

From 1988 to 1995 port visits by even the small and "pocket" size vessels declined to an all-time low of three, carrying only 227 passengers, in 1995. The following year the Port Corporation suspended the passenger head tax that had been instituted in 1977 at the insistence of the National Harbours Board, ostensibly to pay for the minimal repairs to the Ocean Dock. This tax had been a continuing source of irritation to cruise vessel operators, especially in the light of the totally inadequate facilities offered their customers. Clearly, however, until an appropriate dock and terminal could be provided, cruise vessel visits, large or small, would continue to be "few and far between."

With the demolition of the old grain terminal in 1987 the possibility of using that area and the remaining long wooden dock for a cruise ship facility became a matter of active interest. As always, any major development on the waterfront ran into the problem of the CNR rail yard. Moving the yard to Ridley would cost $9 million, according to the CNR who were certainly not willing to use their own funds. In 1994 the City proposed offering a land swap to the CNR in return for removing two rail lines along the shore, which were blocking a new "Skeena Landing" concept. Frustrated by news that Ketchikan had 454 port calls from cruise ships carrying 440,000 passengers, proponents of "Skeena Landing" envisioned a rather grand plan, which would even include a new site for Northwest Community College. However, by late 1994 "Skeena Landing," too, had succumbed to harsh reality.

The Prince Rupert Port Corporation (PRPC), about to become a relatively autonomous Port Authority with a mandate to be responsive to local needs and priorities, moved decisively to create a new and effective small vessel berth and terminal. Between 1998 and 2001 the port spent $6.2 million to acquire the former Atlin Fish plant, provide it with a new floating dock suitable for small cruise vessels, develop a fine passenger reception facility with tourism related commercial activities on the main floor, and convert the second floor into administration offices for the Port Authority. Operators responded favourably to this special facility for small cruise ships, so that by 2003 the port hosted 33 vessels carrying 3,034 passengers to the new cruise centre.

The 1999 entry of Seattle as a base for Alaska bound cruise vessels offered a very real potential for Prince Rupert to serve as the obligatory foreign port call on their itinerary. Norwegian Cruise Lines, one of the first companies to base a vessel in Seattle, sent their *Norwegian Wind* on a trial visit to Prince Rupert on May 4, 1999, lightering their passengers ashore. In response to the clear need for a large vessel tie-up berth, the Port Authority and the City of Prince Rupert jointly devised a "Cruise Ship Facility Development Plan" in 2000. With financial assistance for the project promised by both the province and Ottawa they awarded a contract to design a docking facility that would suit the needs of the largest vessels in the Alaska cruise market.

Built at a cost of $9 million the new Northland Terminal received its first vessel, the *Superstar Leo (Norwegian Spirit)* on May 20, 2004. A further $3 million was spent on upland improvements and an impressive array of excursions developed for landed passengers. Like the small ship facility, the new terminal was well received and Prince Rupert citizens enthusiastically welcomed 62,045 passengers from 32 large and 23 small vessel port calls in 2004, a huge increase over the previous year.

THE FERRY TERMINALS

By 1992 the Alaska Ferry Terminal, built by the federal Department of Public Work in 1962–1963 was in dire need of a major upgrade. To achieve this the PRPC purchased the water lot in 1992 and arranged with the City of Prince Rupert to build a new passenger terminal for lease to the Alaska Marine Highway system in time for the 1993 summer tourist season. The following year the B.C. Ferry Corporation opened a new passenger facility on their adjacent terminal.

THE CONVERSION OF FAIRVIEW GENERAL CARGO TERMINAL

A greater source of optimism for the port's future stemmed from in-depth studies initiated in 1996 by the port staff into converting the existing break-bulk terminal at Fairview into a container handling facility. This initiative was given a boost by the 1997 report of the federally appointed task force assigned to study the Northwest Transportation Corridor. It designated Prince Rupert as a "Key Pacific Gateway" with the development of a modern container handling facility a top priority. As lumber throughput continued its steady decline and the pulp handling initiative faltered, it was abundantly clear that the port had either to enter the container age, or watch traffic through its $73 million Fairview Terminal dwindle to insignificance. Though declining sawmill production in the port's hinterland and changing markets accounted for some of the steep reduction in lumber and pulp throughput, it was also evident that more and more forest products of all types were being stuffed into otherwise empty Asia bound containers and being exported at favourable shipping rates. Other traditional break-bulk and bulk commodities, too, were increasingly caught up in the "container revolution." There could thus be little or no future for an export oriented break-bulk terminal in an isolated port with no container handling ability.

An attempt had been made in 1990 by the White Pass and Yukon Railway to establish containerized traffic out of Prince Rupert using Fairview Terminal and their small container vessel *Frank H. Brown*. That year 6,800 tonnes of BC Packers products were stuffed into 375 containers in Prince Rupert. These containers were then picked up by the *Brown* and moved to Vancouver for transfer to overseas markets by one of the container shipping lines calling there. Company efforts to market this concept to other commodity producers in north central B.C. were unsuccessful and the exercise was not repeated.

Clearly, a successful container terminal requires both inbound traffic and stuffed boxes for export, if it is to attract major container ship operators. Hence, the port staff had to identify a market that would benefit from Prince Rupert's advantageous geographic proximity to Asia and it's grossly under-utilized, but first class rail corridor connection to virtually all North America.

In the spring of 1996, the port engaged the services of a highly respected New York transportation consultant, C.R. Cushing & Co. Inc. to examine the feasibility of "Project Silk," a reincarnation of the old land bridge idea that so enamoured the early railway builders. This concept proposed moving Europe bound containers from Asia to Prince Rupert and thence, by rail to Halifax, for reloading on a container vessel for the transatlantic crossing. Cushing's report, received in August 1996, concluded that this arrangement could not compete with vessels carrying containers directly between Asia and Europe via Suez, due mainly to the extra costs of double handling. The report did, however point out that both the cost and the transit times required to move containers from Asia to the U.S. Central and Mid-Atlantic states were significantly less through Prince Rupert, using Canadian railroads, than via U.S. West Coast ports and U.S. railroads, or by the all-water route to the U.S. east coast via Panama. They further recommended that the PRPC pursue the possibility of establishing an entry point for U.S. and Canada bound containers moving from Asia.

At the subsequent request of the port, Cushing expanded on their recommendation in a second report dated April 1997. This report stated that a modern container facility in Prince Rupert would "enable Prince Rupert to become the quickest and lowest cost service link to and from the Far East and the middle of the North American intermodal container market."

This solid expression of faith in the potential for the port was indeed encouraging. However, with the steep decline in port revenues, the port was forced to reduce staff, so that the burden of resolving the many hurdles associated with bringing such a project to fruition fell on the remaining eight people. There were scoffers aplenty. All existing North American Pacific container ports serve a large local population as well as far away markets. At the Southern Gateway terminals about one-third of containers are moved between the facility and local destinations by truck. In fact, this is a major source of inefficiency at these terminals. Rather than an obstacle, the absence of a local market gave Prince Rupert the opportunity to create a unique, pure rail intermodal operation, modern in every respect, with no interference from road traffic or from congestion on its excellent rail link.

The affirmation of potential was one thing, but success would depend on a number of factors, and by no means were all of these under the control of the port. Of crucial importance would be:

- Support of the CNR
- Financial assistance and cooperation from senior governments
- Selection of a terminal operator
- Recognition and utilization by a major container shipping line

The President of the CNR, Paul Tellier, responded positively to a presentation in early 2002 by Don Krusel, President and CEO of the Prince Rupert Port Authority, outlining the potential for the port and the railway, if joined in a partnership, to move containers from Asia to eastern Canada and the U.S. Midwest. Hunter Harrison succeeded Tellier a year later and he, in turn, became an enthusiastic and very strong proponent of the project. Freed at last by their 1995 privatization from political constraints, the CNR's focus had moved from an east-west to a new north-south orientation, as confirmed by their purchase of the Illinois Central R.R. in the U.S. They could see in Prince Rupert's project a superb opportunity to increase lucrative long-haul Asian container traffic over their lines to the U.S. Midwest. Moving traffic from a state-of-the-art, pure rail intermodal facility over their grossly underutilized, but high quality Northern Corridor, as opposed to the continual struggle with port and rail line congestion in the south, could only be attractive.

With their oft-proclaimed keen interest in the Asia Pacific Gateway, the federal and provincial governments also found the Prince Rupert project much to their liking and became strong supporters. Their financial contributions and concessions were essential in allowing the project to succeed. Local long shore labour, direct victims of the collapse of the port's traffic, were enthused and eager to learn the sophisticated techniques involved in a new state-of-the-art container terminal operation.

As first conceived, a modest conversion of the terminal could be achieved at a cost of $28 million, plus an additional $10 million for equipment and another $10 million for modifications to the CNR rail tunnels to accommodate double-stack container trains. This concept, embodying the purchase of second hand cranes and use of the existing dock face, envisioned handling vessels in the 3,000–4,000 TEU range only.

As planning progressed, it became apparent that a much more robust conversion would be needed to capitalize on the port's deep-water advantage. Container ships were getting ever larger and naval architects were already designing vessels able to carry 13,000 TEU. With its deep natural harbour and second deepest ship channel in North America, the port could very comfortably accommodate these future behemoths, without having to mitigate the environmental consequences of dredging. Clearly, the conversion of Fairview Terminal should be planned and equipped to take advantage of this benefit. By early 2004, marine design consultants recommended a dock face extension using steel pilings with a bridge deck to the existing caissons. The new dock face would be in water 18.7 m (62.3 ft.) deep at low tide. This would enable the terminal to handle the largest container ships afloat, or being designed.

One of the crucial elements in bringing this project to fruition was the selection of operator for the completed terminal. Canadian Stevedoring, long-term operators at Fairview, had been sold to P&O Ports Canada and their lease on the terminal expired December 31, 2004. A number of terminal operators responded to the port's call for submissions, but one stood out as the most enthusiastic and acceptable. Maher Terminals of New Jersey had 60 years of experience in terminal operation, operated the largest container terminal in the U.S., and had no terminals on the West Coast, a most important point in avoiding conflict of interest. On July 26, 2004 the port was able to announce agreement in principle with Maher as the new operator of Fairview Terminal effective January 1, 2005. The association of the project with this highly respected operator immediately gave it credibility in the marine community.

Thus, by the end of 2004, the port was nearing completion of plans for a total conversion of the existing Fairview Terminal to a state-of-the-art facility that would be operated by a very experienced operator. Concurrently, planning was underway for a second phase project that would more than triple the initial 500,000 TEU annual capacity of the terminal. Assuming completion of engineering, environmental reviews, funding arrangements, and First Nations consultation, it was anticipated that tenders for initial work on the project could go out in mid-2005.

PROPOSED PETROCHEMICAL AND LNG TERMINALS

The intense flurry of interest in the early eighties in establishing petrochemical, liquid bulk, or LNG terminals in Prince Rupert persuaded the Port Corporation to seek to acquire a 26 hectare (65 acre) parcel of the B.C. Development Corporation property on southwest Kaien

Island adjacent to Ridley Island. The purchase of the site was finally concluded in September 1990 for $1.2 million.

The passage of the *Clean Air Act* in the U.S. sparked a new interest in producing chemicals that could be blended with gasoline to allow cleaner burning and thereby reduce noxious emissions.

In mid-1993 EcoFuel, a subsidiary of state owned Italian oil giant, Eni S.p.A., approached the Port Corporation with a proposal to construct at $350 million plant to produce the gasoline additive methyl tertiary butyl ether (MTBE) on the southwest Kaien site. Shipping facilities were to be included and California would be the main market. A few months later another company, Mundogas America, proposed a deep-water loading facility for liquid butane and propane destined for Central and South American markets. They first proposed to store these products in a floating tanker vessel secured close to shore, for transfer to vessels that could tie up outboard for loading. Canadian regulatory agencies rejected this idea. Mundogas then devised a plan to rail in butane and propane, compress it in a plant on the southwest Kaien site, and ship it over Ridley Terminals' facility at a rate of four to five vessels per month. Their plans never developed further.

Ecofuel kept working on their proposal with active assistance from the Port Corporation, which spent over $250,000 on site studies of the southwest Kaien site. Ecofuel intended to secure methanol from the Methanex plant in Kitimat and isobutene from Amoco in Alberta. They formed an alliance with two American companies including Kiewit Fuels and together they worked on a pre-feasibility costing study until early 1996 when changing markets for MTBE resulted in collapse of the project.

Another entity entered the picture in early 1995, Pac-Rim of Calgary. They appeared to be revitalizing the Dome LNG project and were looking at Prince Rupert and the Kitimat area as potential sites for a $1.1 billion LNG plant and tanker terminal. By September 1996 they had secured a letter of intent from South Korean customers and their planned expenditures had escalated to $1.4 billion. Finally, in December 1996 they announced Kitimaat Village as the preferred site with work to start in 1997. Their site choice was influenced, they said, by the difficulty and excessive costs of building a pipeline between Terrace and Prince Rupert. This project, too, failed to materialize.

Late in 2004, Calgary based WestPac Terminals Inc. signed an agreement with the Port Authority to use a 100 hectare (250 acre) site on Ridley Island adjacent to the coal terminal for the proposed construction of an import LNG terminal. The projected $200 million terminal was to include storage tanks, a regasification plant, and dock facilities. From this hub, gas was to be trans-shipped by rail, road, ship, barge, or pipeline to North American markets.

A Visual Record of the Gateway Ports and the Men Who Moved the Cargoes 1919 to 2010

THE GATEWAYS FROM 1919 TO 2010

New Westminster from 1919 to 2010

During the first two decades of the twentieth century, foreign cargo handling continued to languish at the river port. In 1918, New Westminster moved only 1.4 % of the total overseas traffic passing through the West Coast. The situation changed quite dramatically in the early 1920s and, by 1926 New Westminster was loading a quarter of all B.C. overseas lumber exports. Deep-sea-vessel calls increased from 13 in 1921 to 509 in 1939 and then dropped by half during WWII.

To handle this increased traffic, existing wharves and their backup facilities on the city waterfront were expanded in 1925 and again in 1928, this time with the inclusion of a large cold storage plant for agricultural products. Products handled included forest products, canned salmon, apples, fertilizers, bar metal, and metal concentrates. In addition to these conventional facilities on the city waterfront, a small grain terminal was completed on the south bank of the river in 1928.

By 1947 deep-sea traffic resumed its pre-war level. Then, over the next 25 years, throughput slowly increased from one to one and a half million tonnes annually of primarily resource commodities, including forest products, canned salmon, apples, metals and fertilizers. A major new facility to handle bulk and break-bulk cargoes was completed on the south bank of the river in 1964 and, a decade later, this terminal added a dedicated and fully equipped container terminal on adjacent property. Unfortunately, that facility failed to prosper during the next three decades. Two auto terminals were completed on riverside locations in the early seventies. Both were successful and later expanded.

In 1978 the B.C. Development Corporation purchased the New Westminster waterfront facilities of Pacific Coast Terminals and, after 1982, all deep-sea traffic berthed at the extensive wharf complex on the south side of the river, or at the auto terminals. International cargo tonnage continued to grow through the seventies and eighties, reaching a new high of 5.3 million tonnes in 1993. Container traffic underwent a short but spectacular increase from 1996 to 2005, before its sudden near collapse. Domestic cargo moving on the river has fluctuated with the domestic economy, but has continued to be a multiple of two to three times foreign traffic.

In 1982 the Port Authority inaugurated a Land Acquisition and Harbour Development Fund. From this fund, rail-served riverfront properties in Richmond and Surrey were acquired and consolidated. These have successfully attracted an increasing number of logistics companies.

Responsibility for maintaining the navigable river channel was assumed by the Port Authority in 1999 and since then the channel has been maintained at approximately 11.4 metres (38 feet).

After vigorously resisting union with the Port of Vancouver for at least three-quarters of a century, the two Fraser Port Authorities and the Vancouver Port Authority were combined to form the Vancouver Fraser Port Authority in 2008. The future of this land-rich river port within Port Metro Vancouver now focuses primarily on the further development of its logistic facilities and their increasing role in short sea shipping from the port's deeper water terminals.

NEW WESTMINSTER, 1919 TO 2007

Frank Leonard photo, Vancouver Public Library VPL 10598

PLATE 104 *New Westminster Harbour Commission Elevator No. 1. This small terminal was constructed on the south side of the Fraser River and received its first vessel in June 1929. Over the next 39 years it moved a total of 3.27 million tonnes of grain, much of it consigned as "overflow" from Burrard Inlet terminals. Built on pilings, it developed a lean in 1968 and was closed permanently and demolished two years later.*

PLATE 105 *Loading apples at Pacific Coast Terminals. Receiving, storing, and loading fruit for overseas markets formed a significant part of the port's business in the 1930s. In 1937 a total of 1,313,901 fifty-pound boxes of apples were loaded to vessels at New Westminster wharves.*

PLATE 106 *Loading rolls of paper on the New Westminster waterfront in 1938.*

PLATE 107 *Aerial view of the New Westminster waterfront in 1946.*

Courtesy Port Metro Vancouver

PLATE 108 *Loading bagged fertilizer at Pacific Coast Terminals in 1955. Fertilizers constituted a major commodity movement for the port.*

Vancouver Public Library VPL 56191

PLATE 109 *Wharf and warehouse facilities in front of the downtown core in 1959. This location offered very limited backup land, as well as congested access.*

PLATE 110 *The extensive Surrey and Annacis Island holdings of the New Westminster Harbour Commission in 1961. Note the "lonely" little grain elevator on the south bank of the river.*

PLATE 111 *Dredging in the mid-sixties to create a site for an auto terminal at the north end of Annacis Island. Virtually every terminal development at the Southern Gateway Ports has involved extensive dredging, both to create land and to provide adequate water depth for berths.*

PLATE 112 *The first stage in the development of Fraser Surrey Docks, as seen from the air in May 1963. The development surrounds the old grain terminal, which was still operating.*

PLATE 113 *Fraser Surrey Docks in May 1969 showing recently built infrastructure and warehousing, as well as terminal expansion underway south of the idle grain terminal.*

PLATE 114 *Aerial view of Fraser Surrey Docks in May 1972. The elevator has been demolished and a large cargo shed built on the site. Preparation of a new construction site is underway to the south.*

PLATE 115 *Initial development of Fraser Wharves Auto Terminal in Richmond, in 1971.*

PLATE 116 *The newly opened Annacis Auto Terminal in 1973. Developed on reclaimed land, this terminal has since undergone a number of expansions, including a second berth. It is now operated by Wallenius Wilhelmsen Logistics.*

PLATE 117 *Aerial view of Fraser Surrey Docks taken in June 1978. The container terminal section opened in December 1974 with two berths, two Paceco cranes, ample backup land, and excellent rail connections. It saw little use for the next 25 years.*

NEW WESTMINSTER, NOW PART OF PORT METRO VANCOUVER, 2008 TO 2010

Courtesy Port Metro Vancouver

PLATE 118 *Annacis Auto Terminal and Fraser Surrey Docks in 2009 after further development, including new intermodal facilities adjacent to the Fraser Surrey terminals.*

Courtesy Port Metro Vancouver

PLATE 119 *Partial development of the port's Richmond Properties division, as seen in 2010. This site continues to be developed to serve intermodal and logistics activities, including those related to short sea shipping.*

Vancouver from 1919 to 2010

WATERFRONT DEVELOPMENTS ON BURRARD INLET, 1919 TO 1929

In 1919 Vancouver finally passed Victoria in terms of the total overseas cargo tonnage handled. The new post-WWI ability to access Atlantic markets via the Panama Canal was the prime reason for the spectacular boom in port traffic and facility development between 1920 and 1929. This was especially apparent in the construction of terminals for the new bulk movement of prairie grain.

Stuart Thomson photo, City of Vancouver Archives CVA 1123-13

PLATE 120 *Vancouver's first grain elevator, Dominion No. 1, and the Government Pier, later called Lapointe Pier, located at the foot of Commercial Drive. These two facilities were funded by Ottawa and completed in 1915/1916. The picture is dated 1919.*

PLATE 121 SS War Viceroy *sailed for the United Kingdom on November 13, 1917 with 2,700 tons of wheat loaded at Dominion No. 1 elevator. This was the first of five shipments organized by a federal government agency to determine the feasibility of shipping grain from the West Coast to Atlantic markets via the Panama Canal.*

PLATE 122 SS Effingham *was the first vessel to carry bulk grain, purchased on a commercial basis, from the port to a buyer in the United Kingdom. She loaded at Dominion No. 1 elevator and sailed January 7, 1921.*

PLATE 123 *One of three locomotives belonging to the Vancouver Harbour Commissioners Terminal Railway. The railway, which began operating in 1923, was conceived as a solution to the problems arising from the congestion and the conflict between competing rail jurisdictions that were plaguing the south shore waterfront facilities.*

PLATE 124 *Ballantyne Pier, completed in 1923, with the loading gallery for Vancouver Harbour Commissioners elevator No.2. The elevator was demolished in 1979 and the pier was extensively rebuilt in 1995. Immediately beyond Ballantyne is the Great Northern pier, built in 1914. This aerial photograph was taken circa 1940.*

PLATE 125 Empress of Canada *and* Aorangi *at CPR Pier A (formerly Piers A and B) in 1925.*

PLATE 126 Empress of Canada *berthed at Pier D in 1923. This pier was completed by the CPR in 1913 and extended in 1917. The liner* Empress of Australia *(ex* Tirpitz*) is berthed at the wharf. Their black hulls were painted white in 1926.*

Dominion Photo Company, Vancouver Public Library VPL 30368

PLATE 127 *The first road/rail bridge across second narrows was completed by the Burrard Inlet Bridge and Tunnel Company in November 1925.*

Frank Leonard photo, Vancouver Public Library VPL 2801

PLATE 128 *Another view of the original bascule type bridge at second narrows. The location of the open span was blamed by mariners for the many accidents at this site.*

PLATE 129 *Vancouver Harbour Commissioners No.1 elevator (ex Dominion No. 1) with its new annex and the adjacent Vancouver Elevator Company (Spillers) terminal in 1927. These terminals were later consolidated to form Pacific Elevators.*

PLATE 130 *Vancouver Harbour Commissioners Elevator No. 3 after its first expansion in 1927. This terminal was leased to the Burrard Elevator Company Ltd., a consortium led by United Grain Growers. After further expansion and upgrade, UGG bought the terminal from the National Harbours Board for $3.5 million in 1967. It currently operates as the Alliance Terminal.*

PLATE 131 *The new Alberta Wheat Pool Terminal as completed in 1928. The terminal has been increased in size and upgraded many times since. It is currently operated as Viterra Terminal.*

PLATE 132 *Midland Pacific Grain Elevator on the north shore, as first completed in 1928. After expansion, partial destruction by explosion and fire, and then rebuilding and extensive modernization, this terminal now operates as James Richardson International terminal.*

PLATE 133 *Site of the former Hastings Sawmill, acquired by the Vancouver Harbour Commission in 1929. Centennial Pier opened on this site in July 1960.*

PLATE 134 *A section of the disaster prone second narrows road/rail bridge collapsed after the hulk* Pacific Gatherer *collided on September 19, 1930.*

PLATE 135 *The second narrows bridge was taken over by the Harbour Commission and redesigned with a central lift span. It finally reopened on June 1, 1934 and served until it was replaced by a new CNR bridge in 1969.*

PLATE 136 *Vessels loading flour from Terminal Dock in 1927. Flour was a major export commodity for the port between 1925 and 1970. Terminal Dock, located just east of Nanaimo Street, was built in 1925 and demolished in 1983.*

Vancouver Maritime Museum

PLATE 137 *Loading sacked flour at Terminal Dock in 1926.*

Vancouver Maritime Museum

PLATE 137A *Stowing the sacked flour in the hold of a conventional cargo vessel. In addition to flour, this vessel carried lumber stowed both below and on deck.*

PLATE 138 *The recently completed CPR Pier B-C between Pier A and Pier D in 1927.*

PLATE 139 *The largest shipment of baled silk ever received in the port being unloaded at Ballantyne Pier in May 1929.*

Frank Leonard photo, Vancouver Public Library VPL 16641

PLATE 140 *The* Canadian Observer *in the new Burrard Dry Dock in 1926. The dock was built with a 70% federal subsidy and lifted its first vessel in March 1925.*

City of Vancouver Archives CVA Out P17

PLATE 141 *The IOCO refinery east of Indian Arm on the north shore of Burrard Inlet in 1920. The refinery opened in 1915.*

PLATE 142 *The mouth of the Capilano River in 1928.*

The Vancouver Waterfront from 1930 to 1945

Momentum stalled during the depression years with very few new waterfront developments and little growth in cargo movement. During the war years, activity was focussed on shipbuilding on both shores of Burrard Inlet and also in False Creek.

PLATE 143 *The CPR piers and Coal Harbour in 1930.*

PLATE 144 *The grain terminals on the south shore in 1930, looking east from Ballantyne Pier.*

PLATE 145 *The "Jungle" of 1931. Unemployed men making makeshift shelters on the site of the former Hastings Mill, now occupied by the Centerm container terminal.*

PLATE 146 *Aerial view of Burrard Dry Dock in 1930.*

PLATE 147 (above) **& 147A** (below) *Scenes from the "Battle of Ballantyne Pier," June 18, 1935, the blackest day in Vancuver's waterfront labour history.*

Courtesy Port Metro Vancouver

PLATE 148 *Waterfront worker Charlie Lomas is seen here driving a three-wheeled Harley Davidson "Trike," pulling carts loaded with chests of tea unloaded from the* Empress of Japan. *The picture is dated 1937.*

Joseph Bertalino Photo, City of Vancouver Archives CVA 1376-40

PLATE 149 *The destruction of Pier D by fire on July 27, 1938.*

PLATE 150 *Building and outfitting "North Sands" type freighters at Burrard Dry Dock in late 1942.*

PLATE 151 *Building freighters at West Coast Shipbuilders' yard on False Creek in 1943.*

Vancouver Developments from 1946 to 2010

Bulk terminals had to be developed in the fifties and sixties to meet the new export demand for bulk raw materials to feed the burgeoning post-war Asian industries. At first, these were built on sites on the less developed north side of Burrard Inlet. Eventually, it became necessary to extend the harbour limits and to create a new "superport" at Roberts Bank. In the seventies, new and very efficient break-bulk terminals were added to handle the massive increase in forest product exports from new and expanding mills in the interior of the province.

The port's early response to the container revolution was sluggish and timid. As a result, it lost momentum to aggressive competitors in Puget Sound. From the opening of the first, very modest facility in 1970, it would take 25 years to reach an annual throughput of 500,000 TEU.

Since 1985, the port has focussed on expanding its container and cruise business and has spent heavily to develop very adequate facilities for both. However, the movement of bulk and break-bulk commodities still comprises over three-quarters of the total tonnage handled by the port.

Jack Lindsay Photo, City of Vancouver Archives CVA 1184-3429

PLATE 153 *Aerial view of piers on the south shore of Burrard Inlet in 1948. From the top down, they are Piers A, B-C, Union Steamships, Pier H, Evans, Coleman and Evans, North Vancouver Ferry Terminal, and the CNR (former GTP) Pier.*

PLATE 152 *Handling lumber at Terminal Dock in 1946 — an improvement on the tall ship days, but still very labour intensive. In the seventies, lumber increasingly arrived on the dock in wrapped bundles for loading onto specialized forest product carriers, which greatly increased efficiency. Now, a substantial percentage of exports of lumber and other forest products move overseas stuffed in containers.*

PLATE 154 *MV* Clifford J. Rogers *in 1956. This new and specially designed vessel inaugurated the age of containerization for marine cargoes when she sailed for Skagway, Alaska, on November 26, 1955.*

PLATE 155 *Lowering the specially designed containers into the hold of the* Clifford J. Rogers *in 1956.*

PLATE 156 *The second generation container vessel built for White Pass, the* Frank H. Brown, *berthed at Skagway in 1970.*

PLATE 157 *Bagging potash for export at Vancouver Wharves in the early 1960s.*

PLATE 158 *The first vessel to load at the new Saskatchewan Wheat Pool Elevator on the north shore on May 29, 1968.*

PLATE 159 *The early development of Neptune Terminal and site preparation for the future Seaboard Terminal, pictured on August 26, 1969. These sites were created for the National Harbours Board by dredging 3.2 million cubic yards (2.45 million cubic metres) of sand, gravel, and boulders from the adjacent harbour bottom.*

PLATE 160 *An aerial view of Vancouver Wharves in 1969. This bulk and break-bulk facility opened in 1960 on land developed just east of first narrows on the north shore of Burrard Inlet. Much of the site was created with fill material gained by dredging the adjacent harbour bed. The facility is served from the north and east by the CNR. The present much expanded and upgraded terminal is now owned and operated by Kinder Morgan.*

PLATE 161 Snow White, *the first vessel to load coal at Westshore Terminal on May 4, 1970.*

PLATE 162 *The first development of the Roberts Bank "Superport," as seen on May 6, 1970. Pod 1 was leased and developed by Westshore Terminals.*

PLATE 163 *Neptune Bulk Terminals in 1971. This terminal was built on land created by using fill material dredged from the adjacent seabed. Part of the site was subsequently leased by the National Harbours Board to Neptune for development and the new facility unloaded its first vessel in December 1968.*

PLATE 164 *The port's first container handling facility consisted of a single crane placed on Berth Six at Centennial Pier in 1970. In 1977 Centennial was renamed Centerm and in 1984 this terminal received its second container crane.*

North Vancouver Museum and Archives 8512

PLATE 165 *Explosion and fire at the Pioneer Grain Terminal in October 1975.*

North Vancouver Museum and Archives 4516

PLATE 166 *The rebuilt and enlarged Pioneer Grain Terminal in 1980. This terminal now operates as the James Richardson International Terminal.*

John Denniston photo, North Vancouver Museum and Archives 15598

PLATE 167 *Damage to the new CNR Second Narrows Rail Bridge after being struck by the* Japan Erica *on October 12, 1979.*

PLATE 168 *The Seaboard International Terminal in 1980. Considered the largest specialized wood product assembly and loading facility in the world, it loaded its first vessel in mid-1971. This terminal was located immediately east of Neptune's terminal and was built on the balance of the original site created by the National Harbours Board.*

PLATE 169 *The first vessel lifted in the new Burrard Dry Dock in late 1981. This new facility, capable of lifting vessels up to 75,000 tons dwt., arrived from Japan in August 1981 and replaced the old wooden dry dock installed there in 1925. Its initial cost with support facilities amounted to $63.3 million, two-thirds provided by Ottawa and Victoria. In 1992, the federal and provincial governments provided another $14 million to "save the dry dock" from being sold to Asian interests.*

PLATE 170 *The Vanterm Container Terminal in February 2002. Opened in 1975, the facility has under-gone modifications and upgrades since but, hemmed in by grain elevators, the terminal has little scope for expansion.*

PLATE 171 *Canada Place with two berths — as it appeared when first opened in 1986.*

PLATE 172 *Canada Place after the extension was completed in 2003.*

Courtesy Port Metro Vancouver

PLATE 173 *Ballantyne cruise facility, developed as part of the $49 million 1995 refurbishment of the seventy-year-old pier. It is now connected to Centerm on its west side.*

PLATE 174 *Deltaport Container Terminal, which was originally opened in 1997 on Pod 4, shown here after the expansion in 2000 onto Pod 3.*

PLATE 175 *On January 1, 2003 gale force winds destroyed one ship loader on Berth Two at Westshore coal terminal and extensively damaged the other. The berth was out of service for seven months.*

BURRARD INLET AND ROBERTS BANK TERMINALS TODAY

Courtesy Port Metro Vancouver

PLATE 176 *Westshore Coal Terminal and Deltaport after completion of the Third Berth Project in January, 2010.*

Courtesy Port Metro Vancouver

PLATE 176A *Burrard Inlet terminals today.*

PLATE 176B *Aerial view of Burrard Inlet looking west from Chevron's tank farm to English Bay.*

PLATE 176C *Burrard Inlet east of second narrows with the entrance to Indian Arm across from the Westridge oil terminal.*

PLATE 176D *The south shore of Burrard Inlet further east of second narrows from the Petro Canada Terminal to the Pacific Coast Terminal and Port Moody.*

Prince Rupert from 1919 to 2010

PRINCE RUPERT, 1919 TO 1945

The Grand Trunk Railway was unable to honour its guarantee on the securities of its subsidiary, the Grand Trunk Pacific Railway. This led to the nationalization of both railways and their subsequent amalgamation into the Canadian National Railway on January 19, 1923. The Prince Rupert Shipyard and Dry Dock had been completed before the financial collapse, but most of the other development plans for the new northern port were abandoned.

In the inevitable rationalization that followed the absorption of six failed railways into the new national carrier, the Canadian Northern line from Red Pass Junction to Vancouver was designated the main line. The Grand Trunk Pacific line west from that point to Prince Rupert was relegated to the status of a seldom-serviced branch line.

With minimal support from senior governments or the new, publicly owned railway, the new gateway port with its manifold natural assets was allowed to languish for the next six decades, except for a short burst of activity during World War II. The risk inherent in relying totally on one corridor to one port for Canada's overseas trade through the West Coast was accepted, apparently without question.

The Panama Canal opened Atlantic markets to exports from the West Coast and was the main stimulus for the spectacular growth of the Southern Gateway during the 1920s, but it offered little or no benefit to the new Northern Gateway. Transpacific trade, which Prince Rupert was ideally located to serve, failed to materialize to the extent anticipated, especially during the long period of Asian wars from 1930 to 1954.

Deep-Sea Terminals

PLATE 177 *View of the Ocean Dock and freight shed, as completed in 1920. It was extended by the U.S. Military in 1942.*

PLATE 178 *The Canadian Government Grain Terminal, as completed in 1926.*

PLATE 179 *The first two freighters to arrive at Prince Rupert's new terminal to load grain in October 1926. After 1928 the terminal was consigned to an "overflow" role to Vancouver's facilities and, during 11 of the next 23 years, received no grain for shipment.*

John R. Wrathall photo, Prince Rupert City and Regional Archives & Museum of Northern B.C. WP997-81-13582

PLATE 180 *The Prince Rupert waterfront northeast of the grain elevator in 1935*

Fish Plants and Wharves

William W. Wrathall photo, Prince Rupert City and Regional Archives WP996-36-10546

PLATE 181 *The Canadian Fish and Cold Storage Co. plant at Seal Cove in 1928. This very large facility was a major asset to the North Pacific halibut fishery.*

PLATE 182 *The Atlin Fisheries and Northern Fishermen's Cold Storage plants in 1938. The fishing industry kept Prince Rupert alive during the 1930s. In 2001, the Atlin Fishery building was converted into a passenger reception area for small cruise vessels and offices for the Prince Rupert Port Authority.*

PLATE 183 *Fish docks on the waterfront in 1941.*

Prince Rupert Shipyard and Dry Dock

Prince Rupert City and Regional Archives P996-119-11849

PLATE 184 *The Prince Rupert Shipyard and Dry Dock in 1925. This substantial facility and port asset was completed in 1916 by the Grand Trunk Pacific Railway on the promise of a $2 million federal subsidy.*

PLATE 185 *Launching the second steel freighter, the* Canadian Britisher, *for the Canadian Government Merchant Marine on October 6, 1921.*

PLATE 186 *The Prince Rupert Shipyard and Dry Dock in 1940.*

PLATE 187 *Prince Rupert Shipyard and Dry Dock at its peak of activity, 1943–1945.*

PLATE 188 *Harbour trials of one of the 15 freighters completed in Prince Rupert during WWII. Thirteen of these freighters were variants of the basic British "North Sands" design that was common to all 354 ten-thousand-ton freighters built in Canada, as well as to the 2,710 "Liberty" ships built in the U.S. during WWII.*

Wartime Developments at Prince Rupert

Between 1942 and 1945 the port was utilized by the U.S. military to move 1,121,653 tons of military cargo and 73,884 personnel to the Pacific Theatre. Most of the temporary facilities built by the Americans to supplement existing facilities were demolished shortly after the war.

PLATE 189 *The gun emplacement at Barrett Fort was one of several protecting the main entrance to Prince Rupert harbour during WWII. Work on the fixed artillery installation here and at Fort Frederick on Digby Island commenced in 1938.*

PLATE 190 *U.S. Army warehouse and overhead ramp to the Ocean Dock. This was one of many temporary facilities constructed in Prince Rupert by the U.S. military at a total cost of $16 million during the port's wartime stint as their "Sub-Port of Embarkation."*

PLATE 191 *Wartime camouflage on the large warehouse built by the U.S. military on Prince Rupert's waterfront. This was removed shortly after the end of WWII.*

PLATE 192 *Unloading military supplies at Ocean Dock in 1943.*

PLATE 193 *The U.S. Military's ammunition wharf at Watson Island in Porpoise Harbour. Celanese Corporation of America made use of this war-built wooden dock and the adjacent site on Watson Island when constructing the Columbia Cellulose pulp mill shortly after the war. The dock was destroyed by fire February 14, 1967 and replaced with a concrete structure.*

PLATE 194 *Unloading bombs from an ammunition ship at Watson Island in 1944.*

DEVELOPMENTS SINCE 1945

After three wartime years of unaccustomed port activity, the northern community very quickly returned to relying on the fishing industry for survival. Its population shrank by two-thirds. Further decline was only halted by the construction of a pulp mill by the Celanese Corporation at the Watson Island site that the U.S. military had developed and which included a wooden dock that they had used for loading ammunition. The aspiring port suffered two further blows, first in 1955 when the treasured floating dry dock was sold off to a Seattle firm and the shipyard was dismantled, and later when the Ocean Dock was destroyed by fire in 1972.

As a result of active local lobbying, an annex was added to the grain terminal in 1968. Concurrent huge grain sales to China and the USSR ensured that the enlarged facility began to be used fairly consistently, though at a level far below its capacity.

Frustration at the lack of any modern cargo handling facility led community leaders to pressure Ottawa to take positive action. This led, albeit painfully slowly, to the completion of the Fairview General Cargo Terminal in 1977. In response to increased lumber traffic from mills west of Prince George, the terminal was expanded in 1986.

Convinced that a major road to port development lay through the grain industry, the writer undertook an intensive and long term campaign for expansion of the port's grain terminal capacity and for the integration of the port into the overseas movement of grain through the West Coast. This eventually resulted in the completion of a modern high throughput grain elevator on Ridley Island in 1984. This facility brought the infrastructure to this valuable greenfield site that was also needed for the development of the coal terminal.

With three modern facilities operating by 1985, the port prospered over the next decade with throughput peaking at 13.8 million tonnes in 1994. A decade of decline followed with throughput falling to a low of 4.03 million tonnes in 2003.

A number of factors have since caused traffic to quadruple and the port is beginning to achieve the position envisioned for it a century ago. These include: new coal developments, the CNR's new policy directed at utilization of their north corridor line, the support of senior governments for converting Fairview Terminal to a modern rail-oriented container terminal and, above all, the increased dominance of transpacific trade.

PLATE 195 *Prince Rupert's waterfront, as seen looking northeast from the Ocean Dock in 1948.*

PLATE 196 *The inactive shipyard and dry dock in 1950.*

PLATE 197 *The first pulp mill on Watson Island and the wharf on Porpoise Harbour built by the U.S. military during WWII.*

PLATE 198 *A very sad day in Prince Rupert! In 1955, the tug,* Salvor, *towed the floating dry dock to its new owner in Seattle. For some, this seemed to symbolize the end of Prince Rupert's hopes to become a major port.*

J.R.Wrathall photo, Prince Rupert City and Regional Archives & Museum of Northern B.C. WP993-15-7169

PLATE 199 *The Canadian Grain Commission elevator with its newly completed annex in 1969.*

J.R. Wrathall photo, Prince Rupert City and Regional Archives & Museum of Northern B.C. WP997-38-12787

PLATE 200 *After the dry dock was sold and the shipyard buildings demolished, the site was used for several years by Prince Rupert Sawmills who loaded their export lumber on freighters at the former shipyard dock. The old wooden dock was declared unsafe by the WCB in 1968 and subsequently demolished.*

PLATE 201 *Seafloor drilling for hydrocarbons in Hecate Strait, May 16, 1968.*

PLATE 202 *The tug,* Comet, *with her rail barge, moved CNR cars loaded with pulp in Ketchikan to Prince Rupert for forward delivery by rail to the "lower forty-eight" over the 20-year period from 1954–1974.*

Courtesy Canadian National Railway

PLATE 203 *In 1982 the tug* John Brix *and new 55-car barge* Aquatrain *replaced earlier smaller vessels on the service connecting Prince Rupert with the Alaska Railroad terminal at Whittier, Alaska. The service has been operated by the CNR since 1962.*

Prince Rupert city and Regional Archives P988-4-3752

PLATE 204 *Fire destroyed the Ocean Dock on June 10, 1972.*

PLATE 205 *Aerial view at low tide of the harbour foreshore from Wahl's Boatyard to Casey Point. This is the site Western Wharves selected in 1967 for development as a general cargo terminal. The terminal was converted in 2003 to become this port's first container terminal.*

PLATE 206 *Fairview General Cargo Terminal, which opened in early 1977, approached capacity in the mid-1980s. A decision was made to enlarge the terminal in 1986.*

PLATE 207 *The expanded terminal at Fairview as seen in 1991.*

PLATE 208 *A nearly deserted Fairview terminal with its new pulp warehouses in May 2000.*

PLATE 209 *Provincially owned Ridley Island before any development.*

PLATE 210 *Loading the* World Prize, *the first vessel to berth at the new, high throughput grain terminal on Ridley Island in March, 1985.*

PLATE 211 *The new grain and coal terminals on Ridley Island loading large bulk carriers in mid-1999.*

PLATE 212 *Atlin Cruise Dock and Terminal. This fine facility for handling "pocket-size" cruise ships and large pleasure craft was completed in 2002.*

PLATE 213 *The Northland Cruise Terminal, comprising extensive shore side facilities and a berth for the largest vessels operating Alaska Cruises, was completed in May 2004.*

PLATE 214 *Fairview Container Terminal, key to the new "Northern Express Gateway and Corridor" link in the supply chain between Asia and North America began operation with the arrival of the* COSCO Antwerp *on October 30, 2007.*

PLATE 214A *The* COSCO Antwerp *berthed at the new Fairview Container Terminal on October 30, 2007, inaugurating the new service.*

PLATE 215 *The design of the new container terminal offers the operator the opportunity to move many containers directly from vessel to rail car.*

PLATE 216 *Twelve days after leaving Asia these containers arrived in Chicago on the first unit container train from Prince Rupert.*

PLATE 217 Wan He *departing Fairview Container Terminal for Vancouver and Seattle.*

PLATE 218 *A recent aerial view of the high throughput Prince Rupert Grain terminal on Ridley Island.*

PLATE 219 *Ridley Island Industrial Park. This flat, rail served, 450 hectare (1,124 acre) island is one of the very few rock based parcels adjacent to deep water on the B.C. coast that are available for major industrial developments.*

PLATE 220 *The* COSCO Prince Rupert *arriving April 8, 2011 at Fairview Terminal on her maiden voyage.*

Courtesy Lonnie Wishart Photography

PLATE 220A *The* COSCO Prince Rupert *on April 8, 2011 at Fairview Terminal on her maiden voyage.*

Courtesy John McDonald, Prince Rupert, B.C.

PLATE 221 *Canada's second Pacific Gateway, located on one of the world's finest natural deep-water harbours. Its proximity to Asia guarantees its future.*

CHAPTER NINE

The Gateways Since 2004 — Opening the Northern Corridor and Gateway

A dominant feature of this period has been the provincial and federal governments' enthusiastic attention to the potential for expanding Canada's role as the Pacific Gateway of choice, for rapidly increasing Asian trade with both Canada and the U.S. This attention has been backed by their apparent willingness to spend billions to achieve that goal. A major motivating factor is Ottawa's renewed awareness of the need to diversify Canadian trade, long centered on the U.S., toward other Pacific Rim countries. Another is its desire to complement British Columbia (B.C.) initiatives directed at assisting West Coast ports to capture more of the container traffic moving through U.S. Pacific ports to inland U.S. destinations.

The Ports Competitiveness Property Tax Initiative was first introduced by Victoria in November 2003 to cap municipal taxes on privately owned port facilities for a 5 year period. Later, it was extended to 2018, under legislation introduced by the Finance Minister in September 2007. In addition, it was amended so that the cap was indexed to inflation. This move confirmed the provincial government's intent to protect existing and potential investment in port facilities from excessive local property tax burdens, as well as to help reduce the heavy municipal tax burden carried by B.C. terminal operators, relative to their U.S. competitors.

The merger of the three lower mainland Port Authorities, first recommended by Sir Alexander Gibb in 1932, and many times since, was finally accomplished and became effective January 1, 2008. This event — of very great importance to the future of the Southern Gateway and achieved relatively smoothly — was enabled by provisions included in amendments to the *Canada Marine Act* that followed its mandated fifth year review. The merger has been accompanied by demands for senior governments to fund major infrastructure projects to ease road and rail congestion issues. These demands, which will cost billions to realize, came from virtually all organizations involved in operating Southern Gateway facilities. The merger also enabled new emphasis to be placed on short sea shipping to transload and distribution centres located along the Fraser River to further ease terminal access congestion.

Continuing concern with port security and a mounting focus on "Going Green" have become issues of prime importance to port administrations, reflecting the positions taken by local, regional, and senior governments worldwide.

This period has seen a major reshuffling of ownership or operating control for many of the terminals located on the lower mainland, including those handling grain, bulk, and break-bulk commodities and containers.

Expansion and upgrade programs at all four of the lower mainland container terminals were completed between 2004 and 2010 at a cost approaching $750 million. These projects have increased the handling capacity of these terminals to an estimated 3.7 million TEU annually. Throughput in 2010 recovered from the 13.6 percent slump in 2009, although the new figure of 2,514,309 TEU represents only a 0.0075 percent increase over the former peak year, 2007.

Foreign cargo moving through Southern Gateway terminals in 2010 reached a new high of 93,260,109 tonnes with the largest increases contributed by coal and fertilizers. Almost all traffic sectors showed recovery from their weakness in 2009, which had resulted from worldwide economic turmoil. Only cruise traffic continued its steep decline.

In 2004 the Northern Gateway began to recover from the series of blows encountered during the previous six years, aptly described as "the perfect storm." Throughput tripled between 2004 and 2009 with grain and coal traffic restored and with the very successful operation at Fairview of the new, purely rail oriented container terminal. For the first time in over eight decades, active support for the Northern Corridor and Gateway from the CNR and both levels of senior government was clearly evident. The rail line east to Red Pass Junction, designated a branch line since 1924, had at last achieved the status of a second main line to the Pacific. No longer would the Northern Gateway be restricted to drawing traffic from local or limited regional sources for solely export commodities. A century after its founding, the port city began to assume its destiny as a factor with considerable potential in transpacific export and import trade.

THE ADMINISTRATION OF NATIONAL PORTS

The *Canada Marine Act* achieved Royal Assent in 1998 and became effective January 1, 1999. It established, for the first time, comprehensive legislation governing many aspects of Canada's marine activities with a view to making the port system competitive, commercially oriented, and efficient. The Act required the Transport Ministry to complete a review of its provisions and operation, and report back to Parliament by the fifth anniversary of its passage.

To meet this requirement a review panel, appointed by the Minister, consulted with stakeholders and prepared a report that was tabled in the House of Commons in June 2003. Based on the report's recommendations, amendments were introduced to the House on November 16, 2007 and were passed in mid-2008. These amendments included provisions dealing with potential amalgamation of Port Authorities, measures to promote greater financial flexibility for the marine transportation sector (by streamlining the process for borrowing by major ports), and changes to enhance flexibility in the management of port lands. These moves were of special interest to West Coast ports. They had been by far the strongest lobbyists for changes to the 1998 Act because of their urgent need to get on with massive infrastructure projects in response to the continuing shift in world trade to the Asia Pacific region.

By late 2008, the Trans-Canada Port Divestiture Program, initiated under the National Marine Policy provision of the 1998 Act, had dealt with 472 out of 549 local and regional ports, mostly by turning them over to local ownership and control. Many of these were situated along the coast of British Columbia. Only a few very remote ports were expected to be retained. When completed it was estimated that this program would save Transport Canada $210 million annually.

PORT SECURITY PROGRAMS

Transport Canada has continued to actively support measures to enhance the security of Canadian ports in close harmony with security requirements in the United States. Its Marine Security Contribution Program funds up to 75 percent of the costs of modernizing and strengthening security systems and programs at Canadian ports and marine facilities.

The Marine Transportation Security Clearance Program, initially perceived to be over-zealous, was amended and implemented at Vancouver and Fraser Port on December 15, 2007 and at Prince Rupert a year later.

The Canadian Border Services Agency is also very involved in maritime security measures, particularly through its Container Services Initiative and Advanced Commercial Information Project. These multinational initiatives seek to identify, target, and intercept potential threats before they reach Canadian shores. Under the Advanced Commercial Information project, all goods shipped to Canada by sea must be electronically reported to the Border Services Agency at least 24 hours before loading on a ship at a foreign port. This information is then subjected to sophisticated risk analysis. Furthermore, every vessel approaching a Canadian Port is now required to send an electronic manifest detailing where it is registered, details of its crew, brokers, and cargo.

Concerns that the proliferation of security measures would surely decrease the efficiency of cargo handling at port facilities have been expressed, but there are clear instances where efficiency has been substantially increased. Closure of the waterfront road on the south shore of Burrard Inlet to public access in the interests of security has resulted in a reduction in traffic congestion in this vital area.

"GOING GREEN"

In recent years there has been a very marked increase in public awareness and worldwide concern over the issue of air pollution from marine traffic and port terminal operations.

Oxides of nitrogen and sulphur, as well as particulate matter released into the air by marine diesels burning low quality fuel have been identified as the most noxious pollutants. With 50,000 commercial vessels operating on the seven seas a resolution of this problem will be neither quick nor cheap.

North American ports are taking measures within their boundaries to reduce emissions from both berthed vessels and wheeled traffic operating on their terminals. To extend anti-pollution measures offshore, the IMO has declared all U.S. and Canadian waters within their respective Economic Exclusion Zones — extending 200 miles offshore — to be Emission Control Areas (ECA), effective July 1, 2010.

ANTI-POLLUTION MEASURES AT PORT TERMINALS

Measures taken to reduce noxious emissions from port terminal operations include using cleaner, or alternative fuels in terminal equipment and scheduling truck traffic to reduce long periods of idling diesel engines.

The problem of marine diesel emissions from berthed vessels has been approached by offering alternative marine power (AMP) at selected locations. This idea is not new. Naval vessels have long "plugged in" to shore installations, enabling them to shut down their internal diesel power plants and go "cold iron." Princess Cruises and Holland America Line were pioneers in equipping their cruise vessels to operate on shore power and the first port on the west coast of North America to provide "plug in" terminals was Juneau, Alaska, in 2002. Since then cruise vessel berths in Seattle and Vancouver have been equipped to offer this service. Vancouver's Canada Place facility completed its two-berth shore power project in August 2009. The $9 million cost was one-third funded by two federal agencies (Western Diversification Fund and Transport Canada), one-third by the Province of B.C., and the balance from B.C. Hydro, Port Metro Vancouver, Holland America and Princess Cruises. This shore power installation was the first to be completed in Canada.

Installation of shore power at cargo terminals is underway at some ports and especially at the twin ports of Long Beach and Los Angeles, where emission of air pollutants is a politically sensitive issue. The BP oil tanker terminal has been equipped with AMP at a cost of US$23.7 million, three-quarters of which was provided by the port. The twin ports have set aside US$180 million to provide for 25 more "cold iron" berths by 2011. Most of these will be container vessel berths.

Prince Rupert's Fairview Container Terminal will be the first in Canada to make marine shore power available to berthed container ships. This project, scheduled for completion in mid-2011, has received half its $3.6 million funding requirement from Transport Canada's Marine Shore Power program, a division of its ecoFREIGHT initiative designed to encourage using technology to reduce air pollution resulting from freight movements in Canada.

OFFSHORE MEASURES TO REDUCE AIR POLLUTION

The 50,000 horsepower engine of a Panamax sized container ship moving at 24 knots burns about 140 tons of fuel every 24 hours. This fuel may contain as much as 4.5 percent sulphur and thus constitutes an unacceptable source of the particularly noxious pollutant, sulphur dioxide. The IMO has set a global maximum contaminant level for marine fuel at 3.5percent sulphur but, for vessels operating within the Emission Control Areas off the North American coast, this standard has become very much stricter. By August 2012, vessels moving within the ECA off Canada and the US must burn fuel with less than 1 percent sulphur content and, by 2015 this limit is reduced to 0.1 percent.

Understandably, ship owners have expressed concern, not only about the extra costs involved to meet this standard, but also about the availability of such ultra-low sulphur fuel at many of the world's bunkering facilities. Owners of "tramp" bulker fleets are particularly concerned, protesting that their industry is by far the greenest if emissions are measured against tonnage carried.

THE RENEWED FOCUS ON PACIFIC GATEWAYS AND CORRIDORS

The concept of Canada's Pacific Coast as a gateway between Asian countries and North America has a long history.

Captain Cook's crews traded with the locals for sea otter pelts during their 1778 visit to Vancouver Island's west coast and later reaped handsome profits from the sale of these much-coveted furs in China. With the arrival on the B.C. coast of Captain James Hanna's *Sea Otter* in 1785, a regular trade in furs began with buyers in Canton. Between 1790 and 1812 up to 24 vessels were annually engaged in acquiring these pelts from hard bargaining natives and then selling them in China.

The promoters of all three Trans-Canada railways used the prospects for their western port terminals — as entry points for Asian trade to both North American and European (via land bridge) markets — as one justification for building their lines. All three, in addition, planned fleets of transpacific liners to provide traffic to and from the Orient through their ports to their railways. Only the Canadian Pacific Railway succeeded.

In 1909 the Vancouver Information Bureau promoted the city as the "British Pacific Gateway: British Columbia, the treasure house of Canada and Vancouver, its greatest seaport," and early issues of *Harbour & Shipping* magazine, first published in 1918, carried the slogan "Published at Canada's Gateway to the Pacific" on the masthead.

Japan's post-war recovery catapulted it to a position as one of the world's great trading nations and its heavy dependence on raw material imports gave great impetus to transpacific trade, as well as to the development of the Southern Corridor and Port of Vancouver. This trade soon replaced the traditional dependence on transatlantic trade via Panama, which had limited the rate of port development and had virtually precluded the development of the Northern Gateway Port. Then, under new and pragmatic leadership in the 1980s, reforms in China released that huge population's impressive entrepreneurial skills and motivation. China's economic renaissance quickly spread to other densely populated nations in Southeast Asia and India and soon vast quantities of consumer products flooded into overseas markets.

Aware of the enormity of this change in world trade patterns, ports on the west coast of the U.S. and the lower mainland of B.C. scrambled to provide specialized terminals to cope with the increasing movement of both bulk and break-bulk commodity exports, as well as increasing numbers of containers filled with imported consumer goods. The new container terminals needed intermodal yards to transfer containers efficiently from ship to railcars or trucks. Ideally, they also needed an uncongested passage to expedite the movement of those containers to both regional and distant destinations. Railways, too, had to make large investments. Not only did they need to efficiently move huge tonnages of bulk commodities to the coast; they also had to move increasing numbers of containers to and from points across North America where intermodal yards had to be built to collect and distribute them.

Over the past three decades, awareness of the rising economic power of the new Asian "Tigers" and their impact on world trade patterns has led to various government initiatives. Their purpose has been to study this phenomenon and to respond in an orderly manner, tailoring assistance to maximize the benefits for Canada.

Determined to diversify Canadian trade from its near total dependence on the U.S., the Trudeau government, in a 1970 Foreign Policy White Paper, offered the country a "Third Option," which emphasized trade with countries on the Pacific Rim.

The creation of the Asia Pacific Foundation of Canada in 1984 provided a national think tank to foster Canada-Asia relations and promote greater awareness of Asia among Canadians. Then, from 1987 to 1990, the joint Federal Provincial Asia Pacific Initiative, with $6 million in funding, completed 60 studies in areas such as transportation, tourism, finance, and education. In 1997, Canada's "Year of the Asia Pacific" culminated in the APEC summit held in Vancouver and, in 2001, Western Economic Diversification's "Gateway to Asia" project was established to link Canadian goods and services to Asian markets.

The mission of the Greater Vancouver Gateway Council, established in 1994, was to plan the expansion of local infrastructure to provide efficient logistical services that would expedite Asian trade. The B.C. Government, in 2003, initiated a $1.1 billion plan called "Opening up B.C." with a similar mission, although not confined to Vancouver. Two years later, the province launched its Asia Pacific Gateway Initiative, calling for expenditures of up to $12.1 billion on new infrastructure projects, as well as cultural and educational initiatives. The visit of China's President Hu Jintao to the West Coast in September of 2005 added impetus to this plan.

On October 20, 2005 the federal government introduced the *Pacific Gateway Act*. That act established and funded a Vancouver based Pacific Gateway Council to promote consensus among private and public sector stakeholders and to advise decision makers on priorities.

The day after introducing the Act Ottawa released details of its Pacific Gateway Strategy, in recognition of the potential of Canada's West Coast ports to provide gateways for the rapid, seamless, and secure movement of goods to and from the burgeoning Asian economies. It was also a response to active prodding by the BC government. This strategy included plans to spend up to $590 million on projects to enhance the effectiveness of the existing gateway structure. Though strongly focused on the Southern Gateway, the Pacific Gateway Strategy was presented as a pan Western initiative designed to remove impediments to the efficient flow of trade with Asian countries, to the ultimate benefit of all Canadians.

Defeat of the Martin government in January 2006 brought a temporary halt to this initiative. Then, in October 2006, the new Harper government announced a modified version called the Asia Pacific Gateway and Corridor Initiative and increased the funding to $1.1 billion. An additional $2.1 billion was earmarked for infrastructure at gateways and border crossings. This commitment focused strongly on upgrades and additions to Canada's Pacific port infrastructure and on providing assistance to other projects deemed related to improving road and rail corridors in western Canada that served the Pacific ports.

This welcome interest by both senior governments was strongly stimulated by the awareness that other countries were investing heavily in infrastructure and related initiatives designed to take advantage of trade opportunities. The U.S. government for example, approved a five-year plan in 2005 to spend $286.5 billion to provide safe, efficient, and flexible transportation of goods. U.S. Pacific ports expanded aggressively to capitalize on Asian trade growth. Furthermore, Chinese investment in new Mexican port developments, designed to capture a share of North American trade, gave added impetus to the Ottawa and Victoria initiatives.

Direct federal government commitments to projects oriented to achieving the goals of the Asia Pacific Gateway and Corridor Initiative have been supplemented by funding from other federal agencies including the Western Diversification Fund, Border Infrastructure programs, and the more recent Infrastructure Stimulus Fund. By mid-2010, over three-quarters of a billion federal dollars had been committed from these programs to projects at the Southern Gateway, primarily to enhance the performance of the port's terminals by relieving congestion and improving access. These include massive road corridor and bridge projects, road/rail grade separations, dredging programs, barge docks for short sea shippers, and repairs to the roof of Canada Place. Almost all of these projects have been predicated on cost sharing by the Province, municipal governments, the Port Authority, or private partners.

Though the Northern Gateway is proclaimed part of the APGCI vision, federal funding for projects at the Port of Prince Rupert over the same time period totalled only $63.9 million. Of that amount, $30.7 million came from Western Economic Diversification

Fund and $28 million from APGCI funding for a Customs Marine Container Program for the Canadian Border Services Agency, both related to the development of the Fairview Container Terminal.

THE SOUTHERN GATEWAY SINCE 2004

Including the extensive and valuable riverfront properties of the two former Fraser Port Authorities into the merged Vancouver Fraser Port Authority has added impetus to the development of short sea shipping and the expansion of ancillary facilities on the river facilities. In addition, the consolidated Port Authorities combined with Southern Gateway municipal governments to increase pressure on senior governments to fund major infrastructure projects to ease congestion on routes serving present and prospective port facilities.

Since 2004, a number of Southern Gateway terminals have undergone ownership changes as well as significant expansion or upgrade programs. The Berth Three expansion project at Deltaport container terminal was completed in January 2010 giving the port substantial excess capacity. Hence, with 2010 container throughput only 0.0075 percent above 2007 levels, there would appear to be little urgency to proceed with the massive Terminal Two project, at least until a more robust growth pattern is firmly established.

The grain handling and transportation system continues to evolve. For the first time in 83 years, canola displaced wheat in 2009 as the leading bulk grain export through the port and continued at a high throughput level in 2010. Increasingly, grains, and particularly specialty agricultural products, are being exported in containers. This trend will progressively reduce the long held dominance of the conventional grain elevators and may also result in the eventual closure of the two bulk "ag-product" terminals built on the north shore in the early eighties.

Traffic at the port's cruise terminals continued its steep decline in 2010. The loss of half this seasonal business since its peak in 2002 is primarily due to aggressive post 9/11 competition from Seattle, exacerbated in the past two years by the U.S. economic crisis.

The one bulk commodity group to avoid the relatively stagnant performance shown by the dry bulk sector since 2004 has been the liquid bulk group, including petroleum and chemical exports.

LOCAL PORT ADMINISTRATION: 2004 TO 2010

Background

Many would contend that the most significant event of the last decade at the Southern Gateway has been the amalgamation of the three local port authorities into the single Vancouver Fraser Port Authority, dubbed Port Metro Vancouver. This eminently sensible union has been a long time coming.

Until the arrival of the CPR in 1886, port activity on Burrard Inlet depended solely on the export of forest products from sawmills along its shoreline. A boom in river transportation accompanied the construction of the railway, but its completion, followed by the rapid growth of Vancouver, resulted in the new city quickly displacing New Westminster as the chief port and commercial centre on the mainland. To citizens and promoters of the "Royal City," who had already suffered the indignity of it losing its position as the provincial capital to Victoria, this second loss was not taken lightly. Using well nurtured political connections, they were able to extract substantial sums from Ottawa for continuing upgrades to the navigable river channel as far as the city's riverfront docks, and were successful in getting their own Harbour Commission in 1913 at the same time as the Vancouver Harbour Commission was established.

Despite Sir Alexander Gibb's 1932 firm recommendation to Parliament that the ports of Vancouver, North Fraser, and New Westminster be combined under a single port authority, the two Fraser ports managed to retain their independent status, while Vancouver, in 1936, had to reluctantly accept the rigid central control of the new National Harbours Board. In support of his recommendation Gibb had contended, with considerable justification, that the existing competition between Vancouver and New Westminster was artificial, and only made possible by extensive and continual federal funding.

Under the *Harbour Commissions Act* of 1964, the New Westminster Harbour Commission became the Fraser River Harbour Commission (FRHC). Not only had the threat of merger with Vancouver passed, but it retained considerably more freedom to manoeuvre under its mandate than its much larger neighbour — to the considerable chagrin of the latter.

Determined to compete with Vancouver for the rapidly growing container handling business, the FRHC added a fully equipped container facility to its south shore Fraser Surrey Dock complex. This opened in December 1974, six months ahead of Vanterm on Burrard Inlet. For the next 20 years the new container terminal saw very little use but, to the frustration of the Vancouver terminal operators, the Fraser facility made a deal with Puget Sound terminals in 1988 to develop a barge service to move containers between their facilities.

Stung by accusations of weak performance relative to their Puget Sound and California competitors in providing suitable facilities for the rapidly growing container trade, the Vancouver Port Corporation took action. In 1993, it commissioned J. Seymour to study and comment on its relationship to Ports Canada and to the FRHC. Seymour's report strongly recommended merging the two Fraser ports with Vancouver. The FRHC responded with a strong rebuttal to Seymour's recommendation and successfully maintained its independence for another 15 years, despite growing evidence of injudicious spending on some capital programs.

While reconfirming their independence, the *Canada Marine Act* of 1998 changed the designation of the two Fraser Harbour Commissions to Port Authorities with a new obligation to pay dividends to Ottawa. The new Fraser River Port Authority (ex-FRHC ex-NWHC) was also required to assume full responsibility for maintaining the navigable river channel to its facilities, in return for a onetime $15 million grant.

Though the two auto terminals and the Fraser Surrey Dock complex facilities were primarily engaged in foreign import and export trade, by far the largest tonnage throughput for both Fraser Port Authorities flowed from domestic business. The prize assets they could bring to a merger were their extensive waterfront property holdings — wisely accumulated in past years and coveted by the cash rich, but land poor Vancouver Authority.

The Merger

The thrust of the National Marine Policy was directed toward streamlining Canada's major ports and accordingly, it supported the pressures from Vancouver to consolidate all Southern Gateway facilities under one Authority. A "Common Gate" report commissioned by Ottawa confirmed the benefits that could accrue from such a merger, as well as its feasibility. With strong support from the provincial government, the project became a major goal of the Asia Pacific Gateway and Corridor Initiative. The union of the three Port Authorities became effective January 1, 2008 forming the Vancouver Fraser Port Authority with total domestic and international throughput that year of 128 million tonnes. Plans called for $4.5 billion in new infrastructure spending over the next decade to cope with the anticipated growth in Asia Pacific trade.

A portion of the infrastructure spending would be used to create a marine highway for the short sea shipping of containers to riverfront intermodal and distribution facilities, thereby reducing truck traffic in the lower mainland. By reducing truck traffic, pollution — a source of strong citizen complaints — would also be reduced. In addition to the potential benefits of a marine highway on the river, the merger has eliminated competition between the former Southern Gateway authorities and enabled the merged Port Authority to make strategic decisions regarding where and when to place new facilities. Port Metro Vancouver (PMV) terminals should now be able to compete more effectively with their opposite numbers in Puget Sound.

RAIL AND ROAD ACCESS ISSUES AND THE SOUTHERN RAIL CORRIDOR

Problems relating to inadequate rail and road access to bulk, break-bulk, and container terminals at the Southern Gateway have been increasingly evident in the last decade and have damaged the port's reputation. Illustrating this is the fact that over the past decade the segment of the grain-car cycle from Red Pass Junction to Vancouver has averaged 3–3.5 days longer than from the same junction point to Prince Rupert, despite the extra 309 km (192 miles) distance to the Northern Gateway Port. Unquestionably, the greater part of this disparity relates to congestion and access issues in the vicinity of the Southern Gateway's terminals.

The main thrust of the Asia Pacific Gateway & Corridor Initiative (APGCI) and the Provincial Gateway Program has been directed at projects designed to alleviate the twin problems of terminal access and road and rail congestion within the Southern Gateway. Each program has involved cost sharing with various partners, both public and private.

Key components of the Gateway Program are the road and rail access projects extending east from Roberts Bank. The $1 billion South Fraser Perimeter Road, one-third funded by Ottawa, will move truck traffic 40 km east from Deltaport to connect with a number of provincial highways. The $360 million "Roberts Bank Rail Corridor" has been designed to enhance the efficiency and safety of rail operations and accommodate increased traffic. Its funding includes a $75 million grant from APGCI with the balance shared between the B.C. Ministry of Transport, Translink, the Port Authority, the CPR, CNR, BNSF and BCR railways, the affected municipalities, and the Greater Vancouver Gateway Council.

Another major program involves the spending of $225 million on five projects designed to enhance port and rail operations to the bulk and break-bulk terminals located on the north shore of Burrard Inlet. The federal government has committed to a third of this sum through its Asia Pacific Gateway and Corridor Initiative.

Yet another program seeks to improve road and rail access to the south shore terminals by the construction of 11 overpasses at a cost of $125 million. The federal contribution to this project is $49.7 million with the balance from the City of Vancouver, the B.C. Government, the CPR and CNR railways, and the grain and container terminals.[5]

While these and other very large investments, mainly of public funds, will at least partially alleviate the long existing rail and road access problems within the Southern Gateway, they add no new capacity and do nothing to address the capacity limitations on the main rail corridor to the port. Neither do they diminish the inherent danger for Canada's transpacific trade of depending so heavily on the southern rail corridor.

In the last five years the CNR has moved to take advantage of their Northern Corridor to relieve the strain on their line south. The CPR has no such option and its customers have already, on occasion, had to face the consequences of the line's capacity limitations.

THE SOUTHERN GATEWAY CONTAINER TERMINALS SINCE 2004

Traffic through the Southern Gateway container terminals continued its spectacular growth with average annual increments of 11.5 percent, over the two decades from 1989 to 2008. Forecasts of future growth varied considerably. The Vancouver Port Authority optimistically predicted 8.8 million TEU passing through its terminals by 2020, while the Province's B.C. Ports Strategy document, released in 2005, and the follow up, Pacific Gateway Strategy Action Plan projected a more modest combined throughput of 5–7 million TEU for the combined Northern and Southern Gateway Ports by that same year, based on the assumption

---

[5]See Appendix 2 for full list of these programs.

that by then they will have increased their market share to 14–15 percent of North American West Coast container traffic. Others believe that the period of torrid growth has peaked and that, with demand levelling off, emphasis should be placed on improving the efficiency and productivity of existing facilities and their road and rail access corridors, rather than proceeding with another massive terminal development at Roberts Bank. Furthermore, it is most unlikely that the U.S. West Coast ports and their railway corridors will not react in the face of lost market share.

Though impressive, the double digit growth in Vancouver's container traffic up to 2008 has been very heavily oriented to moving containerized cargo within Canada and represented only 9 percent of all container traffic through North American West Coast ports. Unlike Canada's East Coast container ports, where much of their boxed traffic moves to and from the U.S., the West Coast Southern Gateway has been much less successful in attracting U.S. bound boxes to its terminals. Increasing Canada's share of container movement through the continent's West Coast ports from 9 percent to at least 14 percent is a prime goal in the strategy behind the Asia Pacific Gateway and Corridor Initiative.

The stated goal of the APGCI is an annual West Coast throughput in excess of 7 million TEU by 2020. However, not all this hoped for increase in traffic will pass over Southern Gateway facilities (especially if destined for the U.S. Midwest), and many other factors will have their impact, including the state of the North American economy, the value of the Canadian dollar, aggressive U.S. port and rail competition and protectionism, the expansion of the Panama Canal, ocean freight rates, and so on.

Projections are notoriously unreliable and, certainly, few progressions continue their course in a straight line. The 13.6 percent drop in container throughput to 2.15 million TEU at the Southern Gateway terminals in the recession year 2009 has prompted a sober second look at future projections. Earlier optimistic forecasts that growth in transpacific trade would continue at double digit rates far into the future led to massive investments in terminal facilities at the U.S. ports in Puget Sound and at Long Beach, Los Angeles, and Oakland, as well as in the rail lines serving them. These expansions have resulted in painful overcapacity in the face of the downturn in global trade. These ports, together with the two Class I railroads that operate their access corridors, have recently formed a "U.S. West Coast Collaboration Unit" with the goal of capturing more transpacific trade. Canadian terminal operators and railroads will find them very tough competitors, especially for traffic to and from points in the "lower forty-eight."

Centerm

The major expansion and re-equipment program at the port's oldest container terminal was completed in September 2006 by new owner, DP World, who had acquired the operation as part of their acquisition of P&O Ports earlier that year. Although $148 million was spent to double the revamped facility's capacity, limitations in rail access and berth availability restrict its potential to about 780,000 TEU per year. The 29.14 hectare (73 acre) terminal was re-equipped to operate with rubber tired gantry cranes in place of its former "top pick" type of facility, giving it the highest density of any of the Southern Gateway terminals. Its two container berths are served by six new, or refurbished container cranes and offer 15.25 m (50.85 ft.) of water depth. The remaining berths serve break-bulk and general cargo.

Vanterm

Since the expansion program completed in 2005, Vanterm has taken further measures to increase its efficiency and now has a rated capacity of 700,000–750,000 TEU annually on its 31 hectare (76 acre) site. As a high density terminal with half its containers moved in or out of the terminal by truck, it has been especially exposed to the adverse effect of periodic strikes by truckers, in addition to the occasional disruption in rail service. The two container berths are served by six modern cranes and offer 50–51 feet of water depth. A third berth handles break-bulk, project cargo, and liquid bulk shipments.

In 2007, the Ontario Teachers' Pension Plan acquired TSI Terminal Systems, operator of both Vanterm and Deltaport, from Orient Overseas International Ltd. TSI then became a subsidiary of GCT Global Container Terminals Inc. with operations also in New York and New Jersey.

Deltaport

After three years of environmental reviews and public consultation, and after overcoming considerable resistance from opponents to further terminal developments on the Fraser River estuary, the "Third Berth" project got underway in 2007. Completed in January 2010 at the substantially escalated cost of $400 million, the project added 20 hectares (50 acres) of storage and operating area plus a third berth, increasing the terminal's capacity by 50 percent to 1.8 million TEU per year. Trackage was increased substantially and the new berth equipped with three new dual hoist, super post-panamax cranes. In addition, the existing ship channel was deepened and an adjacent tug moorage area created. Completion of this project lifts PMV's estimated annual container throughput capacity to 3.7 million TEU.

Convinced that the Southern Gateway would require the capacity to handle 8.8 million TEU annually by 2020, the Vancouver Port Authority began, in 2007, to plan a second terminal at Roberts Bank that would raise Deltaport's capacity to 4 million TEU. Cost estimates for the project are in the order of $750 million dollars. In the spring of 2008, Maersk/Sea-Land was chosen as operating partner for the project, but Terminal Two quickly ran into strong and vocal opposition from a citizen's group in South Delta who called themselves "Against Port Expansion" with the slogan "Stop Terminal 2 Now." Added to this resistance was the recognition that existing terminals were operating far below their capacity and that investment in more container terminal facilities would be of little use without very substantial improvements to road and rail access. As a result, the project has been delayed, while priority is given to infrastructure upgrades and exploration of more effective ways to move containers within the confines of the Southern Gateway.

Fraserport

Thirty-five years after its opening in 1974, the container handling component of the Fraser Surrey Dock complex began to attract vessels to its recently modernized facility. From throughput of 31,921 containers in 1999, its growth was rapid reaching 372,844 TEU in the year 2005. Based on this new found success, the Fraser River Port Authority, Fraser Surrey Docks, and IDC Distribution Services together invested $190 million in upgrades to the terminal including two new cranes and a 7.5 hectare (19 acre) intermodal yard adjacent to the dock. On completion of this project in 2005, the terminal was deemed capable of comfortably handling 400,000 TEU annually.

Unfortunately, most of the terminal's growth had come from one carrier, CP Ships. When that company was sold to Hapag Lloyd in 2006 the new owner consolidated all its port calls at a Burrard Inlet terminal with the result that Fraserport lost 73 percent of its business (mostly to the Vancouver terminals), with throughput dropping to 94,051 TEU in 2006. The adjacent IDC intermodal facility lost 93 percent of its business in this traumatic event. Fraserport's subsequent aggressive marketing successfully attracted new container lines and throughput recovered somewhat, reaching 191,402 TEU in 2007.

The Fraser Surrey Dock complex, including the adjacent IDC Distribution services intermodal facility was sold to New York based Macquarie Infrastructure Partners in 2007. This subsidiary of Macquarie Bank of Australia also operates Halterm in Halifax and so becomes the first terminal operator with facilities on both the Atlantic and Pacific coasts of Canada. It also has a 40 percent ownership in Hanjin terminals in Oakland and Long Beach, California.

Ancillary Facilities

As the port's container terminals have developed and grown, there has been a parallel development of logistic services designed to efficiently process both inbound cargo and cargo destined for export in containers. A substantial number of containers stuffed with imported goods destined for local, regional, and national markets have their contents removed, sorted, and repacked for onward movement to final destination by truck or rail. Goods received for export in containers, such as lumber or agricultural products, must be properly stowed in an appropriate sized container and then moved to a terminal for vessel loading. Maximum efficiency can be gained when both operations are performed at the same location.

In addition to these logistic services, facilities are also required for the storage, cleaning and repair of containers, the disposal of those no longer suited to normal use, and the thorough examination by the Canadian Border Services Agency of those considered "of interest."

Over the past 20 years, many facilities have been developed in the lower mainland to deal with these requirements. All have road and rail connections and some have waterfront locations either adjacent to an existing container terminal or on riverfront sites with a barge terminal installation. Examples of the former exist in the cluster of logistic facilities adjacent to the Fraser Surrey Dock complex and of the latter, the Modalink Vancouver Gateway Hub in Richmond operated by Coast 2000 Terminals.

Approximately two-thirds of containers moving through the Southern Gateway arrive or leave the port's terminals by rail. The remaining third moves by truck and has, in recent years, caused widespread and escalating concern because of increasing congestion of the Greater Vancouver road and highway network. Air pollution from diesel trucks, perceived to be excessive, and safety issues have added to these concerns.

Much of the spending under the APGCI has been directed at reducing the impact of these legitimate issues. While constituting the primary goal of the APGCI, another initiative aims at encouraging the development of short sea shipping services, utilizing the Fraser River as a marine highway for the lower mainland region.

Short Sea Shipping

Short sea shipping can be succinctly defined as the movement of freight on water without crossing an ocean. The concept is certainly not new and is well developed in Europe and some places in the U.S. as a method to reduce road and highway congestion, as well as the air pollution associated with heavy truck traffic. The desire to have a competitive alternative to the trucking industry has been an added stimulus.

In 2004 Transport Canada, the Vancouver and Fraser River Port Authorities, and the Fraser River Estuary Management Program commissioned a study of the potential for a commercially viable short sea movement of containers within the lower mainland region. The study, released in 2005, concluded that such a service could be commercially competitive to trucking, under certain volume conditions, and stressed the need to acquire strategically located sites to develop barge-served terminals. The subsequent urgency to amalgamate the three Port Authorities largely stemmed from the Vancouver Port Authority's need to access the rich inventory of riverfront land held by the Fraser Port Authorities.

Competition for scarce suitable sites has been keen and the costs of acquiring them very high. Most of the sites considered suitable in the 2005 report were snapped up by developers for residential or light industrial projects. PMV's recent acquisition of the former 18.21 hectare (45 acre) CanFor waterfront site in New Westminster is a case in point and was only achieved after a struggle with the City of New Westminster, which wanted it for other purposes. Another plan to develop a barge-served container terminal on environmentally sensitive wetland in Mission has created considerable controversy in that up-river community.

To assist the development of short sea shipping in the lower mainland region the federal government, in September 2008, offered to contribute $20.9 million from APGCI funds, primarily for five short sea projects. Two of these would build barge berths at Vanterm and Deltaport, while the other three would involve constructing specialized facilities including docks, ramps and other infrastructure handling containers, railcars, trailers, and break bulk cargoes.

Short sea shipping at the Southern Gateway is a work in progress. Its commercial viability and success in resolving issues of road congestion and air pollution wait to be seen.

THE DRY AND BREAK-BULK TERMINALS SINCE 2004

There was virtually no growth in the collective overseas movement of coal, sulphur, potash, pulp, and other forest products over the bulk and break-bulk terminals located at the Southern Gateway in the 20 years from 1989 to 2008. During the recession years 2008 and 2009, exports of forest products and potash were especially hard hit. Despite this lack of growth, these major bulk and break-bulk commodities still form by far the greatest part of the port's tonnage throughput. For all the attention paid in recent years to the container and cruise passenger traffic, PMV is still very much a bulk and break-bulk port, especially when liquid bulk and bulk agricultural products are included. Indeed, despite the growing significance and importance of container handling to the port, it represents only a quarter of the foreign cargo handled, or 20 percent of the combined foreign and domestic tonnage moved over the port's many facilities. The other 80 percent allows PMV its bragging rights as the largest port in Canada and one of the few in the world handling over 100,000,000 tonnes annually.

Kinder Morgan Vancouver Wharves

The BCR Group announced their intent to sell all three components of subsidiary BCR Marine in 2002. Finally, in 2007, the sale of Vancouver Wharves was concluded with Kinder Morgan Canada Terminals Inc., a division of a large, Texas based pipeline and terminal operator. The deal included a 40-year lease on the site.

The terminal's 56.3 hectares (139 acres) contain facilities for the export and import of mineral concentrates, and the export of sulphur, specialty agricultural products, wood pellets, and other break-bulk and liquid bulk commodities. It is equipped with loop tracks and four berths with draft adequate to load panamax-size vessels. Soon after acquiring the terminal, Kinder Morgan embarked on a two-year, $119 million program of expenditures on new trackage and other capacity enhancements. The terminal's agricultural products facility, brought on stream in 2000, has attracted insufficient business to be viable and is being phased out in favour of other bulk products. A new program to expand and upgrade facilities for handling copper concentrates began in 2010.

Neptune Terminals

This terminal is operated by Neptune Terminals on behalf of a joint venture between bulk commodity shippers led by Canpotex with over 50 percent ownership. It is rated as the largest multiproduct bulk terminal in North America and handles coal, potash, agricultural products, bulk fertilizers, and canola oil over its three berths. Plans to spend $93 million to expand potash storage capacity were announced in 2005. Then in mid-2008, Canpotex revealed plans to double potash exports through the West Coast, divided between additions to Neptune capacity and a new facility on Ridley Island at Prince Rupert. The precipitous drop in overseas potash sales in 2009 delayed the execution of this expansion but, in December 2009, the company gave the go ahead to a $37 million expenditure on the existing potash facility, designed to increase its capacity by 1.5 million tonnes per year. Total potash throughput recovered in 2010 to slightly exceed the average of the previous six years.

Reacting to the problems caused by the difficult rail access to the north shore bulk terminals, Neptune has vocally pressed for more balance in infrastructure spending between container and bulk terminals, under the APGCI, and has sought assistance from Gateway funds to develop a deep draft, all weather, covered berth for loading potash. The company has also stressed the need for funding to replace the federally owned and heavily used Fraser River rail bridge, now over a century old.

Lynnterm: East and West Gates

This break-bulk terminal represents the merger of the former Seaboard and Lynnterm facilities straddling Lynn Creek and North Vancouver's Harbourview Park that occurred in 2002. The terminal offers 58.68 hectares (145 acres) of heavy pavement, seven berths, eight warehouses, and a barge ramp. The terminal is owned and operated by Western Stevedoring on land leased from the Vancouver Fraser Port Authority. Western Stevedoring was purchased from long time owners Seaboard International and General Steamship Int. Ltd. in 2005–2006. The purchaser was the SSA Marine Division of Carrix, a company controlled by two Seattle families, with Goldman Sachs of New York holding a 49 percent interest. In the face of declining break-bulk volumes, Western Stevedoring is now combined with Westcan Terminals and Westcan Stevedoring, all members of the "Western Group" of companies owned by Carrix. Carrix also acquired the Coast 2000 terminal in Richmond in 2004.

Long considered the world's largest forest products terminal, the facility has faced difficult times in recent years, as a result not only of the overall reduction in forest products exports, but also because an increasing percentage of these shrinking exports are now moved to markets in containers, rather than in the traditional break-bulk package that is loaded onto specially designed and equipped carrier vessels. In addition to traditional forest products, logs, pulp, paper, general and project cargoes, the terminal now handles increasing amounts of steel, much of it brought to the terminal in forest product carriers.

Squamish Terminals Inc.

This break-bulk terminal at the head of Howe Sound, 32 nautical miles north of Vancouver, primarily serves vessels belonging to its owner, Grieg Star Shipping AS of Bergen Norway. The terminal was built and equipped specifically to load export forest products brought by rail from central and north central B.C. mills onto its owners' specialized open hatch vessels. In the face of falling forest product exports, the terminal now handles imported steel and special project cargoes such as windmill blades and turbines.

Fibreco

Since 1979 this north shore Burrard Inlet facility has been shipping woodchips, primarily to Japan and Europe, from the mills of its owners, a coalition of interior and coast sawmills. In 2005 the terminal added facilities and equipment to handle biomass wood pellets, a product much in demand, especially in Europe. This involved modifying conveyors, car dumper and ship loading equipment, as well as providing six storage silos collectively able to store 27,000 tonnes of pellets. With this equipment the terminal loads woodchips at the rate of 1,000 tonnes per hour and wood pellets at 800 tonnes per hour.

Pacific Coast Terminals

This Port Moody terminal, wholly owned by Sultran, specializes in handling sulphur and bulk liquid ethylene glycol, by-products of petroleum and natural gas processing in Alberta. The 43 hectare (108 acre) terminal stores sulphur in open windrow piles and loads it to vessels at the rate of 5,000 tonnes per hour. It ships an average 3.5 million tonnes annually to world markets on vessels up to 80,000 tonnes. Ethylene glycol is received in tank cars, stored in sealed storage tanks, and then loaded onto vessels averaging in size from 12,000–30,000 tonnes, for an average movement of 750,000 tonnes yearly.

Westshore Terminals

Westshore reached its peak throughput of 23.5 million tonnes in 1997. Since 2002 the terminal has averaged 21 million tonnes yearly, or about 30 percent of PMV's total foreign export tonnage. The terminal is operated by Westshore Terminals Limited Partnership on behalf of the partnership's owner, Westshore Terminals Income Fund. The terminal plays a significant role in the world seaborne movement of coal that reached 761 million tonnes in 2007.

After renewing its lease with the Port Authority on more acceptable terms effective January 1, 2007, Westshore embarked on a three-year, $49 million expansion program in anticipation of growth in coal exports. The project, which included adding a fourth stacker reclaimer, new conveyors, and dumper replacements, has increased the terminal's rated annual throughput capacity from 24 to 29 million tonnes.

Most of the coal shipped over this terminal comes from mines in southeastern B.C. operated by Teck Resources Ltd. and is moved 1,150 km (714 miles) to the terminal in six unit trains daily, each train making a round trip in 80 hours. Teck also ships coal through the facilities of Neptune Terminals, in which it has 46 percent ownership.

Since 1991 Westshore has periodically handled shipments of energy coal from properties in Utah, Wyoming, and Montana. Due to the cost of the very long rail haul, the potential for overseas exports from these mines depends on the world price for the commodity, and this fluctuates over a wide range. Exports through Westshore from U.S. mines reached a record 2 million tonnes in 2009 and have held at about that level since. A planned new bulk terminal at Cherry Point in Washington State would likely handle shipments from these mines in future.

Fraser Surrey Docks LP

This multipurpose break-bulk and container terminal abruptly lost three-quarters of its newly thriving container business when CP Ships withdrew in early 2006. However, the break-bulk and other cargo components of the terminal complex that straddle the container facility were not affected and have continued to move an average of 4 million tonnes of foreign imports and exports yearly, including packaged lumber, pulp, steel, logs, project, and general cargoes. The terminal has excellent connections to the CPR, CNR, BNSF, and Southern railways and can offer 18,000 feet of adjacent holding track owned by the Port Authority.

The terminal facilities depend on continuing programs of river channel dredging to maintain a depth of at least 11 m (36 ft.) to their berths.

GRAIN AND AGRICULTURAL PRODUCTS HANDLING SINCE 2004

Changes in Grain Terminal Ownership Completed

By late 2005 Agricore United had failed to complete the sale of the former UGG terminal that had been mandated by the Competition Bureau four years earlier and, in 2006, a trustee was appointed to manage its disposal. In April 2007 the trustee concluded an agreement with Terminal West Ltd., a consortium of six grain shippers to own and operate the terminal. The terminal was renamed Alliance Grain Terminal and has since doubled its throughput. The relatively shallow loading berths serving both the Alliance and the Pacific terminals preclude complete loading of large vessels and are thus major contributors to the port's high (50–60 percent) multiple berth, bulk grain loading record.

To improve efficiency through specialization the two north shore terminals, Saskatchewan Wheat Pool (SWP) and James Richardson International (JRI), formed a joint venture called Pacific Gateway Terminal, effective July 1, 2005 whereby each terminal would handle specific commodities in larger volume. This was soon challenged by the Competition Bureau as a potential threat to competition for handling these products in the port.

In the spring of 2007, SWP and JRI (backed by the Ontario Teacher's Pension Plan

Board) engaged in a bidding contest to take over the financially distressed Agricore United. This ended in a victory for SWP Inc., after it sold $315 million of the combined assets to JRI and agreed to handle up to 750,000 tonnes of JRI's grain annually through Cascadia Terminal for a period of 10 years. Along with these arrangements, the Pacific Gateway Terminal joint venture was abandoned, ending the dispute with the Competition Bureau.

The newly enlarged SWP Inc. now represented the consolidation of all four, former farmer-owned cooperatives and anticipated annual sales of $4 billion. Though an impressive figure, this pales alongside the $75 billion annual sales of privately owned Cargill or the $37 billion of Archer Daniels Midland.

With this final consolidation, Saskpool changed its name to Viterra in August 2007 and completed the rationalization of terminal ownership in Vancouver by transferring its north shore terminal to Cargill, in return for the latter's half interest in Cascadia plus other considerations. This deal resulted in Viterra owning and operating two of the port's five terminals. Those two south shore elevators have 52 percent of the port's total of 930,000 tonnes grain storage capacity.

Some Facts and Figures

The performance of all components of the grain handling and transportation system depends largely on farm production. Production during the 2001/03 crop years was much reduced by drought and grasshopper infestation and resulted in losses that were a major factor in hastening the Wheat Pools' amalgamation. The 2003/04 crop was substantially better and was followed by five crops averaging 53.5 million tonnes, ranging in quality from low in 2004/05 to well above average in 2007/08.

Over the past 10 crop years, an average of 20,942,600 tonnes of agricultural products moved through terminals at the four primary ports of Thunder Bay, Churchill, Vancouver, and Prince Rupert, ranging from a low of 11.8 million tonnes in 2002/03 to a high of 25.64 million tonnes in 2008/09. Continuing the trend of the eighties and nineties, movement through the two Pacific Gateway Ports continued to take an increasing share of Canada's overseas exports, reaching an all-time high of 73.7 percent in crop year 2008/09. Between crop years 2005/06 and 2008/09, Vancouver's grain throughput averaged 12,272,575 tonnes while Prince Rupert's averaged 4,577,450 tonnes for 27.2 percent of the West Coast total.

Crop diversification that began in earnest with the staged removal of the Crow rate between 1983 and 1993 has continued, and has resulted in very different mix of agricultural products moving through the port's facilities and the partial loss of the conventional grain elevators' traditionally dominant role. Most apparent has been the increasing throughput of canola. Shipments of this oilseed through Vancouver terminals rose from 2.8 to 6.47 million tonnes between 2005 and 2009, displacing wheat as the leading export grain commodity for the first time in 83 years.

The port's five grain terminals have 38.5 percent of the total storage capacity of the fifteen located at the four primary ports involved in the Canadian grain handling and transportation system. These five terminals also represent 82 percent of the storage capacity on the Pacific Coast. At Vancouver's elevators, turnover between crop years 2005/06 and 2008/09 averaged 13 times and peaked at 14.4 times in 2008/09. This looks good when compared to the 4.7 times annual turnover at Thunder Bay, but is substantially below the average 21.8 times turnover at the single Prince Rupert facility over the same period. Indeed, that terminal comfortably achieved a turnover of 26.5 times in 1994. Reduced time in storage means reduced storage charges to the producer.

Over the past six crop years, dispatch earnings have substantially exceeded demurrage charges at the West Coast ports. In Vancouver, however, 60 percent of the vessels arriving to load grain at the port's terminal elevators in the recent crop year had to move to multiple berths to fill their holds, thereby incurring extra costs. Many of the larger ships are directed to Prince Rupert for one berth loading of cargoes that averaged 52,213 tonnes for the Northern Gateway Port during the crop year 2008/09, compared to 35,896 tonnes for cargoes loaded at PMV.

Markets and Ocean Freight Rates for Bulk Cargo

Most agricultural products moving through the Pacific ports, whether grains, specialty crops, or animal feed, are destined for markets in East and South Asia, or the Persian Gulf. Distances to these markets are very great, ranging from 4264 nautical miles (Vancouver to Yokohama) to 10,463 (Vancouver to Bandar Abbas in Iran). Vessels loading at Prince Rupert and delivering to these markets save up to 440 nautical miles. Such long ocean hauls leave Canadian grain marketers at a considerable disadvantage to their competitors in Australia when ocean bulk freight rates are high, especially with respect to points in South Asia and the Persian Gulf. These bulk rates are influenced by the demand for moving iron ore and coal, as grain constitutes only about 10 percent of world dry bulk ocean carriage.

Over the past five years, fluctuations in ocean bulk rates have been dramatic, reaching an all-time high of 11,743 on the Baltic Dry Index in May 2008 and then collapsing to a low of 700 only five months later. When these rates are very high availability of supply becomes a deciding factor for buyers, although they will often defer delivery pending more acceptable rates.

On occasion, container rates to move grain have been lower than bulk carrier rates and shippers have taken advantage of this disparity to move modest amounts of grain to selected markets. It is, however, most unlikely that container carriage will replace bulk carrier movement in the foreseeable future for basic commodities such as wheat, barley, and canola.

Rail Movement of Agricultural Commodities to the Port

Canadian grain is produced much farther from its loading ports than is grain for its main market competitors in Australia, Argentina, or the United States. Geography has dictated that the only economical way to move it to the two Pacific ports is by rail. This dependence on rail is responsible for a tradition among farmers and grain shippers of blaming the CPR and CNR for many of the ills that periodically plague the industry. After World War II, the railways, in turn, had little incentive to move grain from thousands of collecting points, served by little used branch lines, to ocean terminals operated five days a week, for a reimbursement rate established in 1897. This reluctance became even more acute when other bulk commodities such as coal, sulphur, and potash became available for rail movement at profitable rates in the 1960s.

With this creaking system no longer sustainable, the federal government finally terminated the Crow rate and Crow Benefit by 1993 and replaced it with a "cap" on allowable profits for carrying grain by rail. Furthermore, the number of collecting points (at one time nearly 6,000), have been drastically reduced so that by 2007, eighty percent of grain to be moved by rail could be picked up at 91 modern, high throughput delivery points. More than half of these could load out more than 50 hopper cars.

Despite the real progress in many areas involved in handling and transporting grain, as late as 2000, railcar movement from country collecting points to the Pacific Coast terminals and back for agricultural product reload remained mired in a 20–21 day cycle. In a speech in May 2001, CNR President Paul Tellier challenged both the railways and the grain industry to work to reduce this excessively long and wasteful cycle to an achievable 11 days, for the mutual benefit of both.

Continuing pressures to improve grain car cycles to the Pacific ports, applied at all segments of the movement, have produced positive results. During crop year 2003/04, cycle times to Vancouver had dropped to 17.8 days and those to Prince Rupert 13.9 days, the lowest yet recorded on the West Coast. For the 2008/09 crop year, the Vancouver cycle had reached 14.1 days, while the cycle to Prince Rupert dropped to an all-time West Coast low of 11.8 days. These figures are based on railcars carrying the major bulk crops of wheat, barley, and canola. Cars carrying specialty crops, mostly handled at bulk terminals or transload facilities in Vancouver, continue to have considerably longer cycles. The record low figures for the 2008/09 crop year are primarily a reflection of the reduced competition from other export commodities for railway capacity, due to the global financial crisis.

The proportion of grain moved to the West Coast by each of the Class 1 carriers has, in most years, slightly favoured the CPR over the CNR, despite the latter serving both ports.

The Changing Scene in Port Agricultural Product Handling

Despite the major shift in movement of prairie farm products from east to west for overseas shipment, at Vancouver these products have long lost their export dominance to coal, though they still constitute a very important segment of total outbound foreign traffic.

The continuing trend toward crop diversification, which began in earnest in the mideighties, has markedly changed the mix of agricultural commodities moving through the port, as well as the way many of these products are handled. The port's five traditional grain elevators, four of them originally constructed over 80 years ago, still handle over 98 percent of the wheat, feed barley, and canola. Their role in bringing received grain up to Canadian Grain Commission export standards has, however, been significantly reduced, as many of the new, large, high throughput inland terminals have taken over much of that function. In 2008, canola supplanted wheat as the port's leading agricultural commodity export and specialty crops made up over a quarter of the total movement.

Keen competition has resulted in specialty crop handling being divided between the traditional elevators, bulk terminals, and the burgeoning transload facilities. These specialty products include dry peas, lentils, chickpeas, dry beans, and fababeans, collectively called pulses, plus mustard seed, canary seed, sunflower seed, safflower seed, and buckwheat. In addition, by-products such as canola meal and grain screenings are exported as animal feed. As mentioned earlier, Pacific Elevator underwent a $20 million program in 1999 designed to enable it to handle a wide range of these products more efficiently. Vancouver Wharves completed their specialized bulk agricultural products terminal in 2000, touted as the first of its kind in North America, and the following year Neptune opened a $17 million redevelopment of their Berth Three to handle similar bulk products. Concurrently, the Prince Rupert Port Corporation upgraded and expanded the former Conarc facility on Fairview Terminal to function under the name Agport. That facility failed to attract anticipated throughput and was demolished in 2005 to make way for the conversion of Fairview to a container facility.

In 1991 Coastal Containers — a subsidiary of Canada Malting and successor to the controversial Elders Grain project on the south shore of Burrard Inlet — began stuffing up to 80 TEU daily with malting barley, for subsequent loading over the berths of adjacent Vanterm or Centerm. Since then transload facilities for stuffing agricultural commodities into containers have been developed at a number of lower mainland sites including Richmond, Annacis Island, Surrey Properties, and Cloverdale. Each has rail access to receive loaded grain cars from the CNR, CPR, or the short line, Southern Railway of B.C. They then move their loaded containers to one of the container terminals by truck, rail, or barge.

Over 17 percent of the port's total agricultural product throughput moved overseas in 126,733 boxes in the year 2007. A number of factors, including limited availability of empty, twenty-foot containers at product source points have resulted in 73 percent of these containers being filled at or near the port. Over half of the 3–4 million tonnes of specialty products moving through the port in recent years has been shipped overseas in containers.

Controversy over the Canadian Wheat Board's Role

The Canadian Wheat Board (CWB) celebrated its seventy-fifth anniversary in 2010. In competition with huge multinational grain companies many times its size, it had sold over 1 billion tonnes of grain for prairie farmers to over 70 countries, since established in 1935. Since 1989 it has functioned as the sole marketing agency for wheat and barley. In 1998 its management structure was changed from five federally appointed commissioners with an advisory committee of elected grain farmers to a 15-member board of directors, including 10 elected farmers and four members appointed by Ottawa. The President and CEO is chosen by that Board with the approval of the federal government. With this new structure the CWB ceased to be a Federal Crown Corporation with its own Cabinet Minister.

Demands, especially from Alberta farmers, for more choice in marketing their grain, which would include dismantling the "single desk marketing" monopoly of the CWB, stimulated the newly elected Harper government to attempt another restructuring of the Wheat Board. The Minister of Agriculture removed the resisting President and CEO, resulting in acrimony. Then, a year later, the Minister made an abortive attempt to remove barley marketing from the exclusive jurisdiction of the Board, leading to temporary turmoil in marketing this product. Another attempt to curb the powers of the CWB by amending the CWB Act died on the order paper in September 2008.

This feud over "single desk marketing" of wheat and barley has strong supporters on both sides of the issue and has yet to be resolved.

LIQUID AND CHEMICAL TERMINALS

In contrast to the relatively lackluster performance of the dry bulk and break-bulk sectors in recent years, the liquid bulk and bulk chemical groups have shown impressive growth with annual throughput in excess of 10 million tonnes since 2008. Growth has been especially dramatic in crude oil exports to Asia, likely a result of the substantial investments Chinese and South Korean companies have recently made in Alberta crude production.

Eleven terminals of varying size and significance handle these products. Four are primarily dry bulk, break-bulk, or container terminals. Pacific Coast Terminals at Port Moody moves a large volume of ethylene glycol. Neptune Terminals stores and loads out canola oil, while Kinder Morgan Vancouver Wharves handles a number of bulk liquid commodities. Vanterm moves exports of both canola oil and the by-products from rendering animal waste at the adjacent facilities of West Coast Reduction Ltd.

Univar Canada Terminal, the former Dow Chemical terminal, exports ethylene glycol and caustic soda over Lynnterm's adjacent Berth Seven. Located just east of Seymour Creek and the second narrows bridge, Canexus Chemicals Canada Ltd. imports salt and produces a range of chlor-alkali products used in the production of pulp and paper, steel, oil, and plastics. These products, plus large quantities of sodium chlorate produced in related plants in Alberta and Saskatchewan are loaded to vessels berthed at the company's own wharf. Canexus has recently completed a $228 million modernization of its production facilities, designed to reduce noxious emissions.

The remaining five terminals handle petroleum products and all are located on Burrard Inlet east of second narrows. Stanovan Terminal is used to export gasoline, diesel, jet fuel, and asphalt from the nearby Chevron Canada refinery. Shellburn Terminal exports petroleum products and styrene and the Petro-Canada Terminal has two small docks for loading petroleum products. Westridge Terminal is the port's main exporter of crude oil. This terminal was built in 1956 by Trans Mountain Pipeline and shipped its first Alberta crude to California that year, thereby reversing the flow of oil which had long been imported from that state. The terminal is now owned and operated by Kinder Morgan Canada, who purchased Trans Mountain Pipeline in 2007. The capacity of the pipeline has since been increased from 225,000 to 300,000 barrels per day and the company wants to further increase this to 700,000 barrels daily. Depth restrictions at second narrows and the approaches to the berth preclude full loading of Aframax tankers (up to 120,000 tonnes and 875,000 barrel capacity), but the Port Authority is considering plans to deepen the channel by dredging to allow the full loading, not only of Aframax, but eventually of Suezmax size vessels (up to 150,000 tonnes and 1,100,000 barrel). This terminal also imports jet fuel from refineries in Washington State to move through its pipeline to Vancouver International Airport. Kinder Morgan opposes Enbridge's Northern Gateway Pipeline Project with its terminus at Kitimat.

On the north side of Burrard Inlet, IOCO has a tank farm and loading wharf. This terminal supplies fuel for freighters and cruise vessels, which has been produced by blending bunker fuel railed in from Alberta with diesel fuel that has been barged in.

THE AUTO TERMINALS

Taken together, the two auto terminals situated on the Fraser River constitute the largest dedicated facility in Canada and are North America's third largest. Between 2004 and 2008 the terminals handled an average 450,000 units annually, but experienced a drop off to 387,230 units in the 2009 recession year. Traffic in 2010 continued subdued and well below the peak year, 2007. Privately owned Fraser Wharves, located on the north bank of the main channel of the river in Richmond, has a single berth backed up with 107 acres of land capable of storing 14,000 vehicles. Annacis Auto Terminal, situated on 145 acres leased from the Port Authority on Annacis Island is operated by Wallenius Wilhelmsen Logistics, a major operator of car carrying vessels and auto terminals. This terminal offers two berths. Both terminals are fully equipped to process and load out imported vehicles to truck or rail, as required.

THE CRUISE TERMINALS

Vancouver's cruise traffic peaked in 2002 at 1,125,252 passengers, the culmination of two decades of 10 percent compound annual growth. In anticipation of future growth, the Vancouver Port Authority spent $89 million expanding the Canada Place facility, completing the project in early 2003. Instead of growth, however, passenger traffic declined to reach a low of 578,986 in 2010, a level last recorded in 1994. This 50 percent drop from peak year 2002 is primarily due to the aggressive post-9/11 entry of Seattle as the base port for an increasing number of cruise vessels, exacerbated by world economic turmoil in the past two years. It is anticipated that the downward trend will be halted and, probably, modestly reversed in the 2011 season.

Clearly, Vancouver no longer holds a monopoly position as the base for Alaska-bound cruise traffic. Seattle has become a fierce competitor for this business and has made substantial investments in terminal facilities. From a very low base in 2000, the growth in Seattle's cruise passenger traffic has been phenomenal, passing Vancouver's traffic for the first time in 2008. Passengers embarking in Seattle, however, miss the attractions of the Inside Passage cruise up the B.C. coast, instead making a fast voyage outside Vancouver Island and through Hecate Strait to their first Alaska landfall at Ketchikan. This routing is necessitated by the extra 300 nautical miles travelled on a round trip for a vessel based in the Puget Sound port. These vessels make an obligatory call at one Canadian port on one leg of their cruise, albeit in some cases for a very short or inconvenient time. Victoria has been the chief beneficiary of this requirement.

Alaskans have become increasingly unfriendly to cruise ship calls. This is especially true in the panhandle where small communities feel both overwhelmed by and undercompensated for the inconvenience of the huge numbers of passengers disembarking from ever larger vessels during the summer season. In response, the Alaska government legislated a number of "anti-cruise" initiatives in 2006, which included a $50 per passenger charge, a tax on shipboard gambling, a tax on the corporate income of cruise lines, regulations covering shore excursion sales, very rigorous sewage disposal regulations, and requirements for each vessel to carry and pay for monitoring "Ocean Rangers" while in Alaskan waters. These initiatives were challenged by the cruise industry and, after negotiation with a new Governor, they have been diluted somewhat in new legislation passed in April 2010.

PRINCE RUPERT SINCE 2004

OVERVIEW

By the end of 2003, citizens of Prince Rupert must surely have felt that some malevolent spirit had cast a spell on their city. The pulp mill, for 50 years the area's largest employer, remained closed and hopes for its reopening were fading rapidly. The fishing industry continued to be a pale shadow of its glory days. Port related activity — the prime reason for founding the planned terminal city and its hope for prosperity and growth — had undergone near collapse. The city's tax base shrank, retail and service outlets were forced to close, the residential real estate market was a shambles, and many residents were forced to leave the city to seek work elsewhere. The local situation was especially galling because, in much of the rest of the province, the economy was booming.

Though neither apparent to all, nor accepted by Prince Rupert's detractors, by late 2004 there were clear signs that a recovery in most components of port activity was near. Indeed, in retrospect, the year 2004 may well be considered a pivotal year in the port's history, primarily due to clear evidence of a new, strong, and active interest in the Northern Corridor and Gateway by the CNR and by both federal and provincial governments.

Signs of the emergence of a new strategy toward the Northern Rail Corridor and Gateway Port began to emanate from the highest executive levels in the CNR. The railroad's marketing policy toward its line west of Red Pass Junction had, essentially, been passive for 85 years.

The CNR's successful purchase of BC Rail operations in 2004 could only benefit Prince Rupert because it would reduce the long standing and virtually total drain of export commodities produced in north central B.C to the Southern Gateway — a drain that had unquestionably stunted throughput growth at Fairview Terminal. With this acquisition the railway confirmed its new intent to make use of the huge advantage it has over rival CPR, namely ownership of an alternative Class One line to a second Gateway Port located significantly closer to burgeoning Asian markets. The railway's new strategy was soon evident in the strong interest and support it showed in the Fairview conversion project, and the steady reductions it applied to rates to haul grain to Prince Rupert. By 2008, those rates had reached the level of a 10 percent discount over the Southern Gateway and port grain throughput was quickly restored.

In addition to this most welcome interest from the transportation component so vital to the port, the new Northland Cruise Terminal facility, capable of handling the largest vessels on the Alaska cruise circuit, opened in May 2004. Later that year, the first trainload of coal from the newly developed deposits in northeast B.C. left the mine bound for Ridley Terminal and, by this time, plans were maturing for an extensive conversion of Fairview with input from the operator selected for that facility.

Through the difficult and disheartening years of collapsed port traffic, the much diminished Port Authority staff had worked on several options for converting the general cargo terminal and were greatly encouraged by Victoria and Ottawa's increasing interest in Asia Pacific Gateway and Corridor projects, evident by 2004. With financial assistance from both senior governments and strong support from the CNR, the Fairview conversion project was completed in the fall of 2007. Reasons for the impressive immediate success of the terminal can be found in the enthusiasm and experience of the terminal operator, the decision of a far-sighted major container shipping line to serve the port, and the total dedication to the project by everyone involved locally. The progress is even more impressive when considered against the dramatic and painful reductions in traffic experienced at other West Coast facilities resulting from the collapse in world trade during 2008–2009.

The new container facility has extended the port's reach to central and eastern Canada as well as to the Midwest U.S. No longer confined to drawing export commodities from northern B.C. and western Canadian grain farms, this new reality has, at long last, made the port a force to be reckoned with in transpacific trade.

The provincial government's cap on municipal taxation of port facilities, enacted in 2004, was a further positive measure for the port. In particular, it helped Prince Rupert

Grain to be more competitive with the Vancouver terminals and encouraged others who might consider investments in port facilities.

From a two-decade low of 4,033,889 tonnes of overseas export traffic in 2003, throughput increased, gradually at first, then jumped to 7,738,252 tonnes in 2006 and 10,432,880 tonnes in 2007. Container traffic, added in late 2007, together with continuing increases in coal throughput lifted total foreign export and import traffic to 12,173,672 tonnes in 2009, nearing the ports all-time peak of 13,824,180 tonnes in 1994. Throughput in 2010 reached a new peak level of 16,424,512 tonnes and is expected to establish another record at or near 20 million tonnes in 2011.

THE NEW CONTAINER TERMINAL AT FAIRVIEW

By late 2004, the Port Authority's plans to convert the nearly idle general cargo terminal at Fairview to a fully-fledged container terminal had made considerable progress. Initially conceived as a modest conversion using second hand cranes and with only minimal change to the terminal itself, the plan had evolved into a thoroughly modern and unique high throughput, rail intermodal facility dedicated to markets in the U.S. Midwest and Central Canada. Support from the CNR was active and by July 2004 the port had selected an experienced and respected operator for the terminal. Even transportation "experts" who had long chuckled at the prospect of Prince Rupert ever achieving its destiny as a major port were beginning, more quietly, to take notice.

Port staff and Westmar Consultants began design and engineering work for the project in early 2004. Concurrently, environmental studies were underway, approaches made to senior governments for financial assistance, and difficult negotiations undertaken with First Nations groups who strongly felt that they had the right to share in any prosperity the project generated on land they claimed to be theirs.

The final design concept for the terminal included a phased development, initially of the existing facility, with later expansion onto the adjacent foreshore. The first phase, converting the existing terminal, entailed removing almost all existing structures, relocating and expanding rail trackage, extending the dock face seaward by 23 m over a length of 400 m, installing three ultra-post-panamax cranes, and upgrading substructure and electrical components. The second phase would expand the terminal to the south by extending the dock face, backup storage, and trackage sufficiently to accommodate a total annual throughput of 2 million TEU.

The Province of B.C., along with Alberta and the B.C. Division of the Canadian Manufacturers and Exporters Association underwrote a study of Prince Rupert's potential by Norbridge Inc. of Virginia, one of the world's premier marine consulting firms. Their report, delivered in March 2005, indicated that the port had the potential to move 4 million TEU annually. It confirmed the many advantages that Prince Rupert possessed as a North American gateway to and from Asia.

The *Canada Marine Act* limited the port's borrowing to a maximum of $22 million and precluded direct federal grants to the port. This latter restriction was circumvented at the insistence of David Emerson, Minister of International Trade, by using the Western Economic Diversification Fund to provide the needed financial assistance. On April 15, 2005 Ottawa and Victoria each announced grants of $30 million for the project. Over half of the B.C. contribution came from the B.C.R. Investment Partnership Fund, which had been established to distribute money from the 2004 sale of BC Rail operations to the CNR.

The federal contribution brought out the usual huffing and puffing from the CPR and some sectors of the Vancouver marine community. Their unenlightened self-interest was clear. The CEO of the CPR, which does not serve Prince Rupert, reportedly opined that "Canada should focus on Vancouver, not remote Prince Rupert" and "we should not be distracted by imitators — dilution is not a solution." These and other objections emanating from the Southern Gateway appeared almost comical in light of the vast sums senior governments have poured into port related developments in the lower mainland over the last century to create terminal infrastructure, grain terminals, bridges, and dredged channels, among many others. While complaining about this comparatively modest contribution to the new Prince Rupert facility, these same parties were loudly insisting that Ottawa and Victoria pour hundreds of millions of dollars into infrastructure projects to ease the accumulation of rail and road access problems plaguing both existing and planned lower mainland port facilities. In contrast, there are no present demands for public funds to resolve such issues at the Northern Gateway.

It is interesting to note that none of the detractors appear to have considered Canada's urgent need for a robust alternative to its single Southern Gateway and Rail Corridor in order to ensure the security of the country's international trade by reducing the chance of its disruption due to natural or manmade disasters.

Maher Terminals of New Jersey, who had assumed the operation of Fairview Terminal on January 1, 2005 with a 30-year renewable lease, committed $60 million for equipment for the new terminal. This included three ultra-post-panamax cranes able to lift up to 66 tonnes and service the largest container ships on the drawing boards.

The CNR committed to $15 million for the terminal intermodal facility plus another $10 million for terminal trackage and further expenditures to their northern line. These included building new sidings and enlarging the clearances under bridges and in tunnels to accommodate double-stack container cars. In addition, the railway placed large orders for locomotives and rolling stock to serve the express route from Prince Rupert to the U.S. Midwest. They planned to vigorously target Chicago and Memphis, points then receiving Asian goods via container terminals in Puget Sound and southern California.

As its contribution, Prince Rupert Port Authority arranged to borrow up to $22 million from a commercial bank to supplement available internal cash resources and wrote off the $10,129,400 book value of existing assets on Fairview Terminal that would have to be demolished.

With financing in place, the Board of Directors of the Authority made the final decision on June 13, 2005 to go ahead with the Fairview conversion. The first contracts awarded provided for structures on the terminal to be removed by year-end. After receipt of an environmental assessment permit early in January 2006, major contracts were awarded for the conversion to a container terminal and work began in earnest. Maher undertook extensive training programs with the full cooperation of the ILWU Local 505. The federal government appointed Bob Plecas, an experienced consultant to attempt to resolve the First Nations issues still threatening the project.

Work proceeded on time and on budget. The project received a tremendous vote of confidence when, on May 14, 2007, the CNR announced an agreement with COSCO Container Lines, whereby COSCO and its CKYH Alliance members would make Prince Rupert their first port of call on their PNWS service to Vancouver and Puget Sound. This virtually guaranteed that containers moved through the new gateway and corridor would reach Chicago and Memphis well ahead of those landed at any other North American West Coast port.

On August 20, 2007 the three ultra-post-panamax container cranes ordered by Maher arrived from Shanghai and were installed on the newly completed berth. Under blue skies and brilliant sunshine, a grand opening ceremony took place on September 12, 2007, attended by many dignitaries, including delegations from Memphis and Chicago, as well as at least half the local citizenry. It was clear that there was wide interest in this new and unique, purely rail intermodal terminal, far removed from the support of any large metropolitan population.

On October 30, 2007 the *COSCO Antwerp* was secured to the new berth and unloaded over 1,000 containers. The first unit train left Prince Rupert carrying 600 TEU the next morning and arrived in Chicago 92 hours later, a mere 12 days after leaving Asia. Thus began the operation of the first rail-dedicated, intermodal container terminal in North America, coupled with a new express connector service to the U.S. Midwest that offered reliability, speed, and efficiency. Clearly COSCO, one of the world's largest container shipping lines, and the CNR, the railroad with the greatest reach and most profitable operation in North America, were totally committed to the success of this new Pacific Gateway.

Designated the "Northern Express Gateway and Corridor," this new supply chain between Asia and North America through Prince Rupert constituted the first new transpacific trade corridor in over a century. With enthusiastic cooperation from everyone involved in moving containers on the new route, the start-up went virtually without a hitch. Strong supporters included the ILWU local workforce, personnel of the Canadian Border Services Agency, tug operators, and Quickload CEF's bonded warehouse staff, as well as the CNR, COSCO, Maher, and the Port Authority.

Further confirming both its commitment to the port and the use of its northern rail corridor to serve the U.S. Midwest, the CNR purchased the Elgin, Joliet and Eastern Railway from U.S. Steel for USD$300 million to facilitate passage around the congested Chicago area. This transaction finally received approval from the U.S. Surface Transportation Board on December 24, 2008.

Well pleased with this new option to serve the North American market, COSCO added a second weekly port visit in mid-2008. This was established as part of their CEN service, with vessels from Asia calling first at Prince Rupert and then proceeding to ports in central and southern California. This decision almost coincided with the severe downturn in the U.S. economy and the resulting dramatic fall in traffic. Certainly, the large container ports at Long Beach and Los Angeles were aware that losing traffic to Prince Rupert was contributing to their plight, which saw reductions of up to 40 percent at Long Beach from their peak in 2006.

Though the deep slump in the North American economy undoubtedly retarded the ramping to capacity of the phase one development at Fairview Terminal, in its third full year of operation the terminal's throughput reached 343,366 TEU, a figure not reached by Southern Gateway terminals collectively until 1990, after twenty years of operation.

Trains carrying import containers move east twice daily along the easiest corridor across the North American Cordillera to inland intermodal terminals operated by the CNR at Toronto, Montreal, Chicago, and Memphis. Congestion is nonexistent and dwell times for boxes on the terminal average less than 48 hours. Loaded outbound containers are a work in progress, gradually increasing in number from an initial 35 percent of the export total. Being the first port of call for loaded inbound containers offers a substantial advantage in speeding their movement to North American consignees.

With continuing growth in throughput of both import and export containers, COSCO has progressively upgraded their service by increasing both the frequency and the size of vessels calling at the port. Further expansion of their service is anticipated in the near future, as is the participation by other operators in the "Northern Express Service." This will trigger a decision to execute already advanced plans to expand the terminal. Furthermore, if the consultants are right and Prince Rupert can expect to eventually handle 4 million TEU per year, a second terminal will be required. The Port Authority has reserved a site for this future facility at the southwest tip of Kaien Island.

Security matters have been front and centre in the design and operation of the terminal with the result that it is considered the most secure on the west coast of North America with 100 percent of inbound containers headed for U.S. destinations being scanned through both radiation detectors and VACIS x-ray machines. Containers of interest to the Canadian Border Agency are removed from the terminal and taken to a bonded warehouse on Ridley Island for complete examination.

The conversion of Fairview Terminal included installing the electrical infrastructure needed to later provide an Alternative Marine Power installation. With federal government support from Transport Canada's ecoFREIGHT program, grants from Western Economic Diversification, B.C.'s Climate Action Program, and equal contributions from the Port Authority, CNR, and Maher Terminals the $3.6 million "green" project is scheduled for completion in mid 2011. Fairview will then be the first container terminal in Canada in mid 2011 equipped to offer "plug in" power to berthed vessels.

The CNR opened a new $20 million intermodal terminal and distribution centre at Prince George in 2007. The terminal has 10 acres of outside storage, a large warehouse, two 2,400 ft. tracks, and trucking and pickup facilities. Together with other CN intermodal terminals on the Great Plains, Central Canada, and the Midwest U.S. it will generate containerized cargo for export via the new Northern Gateway container facility.

THE GRAIN TERMINAL SINCE 2004

Premiums added to rail rates for moving grain to Prince Rupert following the port's loss of parity peaked at 13 percent in the 1999/2000 crop year with predictable results. Prince Rupert's modern terminal reverted to the role of residual facility, used only when the Vancouver terminals were unable to cope with grain flows, such as during their long strike in late 2002. Between 1989 and 1998 the terminal's throughput averaged 4.4 million tonnes annually. Over the next five years it dropped to an average of only 2 million tonnes per year and reached an all-time low of 1,228,982 tonnes in 2003.

The drastic reduction in grain movement added to the loss of coal traffic from northeast mines led the railway to re-examine the multiple components of the cost of moving grain to the West Coast ports with the result that, in 2004, rate parity for grain moving through the Northern Corridor was re-established. It was clear that senior railway management in Montreal was developing a new strategy to benefit from the latent potential in their ownership of a first class alternate line to a second superb natural harbour on the Pacific Coast. The acquisition of BC Rail and the level of support given to developing the Fairview container terminal confirmed this new strategy.

In line with their new policy, the railway began discounting their rate for moving grain to Prince Rupert during the 2006/07 crop year. By the fall of 2007 this discount was set at 8.8 percent, later rising to 10 percent in 2008 and 2009. In addition, the railway held back on rate increases for moving grain to Prince Rupert and provided better car supply for the northern route. As a result, grain flows to Prince Rupert Grain recovered, with average throughput reaching 4.7 million tonnes annually for the period 2006 through 2009. The terminal was restored to its former role as the outlet for about 30 percent of overseas export grain moving through the West Coast.

During the 4-month strike in late 2002 at the Vancouver terminals, 10,699 CP railcars were unloaded by the Prince Rupert terminal, but with this exception and a few more that dribbled in over the next two years, the terminal is exclusively served by CN Rail.

Grain car cycles to Prince Rupert Grain continue to be shorter than cycles to southern terminals. Comparing a return trip for a grain car cycle between Red Pass Junction and Prince Rupert with that from Red Pass Junction to Vancouver, the Canadian Grain Monitor has reported an average saving over a four-year-period of 2.8 days on the northern route.

The benefit to the railway from the more efficient use of rolling stock is obvious.

Unlike Vancouver, where canola has overtaken wheat as the leading commodity moving through the terminals, the mix of grains arriving at the Prince Rupert terminal is still more traditional with about 85 percent wheat and the rest barley and canola. Whereas, in the past, most grain received at West Coast tidewater terminals required cleaning, almost 60 percent is now pre-processed at one of the new high throughput inland terminals that have replaced the thousands of "prairie skyscrapers." This has resulted in a revenue loss to the ocean terminals.

Turnover at Prince Rupert's modern high throughput facility is double that of the Southern Gateway terminals and 5–6 times that of the terminals at Thunder Bay with related storage averaging only nine days, as opposed to 15 days at Vancouver and 27 days at Thunder Bay. Vessels are loaded at a single deep-water berth at rates up to 36,800 tonnes in a single shift and save 400 to 450 nautical miles on their voyage to East Asian or South Asian discharge ports. This saving becomes more significant when ocean freight rates are high. Vessels leaving the berth at Prince Rupert in the crop year 2008/09 carried an average load of 52,213 tonnes, well above the average grain load of 35,896 tonnes from the Southern Gateway terminals.

For the crop year 2008/09 the Canadian Wheat Board selected the terminal as "Grain Handler of the Year" in the western port terminal category. Criteria for this award include accuracy, timeliness, and the flexibility to adapt to new programs and methods.

The ownership of Prince Rupert Grain has undergone change that reflects the series of consolidations within the grain industry between 1998 and 2007. The six original consortium members are now represented by three with Viterra Inc. holding a majority interest and James Richardson International and Cargill the balance. The respective interests fluctuate within a fairly narrow range based on the historical proportionate share of unloads from each.

The terminal carries a $296 million burden of debt, substantially exceeding its depreciated value. As of the end of the 2006/07 crop year it had paid the Alberta Heritage Fund a total of $347 million. Only $42.6 million of this represented a reduction of the principle amount comprising the original 11 percent first mortgage bonds plus capitalized unpaid interest. This strongly suggests the need for a major financial restructuring. Certainly, the much older competing terminals in Vancouver, individually owned by the collective owners of Prince Rupert Grain, do not carry this burden. With the turmoil within the pool sector of the industry during the last decade, a resolution of this problem has been deferred.

THE COAL TERMINAL SINCE 2004

During the seventies and eighties, approximately $150 million was spent on exploring and evaluating a dozen coal deposits in northeast B.C. This activity was a response to the seemingly insatiable demand of Japanese steel producers and was strongly supported by the provincial government. Based on unrealistic volume predictions and escalating price promises, $3 billion was spent to develop two large mines and supply the transportation infrastructure needed to move the coal to the new high throughput terminal on Ridley Island, near Prince Rupert. Quintette, the larger of the two mines was built on a grand scale with inadequately developed reserves and was soon in difficulty, aggravated by the failure of the Japanese buyers to honour the price agreements they had signed. It ceased operation in 2000. The other producer, Bullmoose, operated by Teck Cominco, managed to reduce costs and continue production until its deposit was exhausted in 2003.

Coal throughput over the port facility on Ridley Island averaged 6 million tonnes annually from 1984–1999, less than half the facility's capacity, and then dwindled to nothing in 2004. During the years 2003–2004 the terminal managed to keep open, handling over half a million tonnes of petroleum coke annually, plus a movement of iron pellets from the U.S. to Asia.

While the two large mining operations were winding down, a new generation of developers began to acquire leases for known deposits, which had reverted to the crown, and commenced their development on a more modest scale. The first new production came from Western Canadian Coal's Dillon mine on their Burnt River property near Chetwynd and the first train from that property left for Ridley on December 6, 2004 loaded with low sulphur PCI coal. During 2005, the terminal shipped 632,365 tonnes from this mine and the nearby Willow Creek mine of Pine Valley Coal. The following year, Western Canadian Coal began shipping metallurgical coal from the newly developed Perry Creek deposit near Tumbler Ridge and groomed another deposit to replace the Dillon deposit at Burnt River. Pine Valley Coal closed their Willow Creek mine in 2006 but another entry, NEMI Northern Energy and Minerals, commenced production of hard coal at their Trend mine, making their first shipment to Ridley Terminals (RTI) in April 2006. This brought total 2006 coal shipments from RTI to 2,325,710 tonnes.

During these renaissance years for northeast coal, Transport Canada became obsessed with disposing of its crown corporation, Ridley Terminals, and started the process with a Request for Proposals on the future of RTI to be submitted to Price Waterhouse by May 16, 2003. The book value of the terminal had been written down to $25 million at the time Fed Nav exercised their "put" and were paid off with $60 million of public funds.

As if unfazed by the unpleasant odour still surrounding the very cozy public-private arrangement that created Ridley Terminals, this same government began a process that led it to attempt an equally unsavoury disposal of this substantial public asset.

Suspicious that the Transport Minister planned to "sell" it to friendly private interests who could limit or dictate access to the terminal, the provincial government attempted to initiate negotiations with Ottawa in early 2005 to acquire the terminal as a part of its Asia Pacific Trade and Gateway strategy. Voicing similar concerns, a resource group that included Teck Cominco, NEMI, Western Canadian Coal, Sumitomo, and Grande Cache Coal formed the "Ridley Shippers Coalition" and made strong representations to the Minister, expressing willingness to purchase and operate the terminal for the common use of all shippers. The Board of Directors and management of Ridley, who had been very actively pursuing lucrative business for the terminal were labeled "rogue management" for their marketing efforts and subjected to a cabinet restraining order. Clearly, the Minister's mind was fixed on delivering the terminal to a newly formed entity, North West Bulk Terminals Inc., a joint venture formed in late 2004 by Federal White Cement of Woodstock Ontario and Fortune Minerals, a small junior mining company based in London Ontario. The common denominator to these two companies was an individual with a reportedly less than sterling business background. The Minister's response to protests included the truculent statement, "Government is the sole shareholder and we are going to get rid of this thing."

It soon transpired that the offer of this "preferred bidder" was a paltry $3 million down payment followed, seven years later, by annual payments of $500,000 for the next 33 years. Other offers were revealed to have been very substantially better.

Public awareness of this probable giveaway was stoked by an editorial in the Vancouver Sun newspaper dated October 25, 2005 and later commentaries by reporters suggesting a "funny smell" to the impending deal. The Transport Minister failed to get approval from a key cabinet committee to proceed and an influential B.C. Minister weighed in to block the sale, convinced that the terminal asset must continue to be a common use facility, either as a Crown Corporation, as a subsidiary of the Prince Rupert Port Authority, or as a private entity run by a coalition of users. The federal government was defeated in the January 2006 election and, in one of its very first moves, the new government cancelled the planned privatization scheme, bring an end to this sorry episode.

Inaugurating and then maintaining production from the newly developed northeast coal deposits strained the financial capacity of the new operators. Unable to cope with the vagaries of coal pricing on world markets, Pine Valley Coal, owner of the Willow Creek Mine, sought protection under the *Company Creditors Arrangement Act* in late 2006, after closing its mining operation. Their assets were acquired in 2008 by Western Canadian Coal and production of metallurgical coal at Willow Creek resumed in the spring of 2010 at an initial rate of 900,000 tonnes per day.

Western Canadian Coal merged in 2009 with British owned Cambrian Mining to form Western Coal and this company, in turn, has been taken over by Walter Energy of Florida effective late March 2011. The company expects to triple production from its northeast B.C. mines to 10 million tonnes annually by fiscal 2013. NEMI and Hillsborough Resources became minority partners in the Peace River Coal Limited Partnership, dominated by Anglo Coal Canada, a subsidiary of Anglo American plc. In early 2010, this partnership offered its coal assets for sale. Many other deposits in the area are available for exploitation when markets and prices for the product are favourable. In addition to coal from northeast B.C. mines, substantial quantities of both thermal and metallurgical coal from mines southeast of Hinton, Alberta — operated by Luscar Energy Partnership and Teck Corporation — are being directed to Ridley Terminal for shipment to overseas markets.

Since 1992 the terminal has handled varying amounts of petroleum coke from Alberta oil refineries. Over the last 10 years this movement has averaged about 450,000 tonnes annually but, during 2010, the throughput of this commodity has more than doubled to 1.17 million tonnes. Starting in 2007 a third export commodity, biomass wood pellets from northern interior mills, began moving in increasing quantities over the terminal's loading facilities. It appears that this movement, too, has considerable growth potential. Throughput of all commodities passed 5 million tonnes in 2007 for the first time since 1999, but fell to 4,159,678 tonnes in 2009, a result of the worldwide recession. The year 2010 saw a dramatic increase in total terminal throughput to reach a new high of 8.3 million tonnes. The terminal is expected to operate at or near its 12 million tonne annual capacity in 2011. The need to expand this capacity is becoming urgent.

Efforts have failed to reach a final agreement with ICEC International Commodity Export Company to complete the adjacent sulphur handling terminal inherited by RTI in 2002 when the Sulphur Corporation collapsed, after spending $20 million on the facility. Potential exists to convert this unfinished installation to a facility to store, and either ship or receive other chemical products.

In addition to the turmoil associated with the injudicious attempt to dispose of the terminal, there have been three Chairmen of the Board of Directors in three years and a change in management that occurred when the 10-year President and CEO resigned in 2008 under less than pleasant circumstances. Hopefully, the long term ownership and management of this valuable port asset will soon be satisfactorily settled.

PASSENGER TRAFFIC

The Northland Terminal for large cruise vessels was completed in 2004 and received 32 vessel calls that season, in addition to the small vessels using the earlier-developed Atlin floating terminal. Cruise passenger traffic catapulted from 3,034 in 2003 to 62,045 in 2004 and then peaked at 103,630 passengers — carried on the 47 large vessels and 16 small vessels that visited during the 2008 season. The subsequent withdrawal of port calls by one large vessel resulted in a drop to 55,097 passenger visits in 2009 and 53,300 in 2010. In addition to the work of the Port Authority, very substantial and commendable efforts by the City, community, and private entrepreneurs have been directed toward providing a worthwhile visit for cruise passengers, though success in this fickle sector of the tourism business is never assured.

The Prince Rupert terminal of the Alaska Marine Highway continues to handle approximately 20,000 passengers per year and the B.C. Ferries terminal moves another 75,000–80,000 passengers annually on the two main routes connecting Prince Rupert to the Queen Charlotte Islands (now Haida Gwaii) and Vancouver Island.

OTHER PORT TRAFFIC

Logs

The loading of logs from North Coast forests for overseas export dates back to the shipments of "airplane spruce" to the United Kingdom under the supervision of H.R. MacMillan, chief forester for B.C. during World War I. Since then there have been very few years without overseas log exports, which go almost exclusively to Asian markets. During the fifties and sixties, a deck-load of logs often completed the loading of vessels calling at the port for pulp and mineral concentrates. Later, vessels specially adapted to carry logs took over this trade, usually loading part cargoes, while either tied to a berth, or anchored near the east end of the harbour. Over the past decade, an average of 16 vessels have called at the port annually to load 185,000 tonnes of logs from harbour anchorages. During 2010, log exports nearly doubled at 349,473 tonnes.

In 2004 Coast Tsimshian Resources, an enterprise of the Lax Kw'alaams First Nation, acquired the timber holdings of defunct Skeena Cellulose in a court sale. In coalition with other regional licensees they are committed to redevelop the regional forest industry. Initially, they have focused successfully on marketing low grade logs loaded in Prince Rupert harbour to China. Future plans include lumber manufacture and wood pellet production.

Petrochemicals

The extensive conversion of Fairview Terminal left one former installation intact. The Department of National Defence fuel tanks had been acquired by the port in 1996 and adapted for use as storage for petrochemical liquids or edible oils. Since 2000 an annual average of 14,334 tonnes of slack wax has been imported through the facility for transfer by rail to an Alberta customer.

CN Rail AquaTrain

The early movements of freight by rail barge to and from the port served domestic regional customers at Swanson Bay and Kitimat. Service to connect the Alaska Railroad at Whittier to the continental rail network commenced in 1962 and has operated without interruption since. The current 55-car rail barge makes a round trip every eight days from the dedicated barge slip in Prince Rupert harbour, moving an annual average of 40,000 tonnes of chemicals, explosives and LPG to the Alaska.

Potash Terminal Prospect

Overseas exports of Canadian produced potash handled by Vancouver facilities increased from an annual average of 3.9 million tonnes between the years 1994 and 2003 to an average 5.9 million tonnes between 2004 and 2008. This increase has been attributed to changing food patterns in the increasingly affluent populations of China and India, as well as demand associated with the growing of feedstock for biofuel production.

To cope with long term growth projections in world markets the three top producers in Saskatchewan have undertaken major expansion projects. In addition, they and other entries are undertaking exploration, evaluation, or development of new deposits.

Canpotex International is the jointly owned marketing and shipping arm to Asian and Latin American buyers of Potash Corporation, Agrium, and Mosaic. They concluded in 2008 that their terminal facility in North Vancouver would have to be expanded to its maximum potential and that a new facility capable of moving 10 million tonnes of potash annually would need to be built on Ridley Island.

The economic recession coupled with buyer resistance to excessively high pricing resulted in a precipitous drop in throughput at Vancouver to 2.27 million tonnes in 2009. Demand recovered in 2010 with throughput returning to more normal levels at 5.53 million tonnes. However, the reduced demand and collapsed market price during 2009 temporarily stalled the planned expansion of terminals at both gateways. With evidence of potash demand and pricing recovering, Canpotex announced, on October 20, 2009, plans to invest $37.5 million in equipment to increase the speed of handling the commodity at Neptune and has continued to develop plans for the Ridley Island terminal, in close cooperation with the Port Authority.

North Coast Gas and Oil Terminal Proposals

The Prince Rupert Daily News edition dated January 10, 1921 carried a front page report of a proposal to build a pipeline from the newly discovered oil field at Norman Wells in the Northwest Territory to an export terminal in Prince Rupert. This was to be the first of many.

Sixty years later there was great interest in several multi-billion dollar schemes to build pipelines to move natural gas to export terminals in the Prince Rupert area. The grandest of these proposals expired in 1984 with the spectacular bankruptcy of its sponsor, Dome Petroleum. Ten years later there was another flurry of interest, including a proposed MTBE plant on southwest Kaien Island (a unique liquid propane and butane export facility), and an attempt to revive the Dome LNG project. Nothing materialized from these proposals.

Late in 2004 another Calgary based company, WestPac Terminals Ltd., signed an agreement with the Port Authority to create an import terminal for LNG on Ridley Island, designed to be a hub for trans-shipment of natural gas by road, rail, ship, pipeline, or barge to North American markets. WestPac planned to use the Ridley Terminals Inc. berth facilities to transfer LNG from very large specialized vessels to storage tanks. These carriers would bring liquefied gas from Indonesia, Malaysia, Quatar, Russia, and Alaska. By 2007 the company had changed its focus to development of a terminal on Texada Island in the Gulf of Georgia, but market price changes, local resistance, and the economic recession of 2008–2009 have stalled progress there.

Other recent pipeline proposals have been directed at the export of B.C. and Alberta natural gas, crude oil, or tar sands bitumen and the import of gas condensate. All have narrowed their focus to locating ocean terminals in the Kitimat area. These plans all entail massive expenditures, involve complex dealings with First Nations, and face certain strong resistance to tanker traffic in confined waters. In addition, they are heavily dependent for their success on the vagaries of world markets and pricing for the commodities handled.

The current plan of Enbridge Inc. to construct a multi-billion dollar pipeline from Northern Alberta to a deep-water terminal in Kitimat for export of crude oil in very large oil tankers has generated increasingly hostile attention since the British Petroleum disaster in the Caribbean and Enbridge's own pipeline leak in Michigan. As an alternative to a pipeline, it has been suggested by supporters of crude oil exports that it would be safer and more economical to move the oil to a terminal in Prince Rupert in long unit trains of tank cars.

Curiously, this prospective Enbridge pipeline project seems to have engendered far more negative interest than the existing and rapidly increasing transit of Burrard Inlet by dozens of loaded tankers each year! Kinder Morgan, owner of Westridge Terminal, proposes to more than double their current capacity and opposes Enbridge's Northern Gateway Pipeline Project.

CHAPTER TEN

Changing Markets, Economic Cycles, and the Role of Government in the Pacific Gateways

A review of the history of Canada's two Pacific Gateways and their respective corridors underlines the pervasive role of senior governments and confirms the impact of changing global markets and economic cycles on their development and growth.

TWO CENTURIES OF CHANGING MARKETS

The first record of overseas trade from the west coast of what would become Canada appeared in the published account of Cook's 1778 visit to the area. According to this account, Cook's crew acquired sea otter pelts in dealings with the local inhabitants and made handsome profits selling them in Canton. Then, between 1785 and 1825, 170 vessels mostly from New England exploited the Chinese demand for these furs. In the early nineteenth century, land based fur traders became established and the inevitable depletion of this resource brought an end to the first lucrative transpacific trade.

Masts, spars, and lumber soon replaced furs as the leading exports and were supplemented by salmon, at first salted in barrels and later canned. Markets for these export products were readily available in Australia and the Sandwich Islands, as well as in the United Kingdom (U.K.). Movements to the U.K. were, however, limited by the distance via Cape Horn, so they were served mostly by vessels returning from delivering consumer and trade goods to the early colonists on the Northwest Coast.

The distance barrier inhibiting trade from the West Coast to the U.K. and European markets was partially overcome when, in 1886, the Canadian Pacific Railway opened its integrated land bridge service for passengers, mail, and high value cargo moving from Asia to Europe. The movement of bulk and break-bulk commodities in large volumes to the eastern seaboard of North America and transatlantic markets had to await the effective opening of the Panama Canal after World War I. By the mid-1920s grain exports, primarily moving via the Canal to Europe, replaced forest products as the leading tonnage export through the Southern Gateway. Grain held that dominance for the next half-century.

During World War II transpacific trade came to a complete halt. Within a decade after the war ended, the resurgent Japanese and later, South Korean economies required large quantities of basic resource commodities such as coal, sulphur, potash, and mineral concentrates. All needed to be imported and all were available in Western Canada. Food shortages in communist China eventually forced its xenophobic leadership to enter overseas markets, at first confined to very large grain purchases from Canada in 1961. After Mao's death in 1976, more pragmatic leaders gradually opened their vast country to a full range of world trade and released the dynamism of the Chinese people with resulting spectacular effect on world trade patterns. With the addition of China's huge demand for raw materials, Canada's transpacific trade with East Asian nations exceeded its transatlantic trade for the first time in 1983.

To handle the export of these commodities bulk terminals were constructed at the Southern Gateway during the sixties and seventies, first on the north shore of Burrard Inlet and later at Roberts Bank. By the mid-eighties the Northern Gateway, too, had its first bulk terminals on Ridley Island. Forest products exports to markets in both Asia and Europe also expanded dramatically between 1960 and 2000, requiring the construction of break-bulk terminals at both gateways.

Continuing growth in dry bulk export traffic, especially to Asian markets, required expansion of the recently constructed terminals and upgrading of the rail corridors serving them. Exports of most of the basic bulk commodities came close to peaking in 1988 and growth since then has been modest. Grain exports are primarily limited by available supply, whereas the annual tonnage of most of the other dry bulk exports is primarily a function of world demand.

The Southern Gateway's approach to the "container revolution" was timid and, as a result, it initially lost out to much more aggressive ports on the United States (U.S.) West Coast. Adequate port and rail container handling capacity was eventually provided and this, coupled with rapidly increasing containerized traffic worldwide, resulted in double digit annual growth in container throughput between 1989 and 2008. In late 2007, the new and unique container terminal at the Northern Gateway commenced operation and proved immediately successful, despite the double digit decline in throughput at other Pacific Coast container terminals caused by the financial crisis in North America and Europe in 2008 and 2009.

Through the entire twentieth century Vancouver held a monopoly as the base port for the seasonal Alaska Cruise market. The 9/11 terrorist attacks on U.S. soil created fear among American citizens who became reluctant to travel beyond their borders. Seattle took advantage of this and very aggressively and successfully promoted its expanded facilities. In 2008 it exceeded Vancouver's cruise passenger figures for the first time.

While Canada is recognized worldwide as a reliable supplier of many essential basic resource commodities, it has keen competitors. A major factor in the success of overseas marketing efforts by Canadians for these commodities has been, and will continue to be, closely linked to the cost effectiveness and efficiency of the supply chain from the point of production to the loaded vessel. Although unrealistic optimism that leads to flagrantly excessive expansion and over-development is undesirable and expensive, delay in providing adequate corridor and terminal capacity will result in business lost to more aggressive and efficient competitors. The history of the Pacific Gateways offers examples of both.

THE IMPACT OF ECONOMIC CYCLES

In addition to the near total disruption of trade caused by both world wars, recurring swings in the volume of economic activity during relatively peaceful times have a very significant impact on global markets and trade. These cycles are characterized by over optimistic predictions for the immediate future during the good years, only to be followed by the deep gloom that virtually halts capital expenditures during economic downturns.

By 1910 the decade that American historians have called the "Good Years" was coming to an end. This period of rapid expansion in the North American economy was followed by three years of increasing depression prior to the start of the five-year First World War. The post-war "Roaring Twenties" were boom years and growth and development of port facilities at the Southern Gateway was quite spectacular, especially on the south shore of Burrard Inlet. A decade of deep depression followed, ending in another World War lasting six years. After the war, trade recovery had a special impact on the Southern Gateway, creating the need for new terminals to handle the demand for bulk raw materials from the first of the "Asian Tigers." Subsequent peaks and dips in the global economic cycle were less dramatic until the leadership of the financial system in the U.S. and Europe collapsed, trigging a global crisis in 2008 that threatened to rival the Great Depression.

Attempts to predict these economic cycles are, at best, unreliable. In relation to the Gateway Ports, inaccurate predictions have resulted in periods of over capacity alternating with periods of limited ability to serve available markets.

THE INFLUENCE OF SENIOR GOVERNMENTS ON THE DEVELOPMENT OF THE CORRIDORS AND GATEWAYS

RAIL CORRIDORS

The first corridor to the coast, the Cariboo Road, was built for the colonial British Columbia government by Queen Victoria's Royal Engineers and served to open a route into the southern interior.

The CPR was built to fulfill Prime Minister Macdonald's promise to tie British Columbia to Canada by steel rails. Political imperatives forced the railway's financiers to raise capital outside the U.S. and strongly influenced their decision to build the line through the much more difficult southern mountain passes. Federal grants of $30 million cash plus 12 million hectares of prime prairie land and a tax free, 20-year monopoly on Trans-Canada railway building rounded out federal largesse to this company of wealthy Montreal businessmen. To entice the CPR to extend its line from Port Moody to Granville the provincial government, in 1887, gave the railway much of the waterfront on the south shore of Burrard Inlet plus 25 square kilometers of upland, now the business district of Vancouver. The CPR became the federal Tories' pride and joy, and early Vancouver citizens responded with strong support for that party.

The Canadian Northern began as a regional network in Manitoba with the goal of breaking the CPR's monopoly on grain movement to the Lakehead. In its role as the "Farmers' Friend," it had strong support from the provincial and local governments.

The hybrid Grand Trunk Pacific/National Transcontinental railway was built to satisfy Prime Minister Laurier's strong desire to have a Liberal sponsored railway built across the country, a reversal of the party's long held antagonism toward the first transcontinental built by the Tories. Instead of huge land grants, however, government financial support for the second and third transcontinental lines involved guarantees on a high percentage of the bonds issued by the railway builders. Consequently, when both the new lines failed soon after completion, they were taken over and merged with other failing Canadian lines to form a government owned and politically influenced entity, the Canadian National Railway.

Caught up in the late stages of the North American public mania for railway building, the Tory McBride government in Victoria (1903 to 1915) — friend of the CPR and the CNP, but cool to the GTP and Prince Rupert — responded to public demand. It granted bond guarantees of $35,000 to the newly incorporated PGE for each mile of line it built north from Vancouver into the Peace River country in northeast B.C. By 1918 this project, too, had failed and had to be taken over by the new Liberal government in Victoria. For the next 86 years, it became a very costly "political football," until its operations were finally sold to the newly privatized CNR in 2004.

GATEWAY PORTS

As with the railways, the development of the Gateway Ports on the West Coast had very strong political overtones. The colonial government of James Douglas was determined that Victoria would retain its position as the chief port of entry for trade goods from Europe and be the premier loading port for exports of forest products, salmon, and furs collected from coastal points and the interior by HBC vessels. To help achieve this Douglas initially hobbled New Westminster, the rival mainland port, by designating it a customs port, in contrast to the capital city's free port status.

Thwarted by politics and the reluctance of most deep-sea sailing vessel captains to negotiate the Fraser River estuary, New Westminster focused initially on the rapidly growing domestic traffic up river, which served the interior gold rush and agriculture developments in the valley. At the same time, the community began to provide basic navigation aids on the treacherous terminal channels of the river. Determined to become the premier port for mainland B.C., "Royal City" promoters successfully lobbied Ottawa to fund two vital projects. The first focussed on defining and maintaining a navigable channel on the

Fraser River to enable deep-sea vessels to reach the city. The second aimed to remove snags from the river as far east as Hope. Federal funding for these projects commenced in 1882 and continued for well over a century.

During the Laurier years, New Westminster benefitted from federal Liberal government favours and that party's visceral distaste for anything related to the Tory sponsored CPR. Its citizens responded with strong support for the Liberal government.

McBride's provincial Tory government and Laurier's federal Tory successor, Robert Borden (1911–1917) clearly favoured developing Vancouver over either New Westminster, or the new Northern Corridor with its terminal port at Prince Rupert. McBride did, however, provide his hometown on the river with a rail/road bridge in 1904. The rail component of that bridge is still in active use after 106 years.

The port on Burrard Inlet had modest beginnings as a village accommodating sawmill employees. Early overseas export traffic consisted solely of products manufactured from the local forests. The port's status changed dramatically with the arrival of the railway and the subsequent launch of transpacific liner service carrying high value import cargo and passengers. This gave it national and international significance. The marine community's complaints about the perils of the "indifferent entrance" to the inner harbour persuaded the federal Department of Public Works to acquire a new Scottish built dredge in 1910 to widen, deepen, and straighten the channel at first narrows. This would be the first of several federally funded projects to improve the harbour entrance.

Until 1913, the private sector provided and operated most terminals and marine related facilities at Vancouver and New Westminster. In Vancouver, the major wharves, piers, and shore-side installations belonged to the CPR. There was no central administrative body to oversee waterfront planning or control developments.

Vancouver's 100,000 citizens were particularly fortunate in their choice of H. H. Stevens as their Ottawa representative in the 1911 election. Reelected four times, Stevens, who could be considered the "Father of the Port of Vancouver," laboured ceaselessly and effectively to promote the port's growth and development. In 1913 he introduced legislation that created the Port of Vancouver as an official entity to be administered, controlled, and developed by a new Vancouver Harbour Commission. At the same time, the New Westminster Harbour Commission was established and remained independent within the Southern Gateway for the next 95 years.

Stevens obtained federal funding for additional dredging at first narrows and for constructing the port's first government owned pier complex, which was completed in 1915 on a site just east of Hastings Mill. With the opening of the Panama Canal imminent, Stevens envisioned that a substantial quantity of grain from the western prairies would move through the port en route to transatlantic markets. To handle this prospective movement he persuaded Ottawa to fund the ports' first grain elevator, built adjacent to the new government pier and completed in 1916.

In 1919 the federal government established a new policy of loaning funds to Harbour Commissions for port projects approved by the Minister of Marine on the issuance, by the borrowing Commission, of debentures bearing interest at 5 percent. This funding model built many of the structures on the south shore of Burrard Inlet including Ballantyne Pier, the Vancouver Harbour Terminal Railway, two more grain elevators plus an annex to the first, and loading jetties for the grain terminals. Persistent requests from the marine community were rewarded with a 70 percent federal grant toward the $3.75 million cost of the first floating dry dock for the port, completed in 1925.

The New Westminster Harbour Commission completed a small grain terminal in 1928 for lease to operators on the south bank of the Fraser and the City of New Westminster supported Pacific Coast Terminals' wharf projects by offering long term tax relief and a 20-year guarantee on the company's preferred share dividends. In addition, Pacific Coast Terminals received a $700,000 federal subsidy for their cold storage facility.

At Prince Rupert the Grand Trunk Pacific belatedly received a promised federal subsidy amounting to 71 percent of the cost of their shipyard and dry dock project, completed in 1916. Along with the railway, this reverted to the CNR when the GTP went into bankruptcy in 1919. The wooden Ocean Dock was built parallel to the shoreline with federal funds in 1921 and the Canadian Government Grain Elevator opened for a very short burst of activity in 1926.

It is clear that there was no defined pattern or formula to senior government aid for corridor or port developments during the half-century from 1880 to 1930. The CPR was given enormous land grants and cash, while the next two transcontinental railway builders and the PGE received government guarantees on most of their bond issues. Annual Fraser River dredging and snag removal plus periodic dredging of Vancouver's harbour entrance and major projects to enhance the navigable Fraser River channel were all funded by Ottawa. Dry dock projects at Vancouver and Prince Rupert received federal grants covering 70 percent of their cost and the first government pier and grain elevator at Vancouver was fully funded by Ottawa, to be owned and operated by the new Vancouver Harbour Commission.

Between 1919 and 1929 federal funds made available to Harbour Commissions on both coasts (including the St Lawrence River ports) reached $150 million. This funding took the form of repayable interest bearing loans for approved projects. However, only the Vancouver Harbour Commission, recipient of less than one-fifth of that amount, had honoured its obligation to meet interest and sinking fund payments. During the subsequent depression years many of these loans, including a portion of Vancouver's, were written off.

Labouring under the severe financial constraints so prevalent during the early thirties and acutely aware of mounting problems with the national ports, the new government of R. B. Bennett appointed Sir Alexander Gibb in 1931 to conduct an inquiry into the management, operation, and finances of the major Canadian public ports and recommend needed changes. As described in Chapter Four, his recommendations led to the formation in 1936 of the National Harbours Board (NHB) which provided centralized control of the newly created Port Authorities that replaced many of the former Harbour Commissions, including Vancouver's.

Gibb's recommendation to merge the two Fraser River Harbour Commissions into the new Vancouver Port Authority was not followed; neither was his advice that ports be kept free of political influence. Unfortunately for Prince Rupert, his recommendation "that Vancouver should be protected from establishment of a competitive port further north," (with no time limit) was accepted without question, effectively blocking government support for development of the Northern Corridor and Gateway Port for the next four decades.

Whereas the Vancouver Harbour Commission had borrowed public funds to build and operate terminals and the Harbour Railway, under its new status as a Port Authority it was subject to the tight control of the NHB office in Ottawa. From this time on, federal funds were used primarily to prepare sites that could be leased to private entities for development and operation. Later the NHB added throughput charges on all traffic over their leased sites. The charges included escalation clauses and were to be paid in perpetuity, thereby creating the "gift that keeps on giving" and providing handsome revenues to the Port Authorities.

From 1930 to 1945 federal funding for non-military west coast port projects was minimal. New Westminster continued to receive funding to maintain its river channel and in 1934, shortly before its conversion to a Port Authority under the NHB, the Vancouver Harbour Commission rebuilt and assumed ownership of the second narrows bridge, which had been out of service for four years. After 1936 the new Vancouver Port Authority required approval from NHB headquarters in Ottawa for expenditures over $10,000. Certainly on the West Coast, the NHB's policy for the next two decades would be one of retrenchment.

Continuing concern with the navigation channel at first narrows led to federal funding of further major dredging projects in 1953 and again in 1969–1970.

Two developments made it feasible for private developers to build bulk terminals on the north shore of Burrard Inlet in the fifties and sixties. The first was the extension of the provincially owned PGE Railway into North Vancouver in 1956. The other was the major investment made by the federally owned CNR to access the north shore, starting with their purchase of the second narrows bridge in 1952. The site for Neptune Terminals (and later Seaboard) was prepared by the NHB in 1966–1967 and a decade later this site was expanded to the east for lease to Lynnterm.

On the south shore of Burrard Inlet, Centennial Pier was completed by the NHB/VPA in 1959. Substantial rail and road access improvements were made to most south shore terminals in 1966 and the thorny issue of the waterfront ownership finally settled with the CPR. As part of that settlement, the Port Authority acquired the CPR's Pier B–C.

Also in 1966, the NHB extended the limits of Vancouver harbour south to the U.S. border in response to vigorous prodding from B.C.'s Premier Bennett. The board then created an offshore, 20 hectare "island" (with connecting causeway) at Roberts Bank and leased it to Westshore Terminals. This new coal terminal was served by a rail line constructed by the B.C. Harbours Board. Then in 1984, the NHB embarked on a second major initiative. It quadrupled the size of the artificial island, created from dredged silt, and added a second deep-sea berth for the coal terminal.

Seeking to improve Vancouver's ability to handle expanding transpacific wheat sales, the Canadian Wheat Board, in 1976, offered a generous Storage Incentive Program to terminal operators willing to substantially increase their terminals' capacities. With this stimulus Alberta and Saskatchewan Wheat Pools each added an annex to their elevators; Pioneer Grain rebuilt, enlarged, and modernized their extensively damaged Burrard Terminal, and United Grain Growers extensively modernized their terminal over three years. When completed, these additions increased the port's grain terminal storage capacity by 40 percent.

Although the NHB was aware that container terminal development at U.S. West Coast ports was progressing rapidly, it was slow to act at Vancouver. A very modest facility created by modifying part of Centennial Pier and supplying it with one crane opened on June 1, 1970, but it would be another five years before the port could offer a purpose built facility and that opened several months after the new container terminal on the Fraser River.

A new and much larger floating dry dock was installed on the north shore of Burrard Inlet in 1981. Two-thirds of the completed cost of $63.3 million was provided by grants from Ottawa and Victoria. Just 10 years later the two governments contributed a further $14 million to prevent the facility from being sold by its bankrupt owner to Asian buyers.

Under the *Canada Ports Corporation Act* passed in 1983, the Vancouver Port Authority was replaced by the Vancouver Port Corporation (VPC). This new Crown Corporation was provided with a modest increase of freedom through its new spending limit of $5 million. Despite the name change, however, there was little evidence that the controlling mindset of the bureaucracy at Canada Ports Corporation head office in Ottawa had changed. One of the first projects the VPC undertook was the development of the Canada Place cruise terminal on the old Pier B–C site. This project was completed in time for the opening of Expo '86. In 1993 the Canada Harbour Place Corporation, developer of Canada Place, became a subsidiary of the VPC and in 2003 the cruise facility was extended to accommodate an extra vessel.

The Southern Gateway's original port at New Westminster escaped being merged with the Vancouver Port Authority, despite the recommendation contained in the Gibb Report. Under the *Harbour Commission Act* of 1964, the New Westminster Harbour Commission became the Fraser River Harbour Commission with more local representation and it continued to operate free of the rigid central control imposed on the Port Authorities. The Harbour Commission redeveloped their site on the south bank of the Fraser River formerly occupied by the riverside grain terminal. They then leased it to Fraser Surrey Docks who commenced operation in 1964. When this site was expanded the Southern Gateway's first specialized container terminal with accessible and uncongested rail connections was developed. The Commission's contribution to this project was funded through loans from a commercial bank. In addition to the container terminal, the Commission also developed riverside sites in 1971 and 1973 for two auto terminals and expanded both sites as business developed. By the early 1980s the Commission was heavily focused on assembling more parcels of riverside property suitable for future marine related developments. It consequently gained the reputation of a property rich port.

In 1988 Fraser Surrey Docks accepted a $9 million loan from the Government of Alberta. When they defaulted on the loan provisions, Alberta assumed control of the facility, but their operation was not successful and the terminal was sold at a substantial loss to Hong Kong investors in 1992.

Under the provisions of the *Canada Marine Act* of 1998, the Fraser River Harbour Commission became the Fraser River Port Authority (FRPA) with a mandate to operate in a manner similar to the other Port Authorities, while still retaining its long cherished independence. The new FRPA continued to focus on acquiring and developing riverside properties, especially the large and valuable Richmond and Surrey parcels. In 2004 the Port Authority participated in the ill-starred $190 million container terminal expansion. Finally, in 2008 the long deferred merger took place and the two Fraser Authorities merged with the Vancouver Port Authority to form the Vancouver Fraser Port Authority. This ended 95 years of rivalry and frequent unseemly competition within the Southern Gateway.

The 1988 U.S. Canada Free Trade Agreement and NAFTA, passed in 1994, created new opportunities for Canadian trade within North America. The subsequent privatization of the CNR followed by its merger with the Illinois Central Railroad created a Canada based, business oriented, railway colossus with the greatest geographic reach of any North American railroad. These events would hold special significance for the future of the Northern Corridor and its Gateway Port.

Recognizing the impetus to transpacific trade resulting from the tremendous changes taking place in the economies of China, India, and other south and Southeast Asian nations, both the federal and B.C. governments acted. Beginning in 1984, they began a series of initiatives designed to foster trade with these new economic powerhouses and to enhance the ability of the western gateways to handle increasing transpacific traffic. These initiatives culminated in October 2006 when the new federal government announced the Asia Pacific Gateway and Corridor Initiative (APGCI) with billions in funding for gateway and road/rail corridor infrastructure projects. In 2009 this funding was supplemented by funds from an Infrastructure Stimulus Fund created to stimulate employment during the sharp economic downturn. Federal funding commitments to projects specifically designed to enhance the operation of facilities within the Southern Gateway exceeded $750 million by mid-2010.[6]

Between 1994 and 1997 the VPC developed Deltaport, a third container terminal for the Southern Gateway located at Roberts Bank. Later, based on traffic projections, a third

---

[6]See Appendix 2 for details.

berth was added to this facility along with increased backup land. This project was completed in early 2010 at a cost of $400 million.

With passage of the *Canada Marine Act* in 1998, the Vancouver Port Corporation was renamed the Vancouver Port Authority, but this time the name change was accompanied by more autonomy, the organization was mandated to operate in a commercially oriented manner, and its borrowing limit was increased to $225 million. A decade later it merged with the two Fraser Port Authorities to form the Vancouver Fraser Port Authority with control over the entire Southern Gateway.

Since September 11, 2001, port security has become an issue of prime importance and the federal government has provided successive grants to ports for security related projects, especially at container terminals. Along with security, there is also an increasing focus on "going green" as it relates to port operations and visiting vessels. The federal and provincial governments contributed two-thirds of the $9 million cost of providing the Canada Place cruise facility with two alternate marine power installations, a project completed in August 2009.

To counter the increasingly inequitable municipal tax burden applied to port terminals and related facilities the province introduced the *Ports Competitive Property Tax Act* in 2003. This Act, which has since been extended, has provided a measure of stability to existing and potential private investors.

THE NORTHERN GATEWAY

At Prince Rupert the Canadian Grain Commission added a 1 million bushel annex to the local elevator in 1968 and in 1970 the NHB acquired the leases that Western Wharves Ltd. had assembled at Fairview, promising the early completion of a general cargo terminal on that site. In 1972 Prince Rupert was proclaimed a national harbour and the B.C. government transferred Ridley Island to Ottawa with the understanding that it would provide the infrastructure needed for the early development of bulk terminals there. Despite the loss of the port's only general cargo facility in the Ocean Dock fire in 1972, progress at Fairview remained painfully slow. The new general cargo facility was not completed until early 1977.

The potential for growth in throughput over the long delayed Fairview facility was very substantially reduced by two factors. The first was the collapse in 1977 of the federal-provincial "Grand Plan" for railway building in the northwest sector of the province. The second was the unwritten obligation of forest products producers at sites served by the PGE/BCR to ship via that line to Southern Gateway Terminals.

The Prince Rupert Port Authority was established in 1975 with an NHB-imposed-leash that was so short that the port could exercise "authority" in name only. It was eventually authorized to spend $0.5 million to minimally rehabilitate the remainder of the Ocean Dock and then only with the proviso that the costs be recouped through a tax on cruise vessel passengers. Given that no passenger amenities were offered in return, cruise vessel operators resented the charge and this contributed to the loss of this seasonal business for the port.

The Province of B.C., through the B.C. Development Corporation, acquired a large parcel of waterfront property on the west side of Kaien Island in 1976 and used it primarily to goad the NHB into the timely provision of coal and grain terminal infrastructure on Ridley Island. These terminals were completed in 1984 and 1985 respectively. The provision of the road, rail causeway, and other basic infrastructure to the island flowed from the Memorandum of Understanding signed on July 30, 1979 between Ottawa and the consortium of grain companies that formed Prince Rupert Grain. The road from Highway 16 was contributed by the B.C. Department of Highways. Funding for the rest of the infrastructure was provided by way of grants from the Province of Alberta and a mix of grants and recoverable expenditures by Ottawa. Eighty percent of the funds required to build the grain terminal were provided through long term loans to Prince Rupert Grain from Alberta, whereas funding for the coal terminal was eventually financed in full by Ottawa and operated as a Crown Corporation. Both terminals were built on land leased from the Prince Rupert Port Authority, payable as a throughput charge on the volume shipped through the facilities.

The 1995 legislation that finally eliminated the Crow Benefit included the loss of port parity for moving grain to Prince Rupert. In response, the CNR initially substantially increased its charge for carrying grain over the Northern Corridor with the inevitable result that grain throughput for the northern port was drastically reduced. Eventually, new thinking at CN headquarters produced a gradual return to parity with Vancouver and later a substantial discount over the Southern Gateway, restoring grain flows to approximately 27.5 percent of West Coast exports.

When the Prince Rupert Port Corporation became the Prince Rupert Port Authority under the *Canada Marine Act* on May 1, 1999, it had considerably more autonomy and a mandate to operate in a commercially oriented manner. Its borrowing authority, however, was capped at only $22 million and, as with all other Port Authorities, provisions of the Act preclude the port from borrowing against its assets, seeking government guarantees on borrowing, or receiving money from an appropriation by Parliament. While the restrictions pose little or no problem for a cash rich port like Vancouver with abundant income from multiple revenue streams, they have placed the Northern Gateway Port at a distinct disadvantage in attempting to fund even basic infrastructure, let alone the new port facilities required for it to fulfill its long overdue role as Canada's second Pacific Gateway.

The Port Authority opened a $9 million, large cruise vessel terminal in 2004 with funding assistance of $1.5 million from the Western Diversification Fund plus contributions from the province and the City of Prince Rupert.

Ill-considered attempts by the federal government to dispose of the Ridley Island coal terminal in 2004–2005 were fortunately blocked by a new administration in Ottawa early in 2006.

The federal and provincial governments each contributed $30 million toward the cost of converting the Fairview General Cargo Terminal into a unique rail served container terminal. This major undertaking was completed in September 2007 and has been very successful, despite the double digit slump in throughput felt at other West Coast terminals during 2008 and 2009. In early 2011, the terminal will became the first container terminal in Canada equipped to provide berthed vessels with alternative marine power. Seventy percent of the funding for that project was provided by federal grants.

SUMMARY

This review clearly demonstrates the dominant role of senior governments in controlling and funding the destiny of both "National Gateway" ports on the Pacific Coast. Administration of these ports has evolved over the last century, as have the ways of providing funding for their development.

It would probably be impossible to determine with any accuracy the sum total, in current dollars, of senior government expenditures by way of grants, equity, loans, and other forms of assistance to the development of the Pacific Gateway Ports since the first federal funds were used to dredge the Fraser River in 1882. It is certain, however, that all but a relatively tiny portion has been spent on projects at the Southern Gateway Ports, now consolidated into Port Metro Vancouver.

CHAPTER ELEVEN

The Gateways Today and Tomorrow

I n the shipping world ports are judged in terms of cost, efficiency, and reliability. Efficiency is measured largely by the ability of the port's facilities to send arriving vessels back to sea in the fastest time possible. Optimum efficiency in the transfer of cargo between a berthed vessel and its source or destination requires smooth terminal operation, uncongested road or rail movement within the "last mile" of the terminal, and reliable rail service in the port's main corridor. If any one of these supply chain components operates inefficiently, it affects the whole movement and will eventually reflect negatively on the port's reputation.

THE CORRIDORS

At both Pacific Gateway Ports the movement of bulk and break-bulk commodities destined for overseas markets dominates their tonnage throughput. Most of these products are sourced at a distance from tidewater that precludes all but rail movement to port terminals.

The movement of high-content-value import containers from a berthed vessel to distant destinations is especially sensitive to the reliability and cost effectiveness of rail service. Speed is of paramount importance. The performance of the rail component to, from, and within the Gateway Ports is therefore critical if the segment of the global supply chain passing through Canada's West Coast ports is to function optimally. Competition from United States Pacific Gateways and their rail corridors is keen and is not likely to weaken.

THE DOMINANCE OF THE SOUTHERN CORRIDOR

During the four-year period ending December 31, 2010, a total of 387 million tonnes of foreign import/export cargo moved over the terminals of Canada's two Pacific Gateway Ports. Of that total, 85.3 percent was handled by terminals within Port Metro Vancouver and most was moved to or from the port by rail, through the Southern Corridor. That figure represents a significant drop from the near total dominance of the Southern Gateway and Corridor through most of the twentieth century. In 2010, the Northern Gateway's share of total Pacific Coast foreign cargo movement reached 15 percent and will likely exceed that proportion in 2011.

Many of the reasons why the Northern Corridor and Gateway Port were virtually abandoned until the mid-1970s are examined in Chapter One. It would appear that Canada, so very dependent on export trade, has long been in denial about the risk of funnelling such a high proportion of its transpacific trade through one corridor to one port. In Eastern

Canada, such dominance has never existed, nor would it have been tolerated in a region where many ports serve the country's transatlantic trade.

With the relatively recent and dramatic shift in world trade to the Asia Pacific region senior governments have begun to show more interest in the eminently viable Northern Corridor and the superbly located Northern Gateway Port.

RAIL LINES TO THE PERIPHERY OF THE SOUTHERN GATEWAY

Three Class One railways move goods to and from Southern Gateway terminals. The Burlington Northern (BNSF) enters Port Metro Vancouver (PMV) from the south. It is a relatively small player that moves mostly forest products south and U.S. sourced coal north to Westshore Terminal. The Canadian Pacific Railway (CPR) and Canadian National Railways (CNR) move over 95 percent of foreign cargo entering and leaving the gateway.

With the exception of the CN operated former BC Rail line, these two Class One main lines share a common corridor for the last 400 km (250 miles) of their route to the coast. This common corridor passes through the narrow valley of the Thompson River and the spectacular Fraser River Canyon over a distance of 160 km (100 miles) and is vulnerable to blockage as a result of natural or manmade disasters. In 1965 a minor earthquake triggered a slide, estimated at 46 million cubic metres of rock, earth, and snow that buried 3 km (1.8 miles) of the southern trans-provincial highway to a depth of up to 70 m. The slide occurred at a point only 19 km (12 miles) east of Hope, the community located at the southern entrance to the Fraser Canyon. Further confirmation of the adage, "every mountain wants to meet the sea," occurred in August 2010 with the collapse of a section of Mt. Meager, located 128 km (80 miles) west of Lillooet at the north end of the Fraser Canyon. At an estimated 40 million cubic metres, this avalanche of rock, ice, and mud is second only to the Hope Slide as the largest recorded in Canada.

It appears obvious that there is a very real potential for a massive slide in the geologically unstable Fraser canyon, which would result in a long term blockage to one or both rail lines and a catastrophe for exporters of Western Canadian bulk commodities. To ignore or deny this risk is irresponsible. The folly of relying on this vulnerable corridor to move such a high percentage of the country's Asia Pacific trade must surely be disturbingly evident to importers and exporters, both here and abroad.

Further to concern over the fragility of this common corridor is the question of the railways' ability to substantially increase traffic over the long stretches of their necessarily single track. The agreement between the CN and CP, which provides for directional running from Mission to near Ashcroft, has eased capacity constraints during the past decade. To achieve a further capacity increase of that magnitude over that sector of their common corridor would surely be both difficult and prohibitively expensive. No other practical route across the rugged mountain terrain of southern British Columbia (B.C.) is available.

THE UNDERUTILIZED NORTHERN RAIL CORRIDOR

The CNR line in this corridor, completed in 1914 by the Grand Trunk Pacific Railway to high standards of grade and curves, was upgraded to accommodate unit trains carrying coal and grain in the early 1980s. From the point where this line departs from the CNR line south to Vancouver at Red Pass Junction, it follows a water grade west to Prince Rupert across the much gentler terrain of central and northern B.C. Its builders faced none of the extreme difficulties and hazards of constructing a line through the Fraser Canyon, or the much higher mountain passes of Southeastern B.C. Indeed, the Northern Rail Corridor is considered by many to be the easiest and best route of any built across the North American Cordillera.

The distance by this corridor from Red Pass Junction to Prince Rupert is 309 km (192 miles) longer than the distance from that point to Vancouver. Although this would appear to be a significant disadvantage, several compensating factors have persuaded the CNR to offer substantial rate discounts on grain traffic moving via the Northern Gateway in recent years.

Another issue with the Northern Corridor is its dependence on a single rail line and operator. While this point is valid, the single rail operator is in a position to work very closely with the terminals to achieve maximum efficiency and productivity. With only one rail operator, there is none of the chronic squabbling between competitors that often hampers operations at port terminals served by two or more railroads. Frustration with that issue has periodically led the Vancouver Port Authority (VPA) to consider recreating and operating its own harbour railway.

Indeed, though two Class One lines carry most of the traffic to and from the Southern Gateway, they use the same corridor for the last 250 miles of their route and operate on each other's tracks over two-thirds of that section.

When the federal government has considered it to be in the national interest it has shown willingness to exert pressure at the highest levels of both Canadian railways to ensure they cooperate to keep key traffic moving. For example, during the four-month grain workers strike in Vancouver in 2003–2004, a total of 10,669 CP cars were interchanged with CN for onward movement to Prince Rupert Grain via the Northern Corridor.

A more permanent solution to satisfy a future perceived need for rail competition on the Northern Corridor might involve a change in the *Canada Transportation Act* to allow open access to other rail operators. This was one of the recommendations contained in the 2005 B.C. Port Strategy document. Another option could involve creating a senior government authority to acquire ownership of the track and rail bed to allow for common use of the corridor. At the present time, however, there is no apparent need for either of these options to be considered seriously, as the Northern Corridor line operates far below its capacity and has ample room to increase capacity when traffic warrants.

THE PACIFIC GATEWAY PORTS

Canada's two Pacific Gateway Ports provide the vital link in the movement of bulk, break-bulk, and boxed cargo between distant overseas ports and regional, national, and international origins or destinations. Their facilities and related infrastructure are assets of national importance and, if Canada is to benefit fully from its favoured location on the Pacific Rim and its economic and political relationships, it is essential that they operate efficiently and reliably.

Historically, the Port of Victoria dominated both of its two mainland rivals in terms of the tonnage of cargo handled, until Vancouver passed it in 1919. From then until the first modern bulk and break-bulk terminals were completed at the Northern Gateway between 1977 and 1985, Vancouver held a near monopoly on the movement of almost all categories of export and import cargoes.

Port Metro Vancouver will undoubtedly retain its position as the leading Pacific Gateway, but its dominance will almost certainly decline as the ease with which trade moves between Asia and mid North American points, through the more favourably situated Northern Gateway, becomes more widely recognized.

PORT METRO VANCOUVER, THE SOUTHERN GATEWAY TODAY

Since the arrival of the first CPR chartered vessel bringing cargoes of tea to the new rail-served port, Vancouver has considered itself the exclusive Western Canadian Gateway for transpacific trade. The port saw spectacular growth and development in the 1920s based on the bulk movement of prairie grain to transatlantic markets via the Panama Canal. A second era of rapid development in the port's inventory of terminals took place in the sixties and seventies when it began to export very large tonnages of bulk and break-bulk commodities to burgeoning Asian markets. These two periods of growth gave Vancouver its reputation as "The Port that Bulk Built." In the last two decades the main growth areas have related to the movement of containers and cruise passengers.

Over the past 125 years, the port has grown to become the largest in Canada and, in terms of foreign exports, is considered the fourth largest and most diversified port in North America. Approximately 95 percent of its throughput serves Canadian import/export demand.

The January 1, 2008 merger of the Vancouver and Fraser Port Authorities not only removed the long standing irritant of intraregional port rivalry, but also added a very large domestic cargo movement to the combined port's total tonnage and provided much needed river front sites for future port developments.

With development spanning well over a century this mature, full service port is now facing several difficult issues that could significantly affect its future development.

Sea Access to PMV Terminals

Like the Puget Sound ports of Seattle and Tacoma, Port Metro Vancouver can almost be considered an "inland" port. Vessels approaching these ports from the open ocean have a long distance to travel under increasingly stringent Emission Control Area regulations. A vessel destined for a Southern Gateway berth is required to carry a professional pilot during the final 128 km (80 miles).

The majority of the port's terminals are located on the shores of Burrard Inlet and to reach most of them a vessel needs to move only a short distance past the harbour entrance at first narrows. Water depth there, despite several major dredging projects over the years, still limits the loaded draft of very large vessels. Furthermore, clearance under the Lions Gate Bridge precludes the latest mega cruise liners from passing.

Second narrows is crossed by a high level highway bridge and a lift span railway bridge. For vessels berthing at the oil and bulk terminals on the eastern extension of the Inlet, transiting this narrow passage is fraught with special hazards and is subject to the Port Authority's very strict rules, which attempt to avoid a repeat of the many previous accidents at that site. The recent, very marked increase in the number of deep laden oil tankers moving through this narrow passage, as well as the pressures to increase the size and frequency of these vessel movements have focused attention on this harbour choke point.

Vessels moving to a berth at the Roberts Bank terminals face no natural obstacles, as long as they stay within the dredged passage. Those terminals are, however, exposed to occasional very strong winds that can disrupt their operations or cause extensive damage, as happened on January 1, 2003. That event resulted in the closure of one of the two coal loading berths for seven months.

Since the first sailing ship master gingerly and reluctantly threaded the shallow and shifting channels of the Fraser River to reach the Royal City, 25 km ahead, the annual deposit of 3 million cubic metres of silt in the outlet channels has complicated the use of the extensive riverfront shoreline for deep-sea terminal development. By 1998, one hundred and sixteen years of federal expenditures on annual dredging, snag removal, and major control works, resulted in a navigable channel 10.7 m (35 feet 8 inches) deep. Subsequent dredging has succeeded in reaching and maintaining a depth of 11.5 m (38 feet 3 inches), which is close to the maximum possible given that the crown of the Massey Tunnel has a low water clearance of 11.9 m (39 feet 7 inches).

Although the VFPA continues to maintain the main navigation channel and ensure access to deep-sea facilities, side channels are rapidly silting in and marina operators are increasingly vocal about needing help to maintain access to their facilities.

Land Access to Port Metro Vancouver Facilities

Greater Vancouver's geographic features, though unquestionably responsible for its spectacular natural beauty, create considerable physical challenges and constraints for heavy rail or road traffic moving to and from the port terminals. Movement is neither easy nor cheap.

Most of the port's 26 cargo terminals line the shores of Burrard Inlet and rail access to them is hampered by the complex tangle of competing jurisdictions and the limited water-front space available for tracks. All rail traffic from the south moving to the north shore bulk and break-bulk terminals must cross the second narrows lift span rail bridge, owned by the CNR. Though traffic there was last interrupted for a prolonged period in 1979, this bridge remains a major concern for terminal operators on the north shore.

The venerable Fraser River lift span rail bridge at New Westminster provides access to Vancouver for the CN and BNSF railways and currently carries an average 46 trains daily. This span, too, is susceptible to accidental damage interrupting rail service, such as the 1975 barge collision that caused a four-month outage and the 1982 fire that closed the bridge for a month. These bridges are indeed the "Achilles Heels" of rail service to the Burrard Inlet terminals. Until the repeal of Murphy's Law they will continue to be!

It is ironic that the terminal complex on the south bank of the Fraser River opposite New Westminster — a terminal whose use is compromised by the depth of its access channel — has easy and relatively hazard free rail access, as well as generous space available for adjacent trackage.

Rail service to the terminals at Roberts Bank is provided by the 38.6 km (24 mile) common user line, built and still owned by the B.C. Harbours Board. Since 1969 this line has provided fair and open service to all three Class One railways.

In addition to serving the 26 deep-sea, bulk cargo and container terminals, the railways serve a large number of widely scattered facilities in the Greater Vancouver area involved in such activities as distribution, transloading, and forwarding. This increases not only the complexity of rail movements, but also public irritation stemming from level crossings, noise, and air pollution. The very marked increase in the movement of large diesel trucks carrying containers between local or regional points and the container terminals has caused increasing public concern, due partly to the trucks' contributions to air pollution and to the congestion on Greater Vancouver's already stretched road network.

Increasing awareness of the mounting problems associated with congested and con-stricted access to port terminals led to the Greater Vancouver Gateway Council being estab-lished in 1994. It was charged with planning the expansion of local infrastructure to provide efficient logistic services for expediting Asian trade. Their activities, strongly supported since 2003 by the provincial government, led to Ottawa announcing its Pacific Gateway Strategy in 2005. A year later, a new federal government recycled and reissued this as the Asia Pacific Gateway and Corridor Initiative (APGCI) with a strong focus on upgrades and additions to Pacific port infrastructure, as well as assistance to many projects designed to improve road and rail corridors serving the ports.

Under the APGCI and a later economic stimulus program, the federal government has committed $792 million to projects designed to benefit the operation of facilities within the Southern Gateway, primarily by easing the existing constricted and congested road and rail access to terminals. Most of these projects have received matching grants from the province, as well as substantial contributions from the private sector. In addition to this massive commitment of public funds to local, port related projects, the Vancouver Gateway Council — actively supported by PMV — urges the early replacement of the federally owned Fraser Rail Bridge at New Westminster, funding for more river dredging, plus other Southern Gateway and Corridor projects. No new terminal capacity is being added. The cost effectiveness of these expenditures in improving terminal performance remains to be seen. Much will depend on whether or not they are accompanied by other measures, both onsite and offsite, to improve terminal productivity. For example, a study released by the Vancouver Fraser Port Authority in May 2010 indicates that 84 percent of port rail customers expressed dissatisfaction with their rail service. Doubtless, however, there are two sides to that issue, which can only be resolved by mutual cooperation.

In August 2010, the VFPA announced a plan to recover its $167 million contribution to a select group of these Southern Gateway infrastructure projects, through an escalating fee on cargo movements over most of the terminals for the next 30 years.

Conflicts over Waterfront Sites and Taxation of Port Authority Assets

Before the Southern Gateway Port Authorities merged, the Vancouver Port Authority was considered "cash rich and property poor," while the Fraser River Port Authority was described as "land rich, but water depth poor." The urgent need for the VPA to expand its access to waterfront industrial land was undoubtedly a prime reason for Ottawa's decision to merge the three Authorities into the Vancouver Fraser Port Authority, effective January 1, 2008.

At the time of the merger, foreign cargo dominated traffic at Vancouver's terminals while the Fraser ports handled mostly domestic cargo. Traffic projections to 2020 anticipate modest growth in dry bulk and break-bulk, growth in container traffic at 6.5 percent per year to 4.6 million TEU, and growth in petroleum exports at 5.7 percent per year. Existing terminals are expected to be adequate to accommodate growth in bulk and break bulk movement and the expected growth in petroleum exports would require little or no new land. The projected growth in container throughput, however, will require some expansion of terminal and ancillary facilities, as well as upgraded access infrastructure.

Though the former VPA had jurisdiction over 233 km of coastline, the location considered best for new or expanded container terminals is at Roberts Bank. Expansion there offers the opportunity to develop short sea shipping to move containers between deep-sea berths and inland riverfront terminals for local and regional distribution, or transloading to rail for longer journeys. This concept, coupled with the planned billion-dollar South Fraser Perimeter Road, is expected to substantially reduce traffic congestion, air pollution, and public complaints.

Since the merger, the VFPA has concluded agreements with the Tsawwassen First Nations that will enable a portion of their expanded land base adjacent to the Deltaport Terminal to be used for future port related industries. There is, however, strong opposition in Delta

Municipality to the further expansion of port facilities at Roberts Bank, based on the perception of the substantial negative socioeconomic and environmental impacts associated with these projects. Though the VFPA, as a federal agency, has the power to override municipal and provincial objections, strong public opposition can cause long and costly delays.

Quite apart from local hostility to further developments at Roberts Bank, there is an increasing clash between the Port Authority, with its mission to retain and develop port facilities and infrastructure to further Canada's Asia Pacific trade, and the municipal councils within the Greater Vancouver conurbation, representing the perceived interests of residents. This is not a new phenomenon. The Gibb Report, presented to Parliament in 1932, recommended removing all sawmills and their loading berths from Burrard Inlet. Pioneer Grain encountered strong opposition to the rebuilding of their North Vancouver terminal, destroyed by explosion in 1975. Then in 1989 the Vancouver City Council and its Board of Variance rejected the proposed Elders Grain waterfront project, a move that the VPC defied. Later the same year, the VPC took a softer line with the North Vancouver City Council when it resisted expanding Neptune's potash facility. In this case, a two-year study by a joint project review panel overcame council's hostility to the expansion. More recently, interminable reviews of environmental studies stalled Deltaport's third berth development for nearly four years; reviews that were hardly all motivated solely by the stated concerns.

The Vancouver City Council under Mayor Art Phillips (1972–1976) completely removed industry from False Creek and converted the area to an urban neighbourhood. The City of Sydney, Australia has progressively removed port facilities and related industries to Botany Bay. Very few remain in that magnificent harbour.

Citizens want parks, condominiums, marinas, restaurants, and tourist attractions on their waterfront and their municipal councils want the taxes that major real estate developments bring. The value of the few remaining parcels of choice waterfront land to developers is soaring as site availability dwindles. The VPFA's recent struggle to acquire a desirable parcel of riverfront industrial land in New Westminster is a case in point.

The VFPA has no Botany Bay to turn to for the large scale development of a new port. It can only attempt to improve the productivity of existing facilities in Burrard Inlet by easing the problems of terminal access — albeit at enormous cost to the public purse — and look to Roberts Bank and the Fraser River for future expansion.

In addition to competition for waterfront sites and conflicts over the location of new port projects, taxation of port properties continues to be an issue between the Port Authority and the 16 lower mainland municipal councils. Municipal frustration focuses mainly on the perceived inadequacy of the payments the VFPA makes in lieu of taxes on unleased properties. These payments, which are based on value assessments unilaterally commissioned by the Authority, are substantially below those made on comparable property by the B.C. Assessment Authority. As a result of this discrepancy, in 2009 the VFPA paid only $5.3 million to all 16 port cities, instead of the $11.5 million billed.

The Municipal Port Property Taxation Fairness Commission, appointed by the Metro Vancouver cities to study and report on the issues surrounding port property taxation, released its final report September 21, 2010. It recommends that VFPA payments should reflect the property taxes that would be paid if the federally owned property were taxable and that the VFPA and the municipalities need to develop a process to resolve valuation disputes.

Hanging over this issue of local taxation on federally or tenant owned port properties is the need to be competitive with nearby, municipally owned U.S. ports.

Environmental Concerns

Security and a desire to be perceived as "green" are, and will continue to be, priorities for port administrations in the developed world. Air or water contamination from terminal activities and from anchored or berthed vessels is increasingly unacceptable to host communities. Measures such as the recent requirement that vessels entering Canadian waters burn progressively cleaner fuel, the anticipated reduction in diesel truck traffic resulting from an expanded role for short sea shipping, and "green" measures at terminal sites are moves which will make some contribution to improving air quality in the port's environs.

The future provision of Alternate Marine Power (AMP) installations at multiple berths in the port will take very much longer to achieve a beneficial effect and will still do nothing to reduce air contamination from vessels filling harbour anchorages. Presently, the port offers two "plug ins" with interruptible power at the Canada Place Cruise facility and these were used a total of 44 times in 2010 out of a total of 177 vessel calls at these berths. Even if every cruise vessel calling at the port made use of AMP, this would represent only 0.06 percent of the total number of vessels calling at the port. In addition, cruise vessels spend only an average 12 hours in the port, as opposed to an average of five days for the 2,800 to 3,000 freighters calling at the port annually. With the exception of some of the newer container ships, virtually no freight carrying vessels are presently equipped to use AMP, even if it were made available (at very considerable cost) at the port's bulk and break-bulk terminals. Thus, it will be many years before AMP can have significant impact on reducing air contamination in the port.

The passage of tankers carrying 11.5 million tonnes of crude oil, other petroleum products, and liquid chemicals the length of Burrard Inlet poses a substantial environmental hazard to the port, despite meticulous planning and strict enforcement of rules designed to prevent groundings and collisions in the harbour, especially at its "narrows." At present the media and environmentalists are intensely focussed on preventing tanker traffic on the North Coast, while this existing traffic in Vancouver's harbour seems to pass almost unnoticed.

The impact of annual dredging programs and increasing port and industrial activity in the Fraser estuary on both marine life and resident and migratory bird populations remains to be resolved.

Exposure to Geological and Meteorological Hazards

As a segment of the Pacific "Ring of Fire," Canada's West Coast has the dubious distinction of being the country's most earthquake prone region. Recent catastrophic quakes in Indonesia and Japan are a clear reminder of the potential for similar events inherent in the geologic instability of the B.C. coast.

The complex interactions between the three tectonic plates within the Cascadia Subduction Zone (from Northern Vancouver Island to Northern California) have the unusual ability to produce earthquakes of several types. Of special concern is the megathrust subduction type, experienced in the Alaska quake of 1964, the Kobe quake of 1995, and the recent quakes in Indonesia and Japan. Tsunamis associated with this type of quake can wreak enormous damage both locally and thousands of kilometres away. Intraplate crustal quakes, both deep and shallow, also occur in the fault lines in Puget Sound and the Gulf of Georgia. These are related to the tectonic activity at plate boundaries offshore.

The violent shaking of the ground resulting from earthquakes not only destroys manmade structures, but also causes landslides and liquefaction of unconsolidated water saturated soils and sediments. Tsunamis associated with megathrust quakes reach heights of 15–30 metres depending on seafloor and shoreline topography.

A major earthquake on the South Coast could result in prolonged closure of the Southern Corridor, as a result of landslides or damage to major bridges. Nearly all bulk, break-bulk, and container facilities at the Southern Gateway are at least partially built on dredged fill and, as such, are susceptible to severe damage, especially from liquefaction of that material. In addition, Roberts Bank facilities could suffer damage from a tsunami generated by a megathrust quake either off the coast, or far across the Pacific.

Hurricane force winds are experienced from time to time along the entire B.C. coastline and the Southern Gateway is no exception. Gale force winds on January 1, 2003 caused extensive damage at Westshore Terminal and on December 15, 2006 hurricane force gusts devastated Stanley Park's trees and seawall.

Terminal Labour Productivity

The report of an in-depth study of the Pacific Gateway delivered to the federal Minister of International Trade in early 2008 recorded that "Reforming the cost structure, efficiency and stability of labour will be the most critical element in the success of the Pacific Gateway." The perception certainly exists that the reason many traditional work rules that are inflexible, dysfunctional, and have long outlived their purpose survive is primarily because competing U.S. port operations are similarly burdened.

One of the main reasons why Vancouver was initially so miserably slow to benefit from the "container revolution" was the "container clause" in the 1970 agreement between the International Longshore and Warehouse Union (ILWU) and the B.C. Maritime Employers Association. Both parties' resistance to change on that issue allowed Puget Sound ports to capture a great deal traffic bound for Canada. The clause was finally removed, effective January 1, 1988, after the federal Minister of Labour received the report of a federally appointed Industrial Inquiry.

An enlightened approach by management and labour when addressing current productivity issues would substantially benefit both and would give Canada's Pacific Gateway Ports a significant advantage over their U.S. competitors. Conversely, without early and progressive action by all concerned in addressing these issues, the anticipated benefits flowing from the massive amounts of public funds recently committed to upgrade the port's infrastructure will be considerably diluted.

THE NORTHERN GATEWAY PORT OF PRINCE RUPERT TODAY

While Port Metro Vancouver attempts to cope with these and other concerns, some associated with maturity, the Northern Gateway, after so many decades of delayed adolescence, is finally beginning to benefit from both its superb natural assets and its logistically advantageous position on the Pacific Rim. Having been the most neglected deep-water port in North America for so long, it is now set to become a valuable link in the burgeoning two way trade supply chain between North America and Asia.

Prince Rupert's natural harbour is widely acknowledged as one of the finest in the world. As the deepest ice-free port in North America it does not require expensive dredging to create, maintain, and deepen navigation channels or to access terminals. The harbour entrance has a minimum depth of 35 m (116 ft.) and a minimum width of 457 m (1,523 ft.). There are no bridges to pass through or under.

The location of the port on the Pacific Rim gives it a significant advantage over other North American West Coast ports for transpacific trade. For example, a container vessel moving at 19 knots on the Great Circle Route between a northeast Asian port and North America will arrive at Prince Rupert a full day sooner than at Vancouver or a Puget Sound port, and 2.5 days sooner than at Long Beach or Los Angeles. This relative proximity to Asia can translate into at least one extra round trip a year for a vessel operator contemplating a pendulum type service across the North Pacific. Likewise, a bulk carrier destined for a South Asian or Persian Gulf port will save over 400 nautical miles if loaded at a Northern Gateway terminal compared with any other West Coast port. Conversely, a vessel sailing from a B.C. port to Panama has to cover an extra 307 nautical miles if loaded at Prince Rupert instead of a Southern Gateway terminal.[7]

The port's major terminals occupy three distinct locations. The small cruise vessel Atlin Terminal and large vessel Northland Cruise Terminal are centrally located on the city waterfront where the surroundings have been extensively upgraded with a view to welcoming ship-borne visitors to the City.

---

[7] See Appendix 1 – Distances from Prince Rupert to selected world ports.

The B.C. Ferry and Alaska Ferry Terminals occupy sites at the southern extremity of the city proper, and Fairview Terminal is located immediately south of these coastal passenger terminals. This facility was completed in 1977 as a general cargo facility and was constructed by using blasted upland rock to fill over a very shallow submarine rock ledge that extended offshore approximately 184 m (650 ft.), before abruptly dropping off to deep water. The original site was expanded and a third berth added in 1990. Subsequently, it was converted to a state-of-the-art, rapid throughput container terminal with its own rail yard in 2007. The site offers potential for expansion to both the north and south, while still well protected from wave action.

Two bulk terminals presently occupy a relatively small portion of the Ridley Island Industrial site located 8 km (5 miles) south of the City. The 450 ha (1,124 acres) of this low, flat island represent one of the very few infrastructure served, bedrock land parcels on the coast of B.C that are adjacent to deep tidewater and available for marine terminal and related industry development. In addition, adjacent locations totalling another 550 ha (1,375 acres) are available for industrial development. These include locations on South Kaien Island, which are served by rail, and on nearby Coast and Lelu Islands, which are yet to be connected by rail. All these are relatively flat bedrock sites close to both deep water and infrastructure.

Deep-sea vessels approaching the port's facilities are obliged to carry a pilot for the final 23–27 nautical miles of their passage.

The port's terminals are well protected from open ocean wave action by the chain of islands that enclose Chatham Sound. They are, however, exposed to the same southeast gales experienced along the entire B.C. coast during fall and winter. Although these storms occasionally cause loading delays at the bulk terminals and temporarily halt crane operation at the container terminal, they have never caused substantial damage to port installations.

Prince Rupert is much maligned for its supposed interminable rain. In fact, its total annual precipitation exceeds the 10-year average of seven recording stations in North Vancouver by a mere 7 percent. Grain loading at both ports is subject to delay caused by heavy downpours.

On the British Columbia coast north of Vancouver Island the Pacific Plate is sliding northwest relative to the North American Plate. This activity caused the largest earthquake ever recorded in Canada, located offshore the Queen Charlotte Islands (Haida Gwaii) in 1949. The shallower crustal quakes common to the Strait of Georgia and Puget Sound area are not experienced between Haida Gwaii and the mainland. The tsunami from the Great Alaska Earthquake of 1964 that devastated some locations further south caused only trivial damage to shoreline facilities in Prince Rupert Harbour. None of the port's terminals have been created by adding dredged material to a deep unconsolidated sediment base.

Prince Rupert has no large, expanding urban population to conflict with the Port

Authority over access to waterfront locations. There are no pressures for gentrifying existing or planned terminal locations, at least in part, because, with the exception of the cruise facilities, these are sited outside the city waterfront. Furthermore, the entire community recognizes the great importance of its harbour and strongly supports its orderly development with modern terminal facilities.

Waterfront and terminal labour is enthusiastic and eager to set records at the port's existing bulk and container terminals. Cooperation between port labour, terminal operators, the railway, the Port Authority, and other ancillary service providers is exemplary and this is widely acknowledged by shippers and vessel operators.

Rail access to the port's terminals is uncomplicated, rapid, and efficient, reflecting one of the prime objectives of those who designed these modern facilities. Future terminals will benefit similarly from almost ideal rail access and service with optimal car turnaround. There are no conflicting rail jurisdictions, no lift bridges to negotiate, and no widely scattered distribution of terminals and ancillary facilities. Future port planning incorporates the concept of concentrating rail and terminal facilities in a very few defined and spacious areas.

At present the port lacks some desirable amenities such as bunkering facilities for visiting vessels. These will be provided as traffic increases and they become commercially feasible.

The issue of the original compensation for the foreshore lands in the harbour area, acquired from the original inhabitants by the Grand Trunk Pacific Railway (assisted by agencies of the federal government and the church), has been outlined in some detail in Chapter One. Although the railway achieved its property objectives for its Pacific terminus, the deal made has increasingly been considered inequitable and unacceptable by the descendants of the original occupants.

With the recent resurgence in port activity and planned expansions, First Nations in the area have given expression to this century old, festering grievance through legal measures used to delay new projects until a full and final settlement of their claims has been achieved. Complicating the issue are disagreements among First Nation bands over the legitimacy of each other's claims.

Several years of negotiation between the Port Authority and the Coast Tsimshian First Nations have successfully resolved these difficult issues. An agreement concluded March 14, 2011 formalizes settlement for the current container terminal, as well as future expansion of the facility and other related activities associated with the handling of containerized cargoes. The agreement includes a future projects protocol, providing a framework for consultation and accommodation for future terminal projects, thus providing proponents greater certainty in considering investments at the port. This agreement is in addition to agreements reached with the Kitselas and Kitsumkalum First Nations located near Terrace. These mutually beneficial agreements have resolved all outstanding issues and clear the way for all aspects of planned and future development of the port.

THE GATEWAYS, 2010 TO 2020

Despite the multiple difficult issues facing the merged Southern Gateway Ports and their main corridor, there can be little doubt that they will continue to handle the major portion of Canada's Pacific Coast overseas traffic for the foreseeable future. They will not, however, have the almost total dominance they have enjoyed over the past 91 years.

Port Metro Vancouver has several considerable advantages: very extensive terminal and support facilities, service by three Class One railroads, a large local and regional population of consumers, extensive traditional overseas relationships, and the apparent political clout to successfully persuade senior governments to pay for attempts to relieve its infrastructure, congestion, and access problems. Time will tell whether these enormous public expenditures, which provide no new capacity, will be seen to be justified by major improvements in terminal performance and reliability.

Prince Rupert, on the other hand, has only recently extended its reach to become a global port, after nursing a century of thwarted ambition to see its destiny fulfilled as the alternate Pacific outlet for Canada's trade. Although the port's terminals are few in number, they are modern, easily accessible, and well located, offering uncomplicated, efficient, reliable and enthusiastic service. No infrastructure funding is needed to enhance their performance, so that if any senior government funds were to be made available to the Northern Gateway, new capacity would be added.

The pattern of future development at the Northern Gateway will not mirror that of its much more mature southern counterpart. Its position on the Pacific Rim and the uncomplicated access by an underutilized transcontinental rail line to multiple deep-water, accessible, hard rock, industrial sites coupled with the absence of a large, encumbering, metropolitan population give Prince Rupert a unique opportunity to expand and develop state-of-the-art facilities designed to optimize efficiency and reliability. Within North America, the port's reach extends across the northern plains and into eastern Canada and the mid-western United States, as well as into the resource rich northern half of B.C. and adjacent Alaska.

THE FACILITIES NEEDED TO HANDLE OVERSEAS TRADE TO 2020

The Southern Gateway

Port Metro Vancouver's foreign traffic growth projections for the period 2008 to 2020 indicate only modest increases in dry bulk and break-bulk throughput, but anticipate annual increases of 5.7 percent and 6.5 percent for liquid bulk and container traffic respectively, with container traffic reaching 4.6 million TEU by the year 2020. That figure appears more realistic than the earlier Vancouver Port Authority prediction of 8.8 million TEU by 2020. The two decades of double digit growth are almost certainly history and the capacity crunch for terminals and vessel operators, which ended in 2007, has been replaced by painful excess for both.

Summer cruise passenger traffic is expected to recover somewhat and auto imports are expected to continue with modest annual growth.

Based on these PMV predictions, existing dry bulk and break-bulk terminals should be able to cope with anticipated business for the next decade without major expansions. Increase in liquid bulk throughput, primarily crude oil exports, will depend largely on public acceptance of increasing numbers of ever larger and deeper laden oil tankers (plus chemical tankers) transiting the length of Burrard Inlet, and the deepening of the navigation channel at first and second narrows. Vancouver's loss to Seattle of its near monopoly on the cruise business raises some doubt about the future need for the auxiliary cruise passenger facility at Ballantyne Pier.

The existing container terminals at PMV have a current rated annual capacity of 3.7 million TEU. A substantial increase in capacity, efficiency, and reliability by relieving congestion and improving access to existing terminals is the prime objective behind the current massive injection of public funds into infrastructure projects around the Southern Gateway. These public expenditures can only be justified if they are coupled with an overhaul of work practices at the terminals, elimination of the disconnect between rail and terminal operations, and other progressive measures including short sea shipping and greater use of inland ancillary facilities. Given the cumulative potential benefit resulting from a realization of all those measures, the existing terminals should be able to cope comfortably with annual container throughput increments as high as 6.5 percent. Using an average of the past four years as the base line, this would take throughput to 4.53 million TEU in 2020.

There would then appear to be little reason to proceed in the near future with the hugely expensive and controversial Terminal Two at Roberts Bank, at least until the full potential can be squeezed from all four existing facilities.

Many factors outside PMV's control will affect growth predictions. These include the 2014 opening of the new, larger Panama Canal locks, the rate and extent of North America's economic recovery, competition from U.S. West Coast ports and the railroads serving them, and the potential preference by some vessel operators and their customers to land or load their containers at the Northern Gateway.

The Northern Gateway

During the next decade, the Prince Rupert Port Authority projects average annual increments in foreign cargo movement of 9 percent for bulk commodities and 20 percent for containers. By 2020 this would take total throughput to 30 million tonnes of bulk commodities and 2 million TEU of containerized cargo. If realized, this amount of traffic would amount to approximately 30 percent of the total overseas import/export tonnage through the two Pacific Gateways, about double the port's present share.

Ridley Terminals — Since delivered from the threat of disposal by a politically inspired giveaway in 2005, Ridley Terminals Inc. has recovered dramatically and throughput has increased from 1 million to 8 million tonnes annually. New coal producers in northeastern B.C. have overcome their initial difficulties, which were much exacerbated by the world economic meltdown in 2008–2009 and they are increasing production from both new and reopened mines. In addition, the terminal is now handling substantial tonnages of coal from Alberta mines — operated by Luscar Energy Partnership and Teck Corporation — as well as product from Arch Coal operations in the Powder River Basin of Wyoming.

Petroleum coke throughput reached 1.17 million tonnes in 2010, double its ten year average. The unfinished sulphur handling facility, which has reverted to RTI, offers potential for conversion to a liquid bulk chemical operation.

The terminal throughput set a record in 2010 at 8.3 million tonnes, surpassing the former record of 7 million tonnes in 1985, its first year of operation. To meet anticipated annual throughput of at least 24 million tonnes by 2020 the terminal has begun to undertake major expansion programs leading to a doubling of present capacity. These include site additions and heavy equipment purchases.

The question of Ridley Terminals Inc. ownership periodically arises with various advocates supporting its sale to a consortium of users (as at Neptune or Sultran in Vancouver), supporting its transfer to the Prince Rupert Port Authority, or supporting its current status as a federal crown corporation.

Ridley Island Industrial Site — Prince Rupert Grain and Ridley Terminals Inc. occupy only a small part of the port's Ridley Industrial Site. The Port Authority plans to extend existing rail and other infrastructure to eventually form a complete utility corridor loop around the circumference of this flat island site. A first stage of this extension would accommodate the new terminal planned by Canpotex for the movement of up to 10 million tonnes of potash to overseas markets each year. Funding for this extension is expected to be provided equally by the Port Authority, the CNR, and the federal government.

Prince Rupert Grain — The port's single, modern, high throughput grain terminal continues to handle about 30 percent of bulk grain moving to overseas markets via the West Coast. Its operating excellence was rewarded by its selection as "Grain Handler of the Year" for crop year 2008/09 by the Canadian Wheat Board in the western port terminal category.

The terminal, although designed to handle 3.5 million tonnes annually, has demonstrated that it is able to move double that amount. Future terminal throughput will depend largely on the amount of farm production available for overseas sale, a continuation of favourable rail rates, and the fate of at least one of the old terminals at the Southern Gateway.

Fairview Container Terminal — The concept for Prince Rupert's first container terminal was developed and brilliantly executed during a period of extreme difficulty for the port and its host community. It opened for business shortly before the bubble burst on the western world's economy, an event which brought growth at all other Pacific Coast container terminals in the U.S. and Canada to an abrupt halt and which was followed by a double-digit drop in throughput after 20 successive years of double-digit growth. Despite many scoffers and what might be considered very unlucky timing, this project has proven a resounding success. Now in its third year of operation, this pure rail intermodal facility handled 343,366 TEU in 2010, a figure not reached by Southern Gateway terminals collectively until 1990, after 20 years of operation.

The new terminal has a number of distinct advantages besides its very favourable location on the Pacific Rim. Designed as a high throughput rail intermodal facility dedicated primarily to distant markets, the terminal and its uncongested rail corridor have proven able to offer a seamless service that is faster, more reliable, and more efficient than that available elsewhere. The project has very strong support from the CNR, which is eager to capture more lucrative long-haul intermodal business and make better use of its second line to the coast. Support from the highly motivated and enthusiastic terminal workforce and from the community has also been very strong. Maher Terminals, the terminal operator, is highly respected in the shipping community and has no other competing operation on the Pacific Coast of North America.

Without doubt, container shipping lines and their customers are constantly looking for better alternative options, especially if they are unhappy with their current terminal service provider. The CKYH Alliance of shipping companies from China, Japan, Taiwan, and Korea inaugurated service to the terminal in October 2007 and, despite the severe economic recession in 2008–2009 they have since more than doubled that service. As the North American economy recovers, and with it the container shipping business, it is highly likely that other vessel operators will seek to use this new very efficient terminal.

The terminal is currently operating at two-thirds its rated capacity of 500,000 TEU and with some modification could handle 750,000 TEU annually. Developing the site to increase its annual capacity to 2 million TEU is possible and can be achieved either incrementally, or all at once.

Increasing Canada's share of transpacific container trade to 14 percent or better is a prime objective of the Asia Pacific Gateway and Corridor Initiative. Expanding the Fairview Terminal offers the least controversial, the cheapest, and the quickest way to achieve that goal. Peter Hall, Chief Economist for Export Canada recently stated that the early expansion of the terminal is necessary to prevent Canada from falling behind in trade growth compared to its trading partners. The committee appointed in 2008 by the Minister of Trade to study the APGCI recommended that policy makers develop container capacity in Prince Rupert, before making further investments in Vancouver. However, for the Northern Gateway to develop as a major new component of the supply chain linking Asia and North America and to absorb a substantial and disproportionate share of future growth, some of the existing constrictions in the *Canada Marine Act*, which limit the Port Authority's ability to finance rapid growth, may have to be addressed or circumvented.

The decision to expand Fairview Terminal will depend primarily on continued strong support from vessel operators, their customers, and the CNR. Whereas at PMV container terminals a substantial proportion of containers are trucked to and from local and regional destinations, at Fairview all loaded import boxes are moved by rail to Central Canada and the U.S. Midwest and a significant proportion of these containers are returned loaded from these distant points with commodities for export via Fairview. Hence the continued, relatively free movement of freight via Canada into the U.S. is critically important to the future health of Fairview. Doubtless, the southern California ports and the railways that service them will attempt to pressure politicians in Washington to find a way to limit, or eliminate the passage through Canada of transpacific traffic moving between Asia and U.S. points. The probable losses those ports will suffer to Gulf Coast facilities after the Panama Canal locks expansion project is completed in 2014 will likely heighten their concerns.

A WORD ON "MANAGED GROWTH" AND RESTRAINED COMPETITION

Recent comments by some members of the marine community at the Southern Gateway have stressed the desirability of "Managed Growth" and the restraint of competition between West Coast ports. Some proponents of this view even imply that competition between the two Pacific Gateways located 804 km (500 miles) apart is somehow against the national interest, if not unpatriotic! That position, of course, is a very thin disguise for the desire to control and limit growth at the only competing national port on the Pacific Coast and keep it an "outport" of the Southern Gateway. It would follow logically that if this were a worth-while position, then all competition should be made to cease between the national ports on the St. Lawrence River and those located on the Atlantic Coast with either Halifax or Montreal alone controlling the development of all the ports engaged in the nation's Atlantic trade. Taken a step further, ports like Montreal and Quebec City should be amalgamated, as also Halifax and St. John!

While some degree of the management of where and when new developments take place may be desirable, the question will always arise as to the impartiality of the manager. With reference to healthy competition between national Gateway Ports, whether located on the St Lawrence River, the Atlantic Coast, or on the Pacific Rim, surely this is the best and only real way to assure that they function at maximum efficiency in all levels of activity. Following the recommendation contained in the Gibb report to Parliament in 1932, Vancouver was thoroughly shielded from the potential competition of an alternate Northern Gateway Port for over half a century. Surely it no longer needs that protection!

Restraining competition by any means, however subtle, is a dangerous concept. Mediocrity, sloth, and stagnation are the certain long term outcome of any artificially created monopoly. The 2007 Pacific Coast Terminal Competitiveness Study undertaken for Transport Canada stresses the essential nature of competition to the success of the gateways and their corridors. Indeed, under the *Canada Marine Act*, the administrators of both Gateways are obligated to make their ports competitive, commercially oriented and efficient. Hobbling competition is the antithesis of the intent of that legislation.

Barring extraneous interfering influences, the greatest relative growth over the next decade will be experienced by the gateway whose terminals and corridor are best able to offer the most productive, reliable, efficient and timely service to customers in both Canada and the United States.

Selected References

Bunker, J.G. (1972). *Liberty ships*. Annapolis, Maryland: Naval Institute Press.

Canada Grains Council. *Statistical handbooks*. Winnipeg.

Canadian Grain Monitoring Program. *Annual Reports, 1999/2000 – 2008/2009*. Edmonton: Quorum Corp.

Canadian Wheat Board. *Annual Reports*. Winnipeg.

Carpenter, R. (1971) *Container ships*. Hemel Hempstead, Hertfordshire: Model & Allied Publications.

Cox & McIntyre (1969). *Yukon Railway feasibility final reconnaissance report*. Canadian National Railways.

Cudahy, B. (2006). *Box boats*. New York: Fordham University Press.

Encyclopedia of British Columbia. Madeira Park, B.C.: Harbour Publishing, 2000.

Friesen, J., Ralston, H.K. (Ed.) (1976). *Historical essays on British Columbia*. Toronto: McLelland & Stewart.

Garden, J.F. (1995). *BC Rail – From PGE to BC Rail*. Revelstoke, BC: Footprint Publishing Company.

Gibb, Sir A. (1931–1932) *National ports survey*. Ottawa: Kings Printer.

Gresko J., Howard R. (1986). *Fraser Port, freightway to the Pacific*. Victoria, BC: Sono Nis Press.

Hacking, N., Lamb, W. Kaye. (1974). *The Princess story*. Vancouver, BC: Mitchell Press.

Harbour and Shipping Magazine. (1918–2010). West Vancouver, BC: Progress Publishing.

Hick, W.B.M. (2003). *Hays' orphan*. Prince Rupert, BC: Prince Rupert Port Authority.

A history of the Canadian Wheat Board. *Grain Matters, July, 1985*.

Hedges, J.B. (1934). *The federal railway and subsidy policy of Canada*. Boston, Mass.: Harvard University Press.

Leonard, F. (1996). *A thousand blunders*. Vancouver, BC: UBC Press.

McCurdy, H.W. (1966). *Marine history of the Pacific Northwest*. Seattle, Washington: Superior Publishing Company.

MacKay, D. (1986). *The Asian dream: The Pacific Rim and Canada's national railway*. Vancouver/Toronto: Douglas and McIntyre.

MacKay, D. (1992). *The peoples' railway: A history of the Canadian National*. Vancouver/Toronto: Douglas and McIntyre.

McLaren, T.A., Jensen, V. (2000). *Ships of steel*. Madeira Park, BC: Harbour Publishing.

Mansbridge, F. (2002). *Launching history: The saga of Burrard Dry Dock*. Madeira Park, BC: Harbour Publishing.

Mitchell, W.H., Sawyer, L.A. (1966). *The oceans, the forts and the parks*. Liverpool, England: Sea Breezes.

Perrault, E.G. (1985). *Wood and water: The story of seaboard lumber and shipping.* Vancouver/Toronto: Douglas & McIntyre.

Prince Rupert Daily Optimist. (May–October, 1910). Prince Rupert, BC.

Prince Rupert Daily News. (1919–1921). Prince Rupert, BC.

Roskill, S.W. (1961). *The war at sea.* (Vol. III, part 2). London, England: Her Majesty's Stationery Office.

Sanford, B. (1981). *Pictorial history of railroading in B.C.* Toronto: Whitecap Books.

Sherman, P. (1966). *Bennett.* Toronto/Montreal: McClelland & Stewart.

Tucker, G.N. (1952). *The naval service of Canada.* (Vol. II). Ottawa: King's Printer.

Western Wharves: *Complete records.* (1966–1971). Prince Rupert, BC.

Wolf, J. (2005). *Royal City — A photographic history of New Westminster, 1858–1960.* Victoria, BC: Heritage House.

Wright, E.W. (Ed.). *Lewis & Dryden's marine history of the Pacific Northwest.* (1895). Portland, Oregon: Lewis and Dryden Printing Company.

Appendix One

DISTANCES TO MAJOR WORLD PORTS

To	From Prince Rupert	From Vancouver	From Long Beach
Balboa (Panama)	4,332	4,025 (-307)	2,912 (-1420)
Bandar Abbas	10,048	10,463 (+415)	11,050 (+1002)
Mumbai	9,102	9,517 (+415)	10,014 (+1002)
Djakarta	6,995	7,417 (+422)	7,899 (+904)
Hong Kong	5,335	5,760 (+425)	6,363 (+1028)
Inchon	4,592	5,031 (+429)	5,630 (+1038)
Kaohsiung	5,084	5,520 (+436)	6,117 (+1033)
Osaka	4,106	4,558 (+452)	5,141 (+1035)
Qingdao	4,669	5,119 (+450)	5,706 (+1037)
Shanghai	4,678	5,114 (+436)	5,708 (+1030)
Singapore	6,667	7,092 (+415)	7,669 (+1002)
Sydney	6,679	6,822 (+143)	6,510 (-169)
Weihai	4,645	5,086 (+441)	5,684 (+1039)
Yokahama	3,825	4,264 (+439)	4,842 (+1017)

All figures in Nautical Miles

Appendix Two

FEDERAL FINANCIAL SUPPORT FOR LOCAL GATEWAY ENHANCEMENTS, 2007–2010

AT THE SOUTHERN GATEWAY:

From APGCI Funds

South Fraser Perimeter Road connecting Deltaport to
Highways 1, 91, 99 . . . . $365 million

North Fraser Perimeter Road to enhance connections between
port and rail yards . . . . 65 million

Dredging at Fraserport to deepen and widen ship channels . . . . 4 million

Roberts Bank Rail Corridor . . . . 75 million

Pitt River Bridge: To enhance movement of international goods
through lower mainland . . . . 90 million

City of Richmond: To improve efficiency of road network
serving gateway facilities . . . . .4.72 million

Corporation of Delta: For improvements to ease truck
movements on Annacis Island . . . . .0.73 million

Projects to improve access to north shore terminals . . . . 75 million

Projects to improve access to south shore terminals .49.7 million

Short Sea Shipping Projects . . . . .20.9 million

From Infrastructure Stimulus Funds

Replacement of "sails" at Canada Place . . . . 21 million

Fourteen PMV projects. . . . . 21 million

Total . . . .$792.05 million

Appendix Two

AT THE NORTHERN GATEWAY:

From APGCI Funds

Prince Rupert Port Container Security Program —
    Canada Border Services Agency . . . . 28 million
From Western Economic Diversification Funds
Contribution to Fairview Terminal Conversion. . . . . 30 million
Marine Shore Power Program . . . . .0.7 million

From Infrastructure Stimulus Funds

Miscellaneous Repairs Atlin Terminal Building
    and Ridley Island infrastructure . . . . .1.5 million

From Transport Canada

Marine Security Contribution. . . . . .1.9 million
Marine Shore Power Program . . . . .1.8 million
Total. . . . .$63.9 million

Index

W

Wallace Shipyards, 67, 76, **128–129,** 259

Wallenius Wilhelmsen Logistics, 217, 292, 387

Wartime Merchant Shipping Ltd, 159

Watson Island, 162, 184, 186, 188, 235, 266, 268, **345–347, 349**

Wenner-Gren, Axel, 36, 43

Westar Industries, 208, 254

Western Grain Transportation Act, 212, 241

Western Stevedoring, 210, 252–253, 379

Western Wharves, 192–193, 219–220, 235, **353,** 411

Westmar Consultants, 390

Westridge Terminal, 181, **355,** 387, 401

Westshore Terminals (*see also* Roberts Bank),
   1946–1970: 170, 173–174, 409
   1970–1985: 205, 207–208, 249, **323**
   1985–2004: 208, 254, 256, **332,** 423
   Since 2004: 380–381, **333,** 415

Westview, 267

Whelan, Eugene, 223

White Pass and Yukon Railway, 42, 174, 175–176, 276, 320

Williston, Ray, 36

Wilson, Sir Charles Rivers, 10, 13

Wisconsin Central Railway, 32, 243

Y

Yellowhead Pass, 3, 13, 15, 17, 19, 56

Young, Doug, 238